PENGUIN BOOKS

O ALBANY!

William Kennedy is the author of the universally acclaimed
cycle of Albany novels, *Legs*, *Billy Phelan's Greatest Game*, and
Ironweed, which received both the Pulitzer Prize and the
National Book Critics Circle Award for Fiction. He is also the
author of *The Ink Truck* (another Albany based novel). In 1984
he received a New York State Governor's Arts Award. Mr. Kennedy and his wife, Dana, still live in the Albany area with their
three children, Dana, Kathy, and Brendan.

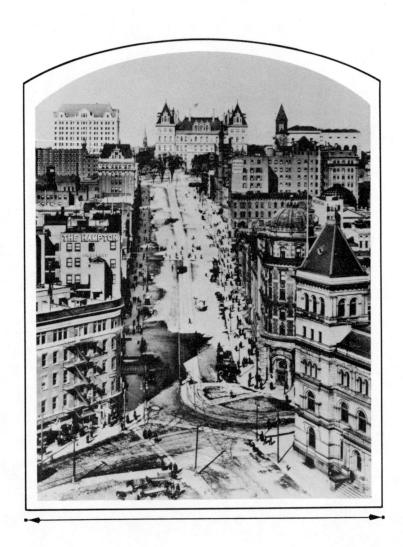

Washington Park Press Ltd.

O Albany!

*Improbable City
of Political Wizards, Fearless Ethnics,
Spectacular Aristocrats, Splendid Nobodies,
and Underrated Scoundrels*

WILLIAM KENNEDY

PENGUIN BOOKS

PENGUIN BOOKS
Viking Penguin Inc., 40 West 23rd Street,
New York, New York 10010, U.S.A.
Penguin Books Ltd, Harmondsworth,
Middlesex, England
Penguin Books Australia Ltd, Ringwood,
Victoria, Australia
Penguin Books Canada Limited, 2801 John Street,
Markham, Ontario, Canada L3R 1B4
Penguin Books (N.Z.) Ltd, 182–190 Wairau Road,
Auckland 10, New Zealand

First published in the United States of America by Viking Penguin Inc. 1983
Published in Penguin Books 1985

Portions of this book appeared originally in *Knickerbocker News*, Capital
Newspapers Group, in different form.

"Everything Everybody Ever Wanted" appeared originally in *The Atlantic*.

LIBRARY OF CONGRESS CATALOGING IN PUBLICATION DATA
Kennedy, William, 1928–
O Albany!
Includes index.
1. Albany (N.Y.)—History.   2. Albany (N.Y.)—
Social life and customs.   3. Albany (N.Y.)—
Politics and government.   I. Title.
F129.A357K46   1985   974.7'43   85-6530
ISBN 0 14 00.7416 3

Maps by David Lindroth copyright © Viking Penguin Inc., 1983

Printed in the United States of America by
R. R. Donnelley & Sons Company, Harrisonburg, Virginia
Set in Trump

This book is dedicated to people who used to think they hated the place where they grew up, and then took a second look.

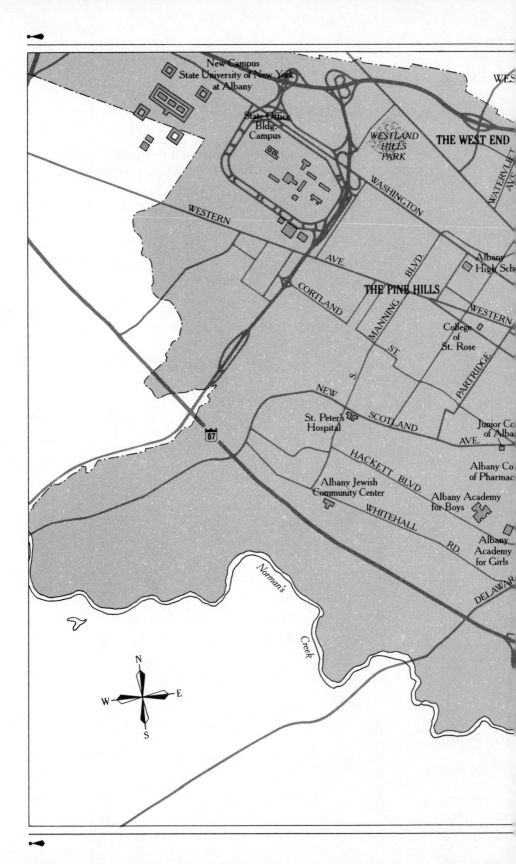

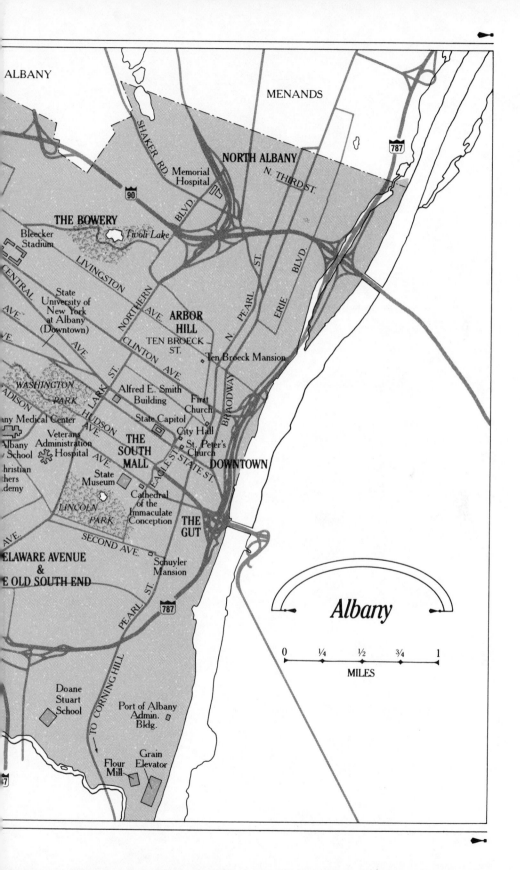

ALBANY

MENANDS

NORTH ALBANY

SHAKER RD.

N. THIRD ST.

787

Memorial
Hospital

BLVD.

90

THE BOWERY

Bleecker
Stadium

Tivoli Lake

LIVINGSTON

NORTHERN

AVE.

PEARL ST.

ERIE BLVD.

CENTRAL

AVE.

State
University of
New York
at Albany
(Downtown)

CLINTON AVE.

ARBOR
HILL

TEN BROECK
ST.

Ten Broeck Mansion

AVE.

WASHINGTON

PARK

LARK ST.

Alfred E. Smith
Building

First
Church

BRADWAY

MADISON

HUDSON AVE.

State Capitol

any Medical Center

Veterans
Administration
Hospital

City Hall

St. Peter's
Church

STATE ST.

EAGLE ST.

DOWNTOWN

Albany
School

THE
SOUTH
MALL

AVE.

hristian
hers
demy

State
Museum

LINCOLN

PARK

Cathedral
of the
Immaculate
Conception

THE
GUT

AVE.

SECOND AVE.

DELAWARE AVENUE
&
E OLD SOUTH END

Schuyler
Mansion

PEARL ST.

787

TO CORNING HILL

Doane
Stuart
School

Port of Albany
Admin.
Bldg.

Grain
Elevator

Flour
Mill

Albany

0   ¼   ½   ¾   1

MILES

～ Contents ～

Common Places, Uncommon Faces, an Album of
Photographs follows page 175.
Maps appear on pages 28, 59, 83,
98, 109, 116, 134, 144, 159, 307.

PART 1

THE MAGICAL PLACES

The Pruyn Library, looking idyllic in the first decade of the twentieth century.

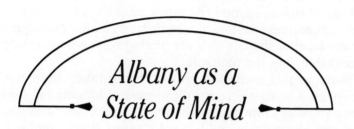

Albany as a State of Mind

I write this book not as a booster of Albany, which I am, nor as an apologist for the city, which I sometimes am, but rather as a person whose imagination has become fused with a single place, and in that place finds all the elements that a man ever needs for the life of the soul.

Maligning Albany is a very old game. The early Dutchmen were targets of derision by visitors who found their city dismal, dingy, and dirty. The English didn't do much better with it. About 1870 the famed architect H. H. Richardson had this to say: "Misery, wretchedness, ennui and the devil—I've got to spend another evening in Albany. Of all the miserable, wretched, second-class, one-horse towns, this is the most miserable."

In modern times the city grew to be a lascivious parlor of Satan, and also what John Gunther in his *Inside U.S.A.* in 1947 described as "a kind of political *cloaca maxima*, beside which Kansas City seemed almost pure." It's true that the city is a famed vortex of state politics, a pinnacle of porkhead bossism, Wasp and Irish. It's true that wickedness has been our lot for more years than any man alive can remember.

But even at its most dismal, wretched, and cloacal moments, it was also something that dyspeptic transients like Richardson and Gunther could not, or perhaps would not, appreciate; and this book is an attempt to strike a balance as to Albany's legend. Even iniquity has its charms: consider what Milton did with Satan. I once thought I loathed the city, left it without a sigh and thought I'd gone for good, only to come back to work and live in it and become this curious cheerleader I now seem to be. But I'm fond of things beyond the city's iniquity. I love its times of grace and greatness, its political secrets and its historical presence in every facet of the nation's life, including the unutterable, the unspeakable, and the ineffable.

I came to this condition slowly, being taken from the city forcibly by a war I never got close to, and longing for Albany's homey vapidity from across the sea. I came home and found it warm and abominable and left it for seven years, coming home yet again for a presumably brief visit to clear up some family untidiness, only to stay, so far, for twenty years on the same corner and commute the twenty minutes to Downtown every time I have an excuse.

As a writer, as an erstwhile student of the Baltimore Catechism, I have found it essential from time to time to ask myself: Why are you here? I was in Puerto Rico writing a novel the first time the question grew pressing, and the question, I supposed then, had merely geographical overtones. For there I was, living in San Juan, a vital city, and waking up every morning to pore through the pages of a picture book of Albany scenes from 1867 and 1842 and 1899 and other such years, trying to understand my life from these photos instead of from the bright, warm, sea-spun life around me. But the fact was that the pictures, more than the Puerto Rican immediacy, were what spun my own imagination.

I was incapable of writing a transient's novel about Puerto Rico—what Eudora Welty calls the Isle of Capri novel. I cared more about the shape of the ball returns in the Knights of Columbus alleys in Albany. For I remembered those ball returns. They were artifacts out of a significant past—my father's, my uncle's, my own—and San Juan had nothing comparable to offer. It was a marvelous place and I will write about it one day, but back then it was not engaging my soul, and that Albany picture book was. It was provoking questions such as: Why was I an only child in a vast family of brothers and sisters and untrackable cousins? (This is a question I am still trying to answer.) Why did my uncles marry so late or not at all? Was there such a thing as culture in Albany? Could you get rich without being in politics? Who was this Van Rensselaer fellow? Why was Eddie Carey called the Squire of North Albany and what precisely was a squire in Albany's lexicon and why did Eddie live at the top of Van Rensselaer Boulevard and why had I always lived at the bottom in one of his houses? Why was the North End, my neighborhood, almost exclusively Catholic, and Irish, and Democratic? How could such a thing happen?

I moved back to Albany partly to get answers, and I vowed that while on this visit I would research North Albany and the city's ethnic blueprints, its political history and the nature of its peculiar people. Before I could make my plans known to anyone, Walter Hawver, an editor on the *Times-Union*, where I'd signed on as a part-time short-timer, asked me to write a series on the city's neighborhoods: how they came to be. I took this as a gift from the great literary editor in the sky and reveled in the four months it took me to write it. The series, I believed, was a masterpiece of durability, but it was about as durable as the flimsy paper it was printed on, or as the neighborhoods that were its subject, for all those neighborhoods have been turned inside out since I wrote of them, a few even atomized as if they'd never existed.

It was in these years that my mind changed on Albany, that I came to see it as an inexhaustible context for the stories I planned to write, as abundant in mythic qualities as it was in political ambition, remarkably consequential greed, and genuine fear of the Lord.

I saw it as being as various as the American psyche itself, of which it was truly a crucible. It is one of the oldest chartered cities in the U.S. and will celebrate its tricentennial in 1986. It was a primeval and savage wilderness to the early settlers—those agents of the first Patroon, and the Dutch West India Company pioneers—just as the Far West would be to the westering American pioneers of the nineteenth century. It had a history as long before the Revolutionary War, in which it was a key city (it was headquarters in the campaign against Burgoyne), as it has had since that war. It was always commercially important, first because of the Dutch fur trade (in 1656 the trappers of Albany— then called Fort Orange—slew thirty thousand beaver for pelts) and because of the Hudson River. Later it became the eastern terminus of the Erie Canal, and later still a railroad center, which made it a cattle town, a bit of the Wild West in the old East. It was a city of foundries and lumber, and its sinful ways made it the hottest town between New York and Montreal.

It was always as much a melting pot for immigrants as was New York or Boston, and it epitomizes today the transfer of power from the Dutch to the English (the city was named for James, Duke of York and Albany, in 1664) to the ethnic coalitions. In Albany the power came to be centered singularly in the Irish, Albany preceding Boston in putting an Irishman in City Hall. But the Irish couldn't have done it without help from the Wasps, most notably a Yankee family whose heir to great wealth and greater significance hold in power until 1983. The Irish-Wasp collaboration created a matchless political record: uninterrupted control of the city since 1921.

The Irish boss who made this happen was a man named Daniel Peter O'Connell. He died in 1977 at age ninety-one. His third chosen mayor, son of the man with whom O'Connell founded the modern party, was Erastus Corning, elected in 1941, and in 1981 at age seventy-two elected to his eleventh consecutive four-year term.

Being a state capital, Albany has also been a springboard to the presidency: Martin Van Buren, Millard Fillmore (he was a state comptroller), Grover Cleveland, Teddy and Franklin Roosevelt among those who made it; Samuel Tilden, Charles Evans Hughes, Al Smith, Tom Dewey, Averell Harriman, and Nelson Rockefeller among the other fellows. Nelson made it to the vice-presidency, that ignominious office of standby equipment he scorned until it was the only bauble left for him. In Albany he was more significant: the builder of the South Mall, that billion-dollar monument he foresaw as a hymn to forever, its vast acres of marble designed to be whispering "Nelson . . . Nelson . . ." to the silent infinity next door, long after the last of us has gone away.

Literarily, what can one say of Albany? Melville was schooled here but went to sea. Cooper hobnobbed with the Patroon. Henry James's grandfather William founded the James dynasty here but Henry came to visit rarely after childhood. Emerson lectured to the Young Men's Association. William Cullen Bryant, one of the forgotten men in American letters, was feted at the governor's mansion by Governor Tilden in 1875 at what was described as "the greatest literary event in the city's history." Bret Harte was born here and left almost immediately, came back as a mature celebrity but was snubbed by the press, left in a terminal huff and died in England trying to forget the place. Harold Frederic worked here as an editor of the *Albany Evening Journal*, Dickens read from *A Christmas Carol* at Tweddle Hall, Mark Twain defended osteopathy at the Capitol, Robert Louis Stevenson passed through on his way to the Adirondacks, Edith Wharton's great friend Walter Van Rensselaer Berry grew up here, Joyce may have referred to the place secretly in *Finnegans Wake*, Hemingway married Martha Gellhorn, who used to work on the *Times-Union*, and William Faulkner died unaware that Albany existed.

Geographically this Albany exists 150 miles north of Manhattan and, during the racing season, 35 miles south of Saratoga. It is centered squarely in the American and the human continuum, a magical place where the past becomes visible if one is willing to track the multiple incarnations of the city's soul. I confront even a single street corner and there emerges an archetypal as well as an historical context in which to view the mutations of its trees, its telephone poles.

It is the task of this and other books I have written, and hope to write, to peer into the heart of this always-shifting past, to be there when it ceases to be what it was, when it becomes what it must become under scrutiny, when it turns so magically, so inevitably, from then into now.

*Legacy
from a Lady*

I awoke in the libraries of the city. This is as anomalous as it always is when a family that doesn't read raises a child who grows up to be a writer. I say they didn't read but I mean books; they all read the paper, my father giving it the last two hours before bedtime, a near-religious ritual with him. I also had an uncle who read books, of a kind not quite suitable for a child, though I read them anyway. My grammar school (P.S. 20) had no library, and my high school (Christian Brothers Academy) was one of, shall we say, modest resources. Every student's crutch in my neighborhood was the Albany Public Library system, and so it was that the John Van Schaick Lansing Pruyn branch on North Pearl Street became my personal point of entry into the beauty and magic of books. Good books. The trashy ones I collected on my own, stored them in the attic, and entered *their* magic with the firm intuition from my uncle that trash is also good for the soul.

I joined the Pruyn (rhymes with *mine*) as soon as I was old enough to take books out by myself. Was I ten? It stood on the southeast corner of North Pearl and Clinton Avenue, across the street from the Grand Theater, kitty-corner from the Palace, one of Albany's busiest intersections in the booming, bustling Downtown Age, when the crowds were six abreast on the sidewalks at high noon and all day Saturday, when all the trolley cars were crowded, and you had to stand in line to get into the movies or to buy two pounds of ambrosia, which in those days came packaged as Martha Washington's dark-chocolate butter creams.

The library was built as a free library by the family of J. V. L. Pruyn, a most eminent nineteenth-century Albanian, on the site of his birthplace. The building was dedicated in 1901, the centenary of Pruyn's birth, by his daughter Mrs. Charles Hamlin, whose maiden name was Huybertie Pruyn, and whose life would intersect my own in 1963, when I began researching the history of the city.

That intersection would mean relatively little to Huybertie Pruyn, for she was ninety years old when we talked, and we only met once face-to-face. But I discovered her further, and with great meaning for me, in her remarkable written record of her life and times in Albany during the last two decades of the nineteenth century, until she moved away.

She never really left the city spiritually, nor can the memory of her father, who died the year Huybertie was born. He was the paradigmatic Dutch Albanian of the nineteenth century. The Pruyn family traced its lineage back to the Schuylers and in a more remote way back to Brandt Aertsz van Slechtenhorst, who in 1646 was a director here of the Patroon's demesne of Rensselaerwyck. J. V. L. Pruyn was a state senator, a congressman, chancellor of the State University, counsel for the New York Central Railroad, a prime mover in the building of the State Capitol (he placed the first stone at its dedication), and a man of great wealth. His love of learning prompted his daughter to create the library as a memorial to him.

The library was a small architectural gem, a brick-and-brownstone structure with elaborate stained-glass windows, a huge revolving door, an iron grillwork railing around a narrow, precarious interior balcony, and fetching step gables in the old Dutch style. Inside, it was silent, solemn, and vast, as much a cathedral to my ten-year-old self as was Chartres in a later moment of awesome reverence for interior space.

The white-haired librarian with the pince-nez, the loose-fitting silk blouses, and the orthopedic shoes was the most soft-spoken, gentle woman I had ever met, including my revered great-aunts, who, though like her in a way, were very unlike her in communicating the nature of softness as a way of life. Her generosity was as impressive as the far reaches of the library's cathedral ceiling. She would give me any book I wanted, give it with a grace and a supreme courtesy I thought unique, but which I have since found to be an archetypal element in certain women who give their lives over to the care and handling of books and book borrowers.

I like to think her name was Anna.

There was another librarian on duty in Miss Anna's absence (Anna was definitely a Miss), and I think of *her* with an upturned nose, steel-gray hair pulled tight, wire-rimmed spectacles riding ominously low, brusque, imperious, and proprietarial about books, and forever shushing people who turned pages with too much flourish or had the temerity to clear their throats with vile-bodied impetuosity. I think of her as Miss Hetty (a Miss for reasons quite different from those which kept Miss Anna from connubiality). She, too, is perpetuated in the oversoul of librarianism.

And so there in the Pruyn Library, softly and without flourish, I made the acquaintance of Tom Swift, O. Henry, Rafael Sabatini, Nordhoff and Hall, Sherlock Holmes, Jack London, Charles Dickens, and that most loathsome purveyor of scandalous language, John Steinbeck. I checked out *Of Mice and Men*, a slim volume suited to my attention span in that day, and had not read more than six pages before I came across a g-d d--n and even more blasphemous utterances, right there on the printed page.

O hallowed trauma!

What was a conscience-heavy child to do in the presence of the occasion of sin? I swiftly took the book back, vowing never again to permit Steinbeck or his filthy ilk to corrupt my days.

But I kept confronting the rancid volume on subsequent walks past the shelf where it lurked, and before long, O puling weakling that I was, I checked it out once again, this time to finish it, to find myself weeping for Lenny, weeping even more vigorously for George, and full certain I would be a Steinbeck freak for years to come, and indeed was. And from then into the age of Joyce and Lawrence, Miller and Mailer, *Penthouse* and *Screw*, I came to adhere most wickedly to a new vow: that no man, no institution, and no abstraction, even one of my own making, should ever again hold censoring power over what I chose to read.

In those formative days, the Pruyn Library was a haven of warmth, a clean, well-lighted place that attracted winos and vagrants, crazies and shopping-bag ladies, and ordinary knights of the road of the Depression years, all lonely old people who would sit for hours looking at an open page of an atlas or the classified ads in the morning paper.

But if they nodded off to sleep, Miss Hetty would come running and usher them streetward, for libraries are for reading, not for sleeping. And the old folks coming off the nod would loudly protest, "I'm reading! I'm reading!" Of course when Miss Anna intervened in such cases, she would nudge the old folks into waking and let them go back to their atlases.

A rose for you, Miss Anna.

The library in an open society is an agency dedicated to the freedom of the mind as a creature comfort, the enemy of all tyranny, and why shouldn't that include the tyranny of isolation? If I ran a library I would recruit aged vagrants and shopping-bag ladies to come and use my facilities and hobnob sedately with the scholars in the far corner. It would give the place tone. It would keep me reminded of the need to preserve what I can of the receding past, and of my function as a keeper of universal and not merely elitist verities.

The wrecker's ball did in the Pruyn Library in 1968. Downtown had decayed into a disaster area, people stopped using the place, and also it interfered with the state's tidy plans for an access road to arterial highway 787. Lewis A. Swyer, an Albany builder who has been involved in a number of cultural contracts, recalled in conversation in the spring of 1983 that he had been a part of the effort to save the Pruyn. Mrs. Frederick deBeer, he said, was a principal figure in trying to rescue the library. A building-mover contractor estimated for Swyer in September 1965 that moving it to the north side of Clinton Avenue would cost $217,000, moving it to Orange and North Pearl streets, $267,000.

Swyer wrote in a letter about all this: "I do recall that the total amount to construct the foundation and basement, install sewer and water connections, electric utilities, and rehabilitate the building, once it was moved, amounted to $425,000." The city would have borne at least some if not all the financial burden for this, but Swyer recalled Mayor Erastus Corning wasn't sufficiently interested. Wrote Swyer: "I find myself feeling uncomfortably that just possibly, with a little more effort, the Pruyn Library would still be there."

But it isn't. Its collection was absorbed by the Albany Public Library system, of which it had long since been a branch.

The name Pruyn remains part of the main Albany library, in a fitting if less spectacular way, as the Pruyn Room, which houses a collection of books, clippings, maps, photos, and manuscripts relating to the history of Albany and environs, a treasure trove for Albany scholars. The Pruyn Room does not house Huybertie's writing, which is owned by the Albany Institute of History and Art in the McKinney Library, the library building itself (the mansion at Dove Street and Washington Avenue) being the former home of Huybertie's sister, Harriet, who married William Gorham Rice. The Pruyns were everywhere, and the pervasiveness of their influence, politically, culturally, and socially, is what Huybertie tells us about in splendid detail. A sampling of her tales appears in the Capitol Hill section of this book.

She was christened Huibertje—pronounced, roughly, she said, *Herbertcha*, with the accent on the first syllable. "But they couldn't swallow that in Saint Agnes School," she told me, and so she changed it to Huybertie, pronounced *Hi-Bertie* and shortened to Bertie by her friends.

She returned to live in Albany in her late, solitary years, and in her apartment on State Street, near Lark, I found her sitting in her own version of the Pruyn Library. She was surrounded by books by Irving, Emerson, Thackeray, by piles of papers and files, clippings and typescripts, by a bust of her father and a photo of Episcopal Bishop William Croswell Doane, and was reading, with the aid of spectacles and a magnifying glass, a letter she had written to John F. Kennedy, who was a friend from her Boston days, and who in a few months would be assassinated. She was a lifelong Democrat and her husband was a leading Boston Democrat who had been an assistant secretary of the treasury under Cleveland before his marriage to Huybertie, and was again under Wilson. He was a Yankee and Huybertie didn't like Yankees, but Hamlin proved to be an exception to her prejudice. She was chauvinistic about the Albany Dutch and talked of Yankees as if they were agents of the enemy, which perhaps they still were in the age she inherited, when people still talked about the Revolution and the Yankees the way we talk about World War I and the Jerries. The talk would now be considered quaint.

"We were not Yankees here at all [in Albany]," she said. "They were just limited to New England. The Dutch always spoke with scorn of the Yankees. It was about two hundred and fifty years that Dutch settlers were here, and even the English who were here then were down on them, for the Yankees wanted the east bank of the Hudson, just as the French wanted to come down and get New York harbor."

Huybertie had summered in Mattapoisett, Massachusetts, since 1900 and still voted from there in 1963. "I'm glad I don't vote in Albany," she said, a reference to the state of politics under incumbent Governor Nelson Rockefeller, who was in the midst of marital strife that would lead to his divorce and remarriage. "I don't have to call at the governor's mansion. You know what they call the mansion now? The woman's exchange."

Politics was central to her life. She lived thirty years in Washington and fifteen years in Boston. But wherever she lived she was an Albanian before anything else. She was born at 19 Elk Street in 1877 and lived there until her marriage in 1898. She became all but fanatical in recording her impressions of the city during those years.

"I always berate people for not knowing the history of Albany," she said. "There's so many interesting things to know about her. There's no place that's had so many interesting people. The Constitutional Convention in 1894 was a very interesting summer here."

Huybertie was, as is obvious from these remarks, extremely alert and not damaged mentally by her ninety years. But in other ways she was almost unbearably old, very near total deafness (I had to talk at double volume, though she spoke at normal level), and her eyesight was poor and getting worse. Her apartment was chilly, and so she wore a sweater and lap robe, warming her crippling body pains, which became visible when she stood up and moved across the room with tiny shuffling steps. There was an abiding grotesqueness in what age had done to this once vivacious and handsome woman, but there remained an aristocratic gauntness in her face: a concave fall to her cheeks. The wrinkles on her forehead were the gentlest of lines, and her mouth was beautiful.

She was not a great writer but she was a good one. I sense she lacked candor, for the work of hers I have read invariably brims with good taste and delicacy, and that takes you just so far and no farther. She also lacked what Proust called "the necessary constriction of a beautiful style," and yet she shared with Proust the mania for reconstituting the past with abundant small detail and nomenclature. But what one seeks from a life is more than detail. She wrote endlessly and yet never centered in on what lay beneath the veneer of her time. So the origin of her impulse was not in literature but in social history. "Munsell," she said (meaning Joel Munsell, the noted Albany printer and history preservationist), "didn't quite fit the bill. He didn't tell what people wore or what they ate. People criticized me for taking too much time on detail, but I did that on purpose."

She was fond of quiet irony but was either indifferent to or incapable of sustaining a dramatic scene. And so the work remains today in its original manuscript form at the Albany Institute and at a library in New Bedford, Massachusetts. She tried to publish it, and one New York publisher after another in the early decades of this century voiced enchantment with the writing, the writer, and the exceptional subject matter, but found it noncommercial.

This did not stop her from writing, for she was still working on manuscripts at ninety. "I once counted that I typed something like two thousand pages a year," she said. "I used to work here for as long as my eyes held out, for hours and hours. I wanted to leave a story of Albany in my time, what we did. My father was very fond of historical matters. He believed strongly in the history of Albany. You know, we're the oldest chartered city in the United States. I always throw that at Boston." (Albany is actually the second oldest; New York City is older.)

One of her stories concerns her meeting with another Albany writer imbued with history, Herman Melville. When I spoke with her I knew she'd written something about him, but I hadn't yet read it.

"He had a long beard," she recalled, "and when my mother and I stopped at Aunt Kitty's house on Washington Avenue [Aunt Kitty was Melville's first cousin, and was married to Abraham Lansing], we found them sitting around an open fire in the living room, and Uncle Abe was measuring out the most wonderful Madeira."

This was 1882 or 1883, and in her written recollection of it Huybertie quoted her mother as saying, "I'm very glad to see you, Herman," and Uncle Abe handed around the wine and toasted "Herman Melville's next book." His next would be *John Marr and Other Sailors*, twenty-five copies privately printed in 1888; his next great one would not be published until thirty-three years after his death in 1891: *Billy Budd*.

"I pulled up a chair next to him," Huybertie recalled, "and he asked, 'What history are you studying in school?' " Huybertie said Paul Revere, and then, she added, "He told me his grandfather was one of the so-called blue-eyed Indians who had given

the Boston Tea Party." Melville told her that when his grandfather's wife cleaned his clothes she found tea leaves in the pockets and cuffs and put them in a bottle. When last Huybertie heard
of the leaves they were in the Old State House Museum in Boston.

She wrote that she never saw Melville again, but asked her
mother on the way home from Aunt Kitty's who he was. "He is
a very curious character," she quotes her mother as saying. "He
wrote a famous work called *Moby-Dick* many years ago but it
seems to be forgotten now. I wonder if it will ever be revived."

We talked about many more things, none more poignant that
Huybertie's contemporary vision of her home on Elk Street, which
is still in use as an office and apartment building, a parking lot
alongside it, a restaurant—the 21 Club—downstairs next door,
another bar-restaurant up the block. The street is much changed
but more intact than anything else that was on Capitol Hill when
Huybertie first saw daylight. Not even the Capitol was up then,
or City Hall. The first three houses on Elk were slated to be torn
down in the early 1970s, to make way for the State Bar Association building, but they were saved—the facades were—because
of preservationist pressure and a brilliant architectural stroke by
James Stewart Polshek, who designed the Bar building with the
facades of the houses forming the southern wall of his otherwise
modern structure. And so at Elk and Eagle streets there is still a
vestigial sense of how it looked in Huybertie's day, although she
would not live to see the preservation. But she would not go near
Elk Street for other reasons, for it was painful. "You drive into
what was our garden," she said. "I don't go down there."

Huybertie Pruyn lived in the past more than most who have
such obsessions. Her childhood, youth, and young maidenhood
were certainly golden times for her, and perhaps after the death
of loved ones her reliving of those days became a form of therapy.
But there was something far beyond that in her. There was the
knowledge that it was important, and irreplaceable.

"Nobody is interested in the Shakers now," she said to me,
"and they have a flying field [she meant Albany Airport] out there
where they used to be. We used to drive out there a great deal,
and I've written a detailed account of their Sunday services. Nobody is interested now, but someday they'll be interested." And
of course she was right.

There is also her fastidious sense of what is the good and proper
life, and so her writing also becomes a handing-on of values. But

most important, she creates a world we can (and often do) walk in, and if she hasn't X-rayed the city's soul, she certainly photographed its aristocratic visage.

My articles about Elk Street and Huybertie appeared in the second week of February 1964. She wrote me a note in a crabbed hand that was almost unreadable but that reflected her graciousness and her acceptance of her declining condition and her solitude.

"I don't write much," she said, "my eyes are too poor. And I can't use them at night anymore. That's the trouble with being ninety. But I always have something to do in the morning, and I like people to come in at teatime in the afternoon. I'm very glad to be alone."

Huybertie died three weeks after she wrote to me. Her estate was auctioned on July 11, 1964, at Hyannis, Massachusetts. The belongings, which included a framed lithograph of Andrew Jackson and a print of Grover Cleveland with his signature on it, brought $15,255, of which the auctioneer took $3,028. Huybertie's posthumous worth, then, was a little over $12,000, but a relative said that at her death she was penniless.

The Romance
of the Oriflamme

*U*nion Station was magical be-
cause it was more than itself, which is how it is with any magical
man, woman, or building. It was more than utilitarian. It was
also an idea, a state of mind, a minor architectural wonder that
led you not only to the trains but to the idea of trains.

It was magical from the beginning and it was meant to be.
Those ceilings, fifty-two feet high, that monumental concourse,
were not casually designed. Space to move in had nothing to do
with the space that reached to the elegant roof. This was the
work of the Ozymandiastic minds of America's industrial cap-
tains: "Look on my works, ye Mighty, and despair!"

Who was ever more powerful than the railroads? Not even the
giants of the world who rode them. William Jennings Bryan was
among the first. His 1900 presidential campaign train rolled through
the station before the building was finished, and a political reporter noted the Great Commoner's common touch: "As the
train passed the new depot, he passed expressions of admiration
at the structure and waved his hat to a crowd of workmen who
were loudly cheering him from their scaffold."

The station was finished a year later when Teddy Roosevelt
came through from a hunting trip on Mount Marcy, changed
trains, and went swiftly on to Buffalo to take the oath as presi-

dent, William McKinley having just died from an assassin's bullet. Caruso, Melba, Diamond Jim bound for Saratoga, Al Smith, FDR, Herbert Lehman, Ike, and Adlai, heroes every one, arriving to cheering crowds, were stars of the moment but only human after all. The railroads were more than that.

When good Americans died in the nineteenth century, they went to Paris. When good American middle-class children of the first half of the twentieth century grew up, they went to Union Station and boarded a coach or, with luck, a Pullman, and rode into the awesome future.

What was a child of modest means and limited ways to make of that? The child knew only that trains passed over the Van Woert Street trestle and chugged up the Cut to the West, knew railroads had magic all right because in his kitchen there hung a sepia print of a grandfather and two granduncles standing beside Engine 151 on a clear day in the century's teens, and he knew the picture was holy. But once on the train what was the child to make of, say, the heavy silverware in the dining cars? What would he make of the black-skinned porters and waiters with coats as white as the dining-car tablecloths? What of the elegant silver coffee service or the plush sofas and chairs in the Pullman car, one even that swiveled like a drugstore stool so a sitter could look out of either window? What was the child to make of portly men with vests and watch chains and white mustaches, who smoked long dark cigars and read the *New York Sun* and drank whiskey out of heavy glasses as the trees and the river sped by at sixty? What was he to make of the elegant woman in the brown felt picture hat who stepped out of a Pullman compartment, looking forever in memory like Madeleine Carroll, that beauty?

The stone exterior of Union Station opened onto a world where such people and things existed. From the first glimpse, the magical connection was established, and the child could never enter through the doors again without the tissue of past awesomeness and present sophisticated anticipation congealing in an excited knot in the stomach. What next? Ah. What a splendid question.

The station was meant to be a wondrous thing, a gift of munificence from the New York Central to Albany. It was built of pink Milford granite and designed by Shepley, Rutan, and Coolidge of Boston, the architectural firm organized to complete the work of H. H. Richardson. Richardson was the great nineteenth-century American architect who designed Albany's City Hall and was a major figure in the design of the State Capitol. The station was meant to rank with these buildings.

The railroad men who stepped officially through its doorways for the first time on December 17, 1900, were as awed as anyone. Frank A. Harrington, superintendent of the Mohawk Division, was the very first, and a *Times-Union* reporter quoted him as saying, "Truly, it was an inspiration to enter the depot and study the beautiful architecture, the handsome ceiling, the mosaic floor, the chandeliers with their many incandescent lights."

Everything that day was magical. General agent Albert Brainerd of the New York Central's passenger department "engaged" John D. Wright to stay up all night and purchase the first tickets at the station so Brainerd could forward the tickets to George Daniels, the general passenger agent, a former patent-medicine salesman who brought showmanship to railroading, the man who invented the *Twentieth Century Limited.*

The first magical moment of that first day came when Wright handed a two-dollar bill to the ticket agent and said, "I want a ticket to Hudson and one to Chatham." The reporter assiduously noted the legendary details: Wright received sixty-seven cents in change—a fifty-cent piece, a dime, a nickel, and two pennies. The reporter listed all the firsts of that day in his story, among them veteran doorman Alfred Booth's calling of the first train. Quoth the reporter: "In a loud and clear voice that resounded all over the building, Booth announced: 'Train for Troy.' Then a little lower: 'Troy train.' "

Trivial?

Certainly. As trivial as a day in December 1968 when Union Station's closing was only days away. The very old dust was trivial then, thick on the walls, and beyond reach. That handsome ceiling was peeling. The mosaic floor was gritty with the tread of sixty-eight years. The redundant sign BAR—COCKTAIL LOUNGE—announcing the availability of strong drink to those benighted ones who might never have confronted a cocktail, and for those too effete ever to enter a mere bar—that sign was dark, the adjacent restaurant closed. Now franks, beans, and Coke were available at a snack bar that served coffee in plastic cups.

Even the great *Twentieth Century*, the train once celebrated in Ben Hecht and Charles MacArthur's play and movie of the same name (John Barrymore and Carole Lombard, magical people, rode the magical train), had faded away. The *Century* had been celebrated also in Alfred Hitchcock's film *North by Northwest*, but celebrated gratuitously, for the train's international reputation needed no embellishment. To go from London to Chicago in a proper manner, you took the *Queen Mary* to New York, the *Twentieth Century* the rest of the way. It had barbers, manicurists, secretaries, valets, bath attendants, gourmet chefs. Lucius Beebe called the train "an oriflamme of romance, a name to quicken the pulse, and its passing in the night a splendor." Now, on this December afternoon, the *Twentieth Century* was gone and the Chicago train was simply Train Number 61.

Trivial?

Of course. Ozymandias, too, is trivial with his head in the desert sand.

Some people now remember the station only as a wonderful place to get warm, to buy the out-of-town papers; or as the place where one night the Sheridan Avenue Gang stole the trousers off a sleeping policeman. The generations that came to Albany through it have their own memories of how it looked: the Jews escaping Russian pogroms and arriving at last at a substantial place from which flight would never again be necessary; the Italians coming to build the latter-day railroads; the World War II soldiers coming home, leaving the New York City brownouts and being cheered by the bright, garish lights of Albany's Broadway, that storied stem of gamblers and hustlers across from the station (that gone, too, now—parking lot now); the Christmas travelers pausing with their luggage to listen while carolers sang from the station's lofty balconies; or the Downtown shoppers picking up parcels the stores delivered to the station's checkrooms as a convenience when Downtown was still alive.

Now, in 1983, Union Station is the on-again, off-again centerpiece of a $100-million hotel and thirty-story office building project; and comparably ambitious developments are being readied up the street. New York State, which bought the station from its last owners, the Penn Central, spent a million to tidy it up, give it a new roof, new street canopy. It also rented the interior to a movie company for the shooting of some scenes in Melvyn Douglas's last film, *Ghost Story*.

One day, they say, if all goes well with all the elegant plans, there will be a railroad museum in the building somewhere, and a classy restaurant, and people passing through. How nice.

But the romance of the oriflamme is dead.

So surely and thoroughly gone, was it just a trick, then?

Oh no.

North Albany: Crucible for a Childhood

*S*ince North Albany is and will remain a place of childhood, then it has no business changing or declining or metamorphosing. I will have none of that, and so you must look elsewhere for its modern particulars, bad cess to them. This is, arbitrarily, capriciously, the way it is with memory: a winter morning in the mid-1930s at 620 North Pearl Street, Eddie Carey's apartment house, and my mother is going down the front stoop on her way to work. She is about the sixth step from the bottom when her foot flies outward and she bumpity-bumps downward, coat twisted, hat knocked cockeyed. She is flummoxed and bruised and her glasses are broken, a newly arrived bundle on the sidewalk ice. Just then a young Greek on his way to work in a meat market up the street comes by and tips his hat to my mother, says, "Good morning, Mrs. Kennedy," carefully steps over her, and keeps walking. My mother accumulates herself, climbs back to our first-floor apartment to restructure her condition, and brings to the family a new understanding of Greek restraint. In the winter of another season we are living across the street at 607 in one of Eddie Carey's one-family houses and I am going out into the cold morning with freshly pressed cassock and surplice that I will wear to carry a candle at my first funeral mass. I will be let out of class at nine-fifteen at P.S. 20 (for this was the age when public schools co-operated with young boys who aspired to sainthood) to be on the altar when mass begins at nine-thirty. Father John J. O'Connor, pastor of Sacred Heart Church, celebrates the mass and then dons a special robe to fling holy water and incense at the dead man's coffin down there in the middle aisle. Back in the sacristy, I stand behind the priest as he starts to disrobe. He presents his back to me, disconnects his collar clasp. I am expected to take the flowing robe from him and fold it, but I am so new at funerals I am utterly unaware of this. "I knew you were dumb, but I didn't think you were numb," the priest says to me and hurls the robe at another boy. Heretofore Father O'Connor mainly bored me. His sermons lacked verve. I didn't like him much but I didn't think negatively about him because in the second grade I had been quarantined with scarlet fever and he came to the house and at our improvised altar gave me First Communion. But as time went on and as I discovered he gave harsh penances in confession (four rosaries, three stations of the cross) and thought me numb and dumb, I reappraised him and realized he was a mean-minded son of a bitch and I was delighted when he was eventually transferred from Sacred Heart to a rural parish for reasons never made public. Father John J. Fearey, the assistant pastor, was the saintly priest you went to for confession. You'd been sinning like a maniac all week: robbing blind people, kicking cripples, coveting eight or ten of your neighbors' wives and daughters, eating hamburgers on Friday, going to movies that were listed Objectionable in Part by the *Evangelist*, and you go in and tell your achievements to Father Fearey and he says, Ah, well, now, be a good boy and say three Hail Marys and a good Act of Contrition. Next? Joe Keefe might have been next but there he was, fighting Dixie Davis, a new kid, up on School 20's athletic field across from my house, and it is one of the great fights of the age. The combatants start at the north end of the two gravel tennis courts where Charlie Bigley and his father are playing singles, and they flail and thwack their way down the field to the other end of the tennis courts, by the school. Joe's nose is bleeding and I am of course rooting for him because he is my buddy. But Dixie is getting in his licks. I think Joe might be winning when his mother appears and says it is time he came home and cut the hedges, which leaves it all unfinished. I vaguely remember Joe and Dixie pledging to resume the combat but I'm not sure it ever happened. Nosebleeds were the badge of victory because the bleeder usually quit. Only Joe didn't. Buddy Salvador said he was not going to let anybody know his nose was his weak spot or that he was a quick bleeder, for they'd go for the nose right away. I never remember anybody going for anything having to do with Buddy because he hit the long ball and was the guy you picked first in a choose-up game and had all the muscles a kid needed on Erie Street. That was the street where Dolly McAuley lived, a little dark-haired spinster (I think she colored her hair on into her seventies or even eighties) with a front room that had the sweet odor of antiquity to it. It probably dated to the 1860s, or earlier, with a huge ornate and always-shining silver stove in its center, great gilt-framed ancestors who overpowered what remained of the little room, and lace doilies and samplers and converted kerosene lamps and brocaded curtains with matching shawls on the horsehair chairs. I sat in this room with six dresses that had to be hemmed for my mother, and four white shirts with collars that had to be turned for my father, and Dolly would say, Yes, you can pick them all up Thursday, and on Thursday she would charge you thirty cents, or maybe sixty. Or maybe it was thirty cents to turn a collar, but how, you wondered, could she subsist on such earnings, unless she was still on the 1860 economy? Jim Yee, the Chinese laundryman on Broadway, charged fifteen cents to turn your shirt from a *sughan*, as my father would say, back into a garment suitable for dinner parties. Witty, toothless Chinaman (as everybody called anybody who looked Chinese, even if they came from Japan), Jim came to Albany after the First World War and survived into the Korean War (and beyond), when China was no longer an ally but the enemy, and so when you talked to him about China he smiled and pressed your shirt. Down the street from Dolly McAuley (she may have been related to Jimmy McAuley the ironworker, one of the toughest citizens the North End ever produced—he was in the Twenty-seventh Division in 1918, and on the ship going to France he fought the ship's champion and licked him) was where Eddie Carey had his North End Contracting Company and next door to him was where Father Francis Maguire established Sacred Heart Church in 1874: a pastor on horseback with a whip in his hand and a powerful fist that was called into use by neighbors in the age before they could ever, or would ever, think of calling in the police to stop a fight. Father Fearey, in a later age, confronted a husband just up the street from us in time to save the wife of the family from another uppercut, and then thrashed the husband to within an inch of the sod, advising him that the laying-on of hands was the province of thy God and my God, the Father. And I, as perhaps you have noticed, must be about my Father's business, so get up and leave the old girl alone. Father Maguire hated Erie Street because of the pigs and chickens that plagued his church during mass every time somebody left the church door ajar. But it was only temporary, for the funding of the real church was under way, and please, no donations over a hundred dollars (an exception being the Cassidy family—William Cassidy owned the *Albany Argus*— who donated the marble altar). Groundbreaking, with the help of mighty backs of the faithful themselves, began in 1876 and the church was finished in 1880, fourteen steps up now to the new sanctuary (at North Second and Walter streets) ensuring that only the most intrepid porkers could make it to mass. Out of that sanctuary in my time came six altar boys I knew well— Jackie Barnes, Red Robinson, Joe Girzone, and the three Kennedy brothers: Mike (I once saw him throw a football two and a half miles), John, and Tom. Jackie, Red, Joe, Mike, and John became priests, Tom a Christian Brother, for wasn't the cloth the grandest thing a young man could wear? I remember aspiring thus, but not beyond seventh grade, for even by then I intuited my embrace of the profane: I was drawing cartoons, printing my own news-paper, fixated on the world of print. I gave up drawing, perhaps in part intimidated by my betters: Billy Callagy, who could copy things and improve on the originals; and Bobby Burns, who in-vented complete comic strips, the hero of one unforgettably named Pimplepuss Perry. Bobby ran a clandestine dart game in his cellar that began to draw postprandial patrons about six-thirty. He was a double-twenty hustler with a spring in his arm and his knee that gave him a three-foot edge on the rest of us, and he financed most of his evenings at these games. Those evenings were usually spent at Mike DeTommasi's grocery store at Broadway and Bon-heim Street, across from the Bond Bakery. On any given balmy night in 1940 or 1941 there might be thirty-five boys on the corner: Joe Sevrons (who worked for Mike), Ray Olcott, Jimsy Burns, Georgie Boley, Neil Gray, Billy Allen, Jack Dugan, Bob Linzey, the Blocksidge brothers, the Kennedy brothers, Ted Flint, Lou Pitnell (the younger), Danny Bobeck, Gordon Jalet with his miniature one-armed roulette wheel, accepting all bets. If it had been a hot summer day probably half the crowd would have been to Mid-City Park to swim. We sifted sand at Mid-City's beach in late May to earn a season pass to swim in Albany's best public pool, owned by Henry Gratton Finn, a bowlegged, curly-white-maned Irish macho who strutted around the pool in his ur-bikini like Charles Atlas. He had once ridden in a circus with Buffalo Bill, and had run off with the Upside-Down Man's wife from one such show, perhaps while the Upside-Down Man was sliding down the wire on his head. Finn also owned Mid-City's skating rink, for which Howard Pugh, whose singular sense of humor often involved a resonant burp, had a predilection. Howard would, incomprehensibly to me, stare down from the rink's small balcony, enthralled by the skaters going round and round, a vision about as exciting to me as watching the weeds turn brown in October. There were girls down there, and I knew that as well as Howard and the rest of our crowd, but I was more enlivened when a carnival came to town—the O. C. Buck shows or the James Strates shows, among many. Gambling for useless gimcracks at these carnivals was very important, as was attendance at the sideshow to see the hydra-headed woman, the alligator-skinned hermaphrodite, and the human fetus kept alive by Spontaneous Electrolysis. The high dive, if they had one, was a high point, but far and away the most significant attraction was the kootch show, where you always watched the outdoor preview on the elevated platform in front of the tent, and sometimes even went inside, unless you were with a girl. I saw my first stripper at the O. C. Buck Show with Bobby Burns. After the first performance (thirty-five cents a ticket) they announced a second and special show for fifty cents extra in the back of the tent, and with some trepidation we paid and entered and saw a voluptuary named Carmen remove the ultimate garment before the eyes of a double dozen of us, I certainly the youngest. Carmen sat on the edge of a chair, then took the hat off a man at the rim of the stage in front of her, and passed the hat provocatively over her body. Some hooted and whistled at this sight, though I think my awe prevented such effusion. My thought was that the man would have to dispose of the hat immediately after the show but from the look of him in memory I wonder now if he perhaps did not take it home and have it bronzed. Walking home, Bob said to me that that was the closest I would ever get to a woman's anatomy until I was married and I thought that rather a pity: What a fate for such a sinner as I. Alas, Bob's prophecy proved incorrect but I will save that story for another day to give it its due. At this point my education in sensuality was largely restricted to party games, most notably at Patsy Selley's house, where Post Office was not only permitted but was the unstated reason that no one ever turned down an invitation, including the most significant and beautiful girls of our set. In what other province of North Albany society could a grammar-school undergraduate gain first-hand experience on how to behave when he found himself alone with a girl in a dark room? Patsy, a beautiful child with long curls like Shirley Temple's, danced on pointe in white toe shoes and tutu whenever our classes were called upon for performing artistry. I played banjo, but not while she danced. Or maybe I did. Maybe I played "The One Rose," and then Bob Burns would draw cartoons on an easel onstage and amaze us all. The vixens among us distinguished themselves offstage in a different style. Jean Pitnell went for older men, high-school freshmen, when she was still in seventh grade. Chloe Wood broke one of Bob Hancox's front teeth with a right cross and it was love in bloom for months thereafter. Ruth Hesser listed her order of preferences: Bill Callagy, then Bob Hancox, and me in the show position. She told us this while all three of us were climbing an apple tree to impress her. The girls of the North End were always a treasure to be zealously guarded—more so, perhaps, in my father's truculent time, and the time of Jack Murray, my next-door neighbor who became postmaster and president of Albany's Common Council. "If anybody came up from the South End and got out of line or started fooling around with the North End girls, then they got more than they were looking for," said Jack. But North Enders ran the same risk when they went to dances on South End turf, for neighborhoods were psychologically sovereign states where any intruder had to prove himself free of inimical design before he was given a visa. The North End lent itself to exclusion by its geography. Only Broadway—the Troy Road—ran through it on its way north. This was the main artery until 1925, when a bill sponsored in the Common Council by then-Alderman Jack Murray approved the cut-through for North Pearl Street, which until that time had dead-ended northbound at Pleasant Street. The cut-through opened Pearl to connect with its North End self, which began again at Emmett Street and ran into Menands. Eddie Carey built about thirty houses on Pearl between North First Street and Lawn Avenue, most of them one- and two-family homes, plus two apartment buildings (I lived in all three types), and created the style for the neighborhood: front and back yards, front and back porches, attic and full basement, garages attached to the one-families. Carey built about fifty houses in all, the first

Mid-City Park* ▢

Hawkins Stadium* ▢

WOLFERT AVE.

BLVD.

LOUDONVILLE

LIMERICK DR.

Wolfert's Roost Country Club ▢

THOMAS ST.

LAWN

HUTTON ST. AVE.

LINDBERGH AVE.

N. THIRD ST.

BONHEIM ST.

MENANDS

To Troy

(formerly Erie Canal)

SHAKER RD.

NORTHERN BLVD. RD.

VAN RENSSELAER

MAGUIRE AVE.

BRADY AVE.

P.S. 20

N. SECOND ST.

NORTH ST.

MAIN ST.

CENTER ST.

N. FIRST ST.

SOUTH ST.

ERIE ST.

Hudson River

Sacred Heart Church

MOHAWK ST.

WALTER ST.

CHAMPLAIN ST.

Lower Patroon Island

ALBANY ST.

EMMET ST.

GENESEE ST.

TIVOLI ST.

PEARL

N. BROADWAY

BRIDGE ST.

BLVD.

LUMBER DISTRICT*

MILL ST.

ERIE ST.

North Albany

*Now gone.

ten completed in 1925, and these, said a newspaper reporter,
"wrought a miracle in the physical appearance of North Albany."
The new School 20 was completed in 1923 on the site of the old
North End School, fronting on North Pearl. And behind it, rising
up to the ridge of Van Rensselaer Boulevard, were the hills that
had been part of John Brady's farm. Before that the land had been
a piece of the Patroon's feudal domain, called Rensselaerwyck,
different from the Patroon's other domain, known as Beverwyck,
the original part of the city. Jeremias Van Rensselaer, son of the
first Patroon (Kiliaen Van Rensselaer), had established Rensselaerwyck with its center about at Tivoli Street. In time a manor
house was built there on fertile flatland east of where Broadway
runs, at the edge of what came to be called the Patroon Creek,
once the main source of city water, and which still courses down
to the river from the western highland. A colony of workers and
servants grew around the Manor House and in time the settle-

ment was called the Colonie, and annexed to Albany in 1815. This was the beginning of the North End. By the 1850s lumber was almost as important to the North Enders as Jesus and a good glass of ale, for the Lumber District had grown up between the river and the Erie Canal. The city was so proud of its leading enterprise that it called itself the White Pine Center of the World. On July 8, 1854, the District had forty-six firms, seven doing more than half a million dollars in business annually, twenty-nine over $100,000. The District ran northward from the sheltered harbor, known as the Basin, along the Erie Canal, to Lock Number 2 at North Street in North Albany. The logs came down the Canal, were turned into lumber in the District's sawmills (their boilers fired by wood shavings) and put on riverboats waiting at the slips that connected the Canal to the Hudson. My father remembered a social group called the Lumber Handlers. "All of Limerick was in that," he said, Limerick being the name of the North End. The Moulders was another such group he remembered, with many North Enders in it who worked at the foundries—Rathbone, Sard's, on Ferry Street, which employed 2,700 workers in 1885, making 220,000 stoves a year. The Lumber Handlers and the Moulders ran annual affairs in Union Hall, Downtown at Hudson Avenue and Eagle Street, until they put in roller polo and spoiled the dance floor's cork center with the skates. They put a new floor in, said my father, but it was never the same. My father and Bill Corbett, who worked for the post office, were almost the same age and both remembered learning to swim in the Canal (you were thrown in and swam or sank). They remembered Lagoon Island, an amusement park that ran down, and then P. J. Corbett, Bill's father, built it back up and called it Al-Tro (for Albany-Troy) Park on the Hudson, a grand place. Later still it was Dreamland, all of these near the foot of Garbrance Lane in Menands, and accessible by boat and foot. The last such place was not on the water but on the Troy Road. It was called Mid-City Park and it had a roller coaster and merry-go-round, pool and skating rink. It was fading seriously in the Depression years, though the pool and rink persisted. It stood next to Hawkins Stadium, the home of the Albany Senators in the Eastern League (Class A baseball). In an earlier age Albany had been in the International and State leagues, its games played at Chadwick Park, about where Hawkins was. Before that the Senators played at Riverside Park in Rensselaer, where Dewey

Begley, a lifelong North Ender, remembers the players knocking the ball into the river. Dewey had a future as a pitcher, and was ready to go with the St. Louis Cardinals when he got such a pain in his back a doctor ordered him to stop playing. It turned out to be a kidney stone, and instead of going to the big leagues Dewey went on the police force for forty-two years, retiring as a captain. Professional ball was also played in Dewey's day at Island Park, where the Menands Bridge begins. The circus pitched its tent near the bridge in the 1930s and 1940s. In earlier eras the circus had come to Peacock Park in North Albany, where the Niagara Mohawk Power Company (the gasworks before it went straight) now stands. In my time the circus unloaded behind Union Station, Downtown, and every year at three in the morning on circus day Lou Pitnell and his father would be on the siding, watching it all happen. I made that scene only once, content generally to sit on the front porch at home and see the line of animals and wagons course through North Albany at a more civilized hour. The circus lions got loose in Menands once, and in the 1950s there was an elephant crisis. *Times-Union* city editor Barney Fowler put through some elephant photos that came from circus press agents and they appeared in print the next morning. Later that day when the circus itself arrived and some elephants broke loose and wandered around Downtown, an intrepid *Times-Union* photographer snapped them on their spree. Barney duly submitted the spectacular photos to Ed Nowinski, the news editor, who rejected them. We had elephants yesterday, said Ed. A vivid moment in my personal animal coverage was the obituary I wrote on Langford, widely known North Albany cat. He'd undergone surgery for a tumor and seemed to be recovering, but then, as his owner, Jerome Kiley, who cleaned beer coils for a living, told a gathering at Jack's Lunch, "Langford took a turn for the worse and they had to gas him." Mourners at Jack's chipped in six dollars for a floral wreath of pussy willows with a bird atop them and a card in the bird's beak with the message to the departed: "I don't have to worry about you anymore." Jim Dempsey, who was ninety-four when we talked, raffled off another cat during a fund-raiser for Sacred Heart Church in the early 1890s. A plaster-of-Paris cat was the presumed prize, but it was really a neighborhood cat Jim had stuffed into a box. Father Francis Toolan was pastor and a crowd gathered as Jim spun the raffle wheel. Professor O'Brien, principal of School 20, won and Jim handed over the box. When O'Brien took the cover off, the cat jumped out and ran away. "Father Toolan laughed till he cried," said Jim, "and Prof O'Brien didn't speak to me for a week." My father remembered another animal disaster: Hunky Bucher, who went hunting in Lamb's Lot with a shotgun taller than himself, shot a goat and had to pay a fine. Hunky stepped off his stoop one night, unaware that Dike Dollard, the paving contractor, had moved it to put in a sidewalk. "Hunky took one step," said my father, "and walked right off the edge. If he hadn't of been drunk he'd have died." More serious problems came in with the winter months. In mid-December in the nineteenth century when the Hudson froze solid and no lumber moved, the North End women smoked and salted meat and preserved vegetables, and men went to work cutting ice on the river, their teams of horses hauling huge blocks of ice up the frozen riverbanks. Jim Dempsey was around in 1890 when electric trolleys replaced the horsecars, but that didn't happen in the Lumber District, where the horsecar continued its run until about 1920; and its departure then meant the District was all through. Lumber supplies from the Adirondacks had already been dwindling in the 1890s, and by 1915 were all but exhausted. Lumber mills closed, the twenty-five-foot lumber piles vanished (Kibbee's was one of the last to go). And then the foundries left, the result of new Western ore sources and their owners' desire to situate their plants near coal mines. "The face of the neighborhood changed," Jack Murray said. The Eastern Tablet Company and the Albany Paper Works, both spin-offs from the lumber, opened up, and the Albany Felt Mill developed, providing new employment for North Enders. Skilled workers found jobs at Simmons Machine Tool, run by Charlie Simmons, a self-made millionaire who started as a machinist in the West Albany railroad shops; or they went with Ramsey Chain, founded by James H. Ramsey. Abetted by the money of millionaire Anthony Brady Farrell, Ramsey manufactured his own invention, the silent chain drive, next door to Simmons Machine in Menands, beginning in the 1920s. Everyone knew the Lumber District was gone for good when Dinny Ronan's Lumber District Saloon closed. His son Andrew kept on with the family grocery business, which had begun by serving canalboats and came to be the North End's largest grocery. Andy was also close to the O'Connells. "He could be very helpful if you were looking for something," said Jack Murray. "You couldn't make a move without him," said my father. Dan and Ed O'Connell came to the North End every Sunday for conferences with Ronan and other North End Democrats—Judge Brady, and Mike Conners (Dick's father), the insurance man, and Big Jim Carroll, my great-grandfather, and Will Cook, a noted orator who nominated Al Smith for governor during a Democratic convention at Saratoga and took a trolley to get there. The men met at the Phoenix Club, a small and pudgy brick building at Broadway and North First Street, a relic that had been the Patroon's land office, and to which the farmers of Rensselaerwyck brought their rent in the form of tribute—corn, produce, hens, and chickens. Bill Corbett remembered the Phoenix Club's interior decor: "A pool table, a card table, and a lot of conversation." Some of the North End Democrats had been leaders before Dan's takeover, during the age when being a Democrat in this city was mostly a badge of honor. It got you little else, for the city was controlled by Billy Barnes, the Republican boss. Yet in the North End the Democrats always boasted that their ward, the Ninth, was the only one that never went Republican in the Barnes years. Homage to this solidarity was paid by the Republicans in the first decade of the century when they redistricted in order to move Gardner's boardinghouse on Broadway, Downtown (near Orange Street), out of the Sixth Ward and into the Ninth, so its thirty-five Republican votes could perhaps tip a scale or two in the solidly Democratic North End—this desperate move recalled by Tim Lyden, a Sixth Ward Democratic alderman in a later age. Irish Democrats might have united against the enemy but they fought one another viciously, Big Jim Carroll once pulling Tom Martin off a trolley in order to knock him down for good and sufficient political reason. Rampant Democratic factionalism was encouraged by Barnes and was one of the secrets of his success. The O'Connells understood this and when they assumed power in the party they imposed a new harmony on it, centering control in their own ward leader, Joe Henchey, who would later become sheriff and remain leader of the Ninth Ward until his death in the 1950s. Henchey was a mystery to me as a child, merely a man with power I didn't understand. But I remember him vividly in a light-plaid, double-breasted suit with high collar, a very tight and carefully knotted tie, and rimless spectacles, walking up from the middle of our block, where he lived, and passing our house on a spring evening—no, it is early summer, but he is nevertheless wearing that tie, and he tips his sailor straw hat to my grandmother, who is sitting on our front porch after dinner, she having watered the geraniums and now waiting for Eddie Cantor to sing to her over the radio. Joe smiles from a face that is wrinkling badly and walks on to only God knows where, around the corner and down to Broadway, perhaps, to catch the Downtown bus. The trolleys were no longer running on Broadway and even the tracks had been taken up to be turned into shrapnel we assumed would be used against the Japanese. Some people were calling Jim Yee a Jap, which brought out the worst in his Chinese vocabulary. Bobby Burns was in the Navy by now, as was Bob Linzey. Charlie Bigley was a Marine, Ray Olcott was in the Navy Air Corps, Russ Blocksidge the Army Air Corps. We who were a shade too young to enlist or be drafted kept up with the progress of our friends through the picture gallery in the window of the elder Louie Pitnell's barbershop across from the carbarns. Snapshots, wallet photos, one or two eight-by-tens (I seem to remember Joe Murphy with a bomber and crew pictured on one of those—I think Joe was a pilot) were pinned up as families brought them along to Lou. Joe Keefe had an ear problem and the services wouldn't take him, so he enrolled in the Merchant Marine Academy and served that way and had the best-looking uniform of anybody in the war. Georgie Boley went into the Navy Air Corps and one day we heard he was dead. Then we heard Charlie Bigley, whose tennis serve I could never return, had caught it on the first wave at Saipan. Shadow Britt, a Marine, also caught it, and Joe Christian, who ran a pretzel business, lost two of his sons to the fighting. The score on all these matters was kept by both Sacred Heart Church and School 20, and for years after when you went to mass or into the school to vote, you saw the names and the gold stars on the Honor Roll. Those rolls are gone now, that war so very far away. Vinny Marzello went into the Navy Air Corps as a V-5 and came out of Quantico and transferred to the Marines as a fighter pilot, fought in the Pacific and survived. In the Korean War as a Marine pilot he destroyed a Communist MiG-15 in aerial combat, flew 142 missions, won eight Air Medals and two Distinguished Flying Crosses, and rose to the rank of captain. Then, in September 1954, on a routine flight as a test pilot, he failed to clear some trees at Atlantic City and never ejected. I liked Vinny a lot (he was a big kid, I was a little kid, and I'd look for him after mass to say hello) because he sold me his record player for fifteen dollars, the best acquisition of my life after my bicycle. I'd already bought a Tommy Dorsey record, "Not So Quiet Please," for the great drum solo by Buddy Rich, even before I owned a player. For two months before I got Vinny's machine I would take the record out and look at it and try to remember how the solo went, for the banjo was going out of style and I'd decided playing the traps was a nobler goal. I was wrong again, but children are supposed to be wrong, otherwise they would be as infallible as adults. This was the age of Glenn Miller and Artie Shaw and Harry James and Bing Crosby, who had a look-alike in my neighborhood: Ben Burns. Ben played golf, too, like Bing, and had Bing's smiling and genial personality. The difference was that Ben was for real and Bing turned out to be an authoritarian punk. The Andrews Sisters were very big and had a record, "Rum and Coca-Cola," that was so popular you couldn't buy a copy anyplace. Also you couldn't hear it on the radio because of the risqué lyrics about a mother and a daughter both working for the Yankee dollar you know how. When my uncle Pete McDonald got word of my deprivation, he convinced a Downtown bartender to take the record off the jukebox, and Pete brought it home to me, scratched all to hell, but invaluable, for playing the new records was a collective pastime as important as baseball or darts or hanging out at Mike's. It was what you did when it was raining or you were too exhausted to do anything else, though I don't remember much exhaustion in those days. The action seemed endless: tennis, ball games always, in all seasons, even playing with the older men, Andy and Jim and Red and Knockout Lawlor, all brothers, and Joe Murphy (not the pilot), who had played, I think, with Elmira, and Walt (Pansy) McGraw and Pete McDonald and Emerson Judge and John (Bandy) Edmunds, maybe the best baseball player the North End ever produced, a shortstop who went off to play in the big leagues but wouldn't put on a uniform, got homesick, came home a week later, and spent the rest of his life as a hoseman at the Engine Eight (Eightsies) Fire House at North First and Broadway, to which his sister Marie would walk five blocks down and five blocks back home carrying him a hot lunch in a picnic basket. These men gathered—not often enough—after dinner to chase flies and grounders and show us how it was done. Andy Kean would show up with a baseball doctor's kit full of thread and needles and thimbles and beeswax and scissors and tape to repair and do preventive maintenance on the assorted baseballs that those stalwarts were so anxious to knock the cover off of the way they used to. In the daylight hours when there was no game there was the wilderness of the old Brady farm, the Hills, which spread out between North Pearl at the bottom and Van Rensselaer Boulevard at the top, and this was a magical setting—

open, grassy slopes that probably had been grazing land for decades and that abutted a gully (we called it the Gully) down which
placidly coursed a creek (we called it the Creek) and up which
you could walk like Natty Bumppo, beginning in the lowland
swamp with its cattails and then into the apple-and-crabapple-
tree zone that was all that remained of what I now assume was
a Brady orchard, and then into the shallow beginnings of the
Gully, where I took my first (and only) chew of tobacco and threw
up, and up the rising gorge toward the Indian Ladder, rather steep
on each side and across which someone, I think it was Jimmy
Becker, felled an oak tree as a bridge, and up farther to the Cowboy
Ladder—loose shale, down and up which you had to climb simply
because it was there, and of course you slid and cut yourself and
ruined your pants but that was what you were supposed to do.
At night there was tennis and if the ball game hadn't started, or
was over, you could take a seven iron and loft golf balls at the
setting sun and the early moon. If no one was around to give you
a game of anything you could take a rubber ball and go to one of
two ledges at the side of School 20 and throw the ball against
them, and if you caught either of the ledges just right the ball
would not bounce back at you as usual but make a pop fly of
itself, and so even in solitude the game was afoot. You were never
solitary for very long, anyway, for it was an Irish neighborhood
that believed in overpopulation. It was the same at the diner in
a later year when you came home from the movies alone on the
bus and stopped for a hamburger or a Danish or buttered toast.
If there was no one there you just waited and they'd come, although you really didn't need them in the diner because there
was always Rex, the English waiter, a witty magpie who showed
off by carrying too many dishes at once, and Herbie Leahy, the
night manager, who had great style. I remember him serving a
cup of coffee with the panache of Humphrey Bogart, though he
looked more like Richard Widmark. The diner was on Broadway,
just north of North Third Street, next door to the Nehi bottling
company. I seem to remember its arriving, all glistening chrome
and red leatherette, one afternoon around 1937. It lasted into the
1960s but its real importance was in the war years, when you
went there as ritual. Rex served my grandmother a French cruller
with her tea one night and because it had vast, uninhabited space
inside it she called it a Gone With The Wind and so did we all,
ever after. Marge Keefe, a dark-haired beauty from Rensselaer,
worked there as one of the first waitresses. She remembered Ralph

Kiner coming in for coffee when he was playing for the Albany Senators and she remembered another player's refusing to sit next to a black man at the counter and bawling out the owner for letting blacks in. H. H. Monette, the owner, often had to provide transportation for his short-order cooks, who seemed to be occupationally drunk most of the time and not always sure what day it was. He would corral them at their fleabag hotel, then stop at King Brady's saloon, across the street from the diner, and get them a few shots to rev them up, at which point they would confront the grill and the frying pans with a smiling vigor, however artificially induced. Marge also remembered one man named Rummy who was cutting baloney with a butcher knife, his hand shaking so badly she feared for his thumb; and when she told Kenny Sharples, the day manager, the problem, Kenny bought Rummy another set of doubles at Brady's and that got him and his thumb safely through the lunch-hour rush. You couldn't always get into Brady's, there being laws against serving alcohol on Sunday before one p.m. Brady's had a side door for customers in severe need but not everyone was let in, and some who weren't brought their own bottle to the diner and spiked their coffee with it after mass while waiting for the oasis to reappear on the corner. Marge remembered that her best tip, five bucks, came from one such anxious customer, whose bankroll matched his gratitude for small favors, like that essential cup of coffee. Marge's good looks and other endowments did not escape the eye of my uncle Peter, who brought his sisters to the diner to meet her, and when they approved he took my grandmother to lunch there to clinch the deal, and Pete and Marge were married fourteen or maybe it was sixteen years later, either figure a normal courting interlude for Irish aspirants to bonding. The diner ran out of food on V-J Night in 1945, not even a slice of bread left, and closed its doors for the first time because of the orgiastic all-night revel in peace. When you think of that peace settling in, and no war to seal the fate of your friends, then you look elsewhere for how people died strangely or prematurely. Alice Moffat, with a doll's face and pigtails, was killed sleigh riding: a car hit her. I think she was in fourth grade. A terrific neighbor, with a marvelous but sad smile, hanged himself one morning while the family was at church, and another neighbor I didn't know took the pipe in his garage. An elderly Irish woman who lived alone and was the best buddy and chief antagonist of my Aunt Libby, died and was buried without a wake: her son hated her and refused her the final farewell of the few friends she had left in the world. Russ Block-sidge died young in the Veterans Hospital. Ray Olcott came out of the service, went to college for a time and drove a cab but didn't like civilian life anymore. He was a cowboy at the wheel and claimed to have made it from downtown Albany to midtown Troy once in twelve minutes, which I think is physically impossible even on superhighways, but maybe not. Anyway, Ray wanted to fly, really, and reupped, in the Air Force this time, and wound up as a pilot in Korea. He was a Lutheran and wrote to Bobby Burns when he was into his fortieth or so mission that Bob should pray to J.C. for him. Bob wrote back that J.C. didn't listen to Lutherans and had an ear only for Catholics, but would pray anyway. The prayer didn't work. On his forty-ninth mission Ray's plane was shot down over North Korea. His two crewmen bailed out but Ray was wounded and went down with his plane. He was listed as missing, and still is, I think, but everybody agreed he was dead except his mother, who lived into the late 1970s insisting he was still alive in China. Bill Corbett's son Billy (called Snorko) was a classmate of mine in grammar school. He was a handsome, loose-limbed lefty who threw his bat after he hit a pitch, and so standing close to him at the plate was risky. He and I skipped school once when we were high-school sophomores and went to a dumb Claudette Colbert movie and got caught and reamed out by everybody. He fell ill with leukemia and lingered awhile in the hospital, but then at the age when the rest of us were heading for college, or a full-time job, Snorko died. The first death I saw close at hand was my mother's uncle, Johnny Carroll, who ran the North End Filtration Plant for the city, built in 1898 under the city's largest contract ever, $300,000, to filter Hudson River water when it was still filterable. But by the 1930s the plant was only standby equipment, a ghostly place where Johnny took me when I was looking for a sink to furnish my chemistry laboratory in the cellar of our house. He found one that probably dated to 1902 and had it trucked to my house and installed; and there the mad scientist of North Pearl Street learned how to use his Gilbert Chemistry Set to make green dye and fizzly gunpowder and to throw around terms like cobalt chloride without ever knowing what it was good for except turning itself purple if you left the top off. Hours and hours passed pleasantly by the sink and I thought only great thoughts of Johnny, who could make me laugh hysterically by shattering half a dozen saltine crackers while trying to butter them. He contracted bronchial pneumonia, coughing painfully and wasting away from the sliver of a man that he was all his life. When he died I cried because I thought I was supposed to cry. But what I didn't know was you can't really cry when you're supposed to if you don't mean it, unless you are an accomplished actor. And I can almost work up a tear now, forty years' distant, when I think what a loss to the family it was when that witty and wiry and wonderful fellow coughed his last. I feel constricted when I think of ending this chapter, for every memory stirs another one and I think of all the people I haven't mentioned. I haven't even mentioned the Paynes, Lottie the seamstress and her brother George, of Main Street, children of slaves, the only black family in the neighborhood on into the 1940s. And Joseph K. (Fritz) Emmett, who was maybe North Albany's most famous resident ever, a German dialect comedian and yodeler who was really an Irish tenor, an international celebrity long before he retired in 1882 to build his castle-style villa at the top of Van Rensselaer Boulevard. Governor David B. Hill took it over after Emmett's tenure and eventually it became the Wolfert's Roost Country Club, the social province of the affluent Albany Irish. The villa burned in 1926 and a new clubhouse was built on its site. And since we are on the Boulevard it is important to mention Bill Carey, son of Eddie, and his story about the noontime rush at Gillespie's saloon at Genesee Street and Broadway during the free-lunch era that gives insight into Irish pragmatism. Bill was five, sitting near the food and twirling one of his gloves. The glove flew through the air and landed in a kettle of Gillespie's famous soup. "Just then the noon whistle blew and the men came in from the gasworks for their lunch," said Bill. "I was crying to get my glove back but they gave me a nickel to keep quiet about what happened to the glove and they kept ladling out the soup." Gillespie's is gone and the old Irish style is changed, but not rapidly enough for some: Richard Shaw, for instance. He is an Irish-Catholic priest who served in Sacred Heart parish during the 1960s, when the Vatican was modernizing the mass and other Catholic rites, and he was pressing vigorously for the changes, following the Vatican lead. But the North Albany Irish refused to change and viewed Shaw as a radical, a hippie. "I was the obedient one, damn it," he said. "I was doing what the church said to do. The old guy with the shock of white hair and jutting Irish chin, and the old biddy saying her rosary, they were the radicals. And the by-product of the battle everywhere was that convents fell apart, the priesthood diminished, people were leaving in droves." He was talking with bitterness, not only about North Albany but of the change-resistant, conservative Irish everywhere. This decline of Catholicism is well documented, and not all of it was the result of Irish knuckle-headedness, though some of it surely was, often at high clerical levels. One little-understood by-product of the controversy is the clarity of Irishness it brought to some Irish Catholics. Peggy Conners Harrigan, daughter of Richard J. Conners, granddaughter of Michael Conners of Phoenix Club fame, remembered her North Albany as being Irish, yes, but that was not all of it: "I felt I had as much affinity with people whose names were Yanni as I did with people with names like McNally. We were all Catholics. I guess it's part of that melting-pot mystique fostered by the church so people growing up in an Irish area like Albany would think of themselves as Catholic and then Irish, rather than Irish and then Catholic." Her grandfather Michael, the first to make a major mark in the Conners family, had been born in 1859 and was so conscious of the discrimination Irish Catholics faced he named his four sons Herrick, Richard, James, and Edgar, "specifically non-Irish," said Peg, "for he felt an Irish first name with the surname of Conners would be a double handicap. It was hard to tell whether people were having problems because they were Irish or Catholic or both in the teens and 1920s. But people certainly weren't pushing Irish-bog values on their children." Quite true. We grew up aware of our Irish connection but more aware of being North End Democrats, really, more aware of being American and Catholic, and eventually resistant to all of it, anxious to break all such ties and assert a vigorous independence of mind and spirit. I walked out of mass during narrowback sermons, refused to sing "Too-ra-loo-ra-lo-ra," registered to vote as an independent, which raised eyebrows at the registration table in School 20, though my father, who was in line right behind me, never blinked, and he always worked these polls as a Democratic inspector. I believed the enemies in the world then were the goddamn Irish-Catholic Albany Democrats, who were everywhere dominant, benighted, and pernicious. I thought myself free, and found out that not only wasn't I free, I was fettered forever to all of it, most surprisingly the Irishness, which was the only element of my history that wasn't organized, the only one I couldn't resign from, and, further, the only one that hadn't been shoved down my throat. My family liked Bing Crosby and Father Coughlin, sang a few Irish ditties when singing was in order, wore green on St. Patrick's Day, but knew nothing of Irish history, rarely spoke of the Irish Troubles then or now (my father sometimes mentioned the Black and Tans), had no more links to relatives there on either side of the family, and if they remembered the anti-Irishness that prevailed in nineteenth-century America, they repressed it. I vaguely remember my uncle's once calling somebody an "APA son of a bitch," those initials being a code word for the enemy, handed on from the 1890s, when the nativist American Protective Association, an anti-Irish, anti-Italian, anti-Catholic group that was more significant for its bigoted oratory than for any lasting changes it effected in law or culture, was active. I remember asking what the APA was, but got no satisfactory answer beyond "a bunch of Protestant bastards." In time such things seemed to fade, and yet with the passing years an Irish quality reemerged. Peggy Conners found herself and her family talking proudly of their Irish heritage, separate from their Catholicism. A pal of mine from Gloversville, Jerry Mahoney, said I got more Irish as I grew older. I think he was suspicious of it. I went to Ireland twice, and last year even started to write a book about the Irish, but that is a dead issue. I am not Irish but I am. I can't sing but I will. Some of my friends, a few years younger than I, reject their Irishness and believe they have made the leap into the great American puddle of ethnic meltedness. I know what they mean. I went to the St. Patrick's Night Dance at the Ancient Order of Hibernians in the mid-1970s and it was great sport, but very exhausting; and all that green made me color-blind for a week. Too much, too much. I am not *that* Irish. But I am not quite anything else, either. The North End made me and nothing exists powerful enough to unmake me without destroying the vessel. I try not to bear witness to the change in the neighborhood, try not to retrace old steps except in memory. It is sometimes true, as Proust said, that the only paradise is the paradise we've lost, and I have lost a bit of it. The loss began in the 1950s when the city housing project, Corning Homes, brought a thousand new people into the North End, right in the middle of the hills where the Gully and the Cowboy Ladder used to be. In their place came an island of strangers. Then Interstate 90 cut through, displacing seventy families, eliminating Genesee Street and Eightsies and the traction company's carbarns and Lou Pitnell's barbershop and Joe Whelan's saloon. The North End lived through this. In 1982 Ted Flint, a lieutenant on the police force and a lifelong pal of mine, was still living there; and so was Billy

Blocksidge, who, like Ted, had put on some weight. Dick Conners is still a North Ender and commutes to the Assembly from Bonheim Street; and Bob Linzey's mother, Anne, still lives on Wolfert Avenue. My father lived on North Pearl until 1970, ten years after my mother died, and came with us for his last five years only after his willful solitude became not unbearable but unmanageable. When we moved him out I no longer had reason to go back. And so it ended there, and what is left to be stated is the synthesis of it all, which is not a bad story. It has politics in it, which North Albany certainly had in abundance, and it has some Kennedys, and it has significant song. It is really a story that goes to one of the mawkish essences of my life: the syrupy, sappy sentimentality that chokes in my gorge and makes me laugh and weep against my will, against all that is intelligent and genuinely holy. It is awful, it is certainly ridiculous, it is bathetic, and it is unpardonable. But there it is in the middle of me, and its epiphany took place at the Albany Institute of History and Art, where Dave Powers, the court jester from Jack Kennedy's administration, was telling funny stories about the long-gone Kennedy years. Just then a white-haired and handsomely attired man rose and asked a three-minute question, posing it in that muggled speech that sounds like George Plimpton speaking underwater. He cited a moment when Jack and Bobby, in their shirtsleeves, were standing on a table with drinks in their hands, arms locked with other friends, all singing "Heart of My Heart." And wasn't this behavior, inquired the man, beneath a president of the United States? Wasn't it little better than the lowbrow political antics that marked the Boston career of the Kennedys' ward-heeling grandfather, Honey-Fitz Fitzgerald? Dave Powers replied to the question before the man could sit down, asking the audience (a full house) how many knew "Heart of My Heart." Then, before the show of hands could be counted, he started to sing it and was joined by almost everybody, or so it sounded, in airing those unconscionable lyrics about being kids, being friends, harmonizing, parting. When the final line about a tear glistening was being sung by us all, Dave Powers shuffled off toward stage right. The man with muggled question, still standing—standing alone—intensified his protest in an ever-rising voice, his index finger raised and raised and raised again to vivify his inaudible point. And as Dave Powers descended the stairs to the auditorium, he, too, raised his index finger, and then rotated it, nail outward, to answer the man, thus resting his case to the thunderclap of applause that followed the final word of the song. I think of that thunderclap not as praise for the Kennedys or Powers or the song, though it was all of that, but as Albany's seal of approval on the mawkish corner of my soul; and bad cess to the critics. And on that note I, too, end my case for the North End, but not without a word for that young Greek fellow who is stepping over my mother on his way to work. On her behalf I forgive him his social delinquency, for it made a great story, which my mother told all her life. And telling stories, of course, was always a favorite pastime in paradise.

The Democrats
Convene, or,
One Man's Family

*A*h yes, Dan O'Connell. He was
Jesus Christ in baggy pants and a brown three-inch-brim fedora
that some silly people like John Lindsay thought was a cowboy
hat. But it was a political hat, and the head of the savior of all
Albany Democrats was under it. When it appeared in public it
told the faithful, It's all right, boys and girls, nothing's changed.
I've still got the same hat. And the city and county, too.

Daniel Peter O'Connell was a major figure in my life, and I
never knew it until I'd gone away from the city and then come
back to it. I spoke with him only twice, once at a political rally
in Polish Hall in 1965 when I asked him a few questions, and
once in his living room when he was immobilized by old age.
And I went to his funeral.

When I was growing up he was important—not personally, but
because he shaped the way everyone around me thought and
behaved politically. I believe it was a common Albany syndrome
for children to grow up obsessed with being a Democrat. Your
identity was fixed by both religion and politics, but from the
political hierarchy came the way of life: the job, the perpetuation
of the job, the dole when there was no job, the loan when there
was no dole, the security of the neighborhood, the new streetlight,
the new sidewalk, the right to run your bar after hours or to open

a card game on the sneak. These things came to you not by right of citizenship. Republicans had no such rights. They came to you because you gave allegiance to Dan O'Connell and his party. The power he held was so pervasive that you often didn't even know it existed until you contravened it. Then God help you, poor soul. Cast into outer darkness.

My family's ties to Dan were probably no greater than those of hundreds of other families, but they were substantial enough to bear inclusion here as an example of patronage as a fine art.

My great-grandfather Big Jim Carroll preceded Dan as a political figure in the city and joined Dan's movement when it began. Big Jim was the tender at the North Street lock on the Erie Canal. He owned a considerable amount of real estate and a saloon called Blue Heaven that was frequented by canalers and lumbermen. Cockfighting went on at the saloon and Dan O'Connell remembered that, remembered fighting his own chickens there. Big Jim was Democratic leader in North Albany's Ninth Ward in the era before Dan, when Billy Barnes ran the city. Big Jim's legend was perpetuated in our family by his son, Johnny Carroll, a Ninth Ward committeeman under O'Connell, and one of *his* sons, Jimmy (the family called him Gorman), became the ward's paymaster for the old men who toiled ever so lightly, cutting and raking grass, in the city's Ninth Ward parks of my own day. Dan once said that taking care of old men "was probably the best thing we did. You pick them up . . . give them independence, they live longer. I went out of my way looking out for them. Did it all my life."

My father became a deputy sheriff of Albany County in the late years of his life and always worked the polls on Election Day. He was a fanatical loyalist to Dan and all he stood for. "The good he's done will never be known," my father said often, echoing the party line. He remembered his own father and uncle and two friends, Dinky Loonan and Johnny Donovan, coming from Van Woert Street to Union Station to meet him when he came home from France in 1919, the year Dan was running for city assessor. "Donovan had a grocery-store book in his pocket," my father remembered, "and was taking up a collection for Dan's campaign."

My mother's uncle, Coop McDonald, a lifelong teetotaler who played baseball for Boston, New York, and Chicago in the teens of the century, ended his days, as did his nephew, Jim McDonald, working in the cashier's office at City Hall. My mother's first cousin, a spectacular fat man all his adult life, drove the Black Maria for the county jail, ferrying prisoners back and forth to court. But he grew even fatter and no longer fit behind the wheel, and so they made him a jail guard. My father's first cousin, Johnny Dwyer, was for years superintendent of the Ann Lee Home for the aged, run by the county, and when he retired, his son, young Jack, took over. I can think of half a dozen more family ties to city or county payrolls, but let me pass on to some neighbors.

Our landlord, Eddie Carey, the Squire of North Albany, was a Ninth Ward committeeman, and his son, Bill, became ward leader, their North End Contracting Company doing a million dollars a year in business with the city in the early 1970s. The State Investigation Commission noted in 1972 that the firm overcharged the city by $450,000 on a landfill contract. One specific overcharge concerned the rental of a used Jeep the firm had bought for $800 and rented to the city for $23,408 for one year, a somewhat heftier fee than usual for used Jeep rentals in cities other than Albany. Carey's firm repaid the $450,000 overcharge, plus a fine, and remained in the city's good graces, which is how it is done in Albany. My next-door neighbor was Jack Murray, who became president of Dan's obedient Common Council for a double decade until he became postmaster. Joe Henchey, the enduring ward leader, lived a few doors down, and Alderman Dick Conners sat in front of me every Sunday in Sacred Heart Church during my formative years and rose up to became a state assemblyman and Dan's candidate for Congress (he lost). A buddy of mine who worked his way through college as a bookie paid off to Joe Henchey to avoid being arrested, and another buddy saw Henchey one day and was a city fireman a few weeks later. The ties were profound and extended beyond Dan and into all realms where Democrats held sway. I remember my mother waking me on post-election morning in 1936, when Roosevelt was up for reelection. She gave me the exuberant news: "It was a Democratic landslide. We took everything." I was eight.

All these events, all these people, were touched by the hand of Dan O'Connell, from the time of his assessorship to his death in 1977. The tenacity of the Machine he built in those years is unique in the history of the country. James McGregor Burns, in his book *Deadlock of Democracy*, wrote that Dan's apparatus "is so well preserved that it should be put into the Smithsonian before we forget what a political machine looks like."

That old Machine, with Dan at the throttle, was on track the evening of July 22, 1965, at a balmy moment just a little while after the supper hour. The occasion was the meeting at Polish Hall on Sheridan Avenue of the 510-member Albany County Democratic Committee. The committee on this night was gathering to formally rubber-stamp the party's nominees for the fall election.

The committeemen were the backbone of the Machine. They were the ones who made the annual door-to-door canvass of their districts to confirm who'd died, who hadn't, who was new, who was in need, who required a car or a wheelchair to get to the polls, who could be counted on and who couldn't. They were the ones who suggested you register Democratic. And if you didn't, the tax assessment on your house might suddenly double, or triple, and you'd have to hire a Democratic lawyer to get it back to normal. They were the ones who did the ward leader's legwork and without them Dan would have had no Machine at all.

Dan was chairman of the Democratic Committee, the only formal title he held after quitting the assessorship. After he and his brothers—Ed, John, and Patrick—first joined with Edwin Corning to form the coalition that took over the party, Dan had been in the limelight. He shared power both with his brother Ed and with Edwin Corning until 1934, when Edwin died, and with only Ed until he, too, died in 1939. Then, with both partners dead, Dan ruled alone over this remarkable construct. Since the early 1920s the O'Connell Machine had swept almost all city and county offices, held control of the county legislature and all local seats in the State Senate and Assembly. In the late 1960s some Republican and independent candidates would temporarily break Dan's hold on some major offices, but on this night his power was inviolable.

Polish Hall was a large, low building, capable of handling Dan's formidable throng, which included my father, Johnny Dwyer and young Jack, Bill Carey, Dick Conners, my miscellaneous cousins and neighbors, and many more. All the boys were out, and a few of the girls. Polish Hall was an organization run mostly for workingmen, which was Dan's speed, and it also existed in the middle of what had been a predominantly Irish neighborhood before it went Polish.

When the Irish dominated, it was a place of poverty and truculence and danger and comedy, the fertile soil for growth and change in which Dan O'Connell found much of his constituency.

It was Canal Street before it was renamed for Philip Sheridan, the presumably Albany-born (he might have been born at sea en route to Albany) Civil War general. It ran east and west along the bottom of one of the ravines on which Albany was built, dodging among the great pools of stagnant water that lay at the foot of the ravine's great clay banks.

The Irish first settled along the pools when the city tumbled the old Irish shantytown of Martinville, and they brought their geese and ganders with them, giving the place a new name: Gander Bay. Mike Dowd, the wandering minstrel of Sheridan Avenue in the early and mid-twentieth century, wrote a song about the place: "It's Gander Bay, good old Gander Bay, where George Gilmore's geese did the rhumba every day."

Mike remembered that the Gander Bay washerwomen could always tell when it was going to rain, for the geese went on parade, screeching and flapping; and the women would haul in the wash. George Gilmore (of the song) and Mike Dillon were both famous ash collectors, Dillon noted for jumping in and out of sixteen empty ash barrels in a row with his arms folded, Gilmore for being bitten by his horse and biting it back. Mickey McManus was a great Gander Bay battler, whose managers, to reduce him by ten pounds for a fight, tied a rope around his waist and had him trot behind a horse and wagon. Mickey made the weight but was so weak he lost the fight. Mrs. Sweeney gave the Irish Cry at every wake in the neighborhood and John Keleher kept his barbershop open until two in the morning.

The Sheridan Avenue Gang was a band of Irish toughs who, by legend, guarded their turf rigorously and let no strangers pass through (except a chosen few, which included my father, an unlikely choice). The gang terrorized outlanders, police, and Republicans and the toughest of their number was not an Irishman but Nigger Dick, a fearful gent who went in and out of white people's houses just like he was a white man, and wasn't that nice? The Oley brothers, Francis and Johnny, came from Sheridan Avenue and grew up to become the city's best-known homegrown criminals. They would both go to jail as members of the gang that kidnapped John O'Connell, Jr., Dan's nephew, in 1933.

Irish dominance in the neighborhood gave way as the Polish immigrants arrived early in this century and settled on upper Sheridan and its tributaries and established the Polish-Catholic church, St. Casimir's, on the street. By the 1960s blacks were moving in and the Polish and Irish were thinning out. Sheridan was freshly blacktopped in 1965—no more stagnant pools—and water ran smoothly down tidy gutters past the Twelfth Ward's World War II memorial (a garish flag billboard), past the police garage, and underneath the Hawk Street viaduct, a popular suicide leap. Polish Hall's log-cabin front loomed up with its frosty red-and-white sign, its barroom just in off the street. And in front of it a mob of newsmen (maybe two or three women) and a moil of pols stood about exuding a steady drone of vitality and anticipation—all of them waiting for Dan. For this was his chief public moment of the year, the one time you could be sure to get a glimpse of him and maybe a handshake, the one time he would pose for photos, say a few words about the upcoming election, the one time the press had privileged access. A handful of reporters who moonlighted as city or county employees could always have access if they needed it, but the two Albany newspapers were Dan's enemies in these years, and when a *Knickerbocker News* editor called Dan at home to ask a question, his reply was "Fuck you and your newspaper" and he hung up.

A police captain in full regalia, brass polished and scrambled eggs agleam, preened in the middle of the street on a menial errand, checking a double-parked car, those scrambled eggs the consequence of his police service during the search for Johnny O'Connell's kidnappers. Any cop who worked for young John's return found himself a likely candidate for promotion in later years on the force, for Dan had a long and grateful memory.

But the captain was only a soldier. The top cop on the scene, dapper in a coconut straw that hid his baldness, was a genial, witty, and nervous Irishman who stuttered when he talked too fast: John P. Tuffey, Albany's chief of police. Tuffey was the son of a cop, his father and Dan's grandfather old cronies, both having come to Albany in a distant emigration from County Sligo. "A good policeman has to want to do that job or he's no good," Dan said once in defense of the coolie wages the city was then paying Albany policemen. "That's the way Tuffey is. His father was the same way. They wanted to be cops."

"When is Dan due?" I asked Tuffey.

"He'll be along," said the chief, and he chatted with a TV reporter about the high cost of educating your kids. Crews were ready with hand-held cameras and Rolleiflexes, snapping the arrivals. Here came Jimmy Ryan, Dan's county purchasing agent and target of a state probe of county purchasing that had prompted one investigator to call Albany "the worst-run county in America"; and Don Lynch, married to Dan's niece, suntanned and hostile to the press, erstwhile county clerk who grew richer than most in the party and resigned his clerkship after the disclosure that he profited substantially from buying land marked for Thruway development, and who would, in later years, move to Florida with his wealth. There came Mayor Erastus Corning, dapper and athletically bouncy, beaming his million-dollar smile at all in radius of its glimmer and drawing the salutes of two uniformed policemen guarding the door.

More pols arrived and time dragged on. "When the hell is Dan coming?" a reporter wondered. "It's after eight."

Tuffey stretched his neck out of his collar and smiled like the cat that had not only eaten the canary but also the parakeet. "Why, he's already inside," said the chief. "Didn't you fellows know? Don't tell me you missed him."

He was indeed inside, surrounded already, having entered through the back way to avoid the crowd, the press, the flashbulbs. Dan loved the caginess of this, the one-upness—never let your left know what your right, etc.—but also he wanted to avoid any streetside katzenjammer activity by a young maverick lawyer named George Harder, a challenger to Dan's authority in two earlier primary campaigns and again this year.

George Harder was not a man to be feared, for he had no chance of winning anything. But then again, he *was* a Democrat, and half-Irish, and an ex-FBI man, and a Catholic, and a communicant in Dan's own parish (St. James's, on Delaware Avenue), and his father *had* been a Democratic regular, and he was smart (no dope like some of Dan's minions), and the press did love to play him up, and he was a phrasemaker (he called Dan's Democratic ticket "One Man's Family"), and what's more, Jews and liberals and progressives and young people liked him, and reformers and professional people aloof from porkhead politics liked him, and family types liked him because he had nine children.

So Dan came in the back way, and now George Harder would not be able to fabricate a pose with him the way he had in 1962, when Dan, in a moment of magnanimity, shook George's hand and said, "You're all right, you did well, good luck," and George had forty-three zillion photos printed up as fliers under the headline GOOD LUCK, GEORGE, for any photo of a candidate shaking hands with Dan, or even standing alongside him, was political bullion, the traditional public way of saying that Dan approved of this fellow. What George was after was the Assembly seat held by Dan's man, Frank Cox, up for reelection. That's what George wanted then; that's what he wanted tonight.

"We flooded the South End with those photos the night before election," Harder recalled, "so they wouldn't have time to counteract them. But they did. They got to the people in front of the polling places when they showed up to vote." Dan's men would collar the voters, whisper Cox's name into their ears. One South End voter, seeing Harder at the polls, chided him for fighting Dan. The old fellow had known Harder's father, who would surely be spinning in his grave, etc. But Harder cajoled him, found he was only making twenty-nine dollars a week take-home, and expounded his reform ideas. "Look," Harder remembered the man's saying at last, "I've got to remain loyal to Dan, but I'll tell you what. I'll cast one for Dan's man and one for you."

Harder lost to Cox, who won the seat in the Assembly. Harder tried again the following year, and when he approached Dan for another handshake, Dan, he said, almost backed over the bar to avoid him. That year at Polish Hall when Harder tried to get the audience of about a thousand people to listen, when he stood up to plead for their attention, they, too, stood up, in a body, made a right-face, and emptied the hall.

Now it was a new year and the hall was full again, with lawyers, clerks, flacks, and lackeys from City Hall and the Court House— a black county supervisor, an Italian police-court judge, a Jewish assistant corporation counsel, an endless flow of party-liners of every stripe. And at the center of this eddy of Democracy, Albany style, were Dan and his hat.

A State Supreme Court judge shook his hand and said, "It's only once a year I see you, Dan, but it's always a pleasure." A man offered a cigar, which Dan refused; the man insisted, Dan accepted. Old women kissed him and young women kissed him. Dozens passed and said only, "Hello, Dan, you're lookin' fine," and shook that most famous, most knobby hand and moved on. Others whispered their loyalty in his ear, or their trouble, for this was the eternal response of crowds to the man, and now and then Dan would palm a bit of the long green and press it into the hand of an importuner. Newspaper and TV cameramen recorded much of this, and then one cameraman set his camera, handed it to a companion, stood shoulder to shoulder with Dan, and fanned out his plumes.

"Get one of me with Devine in it," Dan said when that was

done. "I'd like that." And a photographer grabbed Albany County Treasurer Eugene Devine and steered him to Dan's side.

"Not this Devine," said Dan, "the one over there," and he pointed to John Devine, an Albany Housing Authority employee, a crony of Dan's for fifty years. The cronies, both in hats, posed with easy smiles for the picture. And behind them, trying heroically to prevent his smile from falling through the cracks, stood the extra Devine.

"Make sure you get my cauliflower ear in the photo," said Dan, "and be sure I get a copy."

He spoke softly, in a scratchy voice, constantly lifting a cigarette to his lips, smiling a steady smile, the skin of his neck wobbly where the flesh had fallen away, for Dan had lost weight and his suit hung loosely on him. The suit, a blue double-breasted, was as out of fashion as his high shoes, his wide suspenders, the wide polka-dot blue tie on the soft-collared sport shirt, and his antique hat. His clothing also resisted time and change, belonging as much to the 1930s as it did to the middle 1960s, simply because he said it did.

George Harder and a small band of followers arrived while Dan was holding forth, but the press took no notice. Neither did Dan until George stood up and shouted at Frank Cox, who was by then chairing the meeting in progress, "Point of order!" And a woman snarled at George, "Sit down, ya bum." Dan saw this exchange, then turned his attention from the meeting and back to the crowd at his coattails.

"I'll tell you what," Harder shouted, barely heard in the huge room. "This meeting is contested. It's being run under protest." Amid a barrage of hoots he managed to insist that a quorum was not present, and Cox pointed his finger at George and chanted, "Sit down once, sit down twice, sit down three times." The crowd cheered.

To prove a quorum was indeed present, Cox began a long roll call of the committeemen. Two or three voices responded to every name. Cox then recognized certain party members, who introduced resolutions designating Dan's candidates for office. Among these was State Senator Julian B. Erway, who had recently been called upon publicly by fellow senators to verify his allegiance to the civil rights movement, and he announced that his home had been a stop on the Underground Railroad during Civil War days and that he had recently received a Christmas card from his Negro cook.

Joe McCormick, a Harder man, leaped up and asked for "point of information, point of information."

"If you'll act like a gentleman," said Cox, "and stop jumping up to yell your head off, you can make your point."

"Can we put other men in nomination?"

Boos and laughter answered him.

"It's still a democracy," McCormick said, and Harder then stood and nominated McCormick for state senator, in opposition to Senator Erway.

"You'll like McCormick," Harder told the crowd. "He's a good Irishman."

"Watch that stuff about the Irish in here, bud," a man said.

And then the committee moved on to other business and that was that for McCormick. The new business was Dan's trump: moving Frank Cox sideways into an Assembly district other than the one he had represented, one thought to be safer for him in the primary, with fewer maverick voters to contend with should George Harder's wagon begin to roll. Into the threatened district Dan moved Harvey Lifset, a Jewish attorney, another incumbent with a strong legislative record. Yes, Dan was telling Harder, we are invincible. We have the people, and we spit in your half-Irish eye. But why take chances?

Harder accepted the indirect homage. "The party had to hide Cox someplace," he said.

At the rear of the hall a reporter asked Dan how he thought his candidates would do this year, now that their names were a matter of record.

"Same as usual," he said, his perennial answer to that perennial question. And he would prove to be right.

What advice would he give a young man like George Harder seeking to enter politics?

"Work," said Dan. "Keep fighting. Keep at it." He smiled, this man who thrived on combat and could admire it in a tough young scrapper like George, admire it up to the point where the chin that George was leading with tended to threaten Dan's own testy right hand. He himself had always used fistic imagery to convey his way of life: "Sure, you had your big guys who could make a name overnight, but it was the boys like Bob Fitzsimmons and Jim Corbett who came out of it all right. They were hard fighters who came out clean."

The crowd around Dan moved toward the front door of Polish Hall as soon as he took the lead and made his way out, and at the curb he bent low and slid into a waiting auto.

"God love ya, Dan," a man said in farewell.

And then this nineteenth-century figure, born in the reign of John L. Sullivan and Tammany Hall, this full-blooming heir to Irish bossism—that nineteenth-century urban flower—this survivor from the final century of the living God into the epoch when God was as dead as Kelsey's, this truculent nonesuch sped away down the slope of Sheridan Avenue.

In deference, Polish Hall emptied with a ploosh.

Then the sun turned emerald green and settled itself heavily behind the rooftops of Gander Bay. Ghosts of geese and ganders waddled in their ease. There was and there would be no storm on this blessedly peaceful night.

Elk Street, looking west toward Hawk Street, in the 1880s, when some thought it resembled Gramercy Park.

2

THE
NEIGHBORHOODS

Downtown: Where Things Happened First

*A*lbany looks so good from a distance, journalist Nathaniel P. Willis remarked one day, "that you half forgive it for its hogs, offals, broken pavements and the score of other nuisances more Dutch than decent."

Willis was a brash young journalist when he made that remark in Troy on September 28, 1830, and to say it angered the Albany Dutch would be an understatement. But it stirred no change. Nineteen years later the Common Council would receive a report that "hogs running the streets at large number 4,000."

The ancient custom was to throw garbage in the street and let the pigs clean it up, eliminating the need for garbage collection, and developing fat and sassy porkers. The final crackdown came in 1854, when city officials rounded up fifteen thousand wandering pigs and the citizenry finally got the idea.

Some families had fled the messy neighborhoods and made for the high ground that was to become uptown—Capitol Hill and Arbor Hill—the exodus that really created Downtown; for how can you have a Downtown without an uptown? In the beginning of the nineteenth century there was really only the Town, the center of all life. On Capitol Hill the old Capitol stood at the head of State Street, and beyond it only three residences, one of which is the building now occupied by the Fort Orange Club.

Other forces besides piggery would be causing people to move outward: the turnpikes leading to the West—roads that would become Western and Central and Delaware avenues—all creating small commercial and service communities along their paths; the railroads, which would create the West End; and the Lumber District, which would create North Albany.

Also, the maddening freshets that came in the springtime— the overflowings of the Hudson that bathed Broadway (called Market Street in early days) knee-deep in water: these would continue sporadically until 1930, when the Sacandaga Dam would at last put an end to them. Their effect was to drive merchants up the hill to Pearl Street, where private homes once owned by illustrious Old Albanians were converted to storefronts or torn down to make way for the march of commerce.

The boundaries of Beverwyck, the original stockade settlement of the city, were very close to those of our own age when we define Downtown. The Stockade: Steuben Street on the north, Lodge Street on the west, the river on the east, and Hudson Avenue on the south. Downtown: Clinton Avenue on the north, Eagle Street on the west, the river on the east, and probably still Hudson Avenue on the south, though that boundary is arbitrary. Maybe it should be Madison Avenue, or even State Street. To some, everything south of State Street belongs to the South End. I opt for Hudson Avenue, since that included the Ritz and Leland theaters, both gone now, but certainly part of Downtown's attractions in my time.

The river had been, from the beginning, the lifeline of Albany's trade. Its significance was heightened in 1807 with the first successful steamboat run, by Robert Fulton's *Clermont*, an event that revolutionized water travel in the world. The *Albany Gazette* advertised on September 2, 1807, that the *Clermont* would leave from what is now Jersey City on Friday, September 4, "at nine in the morning and arrive at Albany on Saturday, at nine in the afternoon." Cost for the thirty-six-hour ride: seven dollars. The *Gazette* later noted that the *Clermont* did indeed arrive, and quickly left again for New York "with about 40 ladies and gentlemen." By October 1 the boat was making the trip with sixty (and before long ninety) passengers, and had cut the time to twenty-eight hours.

On a given day in, say, 1822 there might be two hundred sloops, schooners, and steamboats at the city's docks. The Erie Canal

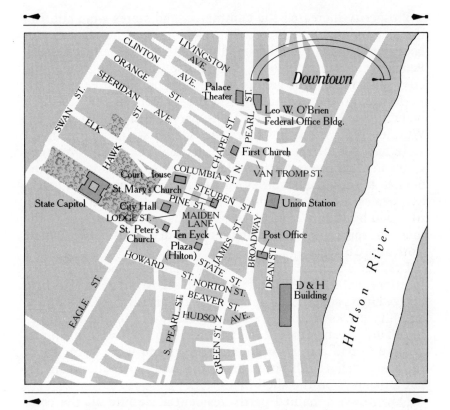

was the great coming attraction, and to cope with all the new traffic, the city, in 1823, began building the Basin, creating a pier that paralleled the shoreline for four fifths of a mile, with bridges from the pier to Columbia and State streets. The pier, eighty-five feet wide, covered eight acres, and the Basin covered thirty-two acres, with harbor space for a thousand canalboats.

The *Albany Daily Advertiser* noted in 1827: "One who is not an eye witness of the fact can scarcely imagine the number of persons who daily arrive at . . . this city in steamboats, and the vast quantity of product that is shipped from our wharves and conveyed to market by steam and wind. Last Sunday Evening (August 26) within one hour there arrived six steamboats . . . three of these having in tow barges, each with freight and passengers. Together they must have landed some 1,600 passengers. There never were more sloops than at present employed on the river, and they all go hence fully freighted."

Prosperity increased the commerce, and stores were built on the pier and on Quay Street. By 1840 some one hundred steamboats were plying the Hudson along with all the sailing vessels. People were coming by boat, train, horse, and foot to shop in the city, and a mercantile genius set up shop on North Pearl Street.

He was William Minot Whitney, sent here in 1859 to run a branch of a New York store. The parent firm pulled out, but Whitney kept on and developed the city's first major department store and one of the first in the nation. The W. M. Whitney Company had the city's first electric lights, elevators, and telephones as supreme novelties for the customers as well as marks of progress; a delivery system was pioneered—with a wheelbarrow; and by 1886 Whitney's was advertising itself as "one of the most conspicuous" retail distributors of dry goods between New York and Chicago.

Drislane's became the city's biggest grocery, operating at two locations on South Pearl and then at 38–42 North Pearl. The firm bragged in its advertising in the 1890s that it employed a hundred and fifty clerks to supply seven thousand of "the best families in Albany." Its biggest era was from 1910 to 1929, with an annual volume of half a million dollars. Liquor and wine were part of the business but Prohibition killed that and supermarkets finally put Drislane's on the shelf in 1937.

Downtown remained partly residential despite all the commerce. Children played on their neighborhood streets—gathering on a winter's day, for example, behind the Kenmore Hotel, where the heat came up through sidewalk gratings. Women pushed baby carriages along North Pearl, and young men such as Timothy Lyden used up their spare time at Duffy's restaurant and Gene Murray's cigar store next door at Columbia and Pearl streets.

Tim Lyden was still living Downtown when I spoke with him, one of a vanishing breed, for Downtown residents in that era were mostly transients, the old-time residential neighborhood having been disestablished. Tim was seventy-four and had lived most of his life either on Chapel Street or in the house where we were chatting, 95 Columbia Street.

"Other people wouldn't live in this neighborhood," he said. "They wanted to move up on the hill. I wouldn't go up on the hill. I wouldn't go above Lark Street for any of them."

Moving above Lark had become part of the great quest for spacious living. When the wealthy merchants and professional men built their homes on upper State Street, Elk Street, and

Washington Avenue, they frequently built without even an alley between the houses. The developers of the Pine Hills in the 1890s would encounter resistance to their planning of large lots, for Albanians just weren't used to spacious grounds around their homes.

But when spaciousness became the fashion, old town houses like Tim Lyden's seemed inadequate. Originally built for one, perhaps two, families, they were chopped into apartments or furnished rooms.

The permanent population hit its lowest point in the 1960s, for Downtown had become a wasteland. In 1962 Tim Lyden was an alderman in the Sixth Ward and had only 283 registered voters in his district, a third of whom were living in the Downtown hotels. Downtown's moribund commerce in a few more years would finally die entirely and go to heaven in the suburban Colonie Center—one of the ten most successful shopping malls in the U.S. The Ten Eyck Hotel would die and on the dust of its bones a few years later the Albany Hilton would be rising. The DeWitt Clinton Hotel would die as a hotel and become an apartment house, chockablock with senior citizens. Tim's home block, Columbia Street, between Eagle and Chapel streets, would, by the late 1970s, have its houses restored to Victorian respectability and families would be moving back to Downtown streets, alive again with trees and quickened traffic. Largely because of the South Mall, every salvageable town house or row house would become a target for rehabilitation. City living, in the age of the shortage and inflated price of gasoline, would once again be chic.

When the city was in the throes of pristine chic, General Philip Schuyler was living at the southeast corner of State and Pearl. Martin Van Buren, the Governor, and soon to be the nation's first native-born President (birthplace: Kinderhook), was living at the southwest corner. Up the street Erastus Corning, fellow member of the Albany Regency with Van Buren, and soon to be Albany's richest citizen, lived at 102 State Street. Ten members of the Van Rensselaer family, including the Patroon, had homes or offices on State Street or Broadway. Philip Livingston stepped outside the house one day and, with almost the same lasting flourish with which he had signed the Declaration of Independence, planted a tree at the northwest corner of State and Pearl. It grew for 142 years, cut down finally on June 14, 1877, for the widening of Pearl Street. Thurlow Weed, manic journalist and a leader of the Anti-Masonic and Whig parties, made his home on Green Street. The socially prominent Bleeckers lived on North Pearl and so did John V. L. Pruyn. The eminent printer Joel Munsell had his modest establishment on State Street, below Pearl. Joseph Henry, the pioneer of electromagnetism, whose work made possible the telegraph and the electric motor (he strung two miles of wire around a magnet in an Albany Academy classroom, sent an electric charge through it all, and rang a bell), lived on Columbia Street. Bret Harte was born down the block from Tim at 15 Columbia, his father a teacher at the Albany Female Academy on North Pearl; but Albany can claim only the first six months of Harte's life, and as far as is known he returned only once, on December 3, 1872, at the height of his career. Local papers carried a seven-line advance notice of his lecture to the Young Men's Association, but they did not cover the lecture, nor did they interview this national culture hero. He left, saddened, never to return. And DeWitt Clinton, on February 11, 1828, died at his home at the southeast corner of North Pearl and Steuben streets, owing—it was revealed a few months later—about six thousand dollars. His property was sold by the sheriff, and of the great pioneer of the Erie Canal a friend wrote on the day of the sheriff's advertisement: "He who added millions to the State of New York, has himself died poor."

To Downtown came many of the notable figures of history: George Washington was given the freedom of the city in 1783; the Marquis de Lafayette in 1824 was received with joy and revisited his headquarters on North Pearl Street. Alexander Hamilton and Aaron Burr both had law practices here. Hamilton married Philip Schuyler's daughter; Burr killed Hamilton in a duel. Henry Clay's remains were escorted through the city by a paramilitary group, the Burgesses. Jenny Lind came to Albany to sing, Oscar Wilde came to prance, P. T. Barnum came to pluck suckers, and hundreds came from afar to see the Van Rensselaers' century plant bloom. General Sam Houston passed through and was feted, as was Edward, Prince of Wales. Alexis de Tocqueville studied Albany's 1831 Fourth of July parade, found our troops lacking in martial spirit and "really quite comic to see." James Silk Buckingham, a member of the British Parliament, saw our parade seven years later and found the military "had really a fine appearance, being well-dressed, well-equipped, and well-disciplined." Buckingham was most moved by the veterans of the Revolution, who passed in open carriages: "The hoary locks which were visible on each, with the associations which their years and services awakened, impressed us more powerfully than anything we had yet witnessed in the country." What Albanians felt for the veterans, he observed, was a "universal sentiment of veneration and respect for their age and character." Susan B. Anthony addressed a convention of Abolitionists, chaired by a local black man. And Steve Brodie, the man who had jumped off the Brooklyn Bridge and lived, started swimming from Downtown on June 24, 1888, and made it to New York in six days and one hour, speedier by nine hours than the previous record.

Downtown was where things happened first. One of the nation's earliest torchlight political parades followed the nomination of Millard Fillmore for president on August 14, 1856. (The torch was lit with oil; you carried it on your shoulder and wore an oilcloth cape for protection against the dripping.) Horsecars ran first in Albany: on Broadway in 1863, on Pearl Street in 1866. The first gaslights replaced the old whale-oil lamps in 1845; kerosene lights followed in 1860, and primitive electric streetlights in 1881. The first velocipede, precursor of the bicycle, arrived in 1869; the first automobile on December 26, 1899, brought by Archibald M. Dedrick. The first telephone "exchange" was established in 1878 with one hundred members; it had been started by seven doctors. And the first telephone pay stations were inaugurated in the city on February 2, 1889.

Tim Lyden was born in 1889, just in time to see the end of an old era and the beginning of a new one. The impact of science was being felt more and more strongly. Electricity, autos, and then skyscrapers like the City and County Savings Bank (they said it would tip over) were revolutionizing Downtown. The old Dutch houses with their step gables were disappearing, almost all of those rare structures now preserved only in photographs. Not everybody missed them. Elkanah Watson, a leading citizen, actively campaigned for their banishment on grounds they spilled rainwater down the necks of passersby.

The horsecar vanished in the 1890s and the new century was only a year and a half old when the great United Traction strike (May 1901) halted trolleys in five cities. Albany was put under martial law, troops camped at Beverwyck Park, and a squad of soldiers rode on every streetcar. E. LeRoy Smith and William M. Walsh were killed when troops opened fire on a violent mob attacking a car at Columbia Street and Broadway. Smith was standing in the doorway of a store, watching the riot, when he was shot.

The gift the trolleys brought was new power and speed and longer runs—extending the city's lifelines, connecting with the lines of other cities, making possible the expansion from the city center. As people moved out of Downtown their institutions either followed them or faded away—certain churches, for instance. Tim Lyden remembered the Second Presbyterian Church at Pine and Chapel streets closing (it merged with two others to form Westminster Presbyterian on Capitol Hill) and the old building's turning into the Capitol Theater, then a skating rink, a wrestling arena, a burlesque house, a movie theater, the Albany Playhouse, a parking lot, and a public garage.

Scotch-Irish Presbyterians from Northern Ireland had built the First Presbyterian Church in 1764 on Gallows Hill (some forty thousand turned out in 1827 to see the city's last public hanging there). The church moved to South Pearl, and in 1850 the congregation built a handsome English Gothic structure at Hudson and Philip streets, modeled after New York's First Presbyterian Church. Then, in 1883, when church leaders decided to move from that building to a new one at State and Willett streets, a rancorous controversy erupted and a number of families left the congregation.

Also, said Reverend Robert C. Lamar, present pastor of the First Presbyterian, the new church didn't seem like a church at all to some naysayers. A Romanesque brownstone structure, it looked like another work designed by the famous architect H. H. Richardson, who planned City Hall, though it was not his. The church is really quite elegant, made more so with five handsome Tiffany windows installed in a later year, and it's difficult to imagine anyone ever judging it to be anything other than a church. It now looks out from Willett Street onto Washington Park, which had catalyzed the neighborhood (since its creation in the 1870s) into one of substance and prestige. The church survived its internal turmoil of the 1880s and a century later has a congregation of seven hundred and fifty, runs the city's principal coffeehouse, and is a landmark in what is still one of Albany's most desirable neighborhoods.

Downtown was once full of churches, and a few survived the ages, among them the First Church in Albany (Reformed), a Dutch church that as a congregation dates to 1643, as a building to 1798, and that boasts the oldest pulpit in America, made in Holland in 1656. The church, with its twin steeples rising over

Clinton Square, is a handsome antique designed by Albany's premier eighteenth-century architect, Philip Hooker.

The English church, St. Peter's, at Lodge and State, is the third on the site, the Episcopal congregation having been established here in 1705 by the English Society for the Propagation of the Gospel in Foreign Parts. Like other English churches in America it was closed during the Revolution, its rector forced to flee for his life to a British outpost. Philip Hooker designed the second St. Peter's, which was structurally weakened by the steepness of State Street and was demolished. The present building was constructed in 1859–60 and was the principal church of the Episcopal Diocese, which was created in 1868.

The oldest Catholic church Downtown is St. Mary's, at Pine and Chapel streets, and is also the third structure with the same name, the first built in 1797, the current one completed in 1869.

A Catholic historian noted that fifty to sixty baptisms a month were performed at St. Mary's, mostly for Irish parishioners in the years of the second church, from 1829 to 1867. (Nine thousand Irish arrived in the U.S. in 1817, and double that number in 1818, the year 3,000 Irishmen were building the Erie Canal. By 1827 annual Irish immigration was 20,000 a year; by 1832, 65,000; by 1842, 92,000. There were 961,719 Irish in the U.S. in 1850, and in Albany by 1875 one in six Albanians was Irish-born—14,184 of 86,541).

"Families as a rule had from six to 10 or 12 children," wrote Reverend John Dillon in his history of St. Mary's. "What life, what hope this prospect gave to the community; children everywhere . . . and then the young people for the societies, with marriages to follow. What a comparison to the families you hear of now, two or three members, the parents dying . . . the children disposed of, and the family name lost."

Something other than religion was on the minds of Tim Lyden and his friends, who in their Downtown neighborhood were doing what young men were doing all over Albany in the century's early years: forming social clubs. Tim's bunch called themselves the How-You-Do Club and rented rooms on North Pearl Street next door to Van Dyk's, the tea and coffee store (Downtown's worst joke: "Did you hear? Van Dyk got arrested—for teasin' coffee").

The How-You-Doers numbered fifty, and gathered together to play cards and drink "soft stuff." Said Tim, "We moved upstairs over Jimmy Murray's saloon on Sheridan Avenue and Jimmy said he'd starve if he depended on us for drinks." Just before Prohibition, Tim recalled feeling slack and someone told him to go over to Jimmy Murray's and try a glass of Bass ale. "So I went in," said Tim, "and Jim said to me, 'We don't have enough for the old customers and we're not taking on any new ones.' So I didn't drink then and I haven't had a drink since."

Instead of drinking, the How-You-Doers worked themselves up by dancing—they ran dances at the Knights of Columbus Hall, and were also, said Tim, "a great gang for going out to Snyder's Lake for dancing," a common diversion in the new era of motorcars.

There was also a strain of lusty comedy in the How-You-Doers. Tim Lyden recalled their taking a new recruit to meet a fireman's wife, an amorous lady they all knew, and to whose charms access was gained by bringing her a gift of fruit. Armed with apples, peaches, and bananas, the young man was led to a darkened stairway leading upward to Eros. As he ascended he encountered not love, however, but the fireman, played by one of the How-You-Doers, who pop-pop-popped his own armful of electric bulbs as he yelled down at the recruit "Ah-ha, so you're the one who's after my wife." Said Tim of the victim: "He came running down the stairs and down the street, dropping the fruit. He thought he was shot."

Some of the How-You-Doers went off to the Great War in 1916, marching down State Street to board the train at Union Station. Downtown homefolks turned out in great numbers for patriotic events, a notable one being the day the Hip Hip Hooray Girls, a burlesque troupe from the Empire Theater on State Street, drew a crowd of ten thousand to a Liberty Loan campaign at State and Chapel. They danced on a platform with a huge military tank as a prop. An anonymous historian reported: "Thinly clad, they disported before overcoated crowds which jammed the streets and blocked all traffic." Mayor James Watt said he liked their patriotism.

A month and a week later the war ended and a demonstration erupted Downtown unlike anything in history. The Armistice was announced at 2:55 a.m. on November 11, 1918. At 4:00 a.m. there were twenty thousand in a crush at State and Pearl. At 7:00 p.m. fifty thousand were in the streets, and at 8:00, a newspaper reported, "the Downtown district was a sight without parallel. It seemed that every man, woman and child in Albany was taking part in the demonstration." The whole thing would happen all over again on V-J Day in 1945.

Downtown was "a handy place to live" for Tim Lyden, almost everything a man could need only a few blocks away—shops, theaters, restaurants, even the hospital (Homeopathic, on North Pearl just above Clinton Avenue, later to become Memorial Hospital and move to Northern Boulevard in 1957). And Tim worked for fifty-four years only two blocks from home—in the John G. Myers department store, which shared commercial eminence with Whitney's on North Pearl. He remembered vividly the morning of August 8, 1905, 9:00 a.m., just after he arrived at work as a sixteen-year-old cash boy. Suddenly the roof crashed through to the cellar of the six-story building, taking everything with it, killing thirteen clerks who were just about to open the store, burying eighty others under debris. The store was being reconstructed but the shoring in the cellar was insecure where men were digging, and it gave way.

Tim wasn't hurt but he lost his hair, as did others involved in the disaster, blaming it on mortar and cement dust permeating their scalps. Myers' was rebuilt and continued its successful business until Downtown all but died, victim of the escape to the suburbs and the pall that racial tensions of the late 1960s had cast over the city. Also contributing to the troubles of Downtown commerce was the harebrained scheme of Governor Thomas E. Dewey's planners to relocate thousands of state workers from Downtown to the State Campus Office Building complex on Washington Avenue in the Pine Bush, Albany's outer limits. Downtown was bereft of shoppers when Myers' closed its doors forever in May 1970, and the building was razed in January 1980. Where it, and Whitney's, stood—once the city's nerve center— is now the middle of the street in Albany's newest block, Pine Street, between North Pearl and Broadway.

The Myers' collapse was touted as Albany's worst disaster, but it hardly qualified after two and a half centuries of riverboat sinkings, plagues, fires, massacres, wars, and epidemics. Cholera, for instance, killed four hundred in 1832, another three hundred and twenty in 1849. The Great Fire of August 17, 1848, was a tragedy of a different order, not in loss of life, but of property— six hundred homes destroyed in the most densely populated part of the city. It started from a washerwoman's bonnet, says the legend, inside a shed next to the Albion Hotel at Broadway and Herkimer Street. The area, no longer inhabited, now forms part of the arterial highway network. Then it was all houses, down to the Basin and the pier. Thirty-seven acres burned—or one thirtieth of the city—and the damage on Broadway, Church, Herkimer, Dallius, and Hudson streets and the pier was estimated at $3 million. Four days later the Common Council decreed that no wooden building could thereafter be built east of Lark Street.

Edwin Booth, America's greatest tragedian, was in Albany during the fire, as was his brother, the infamous hambone John Wilkes Booth. Edwin heroically fought the fire; John was only a boy of ten at the time. Edwin played here at Tweddle Hall, doing Othello, Shylock, and Hamlet on a bare stage, with a huge American flag dropped as a curtain between acts. John, on February 18, 1861, was in town again, having a few nights earlier played Iago, and on this night taking the role of another villainous character named Pescara, in *The Apostate*, a play created for his father, Junius Brutus Booth. Wilkes Booth, as the newspapers called him, was performing at the Gayety and staying at Stanwix Hall on Broadway, three blocks down from the Delavan House, where the man he would assassinate, President-elect Abraham Lincoln, was stopping overnight en route to Washington.

Lincoln had arrived in the afternoon by train, his car pulled by a highly polished locomotive bearing the name *Erastus Corning, Jr.* (after the son of Albany's premier businessman, Erastus Corning, president of the New York Central Railroad). As the train passed the Central's West Albany shops a signal was flashed to a military unit at the Dudley Observatory on Arbor Hill, and a twenty-one-gun salute then welcomed the President to the city.

Officials met him at the Broadway rail crossing near Lumber Street (Livingston Avenue), but he did not immediately emerge, for the Twenty-fifth Regiment, the first Northern detachment to enter Virginia after the assault on Fort Sumter, was half an hour late to escort him. The crowd grew impatient: "Show us the railsplitter . . . trot out old Abe" were the cries some remembered. Mayor George Hornell Thacher rode with the newly bearded, stovepipe-hatted President in the horse-drawn barouche, down Broadway and up State Street. WELCOME TO THE CAPITAL OF THE EMPIRE STATE—NO MORE COMPROMISE, a banner proclaimed.

"That Negro-lover will never get to the Executive Mansion," said a bystander, and Henry Burns, a Civil War veteran who heard that, said he then saw "a big burly fellow . . . one of the Mullen boys" hit the President's critic, knock him down, and bloody his face. Lincoln doffed his hat, stood and waved to the mob. Burns said, "I thought him the tallest man I ever saw and he didn't seem homely to me." Wilkes Booth also watched Lincoln pass in front of Stanwix Hall, where he, too, had made hostile remarks about the President and been cautioned for it.

Lincoln rode to the old Capitol, addressed the legislature in a brief, undistinguished speech, dined with Governor Edwin D. Morgan, then received the Albany citizenry at the Delavan, which was, said one account, "crowded to suffocation." The *Albany Atlas and Argus*, a newspaper hostile to Lincoln, found his face "indicates more intelligence and less character" than expected, and noted that Albany's "Republican crowd" followed Lincoln around with "vulpine eagerness." Albany—city and county—was Democratic, and had voted against Lincoln, and would again in 1864. The *Albany Journal* noted his departure briefly on page two the following day. On page one it effusively noted Wilkes Booth's performance at the Gayety—"one of the finest bits of lifelike acting we ever saw . . . undoubtedly one of the finest actors this country ever produced."

Had Lincoln noticed Wilkes Booth? Had the President and his assassin-to-be made eye contact, perhaps? Albany asked itself such preposterous questions for an age to come.

Lincoln's tragic death at Wilkes Booth's hand brought on another tragedy involving an Albany couple who were present on that baleful Good Friday night, April 14, 1865, when Booth entered the presidential box at Ford's Theater in Washington. A month earlier, March 15, Booth had given his last performance there in *The Apostate*, the role that had won him a rave in Albany.

Sitting behind the President and Mrs. Lincoln at Ford's Theater were two Albanians: U.S. Army Major Henry Rathbone, twenty-eight, and his fiancée, Clara Harris, daughter of U.S. Senator and Albany attorney Ira Harris. Rathbone's father, Jared, had been mayor of Albany, and his cousin, the precocious John, would grow so wealthy from the enormous Rathbone foundry in Albany that he would retire at thirty-five.

The young Albanians were substitute guests for General Ulysses S. Grant and his wife, Julia, who had begged off joining the Lincolns; and so it was young Major Rathbone, instead of General Grant, who grappled with the assassin after the shooting. Booth stabbed Rathbone with a dagger, inflicting a severe gash on his upper arm. And when Booth leaped from the balcony to the stage it was Rathbone who called out, "Stop that man!"—which no one did. When a young doctor came to the box and diagnosed the President's head wound as mortal, Rathbone spoke the phrase "I'm bleeding to death," but as a newsman wrote, "all medical attention was for Lincoln." Rathbone fainted from loss of blood and was two months recuperating.

He later married Clara Harris and retired from the Army. They stayed in the Senator's home on Cherry Tree Lane in Loudonville, and a legend grew that twice Clara saw Lincoln's ghost sitting in a rocking chair in her room. They lived Downtown for a time, at 28 Eagle Street, Rathbone moving inexorably into melancholia—guilty, said his friends, over not preventing Lincoln's death. His depression turned to violence, and in Germany in 1883 he shot and killed Clara and stabbed himself five times with a dagger, but didn't die. He was tried for murder, but when the German court heard of his response to Lincoln's death, the trial was curtailed; Rathbone was adjudged insane and sent to an asylum, where he died in 1911.

Lincoln came back to Albany after his death (and so did Grant, who died in 1885 at Mount McGregor, near Saratoga, after finishing his memoirs, a grueling task but a legacy to his financially bereft family, whom he knew he was soon to leave—another form of heroism in the man. Grant's bier was on display in the new Capitol for two days). Lincoln's funeral train stopped in Albany en route to his burial in Springfield, Illinois, and his body lay in state for thirteen hours at the Assembly Chamber of the old Capitol. The *Atlas and Argus* was more reverential in reporting on the President this time, noting on April 27, 1865: "Aside from the slow tread of the procession, not a sound was to be heard in the streets. . . . Never upon a sabbath morning did the city present a stillness so complete."

All businesses were closed and no vehicles ran during the procession, which took thirty minutes to pass a given point, so many groups were in line: the Twenty-fifth Regiment (on time), the German Literary Society, the Iron Moulders Union, the Fenian Brotherhood, the St. Andrew's Society, the International Order of Odd Fellows, and many more. Some eighty thousand people were in the city, all hotels full, restaurants open all night to feed the mobs, hundreds of people sleeping in the streets. "Such a mass of human beings . . . was never before seen in the streets of Albany," said the *A and A*.

While the President's open coffin was on view, some fifty thousand people filed past, the line extending from the Capitol to Broadway. When the coffin was closed—with thousands still waiting in line—the procession began anew: up State Street, over Dove Street, down Washington Avenue to State, and up Broadway to the railroad crossing. Eight white horses drew the coffin on its catafalque trimmed in white silk; four bands played "Auld Lang Syne" and "Love Not." And then Lincoln was put into the Hearse Car, which was draped with "emblems of sorrow," and he left Albany forever.

The *A and A* had said that despite the crowds "the city was never more orderly." But on subsequent days it noted that certain disorderly events had occurred during the procession. From 132 Lark Street, burglars took eleven silver spoons; from 187 Hudson, thirty silver spoons; and from 196 Hudson, twelve silver spoons, a lady's gold watch, and a pair of armlets marked FANNIE.

Furthermore, George Murray and William Kennan were arrested for stealing a Mr. Van Vechten's watch on State Street while the cortege was passing, Patrick Roddy and Thomas Brown were arrested for fighting, Betsey Farrell for spitting in the face of Catherine Gray, and Johnson Noble for seducing Ann Miller by proposing marriage.

A famous Albany clergyman, Rabbi Isaac Mayer Wise, whose story is told elsewhere in this book, spoke in Cincinnati about the President and claimed him as a Jew. "Brethren," said the rabbi, "the lamented Abraham Lincoln is believed to be bone from our bone, flesh from our flesh. He was supposed to be a descendant of Hebrew parentage. He said so in my presence. And indeed he preserved numerous features of the Hebrew race, both in countenance and character."

The same day that the *A and A* reported this, it also noted that the *New York World* had said Wilkes Booth was of Jewish descent.

When the national grief passed, Downtown went back to its normal business of growing and changing and being the seeding ground for new heroes. On January 2, 1882, one of the more willful of such company checked into the Delavan House. (Did he stay in the same room Lincoln had occupied? Was there a presidential aura that clung to him when he entered it?) This was the hotel where legislators and politicians had met for years, the cramped quarters of the old Capitol no longer able to accommodate even their official gatherings. This visitor—his name was Theodore Roosevelt—left the Delavan the next morning and walked out into the coldest day of Albany's winter wearing no overcoat. His destination was that cramped Capitol, and he might well have taken a horsecar to it; but coatless, wearing a silk hat, a cutaway dress coat, and carrying a gold-headed cane, he walked along Downtown's streets, climbed the formidable hill to the Capitol's plateau, and stepped into the Assembly chamber with an actor's presence, to dazzle his legislative colleagues.

"I intend to be one of the governing class," he said during his tenure in the Assembly, and his intentions were indeed realized, for after four years as an assemblyman he left Albany, became a hero of the Spanish-American War, and returned to the city as the thirty-sixth Governor of New York State. He was the first to occupy the executive chamber of the new Capitol, the most expensive building ($25 million) on the American continent, and it was as if, said one of his biographers, the structure had been built just for him.

He would spend the next two years in Albany, a vigorous man you might see running up the seventy-two front steps of the Capitol two at a time. He had a standing bet with newsmen, so the story goes, that he would give an exclusive interview to any of them who could beat him up the steps. The story adds that no one ever collected. You might also have seen him walking on North Pearl Street Downtown, or angling through the pathways of Washington Park, or pacing a companion along the sidewalks of Manning Boulevard out in the new Pine Hills. He was a visible ambulatory presence here.

His story continued elsewhere when he left Albany.

Downtown's story, too continued.

Continues.

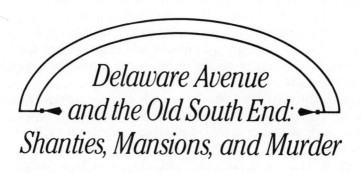

Delaware Avenue
and the Old South End:
Shanties, Mansions, and Murder

*B*ack in the early 1890s, so the story goes, an imaginative landlord named Lackey Doherty advertised a house with running water for rent on Swan Street. What made this unusual was that the house was not a very grand house and the Swan Street neighborhood was not very grand, either. It was Martinville, a notorious Irish shantytown.

So it was with great interest that people trooped over to the Doherty place to see the running water. True to his word, Lackey took the visitors downstairs and showed them the water—the Beaverkill Creek running underneath the house. And there was more than water in the creek. There were geese.

Lackey Doherty lives on in the anecdote, but the geese and the shantytown and even the water have gone. In their place came Beaver Park, now Lincoln Park, an incalculable improvement to the city. The Beaverkill, too, is gone—underground—and lives only in history books, or in memoirs like those of Henry James, whose grandfather founded the remarkable James clan in the Beaverkill's purlieu. Henry, in *A Small Boy and Others*, the first volume of his autobiography, speaks of a relative who visits the Jameses in Manhattan, having come from "the far-off Beaverkill," and he says the man "definitely emerged from rustication—the Beaverkill had but for a certain term protected or promoted, his simplicity."

Simplicity was hardly characteristic of all the Albany folk whose lives touched the Beaverkill, as we shall see. But it was indeed a rustic "kill," the Dutch word for creek, one of five that coursed through Albany. The five all ran east and emptied into the lordly Hudson, which Henry James rather parsimoniously called that "admirable stream."

Taking the kills from south to north, there were the Normanskill, which crossed the Delaware Turnpike (later Delaware Avenue—the main street of this chapter) and emptied into the Hudson at Kenwood; the Beaverkill, which began about where State University is today and ran eastward along Cortland Street, then along Madison Avenue, past the penitentiary (now the site of Hackett Middle School and the Veterans Hospital), down past Martinville, and into the Hudson by the steamboat landing at the foot of Madison Avenue; the Ruttenkill, the ghastliest of the kills, which coursed down a formidable ravine where Hudson Avenue is today and entered the river at State Street; the Foxenkill, discussed elsewhere, which ran parallel to Canal Street, now Sheridan Avenue, and crossed North Pearl Street beneath a bridge; and Patroon Creek, which until the city decided to draw from the Hudson, was the main source of Albany water. That source was created by damming three streams where they merged into Patroon Creek (in the city's far West End), to form Rensselaer Lake, also known as the Six-Mile Waterworks; and by damming the creek farther eastward to create Tivoli Lakes—just north of Livingston Avenue, about at the end of Quail Street—those lakes now gone.

The five kills all exist today but are either part of the city's sewer system or have been buried where they disrupted city life, the lone exception being the Normanskill. That stream derived its name from that of a tobacco planter and sawmill operator, Albert Andriessen Bradt, one of the first to settle on its banks. He was so cruel to his wife and children that he was censured by the first Patroon, Kiliaen Van Rensselaer. He became known as Albert the Norman, and his creek became the Norman's kill.

Patroon Creek, along which the New York Central Railroad built its tracks to the West, derived its name from the fact that it furnished power to mills owned by the Patroon; and also it emptied into the Hudson near his home, the Manor House, in North Albany. Huybertie Pruyn, who wrote extensively about her life in Albany, mentioned an Irish laundress in the Pruyn family's employ, Mary O'Mara, who talked of getting off the horsecar at "Pat Rouin's." The Pruyns at first thought she was talking of a saloon. Finally they translated it from Mary's brogue as "Patroon's"—the Manor House.

The Irish inhabited one periphery of the Beaverkill in the shantytown Martinville, said to have been named for James Martin, its builder, who earlier might have run a grocery on the spot. A photo of Martinville taken in 1892 reveals it as a trapezoidal jungle of about four dozen two- and three-story multifamily dwellings, back a bit from the slip-clay slopes of the Beaverkill ravine, which looks polluted even in black and white. I spoke with three men who remembered Martinville: Walter Stein, John Manifold (who told me Lackey Doherty's story), and Jim Meany— all residents of the Delaware Avenue area.

Walter remembered Martinville as brick houses and shacks aswarm with goats and geese. "You had to be careful," he said. "A goose could give you quite a bite. They'd hiss at you." And Martinville itself? "For a kid it was tough. You didn't linger long when you went through there."

Jim Meany had a different view. He was born on Morton Avenue, across the road from Martinville (he later became a North Ender and then a West Ender), and as to the toughness of his neighbors he said, "They weren't too tough at all. The Irish were there to take their own part and they weren't backing up for nobody. They were rugged people."

One of the saving graces of Martinville was its proximity to Buttermilk Falls, which was noted in history as far back as 1626, when Mohawk Indians ambushed a party of Dutchmen near it, killed four of them, and singled out Tymen Bouwensen to be roasted for lunch. A sawmill, maybe Albany's first, was authorized by the city to be built in 1689, to use "ye fall waters on ye Bevers Kill." In 1800 the cliffs of the Beaverkill ravine were said to be from seventy to one hundred and twenty feet high, and over them at one point cascaded the falls—butterishly milky, no doubt. They foamed into a splendid pool that served during four centuries (not counting Indian centuries) as a New World swimming hole. In the twentieth century it was called Rocky Ledge Pool until it went dry.

The clay on the Beaverkill's slopes was quarried, and several brickyards, with concomitant pollutants, were spawned. Hinckel's brewery, at South Swan Street and Myrtle Avenue, dumped its old suds into the creek, and a swamp took shape. In 1880 the ravine was adjudged a "dangerous nuisance" by a medical society, and in 1883 the Board of Health condemned it. The state legislature, which made laws in the smelly neighborhood, was pressuring the city to redeem the place, and in 1894 the land was cleared and construction was begun on Beaver Park. This also cooked Martinville's last goose and many of the Irish moved north to Canal Street, colloquially rechristened Gander Bay for you know what reason.

Beaver/Lincoln Park was, and is, an oasis in a densely settled part of the city. Rocky Ledge Pool has been replaced by a public swimming pool, and baseball is still played in the park's basin, as it was in the early 1900s when it was the focal point for neighborhood rivalries—the Shamrocks from St. James's, the Peacocks from St. Joseph's, the Schuylers from St. Ann's, the Emeralds from the North End.

On June 3, 1906, it was touch and go whether Sunday baseball, in the park and elsewhere, would be ruled illegal. Several clerics, most notably one from the Fourth Presbyterian Church, precipitated the arrest of young ballplayers active on Sunday, and thus in violation of an old law. I remember this event's still enraging my father forty years later whenever he talked about it. And it was the only time I ever heard him say anything against a Protestant. Judges Rogan and Brady, the latter a North Albanian who was probably a booster of the Emeralds, threw the cases out of court, and on June 17 baseball was back, and Judge Brady was enshrined forever in my father's pantheon as a paragon of judicial enlightenment.

West of where the ball games are now played in the park stood the residence of one of Albany's most famous nineteenth-century citizens: Professor James Hall, who died in 1898 at age eighty-seven. His home is now the Sunshine School in the city school system, used for mentally handicapped students. When Professor Hall built it, it was rustically isolated, just west of the Delaware Turnpike, overlooking the Beaverkill. The professor for half a century made Albany the geological capital of the world, and was honored by numerous countries for his work.

He wrote *The Geology of New York* (1843) and *New York State Natural History Survey* (1847–94), the latter a monumental report on the state's paleontology. He was an authority on stratigraphy and invertebrate paleontology, and his work formed the basis for later geological histories of North America. He housed his geological collections in wings of his house and kept a shotgun on his workbench to discourage interruption.

He was closely associated with the Cabinet of Natural History, created by the state legislature in 1843. In 1870 the Cabinet became the Museum of Natural History, the professor having been its director since 1866. He would continue in that post until 1894.

I remember the museum as it existed in the State Education Building, a vast floor full of wonders: the reconstructed Cohoes mastodon; a housefly enlarged one thousand times; a stuffed timber wolf with bloody jowls; some scantily clad Indians in wonderful tableaus that were, it later turned out, historically inaccurate but nonetheless marvelous; and, not least, a large and memorably boring room full of fossils and rocks.

The boredom, of course, was all my own. Professor Hall no doubt revered every cubic inch. But, it turns out, those were not Professor Hall's fossils I grew up being bored by. In need of funds, he sold his collection to an agent of John D. Rockefeller, the sale price rumored at first to be $30,000, later upped to $65,000; and the collection found its home in the American Museum of Natural History in Manhattan. And so Professor Hall today remains a geological prophet without fossils in his own hometown.

To the west of the professor's home, across the Delaware Turnpike, sitting at the end of a broad access avenue lined with trees, stood "the Castle on the Hill," as the Albany Penitentiary was grandly known. It was authorized in 1844 by the county legislature, and its first section opened in 1846 with 90 cells. As of October 14, 1884, it had 625 cells housing 899 prisoners.

The penitentiary was built with convict labor from the county jail at Eagle and Howard streets, men imprisoned chiefly for offenses against temperance. That crime, in large measure, was what the penitentiary continued to punish for decades, by working the prisoners in shops making chairs, brushes, and shoes. In 1855 it held 801 prisoners, 771 for intemperance. During all of 1884, when not quite one seventh of the prisoners were female, the jail received 2,270 prisoners, 1,894 of whom admitted being intemperate citizens, 376 of whom did not but were jailed anyway. Some 2,000 of their sentences were for six months or less; 128 prisoners were doing one to five years, 13 were in for six to ten, and there was 1 lifer.

As to their national origins, 1,480 were U.S. born, 409 came from Ireland, 115 from Germany, 90 from England, 75 from Canada, and 25 from Scotland, plus a small miscellany. The jail was good business, according to Albany historians George Howell and Jonathan Tenney, who reported that it took in federal prisoners and boarded others from outlying counties, and after covering its $50,000 annual operating costs it still turned $75,000 back to the county exchequer.

The superintendent, Amos Pilsbury (tenure 1844–72), was praised for his management of the prison. But then in 1868 the institution became a target for early penal reformers; District Attorney Henry Smith discovered 50 prisoners, including children, confined in a single room, first offenders mixed with experienced criminals, and more. His findings produced a "profound sensation" in Albany, and reforms were authorized by the county.

Conditions were so bad for one life prisoner that he rigged an ingenious device with a candle, a string, two corks, and two needles. He rigged it to hover over his face, lit the candle, which burned the string and allowed the corks—with needles stuck through them—to fall onto his eyes and pierce his eyeballs, blinding him. He believed being blind would earn him a release from prison, but justice is also blind and he stayed in jail.

The penitentiary was torn down in 1931, when Albany County Jail was built in Colonie on the site of the old Shaker Farm. What turned up in the demolition were solitary-confinement dungeons beneath the floors, iron rings to which prisoners had been strung by their thumbs, and who knows what else. Then on August 20, 1947, Bill McMahon of Eagle Street, a bulldozer operator at work digging into the old penitentiary grounds to build the Veterans Hospital, turned up human skeletons—"a dime a dozen . . . as common as old inner tubes."

It was then that memories were stirred of the prison scandal of 1868, when overcrowding was rife, the water torture—relentless drips on the forehead—was in use, and perhaps even death was in vogue as a quiet form of punishment.

Also raised as a possibility for explaining away the bones was the period when many Confederate prisoners, interred in the penitentiary during the Civil War, fell victim to a plague that ran through the cell block—if that was, indeed, what killed them—and perhaps it was those men who were buried in the prison yard.

It was grotesque indeed to have a penitentiary in the neighborhood—plus a pesthouse at the other end of what is today

Holland Avenue, southeast of where Christian Brothers Academy stands. Jim Meany remembered a horse and wagon's going there early in the century with people said to be smallpox victims. But the cravings of neighborhood nostalgia can be wry indeed. Consider these excerpts from a poem penned by Edward M. J. Morrisey, a resident of the area when the prison was still a fact of life. Morrisey called his poem "A Yen for the Pen":

> I remember the day when the old "Penni-en"
> Held a plentiful measure of joy,
> Embroidering schemes of Utopian dreams
> In the mind of the neighborhood boy. . . .
> The "big hill" where only the bravest would sled
> When winter's white mantle would fall,
> And the stone yard where "robbers and cops" held their
>   chase—
> What enjoyment these memories recall!

Another formidable element in the neighborhood was an institution of a different order—one with extraordinary financial and intellectual dimensions. This was the James family, which had its most significant genealogical juncture in William (Billy) James, father of Henry James the elder, the Swedenborgian theologian who, in turn, fathered William James, the psychologist and philosopher, and Henry James, the eminent novelist.

"Our father's father," the literary Henry wrote in Volume Two of his autobiography, *Notes of a Son and Brother*, "William James, an Irishman and a Protestant born (of County Cavan) had come to America, a very young man, and then sole of his family, shortly after the Revolutionary War" (it was 1789).

Billy James settled in Albany in 1793, the legendary comment about him being that he had "a little money, a Latin grammar and a great desire to visit one of the Revolutionary battlefields" (Saratoga and Bennington weren't far off).

The Albany into which he settled was described by banker Gorham A. Worth as a "third or fourth rate town." Worth said also it was "indeed Dutch, in all its moods and tenses; thoroughly and inveterately Dutch. The buildings were Dutch—Dutch in style, in position, attitude and aspect. The people were Dutch, the horses were Dutch, and even the dogs were Dutch."

James's arrival coincided with an invasion of Albany by New Englanders—or Yankees, as that outlander group was hatefully called by the Dutch. They were outrageously ambitious, and came to be epitomized in a man named Elkanah Watson, who had arrived from Plymouth, Massachusetts, in 1789, and found the city as dismal as had Mr. Worth. "No street was paved," Watson wrote in his journal, "no lamps, no library; not a public-house of any decency." His campaign to pave streets earned him the supreme epithet from a pair of Dutchwomen who wielded broomsticks at his approach and called out, "Here comes that infernal paving Yankee!"

Watson is credited with reviving an old idea, one that dated from the Revolution: a canal connecting the Hudson River and the Great Lakes; and this indeed came to fruition in the hands of ambitious and visionary men. Billy James was one of these, but visionary fits his son and grandsons better than it fits him. He was a single-minded businessman who began as a clerk in what was described in an article about him in the *American Scholar* as "John Robinson's old blue store" at State and Broadway. He moved into tobacco and cigars, then dry goods, and rose like a comet into an opulence "almost beyond parallel" among his contemporaries. He owned an Albany–Utica express firm, bought land in Syracuse and operated a saltworks there, in 1820 was founding vice-president of the Albany Savings Bank—the third such institution in the U.S.—was vice-president of the Albany Chamber of Commerce, and was second in influence in the city only to the last Patroon, Stephen Van Rensselaer. "He has done more to build up the city of Albany than any other individual," said one newspaper report of his day.

His role in the construction of the Erie Canal was both as an early proponent—urging it on the people of the state in 1816— and then as chairman of the Committee of Citizens of Albany (he made a speech) when the Canal formally opened in 1823. (The first Canal water—no boats yet—from Buffalo had mingled with the Hudson's waters at Albany on September 25, 1823, and the first living thing through the lock was a three-foot eel, which was skinned and exhibited in Albany's Lyceum of Natural History.)

The Canal, which cost $7 million to build, quadrupled Albany's wholesale business within a few years. The cost per mile of transporting a ton of freight between Buffalo and New York City declined from almost twenty cents to one cent. Billy James prospered along with many, and more than most. He came to own so much land that his family called him The Patroon.

Henry James, reflecting on his grandfather's younger days, wrote in his autobiography: "I find myself envying the friendly youth who could bring his modest Irish kin such a fairytale from over the sea."

Henry the elder, whose home was not only an old farmhouse but more formal residences, first at State and Green streets, and later on North Pearl, grew up in a strict, Calvinist world where both God the Father and Billy the Father were the causes of a lifelong enmity. Leon Edel, biographer of Henry James the younger, writes of Henry, Sr.: "Henry felt himself a helpless victim of parental disregard. 'I cannot recollect that he [Billy] ever questioned me about my out-of-door occupations, or about my companions, or showed any extreme solicitude about my standing in school.'" As to his home life under Billy, Henry the elder also said: "I was never so happy at home as away from it."

Henry, Jr.'s, view of his grandparents tended to favor his grandmother (Billy's third wife) Catharine Barber: "She represented for us in our generation the only English blood—that of both her own parents—flowing in our veins." Henry liked this, and said if he could have chosen from whom to descend with dominance he would have chosen Catharine Barber. But F. W. Dupee, who edited James's autobiography, points out that Catharine's grandparents both came to America from Ireland, not England. And so Henry was more Irish than he knew, or wanted to be.

Henry quoted his grandfather's obituary in the *New York Post* as saying: "We see his footsteps, turn where we may, and these are the results of his informing mind and his vast wealth. His plans of improvement [for New York] embraced the entire city, and there is scarcely a street or a square which does not exhibit some mark of his hand or some proof of his opulence. With the exception of Mr. Astor . . . no other businessman has acquired so great a fortune in this state." William's estate totaled $3 million, formidable indeed for 1832.

None of the James heirs ever saw fit to work again, and to their leisure we are happily indebted for some of the most glorious writing of the century. Of this eventuality Henry would write: "The rupture with my grandfather's tradition and attitude was complete; we were never in a single case, I think, for two generations, guilty of a stroke of business."

Farther out from the James land, the top of Second Avenue meets Whitehall Road. Second Avenue was originally called

Whitehall Road, for it led upward to Whitehall, one of three mansions in the southern sector of the city linked to noted Albanians and significant American history. The other two are the Schuyler Mansion and Cherry Hill.

Whitehall, named for the palace in London, was British staff headquarters during the French and Indian Wars, when Albany was a key city in the fighting. On the site originally were barracks for British troops and stables for one hundred and fifty horses. Whitehall served as the headquarters of British General John Bradstreet, who enlarged the original barracks. It was a hive of Tory activity during the Revolution, was eventually confiscated by the Revolutionary government, and was sold at auction in 1780 to Leonard Gansevoort, a Revolutionary general who made it a place of formidable elegance and intensive social life at the highest American level—Washington, Lafayette, and Hamilton among his guests.

Gansevoort's daughter Magdalena married Jacob Ten Eyck, and when General Gansevoort died Whitehall passed into the hands of the Ten Eyck family and continued as a site of parties and balls. The mansion had fifty-nine windows, twelve fireplaces, four verandas, and a state dining room. It also had a *dood-kamer*, or dead room, which, one historian wrote, had "a high post bedstead where linen sheets and ruffled shirts were kept in readiness to receive the departed," and which seems the ultimate in both hospitality and tidiness.

Whitehall was 136 years old when it burned to the ground in 1883 and it has seldom been written about. The *Times-Union*'s C. R. (Tip) Roseberry called it "the forgotten colonial manse of the Hudson Valley." A second Ten Eyck mansion was built after the fire, but it lacked the grandness of Whitehall, eventually becoming an inn, a bistro, an apartment house, and what remained of it became 73 Whitehall Road.

The two other celebrated mansions coexisted with Whitehall, but down the hill, eastward from the Delaware Pike. Both were built in extreme isolation, as was Whitehall, and both now are surrounded by some of the city's oldest houses in the crowded South End.

The Schuyler Mansion, on Clinton Street, just west of South Pearl Street, is a state historic site. Philip Schuyler (1733–1804) built it on his 125-acre plot on a bluff overlooking the old pastures of the Dutch Reformed Church, and from this view the mansion took its name: the Pastures. Schuyler built it for his bride, Cath-

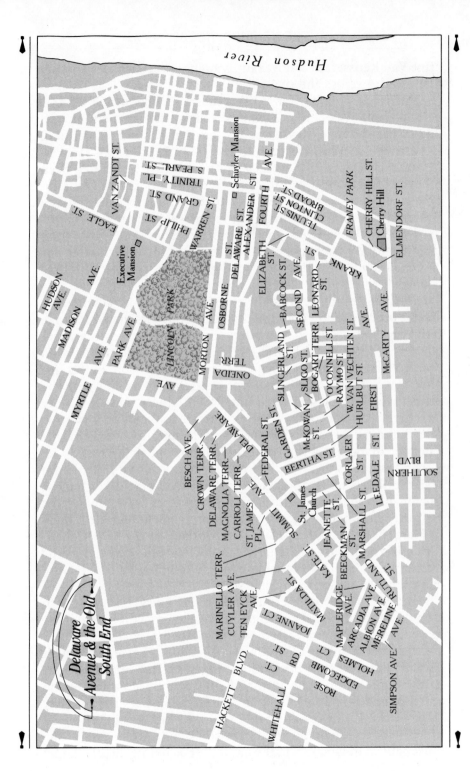

Delaware Avenue & the Old South End

Hudson River

Schuyler Mansion

Executive Mansion

St. James Church

Cherry Hill

LINCOLN PARK

FRANEY PARK

HUDSON AVE.
MADISON AVE.
PARK AVE.
MYRTLE AVE.
EAGLE ST.
VAN ZANDT ST.
PHILIP ST.
WARREN ST.
GRAND ST.
TRINITY PL.
S. PEARL ST.
OSBORNE ST.
DELAWARE ST.
ALEXANDER ST.
FOURTH AVE.
ELIZABETH ST.
TEUNIS ST.
CLINTON ST.
BROAD ST.
MORTON AVE.
ONEIDA TERR.
SLINGERLAND ST.
BABCOCK ST.
SECOND AVE.
LEONARD ST.
KRANK AVE.
CHERRY HILL ST.
ELMENDORF ST.
SLIGO ST.
McKOWAN ST.
O'CONNELL ST.
RAYMO ST.
W. VAN VECHTEN ST.
HURLBUT ST.
McCARTY AVE.
FIRST ST.
GARDEN ST.
FEDERAL ST.
BERTHA ST.
CORLAER ST.
LEEDALE ST.
SOUTHERN BLVD.
BESCH AVE.
CROWN TERR.
DELAWARE TERR.
MAGNOLIA TERR.
CARROLL TERR.
ST. JAMES PL.
DELAWARE AVE.
SUMMIT AVE.
MARINELLO TERR.
CUYLER AVE.
TEN EYCK AVE.
MATILDA ST.
JOANNE CT.
KATE ST.
JEANETTE ST.
BEECKMAN ST.
MARSHALL ST.
RUTLAND ST.
MAPLERIDGE AVE.
ARCADIA AVE.
ALBION AVE.
MERELINE AVE.
SIMPSON AVE.
HACKETT BLVD.
WHITEHALL CT.
ROSE CT.
EDGECOMB RD.
HOLMES CT.
BOGART TERR.

- 83 -

arine Van Rensselaer, whose family home, Fort Crailo, is another historic site across the river in Rensselaer.

Schuyler, a shipping and lumber magnate who owned 125,000 acres of land, was one of Albany's leading citizens—and indeed one of the nation's, having served as General of the Northern Department of Washington's Army in the Revolution. He was, by some accounts, a victim of political injustice, having been relieved of his command during the Battle of Saratoga by politicians who turned it over to Horatio Gates because of the American loss of Ticonderoga to the British. Schuyler was court-martialed and acquitted, and he resigned from the Army. Years later Daniel Webster spoke of the injustice and said Schuyler was "second only to Washington in the services he performed for his country."

His Albany home became the elite prison for General Burgoyne and his officers following the British surrender at Saratoga (where Burgoyne had occupied Schuyler's Saratoga home as his headquarters, then burned it and later apologized to Schuyler, who accepted the apology). It is legend that Schuyler's son, Philip, age nine, playfully flung open the door of a Schuyler salon where the British were dining and cried out, "Gentlemen, you are all my prisoners." One account says the officers looked "very sorrowful." Burgoyne, in thanks for Schuyler's hospitality, presented his daughter Margarita with a pair of diamond shoebuckles.

The Pastures was a focus of revolutionary activity: Benjamin Franklin, Benedict Arnold, George Washington (Schuyler's close friend), Alexander Hamilton, and Aaron Burr were among the visitors. Washington's name appears on the Schuyler birth-book as Margarita's godfather. Hamilton worked on the U.S. Constitution in the library and also married Elizabeth Schuyler in the mansion in 1780. Two other daughters, Angelica and Margarita, eloped out windows with their suitors.

Hamilton, before he met his bride-to-be, Betsy, had written to a friend about the qualifications he sought in a wife: "She must be young—handsome (I lay most stress upon a good shape), sensible (a little learning will do)—well bred . . . chaste and tender (I am an enthusiast in my notions of generosity). She must love neither money nor scolding, for I dislike equally a termagant and an economist— In politics, I am indifferent what side she may be of—I think I have arguments that will safely convert her to mine— As to religion a moderate stock will satisfy me— She must believe in God and hate a saint. But as to fortune, the larger stock of that the better— You know my temper and circumstances and will therefore pay special attention to this article of the treaty . . . as money is an essential ingredient to happiness in this world—as I have not much of my own—and as I am very little calculated to get more . . . it must needs be that my wife . . . bring at least a sufficiency to administer to her own extravagancies."

Hamilton and Betsy stayed together twenty-four years, had four children, and after Hamilton was killed by Aaron Burr in the historic duel, Betsy never remarried. But Hamilton had dalliances with both Angelica and Margarita during his marriage, and his public career came to an end because of a protracted affair with another woman, Maria Reynolds.

And so marriage was a sticky business for this founding father and his in-laws, the Schuylers. But up the road at Cherry Hill, marriage was more than sticky, it was grisly. Cherry Hill was a Georgian-style house built on a nine-hundred-acre farm in 1787 by Philip Van Rensselaer, a grandson of the third Patroon (Hendrick Van Rensselaer), for his wife, Maria Sanders, granddaughter of Pieter Schuyler, Albany's first mayor. The house, which sits back from South Pearl between McCarty and First avenues, was passed on to other Van Rensselaers for two centuries and finally endowed as a museum by its last tenant, Miss Emily Rankin, who died in 1963.

In Miss Emily's will she specified that one subject should not be discussed in relation to the house: the death of John Whipple at the hands of Jesse Strang. Not only has this restriction been lifted, but it was ended with great flourish: Historic Cherry Hill, a nonprofit institution endowed by Miss Emily, published in the late summer of 1982 the complete Whipple-Strang melodrama, *Murder at Cherry Hill* by Dr. Louis C. Jones, director emeritus of the New York State Historical Association. A reception on Cherry Hill's back lawn was given for the book's send-off, with a Dixieland band entertaining the guests and spinning Miss Emily to a two-four beat.

Jesse Strang, a native of Yorktown, New York, had abandoned his family, feigned his own murder, and come to Albany. He was working at Bates' Tavern, just south of Cherry Hill on the Bethlehem Turnpike, the road south out of Albany; and there, in August 1826, he met the flirtatious Elsie Lansing Whipple, twenty-four, a most willful young woman.

Elsie had secretly married an engineer, John Whipple, when

she was fourteen in order to break her status as ward of Cherry Hill's master, Philip P. Van Rensselaer, and thereby gain access to money her father had left her. She lived on at the mansion with Whipple, but evidently not very happily, for twice she tried to poison him with arsenic. The first dose, given to him in his tea, had no effect. The second she mixed with his sulphur (usually taken with molasses as a tonic) and he gave some to his and Elsie's child, upsetting Elsie, although needlessly, for neither husband nor child died this time either.

After Elsie met Jesse Strang, he came to the mansion seeking work and was hired as a handyman. Elsie and Jesse met secretly, passed love notes in the pantry, made love in the hayloft, and at least once stayed together at Hill's Tavern on the Troy–Schenectady Turnpike. The innkeeper later testified they stayed in a room with two beds but "only one bed was tumbled."

Jesse bought a rifle at a gun shop on Beaver Street in Albany, practiced with it, and at ten p.m. on May 27, nine months after he'd met Elsie, he climbed a shed attached to the mansion, wearing, for stealth, he later said, a pair of John Whipple's heavy socks that Elsie had thrown to him from her window. And while Whipple was at his desk going over financial accounts, Strang shot him in the back from nine feet away, then fell backward off the shed roof, leaped up, and said, "Thank God, I'm not hurt." Whipple was mortally wounded. Elsie had been smoking a pipe while her lover was busy.

Jesse's behavior aroused suspicion (he blamed strangers for the crime, showed no interest in the removal of the fatal bullet at the inquest). He was arrested, privately confessed but blamed Elsie as the architect of the deed. Elsie was arraigned as his accomplice. Jesse's trial began July 25 at the Court of Oyer and Terminer before Judge William Duer. On July 27, after a few minutes of deliberation, the jury found Jesse guilty. Elsie was tried separately and Jesse was called as a witness, but Judge Duer refused to let him testify against Elsie, whom the judge found to be "of a character light, frivolous, weak, vain, impudent, and wicked, and guilty to a certain degree; a fit instrument in the hands of a designing man." Elsie was not prosecuted further and on August 3 was acquitted by a jury that never left the box, although she was universally believed guilty. Of this, Jones writes: "The Albany Establishment had closed ranks, however distasteful it may have been to do so, and saved one of their number from the disgrace of a public hanging."

This didn't do anything for Jesse, however. He was ordered hanged, and on August 24, 1827, on Gallows Hill, at the Rutten-kill ravine, a little west of Eagle Street where Hudson Avenue crosses, maybe thirty to forty thousand people lined its ridges and slopes to see Jesse swing. It was said that eleven hundred vehicles had been counted coming from the north alone. *The Confessions of Jesse Strang*, a pamphlet, was circulated among the crowd by some of Jesse's loyal relatives, a St. Peter's cleric prayed with him, Sheriff Conrad A. Ten Eyck cut the rope drop, and then Jesse Strang, he swang.

What happend to Elsie?

She went to New York City, remarried, moved to New Jersey, where her second husband died under mysterious circumstances. She then disappeared into the area of Onondaga, New York, her trail, at this point, somewhat cold.

Jesse's was the last public hanging in Albany. The Ruttenkill ravine (fifty feet deep, three hundred feet wide) had taken its name from the Dutch word for rats (*ratten*), which infested its waters. It was a filthy place and was filled in between 1845 and 1848 by pushing six hundred thousand yards of blue clay from the ravine's hills into its basin. The contractor, who used two hundred and fifty men to do the job, was a former Watervliet man, Charles Stanford, brother of Leland Stanford, builder of the Southern Pacific and Central Pacific railroads.

The modern city was climbing up out of such depths as the Ruttenkill represented. People were moving out onto the turn-pikes, and into new neighborhoods on the high ground up from the river—areas like Delaware Avenue. This had begun, in 1805, as the road the Albany and Delaware Turnpike Company was using as a first leg to the Schoharie Turnpike—through the town of Otego and on to Brink's Mills on the Susquehanna and the headwaters of the Delaware River. But the turnpike failed and was abandoned beyond Schoharie, and in 1865 the segment be-tween Madison and Morton avenues was yielded to the city, extending the city line.

John Manifold, a plumber who was seventy-five when we talked, remembered the plank road that ran from the Normanskill bridge into Park Avenue (cobblestones after that into the city). "In the summer it was all right," he said, "but in the spring of the year it was muck up to your knees. It used to take us three hours to go to church on Sunday, from Besch Avenue down to the cathe-dral."

Cattle drives were a common sight over that planking and through the mud, perhaps four or five herds coming by during a weekend. And when Albany was installing many of its sidewalks, the road was a mass of ruts from the heavy-laden wagons hauling flagstones down from the Helderberg Mountains.

By the time the twentieth century began, Delaware Avenue had been paved and developers were in serious action—men like Jacob Leonard and Joseph Besch. Leonard had acquired fifty acres of Billy James's land and even lived in the James farmhouse (about where Providence Street begins at Delaware). He'd owned the ten acres on which the penitentiary had been built and had donated land for the extension of Beaver Park. He also built Leonard Place, which began modern residential growth, and his son, Jesse, took credit for originating the idea of Hackett Boulevard and Holland Avenue.

Joseph Besch, Republican sheriff in the early years of this century, took up where the Leonards left off and developed along Delaware, from Holland to Besch avenues. He built the second concrete-block building in Albany. I don't know who built the first but it was on Second Avenue and Joe Besch's was on Delaware. People thought they were prisons. Besch also bought three farms and sold lots, creating modern Whitehall Road, previously a muddy wagon path.

Walter Stein, who was eighty when we talked, took a picture of Whitehall Road when it was a plain of rye fields owned by the Ten Eyck family, not far from the old Whitehall mansion. A radio tower, built by one of the railroads, rose high above Ten Eyck Park in the photo, about where Second Avenue meets Whitehall Road.

Walter was a photoengraver by trade, an amateur photographer by avocation. As early as 1902 he was photographing his own neighborhood and other Albany sites. He preserved thousands of negatives on glass plates, taken with a Century camera.

"I knew changes were coming," Walter said. "I thought someday they were going to be antiques and I wanted a record."

There is a splendid quietude in Walter's photos: Hurlbut Street after a rain in 1906, a mud path and open fields about it . . . white fences running along Delaware in the summer . . . the same white fences with snow all about them . . . the dedication of the German church Walter's grandfather helped found as a storefront, and here it is as a real church: Calvary Evangelical United Brethren . . . there's Delaware Avenue in 1919, with so very few houses . . . there's Jacob Stein's farmland in winter, a rolling piece of land where St. James's Catholic Church now stands . . . and there's the traction company's track-welding machine and its crew, repairing trolley tracks at Morton and Delaware avenues on September 20, 1905, a nice day.

The trolley brought some people out to live in the neighborhood, first to Leonard Place, then in 1902 out to Second Avenue, and in 1906 out to Graceland Cemetery.

Walter Stein remembered the opening of the new line:

"Mayor Charles Gaus was in office then, and I think he was on the first car—on a Fourth of July, as I remember. They had a test run the night before and my brother Bob filled a pair of pants and a coat with rags, put a hat on it, and laid it on the tracks. When the light of the trolley shone on that thing, you can imagine what a thrill the motorman got."

The trolley spurred residential development, but Walter heard people say they wouldn't live out Delaware Avenue because there was no church. And going to the Cathedral of the Immaculate Conception, as John Manifold pointed out, required extraordinary commitment.

The first mass in St. James's was said on the last Sunday of October 1913, in a building that would become the latter-day parish hall. St. James's prospered and the Catholic Diocese built the present church in 1931. St. John's Cemetery gave way to residential development, and people stopped by to collect what they thought might be the bones of their relatives, to bury them elsewhere.

The neighborhood produced the most famous one-line politician in Albany history: George Krank, who while running for alderman, campaigned that "I, George Krank, made the water run up Second Avenue." People believed George and elected him. He later ran on a parallel theme: "If I'm not reelected I'll make it run down again."

The Germans, among whom George campaigned, were the first to settle along Delaware, rising up out of what was originally Bonafettle and, to the south, Grosbeckville, German areas at the bottom of the hill, generally referred to as Dutch Hollow. The Irish didn't displace the Germans, but they eventually outnumbered them on Delaware; and as all this settlement thickened, the usual commerce and a bit of industry rose up. The silent-movie houses were the Hillcrest and the Idle-Hour (open-air) on Second Avenue, and later, at two locations on Delaware Avenue, came the Delaware, serving as the city's principal art house in its second incarnation from the 1950s to the 1970s, the age when the movies became cinema.

The grease factory was at Second Avenue and Beekman, the soap factory at Myrtle and Delaware, the old Albany wire works on Delaware. There was a grocery run by Matty Fitzgerald, who cared more about baseball than groceries, for he'd played ten games with the New York Giants in 1906–7. And, most singular of all, there was Peter Kinnear's Albany Billiard Ball Company, which took over the invention of John Wesley Hyatt, who in 1868 found a perfect substitute for ivory, for use in the manufacture of billiard balls. Hyatt invented two items, bonsilate and celluloid. Bonsilate was used to make buttons as well as billiard balls and other such indispensable items, but the real point is that celluloid was the pioneer substance in the creation of plastic, Hyatt's gift to the world. And the inspiration for it came out of an Albany poolroom.

The business people in the neighborhood banded together in 1956 and formed the Delaware Avenue Business and Civic Association, which rarely had more than thirty members, coped with some parking problems, and slid into oblivion. In 1979 the Delaware Avenue Neighborhood Association was still worrying over kids and parking, and for two dollars in annual dues you could join the worrying.

Eleanor Segal Koblenz didn't worry much when she was a kid on Delaware Avenue. Even as a Jew she found nothing to fear, no racism (maybe a little slur now and then), and, what's more, her parents watched her very closely. "I was a very protected little girl," she said when we talked. She grew up thinking the world was made up of Irish Catholics and Jews. She didn't discover Protestants until about fifth grade.

The Jews in the neighborhood were mostly from Russia (though her grandfather had come from Rumania) and lived on Marshall, Jeannette, Bertha, and Hurlbut streets and Summit, Cuyler, and Ten Eyck avenues in the 1920s and early 1930s. They established a new synagogue, Sons of Israel, in a house on Hurlbut, then build a foundation on Federal Street and for High Holiday services erected a tent over it—they couldn't afford a roof.

Eleanor remembers the synagogue's going up at last in 1932—with bricks from the Albany Penitentiary, which had just been torn down. The synagogue is still there, but with new tenants, a fusion of two other congregations that began in the South End—

first Bnei Abraham took it, and Beth El Jacob joined later, making it Beth Abraham Jacob. The old building is now attached to the new synagogue that faces on Hackett Boulevard. The original founders moved Temple Israel to New Scotland Avenue.

The emphatic presence of the Jews and the Irish was superseded in the neighborhood by the Italians, who moved up from Little Italy in the South End. The Panetta family, which ran one of Albany's best Italian restaurants, at Hudson Avenue and Grand Street, lived on Marinello Terrace, where Eleanor later lived. Alfonso Marinello, who built the street's houses (with extraordinary durability), also lived there. By the 1970s the Italian influence was seen in a rush of new pizza parlors, stores selling Italian imports, restaurants such as Armando's and Cavalieri's. Even the Delaware Theater converted to "Carosello Delaware" and showed Italian films without English dubbing or subtitles. But that didn't work. Delaware Avenue wasn't *that* Italian.

It remains a solidly middle-class neighborhood, and Eleanor says it really hasn't changed very much since she was a child. "My sisters both moved out of town years ago," she said, "and the last time they came back, about 1979, they were astonished how it looks so much the same." Eleanor has detected a bit of deterioration creeping up on it recently—"It's beginning to look seedy," she said—and so that's something new for Delaware.

But an era closed in 1977 with the death in his sleep at age ninety-one of Delaware Avenue's (and Albany's) principal political citizen, the Democratic patriarch Daniel P. O'Connell. Dan is explored elsewhere, ubiquitously elsewhere, in this book, but there is more. There is the fact that he moved up from First Avenue in Bonafettle to 142 Whitehall Road. And that street then, and for half a century thereafter, became as famous with Albanians because of his presence on it as the Whitehall Mansion had been when it was Tory headquarters and later when it was the social center of upstate Revolutionary gadflying.

Dan's brothers also lived close by. Edward, the lawyer, who was coequal with Dan in running the Albany Democratic party, lived at 41 Summit Avenue; Patrick, the eldest brother, lived at 15 Besch Avenue; John (Solly) lived at 14 Putnam Street, as did his son, John, Jr., the central figure in the most notorious event in the neighborhood's modern history—young John's kidnapping on July 7, 1933, from in front of his Putnam Street home.

Young John was held for twenty-three days in an apartment house in Hoboken, New Jersey, while his captors sought $250,000

from his father and uncles, on the assumption the Albany political leaders were rich. The O'Connells let out the word that they
were having trouble raising a fraction of that. They offered $20,000
but the kidnappers rejected it as puny. A man who was close to
the O'Connells and their allies in these years told me in 1983
that a high-level county official opened a county safe and offered
Ed O'Connell as much county money as he needed to ransom
young John. Ed's response, said my source, was "Thanks a lot,
but the money is coming in so fast we don't know what to do
with it." Eventually the O'Connells offered $40,000 and the kid-
nappers took it (the bills were marked), and young John was
released unharmed.

Eight men were convicted of the kidnapping and drew long
prison sentences. Among them were four Albany figures: Manny
Strewel, a South Ender, and three men from the Cabbagetown
neighborhood, Percy Geary and John and Francis Oley. Strewel,
said to be the mastermind, was chosen by the kidnappers as the
presumably disinterested go-between; he was in communication
with both the kidnappers and Dan O'Connell, who did the ne-
gotiating for the family. Percy Geary, from Central Avenue, and
John and Francis Oley, from Orange Street, had been involved
with Jack (Legs) Diamond in bootlegging in the early 1930s. Kidnapping had become a popular hoodlum pursuit after the repeal
of Prohibition also repealed the easy money from bootlegging.

Francis Oley's involvement in crime was a surprise to people
who had known him as a youth—Daniel P. Corr, for instance,
who grew up with him in Cabbagetown.

"I can't, to this day," Dan Corr said in 1982, "visualize Franny
Oley participating in that kidnapping. But he apparently went
along with his brother." Franny Oley was a year ahead of Dan in
St. Patrick's School (Oley was class of 1921) and went on to
Albany High School, where he played varsity basketball. "He was
popular," Dan said, "a good basketball player. He didn't seem to
have a criminal nature."

Dan remembered little of Johnny Oley, who was older and the
more seasoned brother in crime, but he recalled Percy Geary as
"goofy, squirrelly, with reddish hair, and cross-eyed—you wouldn't
know whether he was coming or going."

Manny Strewel was the first of the kidnappers arrested and
tried in Albany County Court, and young Johnny O'Connell was
a witness against him. But Johnny's testimony that he could
identify Strewel as having been in the apartment where Johnny

had been blindfolded and chained to a bed was challenged by Daniel H. Prior, Strewel's attorney. (Prior had also been Jack Diamond's attorney in 1931, and would be attorney for some of Daniel O'Connell's associates in the early 1940s during the investigation of the O'Connell Machine by Governor Dewey.) Damaging to Albany's case against Strewel was a newspaper interview with Johnny O'Connell by Leo O'Brien, then a flashy young reporter for the *Times-Union*.

The story, which Leo told me in 1974 and again in 1982, just before his death, was this: Leo had been close to the O'Connells before and during the kidnapping, and had had access to their inner circle. He was such an oracle about what was going on, he said, that reporters from New York—Meyer Berger from the *Times*, James Kilgallen from Hearst's International News Service—would follow him around to see what he'd turn up.

"I was sleeping on a lounge in the ladies' room when Johnny was brought back," Leo said. (He was talking of the anteroom of the ladies' lounge on the second floor of the *Times-Union* building in its old Beaver Street incarnation. Bill Lowenberg, former *Times-Union* newsman, assures me this was not a breach of propriety, for at late evening the couch was up for grabs, there being no ladies on the night shift, or lobster trick.)

The word came to Leo, and he rose from his couch and tracked the O'Connells to their Helderberg summer residence, which was headquarters for the family during the kidnapping. His editor at the *Times-Union*, George Williams, wanted a first-person story when Leo got to Johnny, but, said Leo, "Dan only waved me away." He then called Ed O'Connell, to whom he was close.

"I wanted to go on vacation," Leo said, "and so I said to Ed, 'I got a little stuff from the district attorney—how about faking it?' And Ed said okay." And so Leo put words into young John's mouth, which duly appeared in the *Times-Union*, and appeared again when they were read at Strewel's trial. At one point in the faked interview Leo quoted Johnny, already on record as having identified Strewel, as saying he didn't think he could identify any of his captors.

"Did you say that?" Prior asked Johnny during Strewel's trial.
"No."
"Did you say any part of it?"
"No sir, I did not."
"Do you know a man named Leo O'Brien who works for the *Times-Union*?"

"I know of him."

"He is a close friend of your Uncle Dan, isn't he?"

"I don't know how close."

"You have seen him at Dan's camp, haven't you?"

"Not that I know of."

"Do you mean that?"

"Yes." . . .

"You will admit, though, that this [Leo's story] is a fairly accurate account of what happened to you?"

"Yes it is—some parts of it."

"You mean that some of it is true?"

"Yes sir."

"And you know a story couldn't be written as accurately if you had not talked with a reporter."

"Well, I talked with the district attorney and the police out there."

Leo was not called as a witness, for no one could find him. The O'Connells wanted him to testify that it was a faked story in order to support Johnny's identification of Strewel, but Leo said he declined. "I couldn't defend it," he recalled, "but I didn't know it wasn't true" (that Johnny couldn't identify his captors).

And so Leo stayed home for a week and his wife would let nobody into the house. Strewel was convicted and sentenced to fifty years in prison, but he appealed and won a new trial, and Leo's faked story contributed to that.

The Appellate Division of the Supreme Court found "serious material and prejudicial errors" in calling for a new trial. One point cited by the judges was that the defense did not call newsmen who could have clarified whether or not young John could have identified his kidnappers. Leo also remembered that an element of the judicial argument was that no reputable newspaper would publish a faked story. "But that's bad law," said Leo. "No newspaper story has any weight unless it's corroborated."

Strewel was to be retried, but forestalled that by pleading guilty in 1936 to a charge of blackmail, and drew a fifteen-year sentence.

In early 1937 seven more kidnappers were arrested. Francis Oley, twenty-nine, who had lung trouble, went to Denver and was arrested there on January 20, 1937. A man close to the Oleys offered me a view of Franny different from Daniel Corr's. "He was a pisspot, a squealer," said the man. "They squeezed John's whereabouts out of him." Twelve days after Francis's arrest, John Oley, thirty-six, and Percy Geary, thirty-four, were arrested in New York City, along with Harold (Red) Crowley, thirty-five.

The other four kidnappers arrested—all in their thirties—were Thomas Dugan, John (Sonny) McGlone, Charles Harrigan, and George Garguillo. These, along with Geary and Oley, were sentenced to seventy-seven years in jail. Crowley got twenty-eight years. Franny Oley hanged himself in his cell three months after his arrest. The convictions were all in federal court, Strewel convicted of use of, and conspiracy to use, the mails to extort money. He was given fifty-eight years, which was reduced to twenty-two years. He did his time, went to work on the docks in New Jersey, and was thought still to be alive in 1983. The others were convicted of transport of, and conspiracy to transport, a kidnap victim in interstate commerce. Geary served his time and was about to be paroled when he threw himself under the wheels of a prison truck and died. John Oley was released because he was dying of cancer, and reportedly went to Ballston Spa to die.

Johnny O'Connell married his girl friend, Mary Fahey, while waiting for the federal trial. He became head of the O'Connell family brewery, Hedrick's (which dated to 1852, closed in Prohibition, reopened under Dan's aegis when beer came back, and was sold to Piel's in 1965). Six years after the kidnapping, at age thirty, Johnny was named chairman of the Albany County Democratic Committee, but he was a figurehead. The power was all Dan's. Johnny, at forty-five, died in April 1954, the year after his father died, leaving Dan the only remaining O'Connell with power.

Since Johnny was bludgeoned on Putnam Street and carried off by what the government called the last organized U.S. kidnapping ring of the 1930s, nothing quite so spectacular has happened along Delaware Avenue. But this lull is very likely only a quiet moment Walter Stein might have captured in one of his photographs, for the notorious has a way of recycling itself in this end of town.

Arbor Hill:
Yesterday's Arcadia

*A*rbor Hill is the most mercurial of Albany neighborhoods, a place of Arcadian wealth, gentility, and beauty that became a slum; a peaceable mix of patrician and worker; originally a part of the Patroon's demesne, called The Colonie, and later the site of the Ten Broeck Mansion, which, because of its grape arbors and its lofty position on a hillside, was called Arbor Hill—and this gave the neighborhood its name.

In 1764 the Patroon donated to the city two lots situated between Second and Third streets on Ten Broeck Street, to be used as burial sites. The cemetery remained in use until 1842, when it was closed as a disgrace and turned into a park.

On March 19, 1850, a writer using the pseudonym Knickerbocker had this to say: "Arbor Hill is rapidly improving. Its elevated position renders it one of the most delightful localities in the city. A great many fine residences have been built within a few months, and now that the park is enclosed and men of taste are attracted thitherward, we shall expect it soon to become the most fashionable part of the town."

Thitherward first had gone the Ten Broeck family, who laid claim to the garden spot at the end of the eighteenth century. In time the less affluent did likewise, the Irish being dominant by the first decades of this century. Ultimately it was a homogeneous mix of Dutch, Yankees, Irish, Poles, and Germans, with a few Italians and fewer blacks. Some streets tended to be densely Irish—Colonie and Van Woert, for instance—and by the mid-1920s Northern Boulevard had become heavily Polish, though the principal Polish neighborhood was along Sheridan Avenue.

Not until the 1960s would Arbor Hill be truly ghettoized, inheriting from the exploded South End the dubious superlative of being the city's worst slum. Some people would be erroneously calling the neighborhood the North End during this era, but that was an anachronism. It had had that designation for a time, even into the 1890s, but yielded it to North Albany in this century, a change that carpetbag journalists and transient demographers of the 1960s (and a few in the 1980s also) didn't seem to grasp. The North End is North Albany and Arbor Hill is Arbor Hill and that's that.

It was always residential, with very little commerce and no industry, unless you call a brickyard an industry. It was a grid of mostly narrow streets interlocking with tidy angularity. A black schoolteacher I spoke with remembered it as "a beautiful section, streets lined with elms and chestnuts."

In late 1982 these streets were a disaster. The neighborhood looked bombed out, many houses bulldozed or burned down. Almost two hundred had been foreclosed by Albany County and were boarded up, awaiting the renewal, or perhaps the gentrification, that lurked out there. Of the twenty-six more valuable homes foreclosed on Ten Broeck Street—that short but handsome boulevard once called Millionaires' Row—twenty had been auctioned off to citizens with plans to rehabilitate them. A slogan went with the auction: "Own a piece of the block."

Before it slid into decline, nineteenth-century Arbor Hill was a peaceful place, remote from the rub and roar of Downtown's crowded streets. It was separated on the north by the dead-end chasm of Tivoli Hollow, up which the New York Central would eventually run its tracks to the West, and on the south by Sheridan Hollow, the ravine in which Gander Bay, that dreadful bastion of tough Irish mugs (dreadful if you weren't Irish, or muggish), developed. Not until 1890, when the Hawk Street viaduct opened, was Arbor Hill connected to Capitol Hill. Until that time the chief avenues of entry were Broadway and North Pearl Street at the bottom of the hill, and Lark Street and Northern Boulevard at the top.

The arbitrary boundaries were from Northern Boulevard on

the west to North Pearl Street on the east (though eventually this boundary was extended eastward to the Hudson River), and from Clinton Avenue north to the New York Central tracks. Joe Brennan, an Arbor Hiller who was eighty-seven when we talked, said Clinton Avenue in his day belonged more to Gander Bay that it did to Arbor Hill.

Joe Brennan looked back at his old neighborhood during a conversation in The Closet, a long, thin, high-ceilinged room in City Hall where Joe hung his hat for part of his workday. He was in charge of the city's voting machines, but he also held sway in this curious room where the City Record is kept in cardboard boxes on low and high shelves. It is a room out of City Hall architect H. H. Richardson's Victorian imagination, a room one might encounter in a novel by Charles Dickens.

Joe Brennan himself could have been out of Dickens, a self-made man who had been a poor boy, but he was, in fact, out of

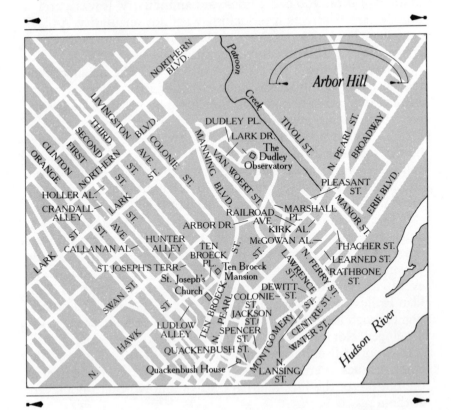

Arbor Hill's Third Street, where he was born in 1894. He lived there, and on Colonie Street, and later on upper Livingston Avenue, which was right at the edge of Cabbagetown, the western extension of Arbor Hill that was inhabited largely by Germans. He went to school at St. Joseph's Academy, commonly called the Brothers School, where my father went a few years ahead of him. It was situated at Colonie and North Pearl streets. (The girls in the parish, in the early years, were divided between two schools— the Industrial School, which taught them sewing and general needlework, and the Day School, where they learned English and music and vocal skills.) After the Brothers School burned in 1906, the new St. Joseph's Academy opened on Second and Swan streets, and was coed until 1911, when the boys were taken into either public school or Christian Brothers Academy. The girls were taught by the Sisters of Charity, and it was in this period that both my mother and my aunt graduated, part of a small class full of physical beauty, if one may judge from a photo of a graduation party.

Joe Brennan ticked off the faculty of the Brothers School for me as if he were reciting what he'd had for lunch. A fellow alumnus, Thomas P. Tooher, who would grow up to put a Reverend in front of his name and become, in the mid-1960s, pastor of St. Joseph's, also remembered the faculty: the principal, Brother William, four other Brothers, and five women teachers. Two boys from the school went across town daily to Christian Brothers Academy, on Lodge and Beaver streets, to bring back lunch for Brother William and his cohorts.

Joe Brennan and Father Tooher remembered the curious discipline the Brothers maintained. "They could lick you," said Joe, who remembered Brother Sebastian's being called Knocko "because he banged us on the head with his knuckles." Father Tooher remembered Knocko's violence as being the result of his impatience: "He was too learned for us. We weren't smart enough for him. Brother William was more our speed. He'd knock you over because he couldn't understand English."

Joe Brennan went to St. Joseph's through eighth grade and almost graduated. But he had to quit, for he found a job in the New York Central Railroad yards, tallying baggage from six in the morning till six at night, for thirty-five dollars a month. He then had to put aside his knickers, which all boys wore, and put on long pants to look like less of a kid in a man's world. But this was a double bind because he didn't want other kids to see him in the long pants, out of uniform, a point of embarrassment, and so he took the less-trodden streets back and forth to work.

Joe went up in the railroad world after a while and earned fifty-one dollars a month as a baggage handler, but left railroading in 1912 for the grocery business, which became his life's work. Late in life he went to work for the city.

There seemed to be no end to his memory of who in Arbor Hill lived where and what they went on to do when. He remembered Michael V. (Dike) Dollard, the contractor from Van Woert Street who paved North Pearl Street with creosote-soaked wooden blocks (they didn't last, and automobiles skidded on them into trolleys), built the foundation for the State Education Building, paved Madison and Western avenues. When Dollard was working on Third Street, Joe and other kids sold ice water out of a bucket to the paving gang—all they could drink for a penny. Joe remembered the Dollard stables (with fifty horses) on Van Woert Street, remembered that Dollard lived on Hall Place, and remembered him riding in a yellow, low-back cart. "They say he didn't have an education," Joe remarked.

Joe remembered the Reverend T. M. A. Burke, early pastor of St. Joseph's, the Irish church, which was finished in 1860 and eclipsed in magnificence only by the Cathedral of the Immaculate Conception (built 1848–52) among Catholic structures. Handsomely gray and Gothic, St. Joseph's has, near its ceiling, hand-carved angels that symbolize figureheads of the ships that brought Irish immigrants to America. Father Burke also established St. Joseph's Academy and went on to become Albany's fourth bishop.

"He was a short, stubby fellow who came to your classroom once a year," said Joe. "He'd pinch your cheek and say, 'I remember your father.' A grand old man."

St. Joseph's Church, at this writing, has an uncertain future. Retired Marine Colonel Bronislaus A. Gill, of Clifton Park, bought it in 1981 for $27,500, preservation his first thought, with the possibility of a conversion to residential use. He has given the Albany Catholic Diocese continuing use of it and the option to buy it back at the same price, but it is not now in use for anything. The pastor, Reverend Nellis Tremblay, says mass in the basement of the rectory, and Father Tooher, who is attached to the parish, said sometimes only fifty people turn up for Sunday mass. The magnificent church is a white elephant, heating alone having cost $35,000 in the winter of 1981–82.

In somewhat better financial shape and formidable still at age 184—thanks to preservation money from even more unlikely quarters—is the Ten Broeck Mansion, up the street from St. Joseph's, at 9 Ten Broeck Place. This house and its occupants are what originally spurred the growth of Arbor Hill as an elite neighborhood. The mansion is in the Federal style and was built by Brigadier General Abraham Ten Broeck (he fought at the Battle of Saratoga) on five acres given him by his father-in-law, Stephen Van Rensselaer, the Patroon.

The general, who later became a state senator and was twice mayor of Albany (1779–83, 1796–98), moved to Arbor Hill in 1798, when his more modest home at Columbia Street and Broadway burned down. He died in 1810 and the house passed through several hands, once being sold for taxes for $6,000. In 1848 it was acquired by banker Thomas W. Olcott, who also built a house at 138 Eagle Street that is now the governor's mansion. Olcott, says one Albany historian, was, "by general consent, the great banker of Albany." He was president of the Mechanics and Farmers Bank from 1836 to his death in 1880, and in 1863 declined an offer from President Lincoln to become First Comptroller of the Currency. At Olcott's death his son, Dudley, took over the bank's presidency.

Dudley was raised in the Ten Broeck Mansion, and it is he whom Joe Brennan remembered as master of the place in the 1890s. Dudley became a member of the city's Park Commission, which developed Washington Park, whose peripheral streets then competed with Arbor Hill as a place of elegant residence; and his bank also financed the real-estate venture that created the modern Pine Hills, another elite neighborhood.

"Dudley Olcott would come home to the mansion every day at three o'clock," Joe recalled, "and as kids we'd go down to see him drive into the gate. He rode with a coachman and a footman, and he always wore a flower."

Flowers were so important to Olcott that he kept a gardener year-round to attend the grounds in summer and the hothouse (long gone) in winter. The gardener's name was Marx and he lived next door to the mansion. Dudley Olcott ensured the health of his flowers by contracting for manure with John Hart, who, said Joe, kept cows at 73 Third Street.

The last Olcott to live in the mansion was Robert, who died

there in 1947. The following year his heirs gave it to the Albany County Historical Association, a private group of history enthusiasts, and it is now a local landmark, open to the public.

The mansion figured spectacularly in the news in 1977, when about three hundred bottles of French wine—Burgundies and Bordeaux bottled in the 1870s and 1880s and still in the original cases—were found in Dudley Olcott's wine cellar. Dudley was a connoisseur and his witty correspondence with his wine merchant has been preserved. About half the bottles proved to be intact, the other half being ullaged (partial evaporation because of cork failure). One wine connoisseur called in to appraise the find compared it to the discovery of King Tut's tomb. The Heublein Company of Farmington, Connecticut, the first firm to conduct wine auctions in this hemisphere, took charge of selling it, and the County Historical Association, according to its president, Charles S. Woolsey, received about $45,000 from the sales. The money has been put toward a new gas furnace, a new slate roof, and restoration of the mansion's chimney, balustrade, and parapet walls. One bottle of the wine, a Mouton Rothschild, said Woolsey, was sold for $2,950.

With the mansion as catalyst, in the very early nineteenth century Ten Broeck Street became a fashionable address, particularly as the century moved along, for the lumber barons found it both socially suitable and handy to their businesses in the Lumber District (Livingston Avenue was called Lumber Street for a time). The names of the lumber barons—Rathbun, Sage, Arnold, Benedict, Kibbee, Hubbell, Vose, Weaver, Dalton, White, Thompson—were of high economic significance in the Gilded Age. Some of them built their elegant brownstones on St. Joseph's Terrace or along Ten Broeck Street. The Irish also began to escalate their position in both wealth and power, and to make their presence felt in the neighborhood, most notably in the person of Michael Nolan, president of Quinn and Nolan Brewing Company, and the first Irish-American mayor (1878–83) of any sizable American city, including Boston. He built his home on Ten Broeck—Millionaires' Row.

Nolan was a singular figure, and the only man ever to be mayor of Albany and a congressman simultaneously. He also was baritone soloist in the choir of St. Joseph's Church from 1855 to 1860, and later became its director during the time when Marie-Emma Lajeunesse was its leading soprano. Miss Lajeunesse went on to become an international opera star under the name Madame

Albani. In 1913 an organ was presented to St. Joseph's in Nolan's name by his son, Frank, then president of the Beverwyck Brewing Company (what the Quinn and Nolan brewery became).

Peter J. Flinn, a flour merchant with leadership qualities in various directions, was another noted Irishman in the neighborhood. He held the title of president of the Albany Board of Education, of the state's first temperance society, and of the Albany Catholic Union. The latter was an organization of wealthy and socially prominent Catholics, a social focus for uptown folk, out of which developed the memorable initials FIF (First Irish Families).

Flinn married Mary Josephine Smith, daughter of Bernard Smith, who ran a grocery on Second Street in Arbor Hill. Theirs was, according to a descendant, the first wedding in the new St. Joseph's Church performed by Father Burke. The couple moved into a former lumber baron's home at 745 Broadway, just below Livingston Avenue, and lived a life of prominence. Flinn turned down an offer to run for mayor, was chronicled in the press voluminously, opened his house and garden for public visitation. His wife bore him twelve children, who studied at Mrs. Brown's private school, or went off to college at Seton Hall, or on the world tour. A daughter, Elizabeth, married James McCabe in St. Joseph's on September 10, 1891, the wedding reported in detail by local newspapers as "A Very Brilliant Affair."

Flinn believed Albany was going to expand northward, and he owned a great deal of property in northern Arbor Hill and beyond. The city surely did expand to the north, but primarily with the working class and heavy industry. The genteel life stopped at the midpoint of Arbor Hill, and one might draw a boundary line through it at Colonie Street.

Colonie started along the river flats of the Basin, the sheltered harbor that began at the mouth of the Erie Canal and ran south to Hamilton Street. Colonie crossed Broadway and rose up the northernmost of the four steep ridges on which the city was built, or it did until 1883, when the first viaduct in the city was constructed—across Broadway at Colonie Street. This interrupted Colonie but eliminated the dangerous grade crossing of the railroad on what was becoming an increasingly busy street—Broadway—the main artery to the north.

After the interruption by the viaduct, Colonie continued an upward course, crossed Ten Broeck, and, still rising, ran westward to all but bump the Dudley Observatory, one of the neighbor-

hood's principal structures, where scientific men of the city cat-
alogued the stars (8,241 measured and recorded for the International
Catalogue as of 1883) atop the same long hill on which the goat
population sometimes ran as high as 150.

The hill was called Observatory Hill where the stargazers gathered, but on Swan Street between Van Woert and Colonie it was
called Goat Mountain, so said my father. "The Van Woert Street
bunch," Joe Brennan added, "used to rally with kids from Swan—
throw stones, cans, fight, punch. They used to fight for Goat
Mountain."

The observatory (Dudley Olcott, and later Robert Olcott, served
as its treasurer) was built with $105,000 from Mrs. Blandina Dud-
ley, widow of Charles E. Dudley, five times mayor of Albany. At
its dedication in 1856, Edward Everett, one of America's most
gifted orators, was the speaker before what was called "the largest
assembly of ladies and gentlemen ever seen in Albany." (Everett's
most famous oration in his own time was delivered at Gettysburg,
when he gave the principal speech that the world little noted nor
long remembered because he was upstaged by Abraham Lincoln's
handful of words, which everybody remembers.)

The Dudley Observatory functioned atop Observatory Hill for
years, impervious to the raucous rallying on Goat Mountain.
Finally the trains thundering along the bottom of the hill in Tivoli
Hollow proved too rattling to the scientific minds and delicate
instruments in the observatory, and in 1893 it moved to South
Lake Avenue. In 1967 it moved again to Fuller Road, where it is
now part of Union University.

Arbor Hill was the center of elegance when the Dudley Observatory was inaugurated, but by the time it moved, the neighborhood was in severe decline. The cause was nothing over which
Arbor Hillers had any control. The changing fashion in neighborhoods was responsible, and the streets around the newly created (1869–82) Washington Park had become desirable residential
turf, far more so than when the park's land had been the city's
burial and parade grounds.

An unexpected form of isolation also took hold in 1890, when
horsecars went out of existence and trolleys came in: the problem
was that they didn't come into Arbor Hill. They stopped at Clinton Avenue, and two decades of frustrating protest by residents
began. Not until 1911 was the trolley to be seen on Livingston
Avenue, and its journey then was not always a blessing. Livingston is a steep hill and on slick and icy days, despite sandings,

the downhill car would sometimes jump the tracks and crash into Grace Methodist Episcopal Church at Ten Broeck, or sometimes into the home of the Sixth Ward's Democratic leader, William Mitchell, who lived across the street from the church—all going to prove that neither God nor the Democratic party had any control over the traction interests.

Barrington Lodge, owner of the B. F. Lodge clothing store, still in existence today at 75 North Pearl Street, lived at 6 Hall Place in Arbor Hill, and on March 27, 1894, he raised his voice on neighborhood problems in a letter to city leaders who were planning a park for Arbor Hill. The Van Rensselaers wanted to perpetuate the arboreal quality of the neighborhood, and so when they donated a large sector of Arbor Hill land to the city, they did so with the proviso that a park eventually be developed there.

Barrington Lodge wrote: "Before the Washington Park was made, the property on Arbor Hill was as valuable as any like property in the city. . . . This was changed by the Washington Park improvement for which the people of the North End helped to pay . . . although it depreciated all their property."

Property values, he said, continued in "steady depreciation," and he asked for the city to set aside a mere $10,000 a year to support the park. He also called for the trolleys to run on Livingston Avenue, and hoped that his ideas would "assume practical form."

But they did not. There is, after all, only so much need for eliteness, and Arbor Hill had become yesterday's garden. Working-class families were crowding in, and they would tend it tidily for two generations. Then the world would change once again: Arbor Hill would grow old and become expendable in a new way, and the slum blossom would take root.

Capitol Hill: A Visit with the Pruyn Family

"*A*s Major Harmon Pumpelly Read was crossing Academy Park late one afternoon he overheard two workmen ahead of him talking. One pointed to the Elk Street row and said to the other: 'See them houses? That's Quality Row—where the big bugs live. Guess if we knew about them people's lives, it would read like a book—guess so—all eaten up with vice and everything.' "

For this social insight we are indebted to Major Pumpelly Read, courtesy of the memoirs of Huybertie Pruyn, both of them denizens of Elk Street. Miss Pruyn's father, John Van Schaick Lansing Pruyn, had chosen, like other leading citizens of Albany, to settle on Elk Street in the mid-nineteenth century.

The street ran along the ravine that plummeted downward to the Foxenkill, a creek that ran below the bed of Canal Street (later Sheridan Avenue). Elk was not a street at all in the early nineteenth century but a goat pasture where during the Revolution Continental soldiers had executed Tories.

Academy Park was a city dump, and when leveled, dumping created Spruce Street in Sheridan Hollow. As the century moved along, people began to buy lots at the ravine's edge and build their stables there, behind their formidable homes, which began to rise, facing south, on Elk Street.

Numbers 13 and 15 Elk were built by Henry C. Wheaton in 1845. J. V. L. Pruyn rented Number 13 in 1847 and leased it to the state as the executive mansion during the tenure of Governor Hamilton Fish in 1849–50. In 1851 Pruyn bought Number 13 for $16,500 and made it his home. In later years the street was renumbered, and the house became Number 19, which it still is today. Elk Street was, in time, paved with cobbles, lit by sputtering carbon lamps, and shaded by trees, and some Albanians thought it had the elegance of Gramercy Park in New York City.

Though Elk Street had the designation of Quality Row, homes of equal elegance, and of even more sprawling design, were being built along Washington Avenue ("a row of perfectly beautiful houses with gardens," Huybertie wrote). People of means still lived on the north side of State Street, below Eagle; three or four monied families lived on Broadway, north of Maiden Lane; a few more lived on Grand Street ("but they were pretty well gone to boardinghouses"); and a few more lived on Patroon Street, later to be called Clinton Avenue.

The latter street was the boundary between city land and the beginning, northward, of the Patroon's vast estate, part of which would become Arbor Hill. When the name was changed to Clinton, Huybertie's aunt would not acknowledge the change and kept Patroon Street as her mailing address. Lancaster and Chestnut streets did not have the status of Elk and State. "It was just a little off," said Huybertie. People went up to Willett Street, but that was "almost out of town, people felt so far away." Dudley Row, a line of brownstones on South Hawk Street, was a distinguished address, the Dudley money having come from Rutger Bleecker, who started the family fortune by confiscating Tory estates after the Revolution. Bleecker passed his fortune on to his daughter, Blandina, who married Charles Dudley and founded the Dudley Observatory. Former two-term Governor Horatio Seymour lived on Dudley Row, and so did William Cassidy, proprietor of Albany's leading newspaper, the *Albany Argus*.

Columbia Street was high-income residential, and at certain moments so were South Hawk and South Swan and streets that no longer exist, such as Park Place and Academy Place, now merely part of the lawns in Capitol and Lafayette parks. The dwellers on all these streets were the Who's Who of Old Albany: Whitney, Townsend, Lansing, Rathbone, Van Rensselaer, Hun, Van Vechten, Banks, Paige, Parker, Sage, King, Reynolds, Van Antwerp, Mosher, Thacher, Vanderpoel, Boyd.

Whitney was William Minot Whitney, the department store pioneer; Reynolds was Marcus T. Reynolds, the architect who designed so many of Albany's great buildings, including the Delaware and Hudson Railroad building—now headquarters for the administration of the State University; Van Rensselaer was Stephen Van Rensselaer, the last Patroon, who bought an Elk Street home for his daughter; Sage was Dean Sage, the lumber baron, who lived on Elk Street in the winter; and so it went.

"I adored Elk Street and never wanted to leave it," wrote Huybertie of her childhood view. "The dwellers therein seemed apart to me from other less fortunate people."

And apart they were. They went to New York to shop, abroad for vacations. Their occasional addresses were Saratoga and Southampton, Bermuda and Newport, London and Paris, Aix-les-Bains. They were the people who founded the Albany Country Club and the Fort Orange Club (the University Club came along in 1901, after the neighborhood had passed its zenith, and established itself in the mansion of William Amsdell, a brewer). They sent their daughters to school at St. Agnes School, their sons to Albany Academy, whose original building, designed by architect Philip Hooker, still stands in Academy Park. A block down Elk Street, at Eagle, where the Court House now stands, the sons and daughters of the less affluent attended the old Albany High School until 1913, when the new school was built on Western Avenue.

With aristocracy went Protestantism: St. Peter's Church on State Street, the First Dutch Reformed Church on North Pearl Street, and the Cathedral of All Saints dominating. The dominating churchman was Bishop William Croswell Doane.

When he was rector at St. Peter's, according to Huybertie, "he was considered very high church," and when he moved to the Cathedral Chapel of All Saints as the first Bishop of the Albany Episcopal Diocese, seventeen leading families left St. Peter's congregation to follow him.

Huybertie has written at length about Bishop Doane ("his sermons were apt to be very long") and about the Cathedral Chapel. "The Corning hothouse would supply orchids and personnel to decorate the Cathedral screen and altar . . . the front settee was reserved for the Governor's family . . . we liked to watch Uncle Erastus Corning [grandfather of the late Mayor] quietly drop a $20 bill in the plate."

Bishop Doane was responsible for the building of Child's Hos-

Capitol Hill
at the Turn of the
Century

pital and St. Agnes School, both on Elk Street, both demolished long ago. The hospital relocated on Hackett Boulevard, the school in Loudonville, and later in Kenwood, where it merged with the Academy of the Sacred Heart to become the Episcopal-Catholic Doane Stuart School. Bishop Doane also began St. Margaret's House and Hospital for Babies after he found an infant on his doorstep. Now situated behind Child's Hospital, it cares for disabled or chronically ill children.

Doane's greatest building achievement was the Cathedral of All Saints, dedicated in 1888, the culmination of his dream to have a great English cathedral in Albany. It has a vast interior, 320 feet long, only 12 feet shorter than St. Patrick's in New York, and was to have appendages, but they were forestalled by the construction of the State Education Building in 1912, which blocks most of the cathedral's southern exterior from view.

A procession moved up Elk Street on November 20, 1888, for

the dedication of the cathedral. The Kenmore, the Delavan, and other hotels were crowded with dignitaries for the occasion and "our house was jammed with bishops," Huybertie wrote. Bishop Doane led the procession.

The Pruyn house was hostel to the elite from the beginning. "Hospitality was a keynote in the lives of my parents," wrote Huybertie. Notables who came to dinner or stayed as guests included General George McClellan; Matthew Arnold (who came to lecture at Martin Hall, but Albanians considered the hall a firetrap and few attended); Mr. and Mrs. James Roosevelt and their son, Franklin; Mr. and Mrs. J. P. Morgan; Mr. and Mrs. Whitelaw Reid; governors galore: Cleveland, Tilden, Hoffman, Dix, Hill, Morton; ministers from Austria, Japan, France, and Denmark; British lords and ladies, including Lady Raleigh, who ate a peanut at the Pruyn home for the first time, shell and all, then advised her son, "Don't try one. They're nasty things."

The menu at a Pruyn dinner held to introduce Governor John Hoffman (1869–72) to prominent Albanians included Julien soup, oysters, pâté (chicken), boiled salmon, sweetbreads and peas, terrapin, asparagus, quail, partridge and salad, Roman punch, roast turkey and chestnut sauce, filet of beef and croquettes of potatoes, cranberries, ices.

"In those days dinners were long and elaborate," Huybertie wrote. "Each place was decorated with endless glasses . . . Roman punch was served in the middle of dinner in glass cups with equally gorgeous saucers . . . little baskets or bouquets of flowers were at women's places and boutonnieres at the men's . . . a dinner usually lasted at least two hours . . . when the tablecloth was lifted onto the table, someone had a hot iron ready and all the creases were ironed out and an absolutely smooth cloth was ready to have the silver gilt service laid on it . . . Mother picked out the China to be used and it was handled with the greatest care . . . the gilt Duke of Sussex rose water basin was often used at one end and perhaps the Louis Philippe hunting cup at the other, sometimes the Cellini cup . . . the forks, knives and spoons were all gilt."

To carry out all this elaborate hospitality the Pruyns employed at least ten servants: butler, housekeeper, cook, laundress, chambermaid, personal maid, kitchen maid, children's nurse, gardener, and coachman.

The coachman, the only servant made obsolete by progress, cut a colorful figure when the family went anywhere in winter.

The carriages were stored away and the mode of travel was sleigh, the horses decorated with bells and foxtails, the coachman atop the four-passenger box in fur hat and gloves and flowing cape. "Everything was on runners," Huybertie wrote, "from the station sleighs . . . and delivery sleighs to the finest type of Canadian or Russian turnout. The whole city presented a gay and charming picture—particularly to the stranger from the South."

Communal sleigh rides were in vogue, a frequent destination being Sloan's old tavern, eight miles out the Great Western Turnpike, for supper and then dancing "on the rickety old floor" to a piano and fiddle. Another destination was the Country Club for ice skating on the lake. Huybertie recalled one incident that just about obliterates the notion that the Elk Streeters were vice-eaten. A skating party of twenty-five persons was almost called off one night when the chaperone couldn't attend. "Some of the 25 were men and women over 30 and 35," Huybertie recalled, "but still none were married—that was the rub." Another chaperone was found and the party "tumbled into the sleigh, having appeased all the parents."

The closest that vice ever gets to intruding on Huybertie's memoirs is in the person of an otherwise respectable lady with a terrible failing—she had been married three times. "And this was quite a problem for Albany in those days, as one marriage had ended in divorce."

Apart from the sleighing, other winter diversions were skating on the Erie Canal, or on the river (Huybertie fell through the ice on a skating expedition to Castleton), or on Washington Park Lake; snowshoeing in Washington Park with members of the Tanglefoot Snow Shoe Club; cutter racing on Western Avenue: "Alta MacDonald was the best-known racer of our day and his fame was national . . . Dr. Cox in a cape coat, his gray whiskers flying, would find time to run his pacer at least once between visits to patients . . . the Bleecker Banks from State Street always had a fine turnout, and from Elk Street came Mrs. James Kidd with her dogs."

Tobogganing on what was said to be the steepest artificial toboggan chute in the country, at the Ridgefield Athletic Club in the Pine Hills–to–be, was still another diversion ("Uncle Erastus Corning in a gray and blue blanket suit was an indefatigable tobogganer") and was often followed by a "galumpf"—defined as "dancing in the toboggan clothes and supper later" at someone's house.

This was a casual pleasure, but a more formal social life was also relished on Elk Street, this probably reaching its acme on January 5, 1892, when Huybertie Pruyn made her debut. Harmanus Bleecker Hall, Albany's greatest theater, later a movie house, and destroyed by fire in 1940, was rented for the occasion. A stage-level floor was installed over the seats and Mrs. Pruyn had the walls decorated with holly and evergreens. Favors, bought in Paris by Mrs. Pruyn and Huybertie the previous year, were stored until the ball, then given to the one hundred and ten couples. There were only two other coming-out balls of comparable scope held at the hall in Huybertie's memory. She never knew how much that grand scope cost her parents.

"It was a wonderful night," she recalled. It was a long night of waltzing for the debutante, followed by long days of visiting. "It was still the fashion for a mother to take her daughter to call on everyone in town that she knew" after the debut.

Six years later, another great social event occurred on Elk Street: the marriage of Huybertie to Charles Hamlin of Boston, described in the press as "the wedding of the year."

Then, seven years later, about 1905, came a traumatic occurrence for Elk Street. Mrs. James Kidd, who had given the city its maple trees for Western Avenue when the street was laid out, and who owned 7 Elk, died, and the new owners converted her home into a boardinghouse. The invasion of Quality Row had begun.

The Row had stood as a symbol, a haven, in Huybertie's words, "from the busy hum of men," a point of impregnability amid a changing scene. The changes were intensifying: Washington Avenue below Swan had grown into a row of small stores and farmers' hotels—the Washington, the Kimball House, then the Borthwick; Park Street (now gone) had a saloon on the corner; another saloon was at Lafayette (gone) and Hawk streets, still another at Capitol Place (gone); tumbledown shacks stood in the shadow of the Capitol; Congress Hall, the noble hostelry where Lafayette, Daniel Webster, and other giants of the American past had stayed, had been torn down long before; Congress Street (gone) had a livery stable on the corner; clanking trolleys ran up Washington Avenue, and so did the new and noisy motorcars.

The exodus began. The quality moved west—to upper State Street, to Englewood Place, to Willett Street, to upper Washington Avenue, to the new Pine Hills ("It didn't really get anywhere until the motors came in," said Huybertie), and to the country—

to get away from the old place and the old-fashioned houses. Governor Al Smith tore down the south side of Elk Street ("just a nest of little houses," wrote Huybertie) to enlarge Lafayette Park.

In time, all of Capitol Hill's cheap housing and little shops would disappear to make way for public buildings, Albany's acropolis. Sleek banks and office buildings would rise in later years and the grand old homes would become headquarters for clubs and societies, doctors' and dentists' offices, coffee shops, nightclubs, and apartments. Then in the 1960s many would fall before the wrecker to make way for Nelson Rockefeller's South Mall. Yet part of Quality Row, much altered, still survives, and so does 19 Elk Street.

"After mother died in October, 1909," Huybertie wrote, "there was nobody to live in the house. Also it was a very expensive place to keep up. It was very hard to have to face the cold facts that it must be sold. . . . It was tragic to have packing boxes in the various rooms—to try to choose what could be kept and used by each of us—to let the rest go.

"Charlie came over for us and on a perfect morning—Monday, June 20th, 1910, we left for good. The place never had looked so lovely, the grass so green, the goose fountain playing and the piazzas so cool behind their vines. And the view from the nursery window—goodbye—goodbye forever."

Pine Hills:
Blue Book Territory

*I*n the first edition of the *New Albany*, a periodical published in May 1891 for the first time, a pair of real-estate developers advertised a new neighborhood this way:

ABOUT PINE HILLS

There is no better city on this continent to live in, all things considered, than Albany, and if you intend to make it your permanent home, here is

SOMETHING YOU OUGHT TO READ

Situated on a magnificent plateau nearly 250 feet above the river, in full sight of the ever beautiful Helderbergs and the distant domes of the Catskills, about two miles west of the Capitol, and a mile beyond Washington Park, lie the extensive properties known as PINE HILLS. . . . It is here that the two magnificent thoroughfares, Western and Madison Avenues, converge and here, with much of the rapidity, but none of the mushroom characteristics of a western city, a resident section is being developed . . . pure air, abundant shade, smooth lawns, asphalt pavements, perfect drainage, detached residences, rapid transit.

Two months later the developers, in another ad, noted that "every house at Pine Hills is a summer resort. The residents there have almost forgotten how the family doctor looks."

The developers were a pair of far-seeing law partners, Louis W. Pratt, an Albany alderman, and Gaylord Logan, who in 1888, with $100,000 borrowed from Dudley Olcott's Mechanics and Farmers Bank, acquired two farms on either side of Western Avenue between where Allen Street and Marion Avenue now exist (the latter named for Pratt's daughter).

Pratt built his own home at 1 North Pine Avenue, the development's first street. Logan built his at 2 Manning Boulevard. They defined their territory with Allen Street as the eastern boundary, Washington on the north, Cortland on the south, and a wavy line between Marion Avenue and Manning Boulevard on the west.

Today the Pine Hills is vastly larger, its boundaries variously redefined by new neighborhood groups that represent it. In my age I would define its eastern boundary as Lake Avenue, along Washington Park, keep Washington Avenue on the north, go as far out as Colonial Avenue for the western boundary, and fudge the southern boundary as a line—much of it swampland until modern times—halfway between Madison and New Scotland avenues.

The Pratt and Logan Pine Hills lots were a spacious fifty by two hundred feet, an audacious size in a city full of shoulder-to-shoulder homes built on old Dutch parcels eighteen or twenty-five feet wide. The space appealed to the young moderns who were expanding out of a cramped city core that was becoming increasingly impacted by ethnic arrivals. Also, advances in transportation—the trolleys and, before long, the motorcar—were making distances a challenge, not a problem.

Pratt and Logan weren't waiting for the trolley, or for the motorcar, either. They were aiming at the carriage trade, seeking to break down the imaginary walls in people's minds that made Lark Street seem like the city limits. In the summer of 1891 they auctioned off "villa lots" for as little as $840. I spoke with Borden Mills, eighty-four, an attorney who served in the last Republican administration this city has known—it was ousted in 1921. He

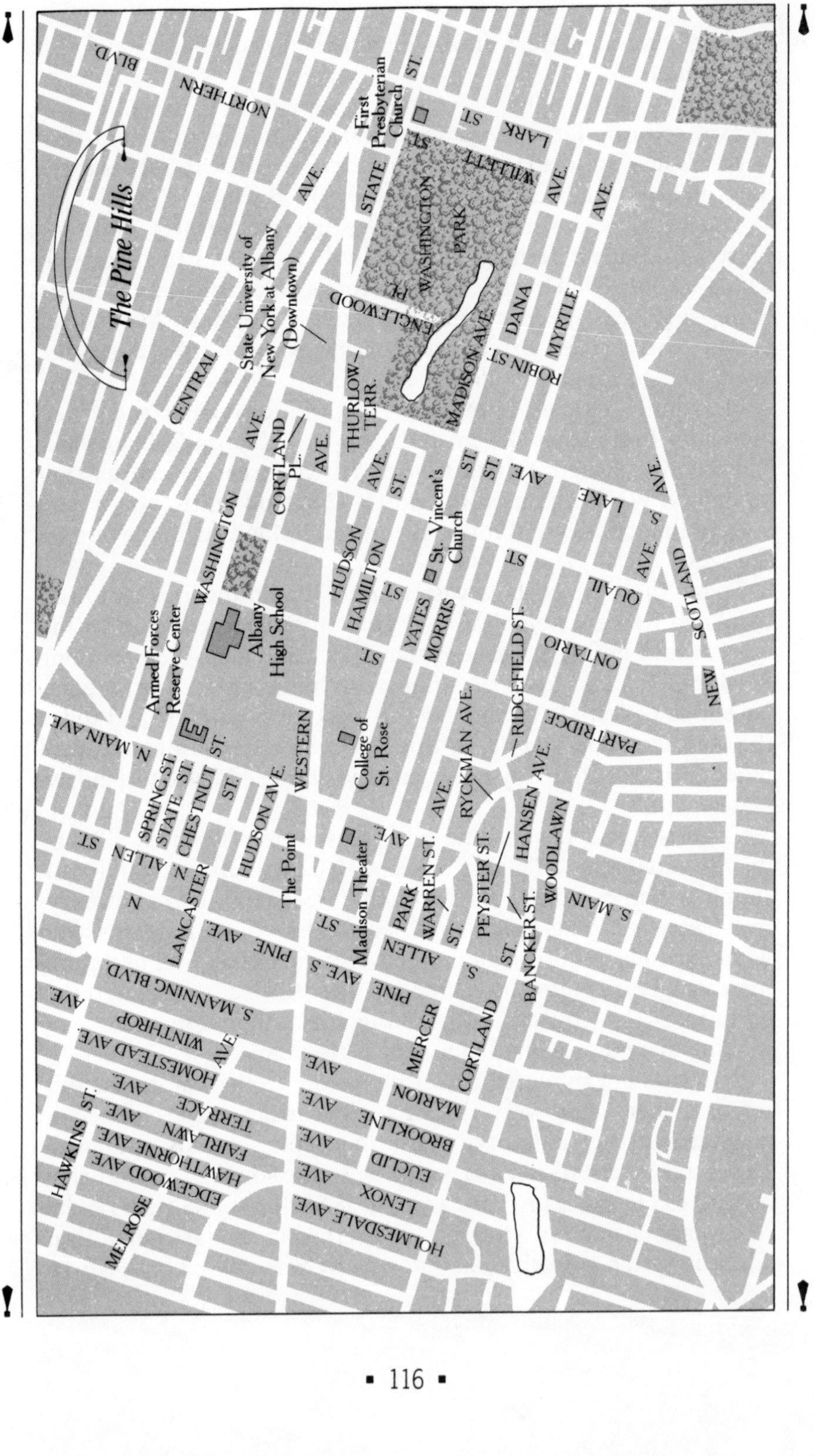
The Pine Hills
NORTHERN BLVD.
CENTRAL AVE.
WASHINGTON AVE.
State University of New York at Albany (Downtown)
First Presbyterian Church
STATE ST.
LARK ST.
WILLETT ST.
WASHINGTON PARK
ENGLEWOOD PL.
THURLOW TERR.
MADISON AVE.
DANA AVE.
ROBIN ST.
MYRTLE AVE.
CORTLAND PL.
HUDSON AVE.
HAMILTON ST.
St. Vincent's Church
LAKE AVE.
S. LAKE AVE.
QUAIL ST.
YATES ST.
MORRIS ST.
ONTARIO ST.
NEW SCOTLAND AVE.
Armed Forces Reserve Center
Albany High School
WASHINGTON
N. MAIN AVE.
SPRING ST.
STATE ST.
CHESTNUT ST.
WESTERN AVE.
College of St. Rose
RIDGEFIELD ST.
RYCKMAN AVE.
PARTRIDGE ST.
N. ALLEN ST.
HUDSON AVE.
The Point
Madison Theater
PARK AVE.
WARREN ST.
PEYSTER ST.
HANSEN AVE.
WOODLAWN AVE.
LANCASTER ST.
PINE AVE.
S. ALLEN ST.
BANCKER ST.
S. MAIN AVE.
S. MANNING BLVD.
S. PINE AVE.
MERCER ST.
CORTLAND ST.
WINTHROP AVE.
HOMESTEAD AVE.
TERRACE AVE.
FAIRLAWN AVE.
HAWTHORNE AVE.
EDGEWOOD AVE.
HAWKINS ST.
MELROSE AVE.
MARION AVE.
BROOKLINE AVE.
EUCLID AVE.
LENOX AVE.
HOLMESDALE AVE.

remembered his father's buying one of Pratt and Logan's first lots on North Pine Avenue, Number 14. The lot cost $1,200, and the house, with two stories, eleven rooms, three fireplaces, a porch, and a large attic, cost $4,500. Consistently, the developers planted pine trees on Pine Avenue, but the trees died and maples were put in their place.

By 1893 the world looked sweet to the developers, and Pratt took his vacation in Europe. Then a depression came, they couldn't meet their mortgage payments, and Dudley Olcott foreclosed. "Pratt went west," recalled Mills, "and the last I heard of him he was secretary of the chamber of commerce in Seattle when it was booming. He was one of those fellows who was about fifty years ahead of his time. The bank auctioned off the lots for peanuts. They would have been millionaires." Other developers took up where Pratt and Logan left off, and in a decade the Pine Hills was a fashionable place to live.

The formation of the neighborhood, before it was the Pine Hills, might be arbitrarily dated to September 24, 1831, the day the first steam-powered railroad in America was inaugurated. That day the *DeWitt Clinton*, the first locomotive on the Mohawk and Hudson Railroad, made its maiden run to Schenectady. It left from The Point—where Madison and Western avenues meet—dragging three stagecoaches full of people, including Governor Enos T. Throops, Patroon Stephen Van Rensselaer, journalist Thurlow Weed, and Erastus Corning, one of the founders of the Mohawk and Hudson.

The new rail line instantly reduced the time of a trip from Albany to Schenectady from a full day on the turnpike to a three-hour run. It also connected the Hudson and Mohawk rivers, circumventing the impassable Cohoes Falls. The railroad would soon supersede the turnpike for overland hauling, and initiate competition with the Erie Canal. The growth of rail traffic would doom the Canal also, but not for several decades.

At The Point, the Albany rail depot would develop, a famous place. Hotels had already been serving Western Turnpike travelers, but now more would spring up. The notable ones in the neighborhood were the Klondike, the Rising Sun, the Speedway at Western and Manning, the West Point House at The Point itself, and Carrick's, catering to farmers who came to market in Albany over the Great Western Turnpike.

That road, like Central Avenue, was a major overland route to the West, and where it entered Albany and became part of the city it was known as Western Avenue. It was a dirt—and, in season, mud—road for years. Planking came along in 1849 and remained until 1876, when landowners appealed for a reprieve from its wretched condition. Granite paving was completed from Washington Park to the tollgate at Manning Boulevard in 1877.

As railroad and turnpike traffic thickened, so did the wayside—but slowly. Borden Mills remembered that as late as 1897 Western Avenue still had great open spaces. He remembered only four houses existing between Ontario and Allen streets. In the new century the open spaces between Lark Street and the real city limits began to fill, inching outward from home base, which was Washington Park.

The park, conceived in 1869, grew as parcels of land were acquired and was fully defined by the early 1880s. As it became visible, the streets surrounding it—Willett and State, Madison Avenue and Englewood Place—became formidable bastions of social prestige. The Rathbuns (lumber) lived on Willett, as did Anthony N. Brady, the city's richest man (called "the Mole of Wall Street"). Robert Pruyn (banking) lived on Englewood, W. Bayard Van Rensselaer (lineage) lived at 385 State, Grange Sard (stoves) lived at 397 State in a house designed by H. H. Richardson, and so it went. It became important to extend westward (but not too far westward) from this klatch of eminence—out Madison, out Western, a street that from the time of the park's creation has been under the care of the park commissioners.

Proximity to the park was also aesthetically important. It offered (eventually) 223 acres of gentility: promenades among the flowers, band concerts, contemplative musings beside the Moses Fountain or the Robert Burns statue, boating in the summer, skating and sledding in the winter, and Arcadia in all seasons. Winter carnivals were in fashion in the 1880s—an enormous ice palace was built at Madison and Lake avenues and dedicated with fireworks.

The horsecar went out Madison only as far as Partridge Street until 1886, and people wanted to extend its run. But the Albany Railway said it would extend only if the folks on Madison bought the rails, which they wouldn't. Then along came the trolleys in 1890 and before long the line ran all the way out to Allen Street in the new Pine Hills. By 1906 it was running to Manning, by 1907 to the Albany Country Club, where State University now stands. Fashion's artery was becoming the longest street in town.

With the old, the new, and the *parvenu* in Pine Hills, the social amenities were observed, and status meant you owned a barn and employed a coachman. Borden Mills remembered one woman who moved to the new Pine Hills and changed her name from Mary to Marie. Many scrambled to get their names in the *Blue Book*, which was not a mythical record but was actually published annually in Albany. It was *Dau's Blue Book*, and in 1898 it offered its readers an "elite family directory" with the best streets and the best clubs listed "for the convenience of our lady patrons." The editor said the book took its title not from the phrase "blue blood" but from the book's blue cover; for blue blood was not always as blue as it looked.

"As society in all large cities is made up of numerous sets," said the editor, "each independent and distinct from the other, the reader will be sufficiently liberal to withhold criticism for the insertion of names which may seem unnecessary, for these may be the friends of your neighbor."

In that 1898 issue North and South Pine avenues in the new Pine Hills were listed, but the society matrons of State and Willett and Madison Avenue dominated as hostesses with "fashionable addresses." By 1916 many more Pine Hills streets would be included, and in time the Pine Hills social swirl would dominate the sepia rotogravure sections of the city's Sunday newspapers.

The Pine Hills Association had been formed in 1900 to perpetuate the elitism in which the neighborhood longed to bathe, and also to guard against incursions by industry and commerce. John J. McEneny, in his history of the city, notes that a major concern of the association before World War I was to ban the dumping of dead horses at a slaughterhouse on Winthrop Avenue.

As to saloons, Pratt and Logan had specified they would be kept out "by covenant," and they were. One had to go east of Allen Street to quench one's thirst. Carrying home a quantity for subsequent quenching presented another problem, for if saloons were gauche, so was the take-home suds pail. But ingenuity proved equal to the problem. A beer container was designed to fit snugly and inconspicuously against the back, beneath a coat, and in Albany it was called "the Pine Hills Growler."

An early moment of panic arose in 1902, when the Hospital for Incurables took an option on land on South Allen Street. Harold F. Andrews, a former historian of the Aurania Club, which stands on that land today, wrote: "The families with fine homes . . . were up in arms at this invasion of their residential area, especially such a hospital, for medicine was not as advanced as now in caring for such patients, and the very word 'incurable' struck terror into the residents. . . . It was a 'menace.' "

Residents held a meeting and formed a club with the idea of buying the site. The city was "combed by an organization committee for prominent citizens of good repute and well-filled pockets to join the new club." This was done, and by June the land was purchased, by November the club was built, and incurability was no longer a threat to Allen Street.

A different sort of exclusion came along with certain streets in the neighborhood—a "gentleman's agreement" to keep out Jews. Marion Avenue was such a street for a time, a status rival for Manning Boulevard and Madison Avenue. Manning had been built as a majestic street with bridle paths on either side and was named for Daniel Manning, a powerful Democrat who had been President Cleveland's secretary of the treasury. Madison was the voguish avenue for the wealthy, including a number of German Jews.

The development of Marion Avenue was recalled by William Kattrein, retired owner of the Watervliet Tool Company, who was eighty-four when we talked. He was part of a group that bought Keeler's farm to create the street as a site for members' homes. Kattrein himself spent $60,000 in 1928 to build his home at 21 Marion, and another $110,000 for later embellishments. Jews were excluded from the street by the agreement, and this situation prevailed until someone sold a plot of land to a Jewish millionaire who planned to build a three-story mansion. Kattrein remembered that a petition was circulated among homeowners on the street to allow the man to build. Kattrein said he signed it, as did other owners. Without that consent the street's private covenant would have prevented construction. The home was eventually built and the barrier fell.

Unencumbered life among the German Jews of the Pine Hills was recalled by attorney Albert Hessberg, who was born on Partridge Street (between Western and Madison) in 1916 and lived there until about 1928; and also by Mrs. Elizabeth Blatner, whose mother, of Irish descent, married into the wealthy Mendleson family, which owned the B. T. Babbitt Company, makers of Bab-O, the scouring powder. The Mendlesons lived at 1006 Madison Avenue, five doors down from South Main Avenue, a house, Mrs. Blatner said, that had "an awful lot of bedrooms" and provided work for a nurse, two maids, a cook, a chauffeur, and a gardener.

Al Hessberg remembered that Madison, in his time, was well populated between Partridge and Manning, mostly by the upper middle class. Instead of exclusion there was mix—Jews, Protestants, Irish Catholics—on his own street. "I liked the kids I played with, liked their families," he said. "Most kids went to Public School Four, or to VI [Vincentian Institute, part of St. Vincent's Catholic parish], across the street. We all played together. It was a good, stable, law-abiding atmosphere in which to grow up."

One neighborhood kid went on to celebrity: Andy Rooney, of the *60 Minutes* television show, who was three years behind Al in Albany Academy, and who was involved with the media even then: at the Academy's summer camp, Rooney edited the newspaper. Rooney still keeps a summer home at Rensselaerville in southern Albany County.

Al Hessberg remembered the neighborhood being self-contained: Graves's drugstore, Evans's grocery, Hagaman's bakery, and the Pine Hills, a silent-movie house and cherished place that died when talkies came to the new Madison Theater. (The Madison is now the city's oldest and most resplendent neighborhood movie house, from any era, and only $1.50 on weekdays, even now.)

As to the Jews, some drove in their carriages or their motorcars, some took the trolley down to the Reform synagogue on Lancaster Street to worship. Among his Jewish neighbors Al Hessberg remembered the Aufsessers and the Levis (brushes), the Barnets (knitting), the Sterns (real estate), and the Mendlesons, among many.

Elizabeth Mendleson Blatner, the youngest of six children, was born on Madison Avenue. Her mother, born Elizabeth Veronica Rooney, daughter of a blacksmith, met Ira Mendleson when she went to work for Babbitt's as a typist. "My father made a pass," said Mrs. Blatner, "and my mother took up her typewriter and went home. He persuaded her to come back and they fell in love." They were married and instantly rejected by both their families for marrying outside their religions. But when their first child was born they were accepted back into both folds.

Mrs. Blatner had a German Lutheran nurse named Louise Schramm who took her to Lutheran Sunday school. (Mrs. Schramm's brother ran a popular Pine Hills tavern, Schramm's, on Morris Street, where one notable customer used to drink his whiskey and then chew the glass.) Mrs. Blatner's parents went to temple mainly on the High Holidays, hobnobbed on their front porch with nuns and priests, and gave generously to the Catholic church.

"Mother became a Jew when they went back into the family," Mrs. Blatner said. "And she was more Jewish than the family. Yet she had a Saint Christopher medal all her life. She was tolerant of all people and all religions. And money didn't corrupt. She hated anyone with pretensions, or who was dull."

Mrs. Blatner went to Albany Academy for Girls; her sister was married at the Ritz-Carlton Hotel in New York. The family was crazy for racing, and in winter they went to the track in Havana, to French Lick for the waters, and then to the Kentucky Derby, the Preakness, the Belmont. In July the whole Mendleson household traveled to Saratoga and took over a mansion on Union Avenue. Nick the Greek was a friend of the family, and so were Helen Morgan and Sophie Tucker.

Ruth Gordon Glavin, product of a predominantly Irish family, lived a few blocks from the Mendlesons and a few doors down from the Hessbergs on Partridge Street. Her grandparents on both sides had lived in Arbor Hill (her grandfather Peter Flinn was a temperance leader, her grandfather Richard Gordon was president of Beverwyck brewery). Her parents married in 1905 and also lived for a time in Arbor Hill, but decided they wanted country and moved to Partridge Street. Ruth Glavin was born at home, delivered by a Dr. Lochner, for her mother distrusted hospitals. When Ruth was about to have her own child at the Brady Maternity Hospital in the Pine Hills, her mother warned her, "You won't bring home your own baby."

Ruth remembered Partridge Street as "an enclave of all religions—the Drislanes, the McEnaneys, the Buckleys, the Hessbergs, the Murrays"—and, like Al Hessberg, she remembered Andy Rooney, who lived next door: "He wasn't Catholic, though he looked it." She remembered other families (drugstores) who got wealthy bootlegging in Prohibition. And she remembered a woman—her husband suddenly rich—who would shop at Van Heusen Charles, a posh store Downtown, and ask the clerk to explain the household equipment. "She was all of a sudden launched through money into what she liked to call Society," said Ruth, "and she didn't know what fork to use." News of the woman's quest to understand forks was circulated in Pine Hills by one of Van Heusen Charles's clerks, whose avocation was gossip. "I knew how much each of my sisters-in-law paid for my wedding presents, and what they said when they bought them," said Ruth.

Not everything was posh and precious in the Pine Hills. The streets east of Partridge, Al Hessberg remembered—Hamilton Street, Hudson Avenue—were home to some less affluent people. Ruth Glavin remembered her mother's telling her as a child, "There are good, decent people on Hamilton Street, but we just don't play with them." Ruth added, "I must conclude from this that my mother was something of a snob."

That area was, in the first decade of this century, populated to a large extent by German and Irish Catholics of the working class, whose presence generated the growth of St. Vincent's parish. The church was established in 1889 in an old Baptist chapel, and grew into the most affluent parish in the city. Far and away the most affluent soul connected to it was Anthony Nicholas Brady, an Irish genius of the interlocking world of business and politics. Among other things, he gave the church its organ and funded St. Vincent's male and female orphan asylums (whose inmates all went to his funeral).

His name still survives on the Brady Building on North Main Avenue in the Pine Hills, which now houses offices of the Catholic Diocese, but which for years was the Brady Maternity Hospital. Brady is worth a book of his own, for he grew from an immigrant Irish boy, born in 1841 in France of Irish refugee parents, to a capitalist potentate of electricity, gas, subways, trolleys, tobacco, and much more; and his estate, at his death in 1913, was worth about $100 million, then judged to be the largest fortune ever left by an American.

Brady came as a child from France to Troy, New York, ended his education at age fourteen, found work, according to legend, splitting oysters, perhaps, at the Delavan House, and rose to the role of bartender, at which point he confronted his main chance: an encounter with a stranger who had imported a great deal of tea but could not pay the duty on it. The legend, recounted by John Corry in his book, *Golden Clan*, is that Brady offered to pay the duty to become a partner, and suddenly he was in the tea business—in Albany, Troy, and eventually New York City.

He moved, not very logically but most successfully, into the contracting business. He bought a granite quarry, paved streets (in the Pine Hills and elsewhere), built sewers, and did the stonework on the Hawk Street viaduct in what was called "the Stone Age" of his fortune. He then moved into streetlighting by manufacturing gas (his "Gas Age"), then into the horsecar, trolley, and subway business (running trolleys so fast they competed with railroads), and branching into Providence, Brooklyn, Queens, Chicago, and on and on and on, in his "Electric Age." He was a Democrat, closely associated with former Governor Roswell P. Flower and Daniel Manning, and was also, according to his obituary writer, "a lifelong friend and admirer of Richard Croker," the Tammany Hall leader.

His funeral, at the Cathedral of the Immaculate Conception, was one of the spectacles of the age, a special train bringing mourners from Manhattan, a platoon of police keeping order in the streets as the sixty carriages in the cortege came and went. Bishop T. M. A. Burke said the mass, with two dozen more clerics on the altar (Brady had donated the altar rail). Brady banks and power companies all over the Northeast closed for an hour during the mass, his subways and trolley lines halted for one minute of reverence, and it took six carriages to carry all the floral tributes to St. Agnes Cemetery, where he was buried in a replica of the Parthenon.

Two of his sons continued the Brady name in high finance, and a grandson, Anthony Brady Farrell, came to be one of midcentury's grandest "angels"—backers of Broadway theatrical productions. Thomas E. Murray, born in Albany in 1860, was a Brady protégé who also amassed a fortune. Brady put him in charge of the Albany Municipal Gas Company's power station in 1887, and Murray, an engineer, began his rise through the Brady companies. He was an inventor who left a fortune that may have been anywhere from $10 million to $50 million—the former was the published figure. He was an associate of Thomas Edison's, and at his death Murray held eleven hundred patents, second in number only to Edison's record. Murray's family story is told in Corry's *Golden Clan* and also in Stephen Birmingham's *Real Lace*.

Education, Catholic and secular, played a major role in the life of the Pine Hills—and does today, perhaps more than ever. St. Vincent's opened its elementary school in 1917, and in 1921 added a high school, Vincentian Institute, which closed in 1977, an era when Catholic education had become economically troubled.

The College of Saint Rose was established on Madison Avenue in 1920 with nineteen female students (it is now coed, with three thousand). Al Hessberg, who remembered the school's being brand new when he was a child, and who later became a member of its board, recalled the acquisition of property by the college as a major development in the neighborhood. Numerous homes on Madison and Western were taken over for dormitories by the new school.

The Academy of the Holy Names was an elite elementary and high school for girls, on Madison across from Washington Park, in the mansion of W. H. Malcolm; and Christian Brothers Academy, a military high school for boys, was a few blocks south of Madison, up the hill on New Scotland Avenue. The educational track for daughters of middle- and upper-class Catholics was first to Holy Names, then to Saint Rose. For boys it was CBA or VI, and then Siena College (which came along in Loudonville in 1938).

Margaret Conners Harrigan, who did her doctoral dissertation at Harvard on family life in Albany from 1850 to 1915, took the Holy Names–Saint Rose track, beginning in the late 1950s, and recalled her classmates as being predominantly Irish and Italian Catholics, with the girls tending to date boys from CBA or VI.

"I think my parents felt it would be better for all of us to marry not only Catholics but Irish Catholics, for cultural reasons," she said when we talked. "So you stayed within that Catholic main line. It was very, very rare to date a Protestant or a Jew." When she went to Saint Rose, she found the girls dated boys from Siena.

"I did date people from RPI [Rensselaer Polytechnic Institute] and Union College," she said, "but I remember you looked at them very warily. It was, how shall I put it, venturing beyond your boundaries to date one of those fellows, and you wouldn't want to get serious because you knew there would be cultural problems. . . . There wasn't much difference between whether the Catholic or non-Catholic boys wanted to sleep with you. They were all the same. The Catholic boy might take no for an answer a little more readily."

Her outlook on religion changed considerably at Harvard, and she moved into progressive Catholicism. But the impact of a Catholic education in the Pine Hills had its effect: she married an Irish Catholic, and so did her two sisters.

As to secular education: Albany High School moved to Lake Avenue and Western in 1912, up from Downtown, and in 1974 moved farther westward to its most modern quarters at Washington Avenue and West Erie Street. The state's first normal school was established in Albany in 1844, was upgraded to a college in the 1890s as Albany State College for Teachers, and, under Governor Nelson Rockefeller, expanded to become the State University at Albany (SUNYA), which still uses the old State College campus between Western and Washington avenues. It also occupies the major new campus in the Pine Bush, designed by architect Edward Durell Stone. SUNYA now brings 960 faculty and 16,000 students (a third of them from New York City and Long Island) to Albany during the school year.

Further, four other colleges exist not quite in the Pine Hills but only a few blocks away, on New Scotland Avenue: Albany Law School, Albany Medical College, and Albany College of Pharmacy, all part of Union University; and Albany Junior College, part of Russell Sage College, in Troy. These, plus the expanded Saint Rose and the new SUNYA, center an enormous student population in the Pine Hills and environs.

To cope with it, many of the handsome old homes, with their numerous bedrooms, have been cut into apartments and made into rooming houses, fast-food shops have opened, and the pub traffic is now formidable.

Back in the 1940s the college and high-school drinking crowds trafficked at Herbert's on Madison, west of South Main, where if you didn't have a draft card you couldn't drink (unless you borrowed one). Girls needed a driver's license. The Madison Tavern, up the block, was a prime focus in the 1950s, and then, in 1963, Mike Flanagan, who'd been playing there as a musician (a champ bassist), bought it and kept it jumping with jazz regulars and visiting heroes, including the young Nick Brignola, George Wettling, Jody Bolden, and Dave McKenna (who played his first local gig there). Flanagan hosted big-band rehearsals on Monday nights, and string quartets on Sunday—the latter, he said, "for little old ladies with blue hair."

The place also drew neighborhood regulars, like the merchant who sat at the end of the bar talking endlessly about the Erie Canal and Man O' War, and drinking Scotch until he grew insensate, fell off the barstool onto the stone floor, hit his head, and went silent. Mike summoned a doctor who was having dinner in the dining room. The doctor bent over the unconscious man and lifted one of his eylids. "Dewar's and water," said the man.

Jazz, food, and drink continued until 1973, when a stranger walked in and found Mike behind the bar. " 'Is this place for sale?' he asked me," Mike recalled, "and I said absolutely, every joint in the world is. I gave him a number and he said it was too high for him to make a decision and I figure that's that. He's back in a month and he says he's very interested and I said that that figure I gave you wasn't for the restaurant equipment and supplies, just the property, and he says of course. And I say, Jesus, what else can I pull out?" The man represented Central Market (which became Price Chopper) and the deal went through. On July 3, 1973, the Madison Tavern/Petit Paris closed and two months later was bulldozed.

In the present age, the voguish places, I am told, are the Partridge Pub, O'Heaney's, the Washington Tavern, Bogart's, and the Lamp Post. The line outside the Lamp Post at two a.m. may include twenty or thirty people waiting to get into the place, which began to do college business only when it got rid of the townies and bikers who had hung out there. O'Heaney's, one of the oldest college bars, was run by Joe O'Heaney, an ex–police reporter. The Washington Tavern had become an Irish bar in recent years, and I never knew it. But it came clear to me the day I walked in with my Albany publisher, who introduced me to the owner, Mike Byron. Byron immediately betrayed his ethnicity by serving me a free plate of corned beef and cabbage. I betrayed my own by eating it.

To get a closer reading on the modern pubbiness of the Pine Hills I spoke to Vincent Reda, thirty, a former resident and a specialist in places where drink and college-age females came together for his pleasure. Reda graduated in 1974 from State University, where he was an All-American in cross-country and also studied somewhat. He went on to become a reporter and a most entertaining columnist for the *Troy Times-Record.*

"Even the most studious guys living off campus got themselves sickly drunk once a month," Reda said. "It proved to the outside world there was a heavy strain on being a student. Off campus was also the place where college girls lost their virginity, or demonstrated again how they lost it last year in East Islip."

Reda found the area a safe one for students, except for the elusive presence of "the Pine Hills Molester," the most cunning sex criminal to unsettle the city in modern times—he's intruded on the homes of forty women to molest but not rape them.

As to Reda's own day as a student, it was a time of "strange people constantly crashing on the couch, wild parties, drug sales, crazy drinking habits. It was your first time on your own and you made dinner for yourself or you didn't eat, and for the first time you thought to yourself, Hey, I've got to get a job someday to continue to live like this. It was a place of pretty tree-lined streets—Western Avenue and Hudson Avenue—a place that felt homey, a nice place to walk outside, to check out where you'd like to live next. The farther uptown you went the denser the trees got and the classier the homes got. And if you got to Manning Boulevard you really didn't feel you deserved it, even if it was for a night."

This sense of significant and elegant place still prevails on part of Pratt and Logan's old turf, and, despite age, some streets seem deeply resistant to decline. John Horton, head of the Department of Oncology at Albany Medical College, has lived on South Pine Avenue since the early 1960s.

"Hasn't changed a bit," he said of his block. "Just a teeny bit older. Nothing new has come in, nothing new is likely to come in. Maybe a few less kids since birth control."

He does bemoan the loss of Mike Flanagan's Petit Paris in the neighborhood and the jazz it brought, for John is a jazz trombonist as an avocation. But he has no serious complaints. Pine Hills is still an enclave.

The A&P is gone, but Price Chopper came in its place. You can still buy a book in the neighborhood—at Clapp's, which has been on Madison for decades since it moved from Downtown. Maybe the greatest loss was the closing of Joe's Restaurant, the sandwich store supreme, founded by the late Joe Kulik, whose Number 19—roast beef, horseradish, Russian dressing, etc.—is one of Albany's major contributions to American culture. Joe died in 1982 and, alas, there are no more sandwiches.

"It's a very peaceful section of town," said Linda Katz, who teaches public speaking and debate at SUNY, and who has lived nine years on Mercer Street. "People don't bother you. There's a lot of huge old trees and peaceful architecture, even though there's a lot of people always going places."

It is to be expected that not everybody has the same positive attitude toward the neighborhood. But not even everybody in the Katz family shares Linda's view. Her husband, Bill, a writer and library scientist at SUNYA, finds the neighborhood noisy to the point of distraction. A curmudgeon whose peace is fragile, Bill Katz perceives it in a state of "constant roar"—of lawn mowers, machines that scrape paint off houses, automatic hedge clippers ("Doesn't anybody know how to clip a hedge without an engine anymore?"), blaring radio music, and noisy garbage collectors: "They drive back and forth and throw garbage cans against my house." Bill's peace is also disturbed by the Pine Hills wildlife.

"I've seen raccoons," he said, "and the other day I saw a squirrel eating a tomato. Nervy bastard, he came right up to the windowsill. Can you believe that? You ever see a squirrel eat a tomato?"

Peaceful or noisy, student paradise or student ghetto, however you find it, the Pine Hills continues, in the main, to be middle and upper-middle class—a concentration of people who form the economic and professional backbone of the city. But it is also a fact that suburban living did arrive in the 1930s and 1940s, places like Delmar and Loudonville became fashion's first line, and the Pine Hills' exclusive blue-bookishness went the way of its plank road and its horsecar.

The West End:
Money on the Hoof,
Money on Wheels

*I*f it were morning again on a summer day in one of the last years of the last century, a young boy might get out of bed in his home at Number 8 Watervliet Avenue and look out the window to watch the cattle go by in the street.

There would come Andy Root in his overalls and leather jacket, the heat or the cold effecting no change in his uniform, guiding a hundred head of cattle just in at the stockyards in West Albany, herding them along the street and then down, or maybe up, Central Avenue, the cattle destined for long life on a local dairy farm or sudden death at a slaughterhouse.

The boy's father—having lost his job as a brakeman on the New York Central after the violent strike of 1890, when the hired Pinkertons fought the strikers, when the cattle died in their railroad cars and sent a stench out over the city—would already be at work in the small meat market he had opened down the street.

There were others like the boy's father. Charlie Feidel, a conductor when the strike came, now ran a grocery up near the West Albany bridge. And Pat Craig had opened a boardinghouse and saloon in the same area not long after the strike cost him his freight conductor's job.

Down under the bridge in Tivoli Hollow thousands of men

would have been at work ever since seven o'clock in the locomotive and car shops, and a boy might lust to play in those fascinating yards where the great trains switched, where the freight cars were strung out over the horizon, where the chorus of anvils and forges and machines and the coupling of cars rose up and spread over the neighborhood like the purr of a healthy lion, which is what the New York Central was. There would be no children playing in the shop area, which was stoutly fenced. A boy could play ball behind the railroad YMCA, one of the first in the nation, or go down by the bridge and watch the West Albany trolley turn around to head back for Central Avenue. Or if he had a penny or two in his pocket he might go over to Mrs. Van Dyke's candy store and add to the riches of an old lady who parlayed penny candy into real estate, so the story went, and in time owned two rows of houses on Watervliet Avenue.

Or if he was without recourse to any action whatever, the boy might go back and sit on his own stoop and watch the ice melt in front of the house next door. The ice, harvested in winter at the pond in Shafer's Grove out by Colvin Avenue and delivered in the summer to one and all, was the joy and the business of Will Shafer, an eccentric iceman. The boy remembered, "If you paid him, all right. If you didn't, all right. He was one of those fellows who was worth knowing."

The boy who remembered these things was Leo Brennan, seventy-one, longtime clerk of Albany's Traffic Court and a resident of the West End all his life. As he talked of his childhood memories the years fell away and Watervliet Avenue was once again what it used to be, the center of one of the most vibrant and thriving sectors of the city.

The West End was one of Albany's frontiers, and like any good American frontier town it was wild and woolly, rich and gaudy, wide open, and then, inevitably, when boom goes bust, populated only by ghosts and memories. It was a double boom and double bust that struck West Albany: railroad shops and cattle, both connected to the New York Central Railroad.

When the Central was created from the consolidation of eight small railroad lines that had developed across the state at mid-century, there was a need for repair shops to service locomotives and cars. Erastus Corning, great-grandfather of the late Mayor, as president of the Central, bought 350 acres for the railroad from the Van Rensselaer estate and from local farmers. What was then called Spencerville, Corning renamed West Albany, and there he established the shops, ten large buildings. The engine house alone cost $65,000 and contained pits for thirty locomotives. Two other shops each had pits for twenty, and the pits were always full.

What followed closely upon this move was the construction of pens (paved with cobbles) and sheds for livestock—cattle, sheep, pigs—that covered twenty acres adjacent to the railroad switch-yards. Albany, which had been the meat market for the Army during the Revolution and the War of 1812, was challenging Chicago and Buffalo to be the major livestock center of the nation. It would become, in the 1850s, "the greatest depot for the whole-sale trade in cattle of any market in the country," according to the *Bicentennial History of Albany*, edited by Jonathan Tenney.

The growth of the Albany cattle market was predicated on one assumption: that cattle must be fed and watered once a day or they sicken and lose weight, and their value declines with their poundage. Albany was a day's journey from Buffalo on the Central line, and therefore strategically located for watering and feeding cattle eastbound to market.

Albany was a sizable market in itself, but far greater possibilities lurked across the river in New England. And on the east shore the cattle could also board freight cars to carry them to the New York City market. The problem lay in getting the animals across the river.

Until 1866 there was no bridge at Albany, the result of effective legislative lobbying by a consortium of special interests protecting the city of Troy against the Central's plan to build one. Troy had the advantage on Albany, for it was bridged over the Hudson at Waterford, and rail lines fed into it.

"It was common practice at first," wrote C. R. (Tip) Roseberry in an article on the cattle market in the *Times-Union*, "to drive the herds on foot from Albany to New York. Before the river was bridged, the cattle had to swim for it. Guide steers would be trained [in Albany] to lead them across the river. . . . In winter, the cattle would be driven across the river on the ice. During the winter of 1855, the ice broke and 69 cattle were drowned. Droves of cattle would also be driven through the woods to Troy via Shaker Road."

Bridge or no bridge, Albany's livestock business boomed.

Slaughterhouses grew up and cattle drives through the city became commonplace. An estimated $5 million changed hands annually in the 1860s, the peak decade. In 1866, a peak year, a thousand carloads of cattle arrived weekly. Until the mid-1880s livestock was king in Albany, with only lumber to rival it in importance to the city's economic life.

An Albanian named Robert C. McCain recalled, in an early 1960s newspaper interview, that "there was more money in West Albany than there is in Wall Street now—cattlemen and farmers with rolls of big bills that'd choke a cow. The streets were the same at 3 a.m. as they were at noon. Everything was wide open and there were lots of saloons—the old kind with the swinging doors, where decent women didn't go."

Exchange Street was the main stem, and along it were George Karl's saloon and Horan's Stockyard Hotel (for three hundred guests, with cattle pens adjoining). There were the Bennett House and, on Watervliet Avenue, the most popular of all, the Arlington Hotel. John Glavin's slaughterhouse specialized in sheep. Rooney's was another big one, and so was McGraw's, and they were typical, for most of the butchers were Irish. And rich.

"West Albany was a rough and ready place, all right, at least it had its tough gangs," Roseberry wrote. "At one time it was much as your life was worth (literally) to cross the bridge from Albany to West Albany on a dark night. More than once, West Albany ruffians were known to toss an intruder over the bridge onto the tracks below. One latter day resident . . . vouchsafed that he was stopped and robbed of a brand new suit, but was fortunate in being permitted to go on home in his underwear."

Life changed for West Albany when new devices were developed for feeding cattle on the cars. Also, the refrigerated railroad car came along, eliminating the need for beef on the hoof. New abattoirs bloomed in Chicago, and from their sidings speedy trains rocketed the refrigerated beef, all but sliced into T-bones, directly to East Coast markets.

Meatpacking continued to exist after the decline of the stockyards (the decline was sharp in the mid-1880s), for Albany was a meat-eating city—a hundred and fifty meat "stalls" (markets) functioning in 1885. Cheap Irish labor had populated West Albany, and as the new century began, Italian immigrants took their place—it is the Italians who dominate West Albany today. They were the backbone of the labor force of six hundred at the Tobin Packing Company (makers of First Prize products, a premium brand in this region for generations), but then a new firm took over Tobin and it went the way of all flesh and closed its doors on November 8, 1981, ending the cattle and meatpacking era utterly.

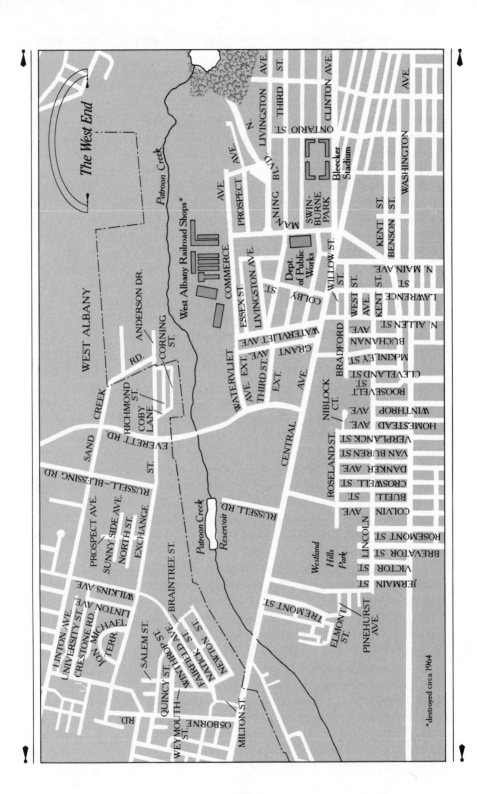

The West End

WEST ALBANY

West Albany Railroad Shops*

Patroon Creek

Dept. of Public Works

SWIN-BURNE PARK

Bleecker Stadium

ANDERSON DR.

CORNING ST.

COMMERCE AVE.

PROSPECT AVE.

N. MANNING BLVD.

LIVINGSTON AVE.

THIRD ST.

ONTARIO ST.

CLINTON AVE.

WASHINGTON AVE.

KENT ST.

BENSON ST.

N. MAIN AVE.

LAWRENCE ST.

KENT ST.

WEST AVE.

WILLOW ST.

COLBY ST.

LIVINGSTON AVE.

ESSEX ST.

WATERVLIET AVE. EXT.

THIRD ST. EXT.

GRANT AVE. EXT.

CENTRAL AVE.

N. ALLEN ST.

BUCHANAN AVE.

McKINLEY ST.

CLEVELAND ST.

ROOSEVELT ST.

WINTHROP AVE.

HOMESTEAD AVE.

VERPLANCK ST.

VAN BUREN ST.

DANKER AVE.

CROSWELL ST.

BUELL ST.

COLVIN AVE.

LINCOLN AVE.

ROSEMONT ST.

BREVATOR ST.

VICTOR ST.

JERMAIN ST.

ROSELAND ST.

BRADFORD ST.

NIBLOCK CT.

Westland Hills Park

RICHMOND ST.

COBY LANE

EVERETT RD.

SAND CREEK RD.

RUSSELL–BLESSING RD.

PROSPECT AVE.

SUNNY SIDE AVE.

NORTH ST.

EXCHANGE ST.

Patroon Creek

Reservoir

RUSSELL RD.

WILKINS AVE.

LINTON AVE.

UNIVERSITY AVE.

CRESTONE RD.

N. MICHAEL TERR.

SALEM ST.

QUINCY ST.

BRAINTREE ST.

WINTHROP AVE.

FAIRFIELD ST.

NATICK ST.

NEWTON ST.

WEYMOUTH ST.

OSBORNE ST.

MILTON ST.

TREMONT ST.

ELMONT ST.

PINEHURST AVE.

RD.

*destroyed circa 1964

What remains in West Albany is residual, St. Francis de Sales Catholic Church serving the Italians as it served the Irish. Some of the same streets are still trod—Watervliet Avenue, Corning, Exchange and Richmond streets (the last named for the Central's second president, Dean Richmond).

The West Albany Industrial Park replaced the Central's railroad shops when they closed, bringing new firms into the neighborhood. A Quality Inn went up between Everett Road and Watervliet Avenue. And an anachronistic social group has endured through it all: the West Albany Italian Benevolent Society, founded in 1909 to provide money to members during illness and extreme need, and a death benefit also. Such societies were endemic among immigrant groups everywhere in America for two centuries, but most went out of existence as a result of the diaspora that always followed the decline of ethnic neighborhoods. It speaks for West Albany's isolation, not only in place but in time, that such a group could continue to exist in the 1980s.

One of the high social entertainments of the West End was offered, not inconsistently, by animals: horse racing at the Speedway. Apart from their functional use (there were ninety-five hundred in Albany in 1880), horses were also raced as a sport by both aristocrats and working people. They raced on the Erie Canal, on several horse tracks around town, and at the Speedway, which came into being by subscription in 1895. Three months later a mile of Washington Avenue, from Quail Street to Manning Boulevard, was graded and rolled with a turf surface, the cost absorbed by the Albany Road Improvement Association, Oscar L. Hascy, president.

Leo Brennan remembered the horses, sulkies attached, racing eastward toward Quail. Jim Meany, a longtime West Ender and a machinist in the West Albany railroad shops until he retired, also remembered the track, not of turf, but topped with yellow sand. Sundays and holidays were racing days until the auto came along and put the horses out to pasture. (In an earlier era trotting races of a high quality were taking place on the Troy Road, two miles north of the city, at Island Park. The track, converted from a private track on land owned by Erastus Corning, went public in 1884, with Corning as president of the Island Park Racing Association. It was a mile track—"one of the finest and fastest in the U.S.," it boasted. The association aimed to improve the breed and the speed of trotters, and horses from all over competed in these grand circuit competitions.)

On the Speedway elegant horses mixed with horses of a different caliber. Jim Meany remembered two: "Pat Fogarty had a horse he used for trucking during the week, and on Sunday he'd race it. There was another fellow who raced a horse with only one ear."

Where Saint Anne Institute now stands, Jim remembered also, you could go over on a Sunday and buy a horse from Gypsy traders, whose caravans gathered there from spring through summer. "People would come and get their fortunes told," said Jim. "The Gypsies made kettles out of copper, and they'd have battles once in a while, fistfights among themselves. It was an attraction."

Quail Street, where the Speedway ended, was the arbitrary eastern boundary of the West End, and it fused there with the Bowery (Central Avenue) and Cabbagetown, to the north of Central. Cabbagetown took its name from the abundance of cabbage patches planted by the heavily German citizenry, and the Bowery was a mix of Irish and German. The West End was the same— these groups dominating—but the West End was not identified by ethnicity. There were Catholics in Blessed Sacrament Church, and Protestants were served by the West End Presbyterian, the Sixth Reformed, and St. John's Lutheran.

The West End was a neighborhood of workingmen who established their homes as close as possible to West Albany and all its opportunities. The railroad shops alone employed as many as five thousand at a peak moment, though the men I spoke with remembered a maximum of three thousand early in this century. Central Avenue and the Pine Hills also grew from the phenomenon, but men actually came from all over the city.

At a quarter to seven on a dark winter morning in, say, 1915, on a railroad siding at the foot of Livingston Avenue, a train would start to move. The engineer—it might have been old John Purcell—would throttle up slowly, for men would still be running to catch one of the six cars or grabbing hold of a rod to ride the rear steps of the engine.

With one engine pulling and another pushing, the train would gain momentum as it moved westward up Tivoli Hollow—the gulch of Patroon Creek—and wheeze and strain perceptibly as it pushed upgrade at the West Albany Cut.

In a few minutes the train would be on a siding beneath the Watervliet Avenue bridge and the six cars would be suddenly empty of perhaps two hundred men, all ready to face another ten-hour day of hard labor.

This was the work train. It brought men from Rensselaer, from Downtown, from North Albany and the South End to the starting point of their arduous day. West Albany trolleys brought others. Many more swarmed along dark streets in the cold morning to reach the hollow where the largest shops in the New York Central system were about to begin another symphony of effort, a hymn composed by the financial giants of the day and played by the workingman on instruments of iron and steel.

There was rhythm even in the jargon of West Albany. There was the locomotive shop, the car shop, the machine shop, the boiler shop, the tank shop, the pipe shop, the blacksmith shop, the finishing shop. The men were machinists, mechanics, brakemen, firemen, switchmen, engineers. They worked in the trimming gang or out on the steam track or in the Upper Department or the Lower Department, or in Shop A, Shop B, Shop C, Shop D, or the Roundhouse. They were bossed by the master car builder and the master mechanic and the superintendent of motor power, and all of them and all that they surveyed were part of a great combine of names: the Big Four—Chicago, Cleveland, Cincinnati, Columbus—and the not-so-big others, like Avis and Depew and Jersey Shore and Buffalo and Frankfort and Selkirk.

I talked with John Parsons, eighty-nine, who was the superintendent of the locomotive shop, the big boss from 1921 until he retired in 1941 after fifty-four years of service. He had fifteen hundred men under him working in the two erecting shops, where the transfer table moved locomotives to any of fifty stalls for repairs. A one-hundred-ton crane raised the locomotives.

The car shop, also called the Upper Department, was separate, and in here the plumbers and painters and carpet men worked inside and outside, over and under the passenger and freight cars, the diners and Pullmans. The master car builder was Garry Carson in John's era, and John Grow replaced Carson and stayed until the end of the shops.

The men worked by piecework, mostly, until around 1948, although Jim Meany was on an hourly rate, twenty-five cents an hour in his early days, and John Parsons remembered his own rate as a machinist at Depew in 1896 as being twenty-two cents an hour. Men took an hour for lunch if they wanted, or they ate on the run if they were doing piecework and were hungry only to fatten their paychecks. Later the lunch period was reduced to twenty minutes and few men went home to eat after that.

A legendary phrase was handed on to my time by people who never went near the shops but who understood the arduous nature of the job and how a man sometimes compensated for hard work and a short lunch by spending as much time as possible sitting on the shop toilet. "I'm going to go take a West Albany" was the line. You can be sure the fellow who inspired it wasn't doing piecework.

When the five o'clock whistle blew, the streets filled with a swarm of men who came up the hill, past the row of company-owned houses on Martin (later Essex) Street where some of the shop supervisors lived, walked through the Watervliet Avenue neighborhood, and fanned out across the West End.

May Meany recalled that when she and Jim first moved to the West End one of the memorable sights was seeing those hundreds and hundreds of workingmen walking together on North Manning Boulevard to get the trolley at Central Avenue, or heading home to places trolleys didn't go.

There was so much work.

"I remember in 1912," Jim Meany said, "they didn't have room enough in the yards to bring the freight trains in. They were lined up from Van Woert Street and North Pearl all the way to the shop, waiting to get in. Miles and miles of them."

Jim, a pal of my father's, was an erstwhile North Ender who in his youth rode freights down from the shop at the end of his workday, leaped off at Van Woert, and walked home to North Albany. He had had pure white hair for as long as I could remember and was a man I always wanted to talk with because of his sincerity. He was a person of simple tastes, generous with words and feelings. He could say "How are ya, Billy" and it came at you like an oversize Christmas gift. One thing I remember is that this man who worked in the shops all his life had fingernails devoid of dirt. When he came home he removed the shop's dirt, all of it, so that you wouldn't know it had been there, a characteristic I find admirable not because of cleanliness but because of the honor it did his private life through a separation of values.

"The railroad was a way of life," Jim said when we talked in his home on Washington Avenue (up the block from Ontario Street), where he'd lived forty years. "Everybody on this hill got their living from it. Children followed their fathers into it. Whole families. Like mine."

Jim's father came to America from Ireland during the Civil War, and Jim and two of his brothers worked all their lives in the West Albany shops. Another brother worked for the Pullman Company at Union Station. Jim went to work in 1905 as a machinist's helper, four years later was a machinist on the floor of Shop C, and in 1928 went into the machine shop and stayed there until 1952, when West Albany went into its fade-away. He took his pension in 1953 after forty-eight years with the Central.

He remembered men who weren't so enamored of this life as was he.

"There was a lot of boomers years ago," he said. "They'd get a job for a few weeks and then boom onto someplace else. There was a fellow named Patsy I remember. He worked four months and then said to me, 'Jim, I've got to go back to the circus. I can't take this.' " Years later Jim went to see Barnum and Bailey when it came to the West End (the circus unloaded in the shops' freight yards and pitched its tents behind the Arlington Hotel) and here came Patsy the boomer. Patsy remembered Jim well and gave him two five-dollar reserved seats for the Big Show. You see what I mean about Jim.

Jim told me a circus joke he said my father had told him.

"There's something I can't see into," says my father.

"What's that?" asks Jim.

"An elephant's ass without a stepladder."

Jim laughed till he coughed and then got us back on the track of the West End and its people. He cited the Brennan family, as had Leo Brennan (no relation to the other Brennans). They both remembered that the Brennan brothers all started with the Central and all later went with the Delaware and Hudson, Jim (Shots) Brennan becoming a master mechanic, a big job.

Leo and Jim, separately, singled out Shots as an exemplary man, and when you asked them why, they gave you reasons: because of the job he ascended to, because he played football, was a catcher in baseball, and boxed, too. They both said he never drank in his life, and Jim said he never smoked and that he'd never heard Shots swear. Leo said Shots was a crackerjack with a shotgun, which was how he got his nickname. He was a religious man, "a good-living fellow," said Jim, "a high type of a fellow," said Leo, who added, "I wish some of it had rubbed off on me." These values now seem as archaic as the West Albany shops.

Jim Meany remembered one of the telltale signs of the shops' decline: when the Roundhouse and yards were moved to Selkirk in the early 1920s, and in 1921 when the whole shop closed down for six months.

"That threw the whole area into a dither," Jim's wife, May, recalled. "These men never lost a day's work before that."

Jim remembered a consolidation of shops when it was late, very late, for the railroad. Buffalo and Jersey Shore men were brought in to work at West Albany in 1945, and many Albany men were laid off. John Parsons remembered a comparable, earlier consolidation: in 1931 when the Avis (Pennsylvania) and Depew shops were closed. Seniority always prevailed and almost five hundred of the affected men were given jobs at West Albany.

"We were laying off young, husky fellows who could do a day's work," said John, "and putting the old men on in their place. I likened it to an orchard where they cut down the young trees that were bearing fruit and left the old ones stand for the good they'd done in the past."

Once, perhaps, there were five thousand men in the shops. In 1950 there were twenty-three hundred. In 1952 five locomotive shops were closed and considered available for lease. In 1954 Central president Alfred Pearlman, deciding that leasing the property was more trouble than it was worth, gave orders to sell. In March 1956 a syndicate, headed by attorney Edward M. Segal, was established to buy the shops. It bought everything—shops and land—for $500,000 and announced plans to attract new industry.

Three months later the new owners sold the shops' equipment and scrap for $291,000. They then sold, separately, the thirty-two shop buildings and fifty-four acres for $750,000. By 1957 the shops were white elephants, useless now, victims of the diesel engine. In November 1962, following litigation over the shops' value, the State Court of Appeals ruled the fifty-four acres were worth $435,000 and the shops had no value whatsoever.

By 1963 windows by the thousands had been broken in Shops A, B, C, and D. Smokestacks on the boiler shop and the tank shop were black and rusted, dead industrial flagpoles in the flagless sky. A tree grew through the roof of one building: the tree shop?

May and Jim Meany hadn't been back to the shops for years but then they took a ride over the Watervliet Avenue bridge and May said, "My God, Jim, look at it. There's nothing there."

Jim Meany remembered that moment when we talked. "It's a way of life that's passed on," he said. "That's all, it's passed on."

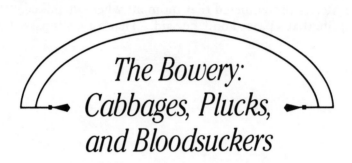

The Bowery:
Cabbages, Plucks,
and Bloodsuckers

The Bowery,
The Bowery,
I'll never
Go there
Anymore

*I*t was part of the Iroquois Trail
and later the Mohawk Trail and the Mohawk Turnpike and the
Schenectady Turnpike. It was the way west out of Albany, and
for an age there was no competing road. "A continuous line of
vehicles crowded its pathway every day," the *Albany Evening
Journal* reported in 1867 about an earlier time. "Some 15 or 20
taverns along its line were crowded with business."

The terminus in Albany was called Bowery Street and later the
Bowery, the name having none of the connotations of New York's
Bowery—that gaudy boulevard of bright lights, swindlers, and
illicit gaiety that turned into the main stem of bumdom. Albany's
Bowery signified something far more pastoral, *bouwerie* being
the Dutch word for farm.

The name remained until July 15, 1867, when Alderman Wem-
ple, impatient with the old Dutch names on his city streets,

racked his imagination and submitted a bill to the Common Council renaming it Central Avenue. Now the Bowery is perpetuated only in history books, and the street is an erratic avenue of boom and bust—mostly bust these days, but with vitality creeping up on it, maybe in the same way decay slowly crept from block to block during the 1950s and 1960s. It'll never be the same, of course, but then it never was. It was at its peak in the 1820s as an artery of commerce, teams of six horses hauling all the westbound freight—all of it—out Bowery Street and over the sandy plain that was the city's western flatland. Then the Erie Canal opened, zapping the turnpike, "and in a twinkling the glory of the Bowery was gone," the *Journal* reported. What little commercial life it enjoyed during winter when the canal was frozen went kaput with the building of the Mohawk and Hudson Railroad to Schenectady in 1831.

The street moldered for a generation and then started to grow. It was graded and paved in 1865, for it had become a new residential area for the Germans and Irish who had been arriving in great numbers. Both groups settled heavily in the South End at first, then expanded outward into the Bowery.

The Irish consecrated a new church in the Bowery in 1868: St. Patrick's, called by the *Albany Argus* "one of the most tasty and appropriately arranged edifices in the country."

The Germans by 1890 had established three Lutheran congregations on or near the Bowery: St. Paul's, St. John's, and the Evangelical Lutheran Church of the Redeemer. The Lutherans had been in Albany since 1649, the oldest congregation of the Lutheran church in America.

The German Catholics placed the cornerstone of their first Bowery church the same year the Irish Catholics did, 1868, and called it Holy Queen of Angels (later, Our Lady of Angels). Despite cold weather, about six thousand attended that cornerstone ceremony, many joining the procession that began at the Cathedral of the Immaculate Conception, on Madison Avenue. Livening up the holy event were Klein's and Greberthuyser's bands, eight military companies from the Tenth and Twenty-fifth regiments, and four civic societies: St. Peter's, St. Joseph's, St. Francisquis, and, in neighborly fashion, the Hibernians. Addresses were given in English and German, and, a newspaper reporter noted, "owing to the lateness of the hour these were short but very effective."

And so the Bowery had become an Irish-German neighborhood, but the Germans predominated as the years went on. They greeted exiled German patriots who came through the city, they paraded to celebrate military and political victories in the Old Country, and they remained ethnically united well into the twentieth century.

I spoke with two men of German descent whose lives and ancestry had long been linked to the social and commercial life of the Bowery: John Pauly, proprietor of Pauly's Hotel and Tavern at Quail Street and Central Avenue, and John R. Hauf, son of one of the street's commercial pioneers, John B. Hauf, who founded his carpet shop in 1897 on the Avenue, or the Hill, as Central was also called.

"Central Avenue was really the only business thoroughfare in the West End," said John R. Hauf, who headed the large furniture store his father's business had become. "The street began in the

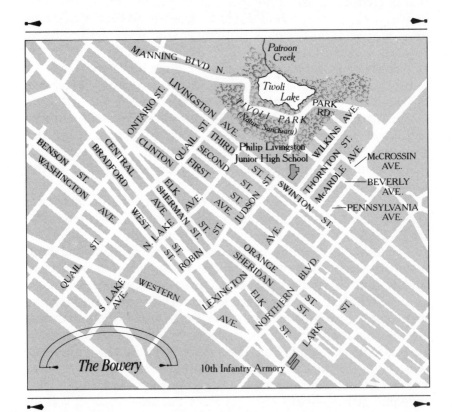

block between Robin and Lake and grew in both directions. It was in continuous upsurge from the nineties until after the First War, and then, when the Depression hit, there was the downgrade."

Commerce had followed the new residents, and the horsecar made the area accessible, the first one running, at three miles an hour, from State and Broadway to Central Avenue and Northern Boulevard on February 22, 1864. The Albany Railway Company's stables were on Central Avenue (and burned in 1879) and in 1888 the company ran the city's first electric car down Central, from Quail to Broadway. The demise of the horsecar era was further symbolized on Central Avenue when in May 1890 the company sold two hundred of its horses in auction at the carbarns.

The Weeber Cycle Works buried the horse even deeper in 1898 with a new symbol: the Weebermobile, the first automobile made in Albany. William Schupp took the hint and converted his huge four-story carriage works and blacksmith shop into a bumper- and fender-repair garage and auto salesroom, where he showed off the first automobile truck to Albany in 1909. With these firms as seedlings, Central Avenue grew into Automobile Row, which it remains today, to a degree.

In 1910 the saloons outnumbered the automobiles in the Bowery, roughly one saloon for every two hundred people, including women and children, who were not allowed into any of them. John Pauly's proved the most durable, founded by a German immigrant, John Klotzbach, in 1861, on the abandoned site of St. Paul's Evangelical Lutheran Church cemetery. Klotzbach sold the saloon to John Ebner, who in 1889 sold it to John Pauly the elder, who furnished it in the Victorian style it exhibits today: pressed-tin walls and ceiling, golden-oak bar, marble columns on the back bar.

John Pauly the younger, with whom I spoke, enlarged the place in 1921 and made it a memorable speakeasy with kick-proof metal plates on the side door (still there); and he also operated it as a seventeen-room hotel. It was an old man's hotel in the 1960s, suffused with antique gloom even on sunny afternoons. An old newsman I knew well, Ray O'Connor, my night city editor on the *Times-Union*, moved his solitary existence from the Kenmore Hotel, Downtown, to Pauly's, and died alone in one of those seventeen rooms.

John Pauly recalled a cheerier era when we talked. "It was all

Germans up this way," he said. "All they wanted to do was drink and sing. Quite often the Germans from Cabbagetown would come over and mix with the Irish on the Bowery. Then somebody'd say, 'You're an Irish this,' and somebody else'd say, 'You're a Dutch that,' and then they'd fight. Then on Sunday they'd mix up out at Shafer's Grove [run by John Pauly's father-in-law at Colvin and Central] and have a good time together."

Part of the saloon culture was the free lunch and a game of euchre or pinochle, the singing societies belting out Old Country tunes, and traveling freaks entertaining the drinking class.

"One man," John Pauly recalled, "would put a brick on his head and another would hit it with a sledgehammer. Some of them stuck pins through their tongues. And there were the old German bands, about five Dutchmen with different instruments playing oom-pah-boom stuff. Then they'd take up a collection."

Lange's Gardens, more than a saloon, was one of the famous places, situated in the Y between Washington and Central avenues at Northern Boulevard. Families picnicked there, watched the gymnasts perform, danced, drank, and sang among the trees. It was the social center of the neighborhood but disappeared in the 1890s, with a reputation that was a shade notorious.

Those gymnasts, hard to find in a saloon anymore—ostentatious joggers warming up at the bar are about as close as we come—are part of a long-gone tapestry of animal energy that once amused drinking men. In the Beehive Cafe, at 256 Central Avenue, Big Jim O'Connor, who had managed Joe Walcott, the welterweight champ (1901–4), taught boxing to customers in a back room that was also given over to cockfights. At Mike Hennessy's saloon at Central and Partridge Street the walls were lined with birds in cages—"every bird known to Ireland." Hennessy also trained greyhounds and on weekends staged his famous rabbit chase, with customers wagering on the time it would take the hound to catch the rabbit Mike released. Races concluded prematurely when the rabbit leaped into one of the holes on Mike's property.

For indoor sports there were the horseroom in the back of George Linter's place on Sherman Street, and the bowling alleys and poolroom (Willie Hoppe gave exhibitions there) in Noodle Fritz Ehrhardt's place on Central, west of Quail Street. Noodle Fritz manufactured noodles, which were sometimes served fried.

More formal entertainment than noodles was available in the

silent-movie palaces of the neighborhood: the Ideal, the Pearl, and the Colonial, the latter surviving into the second era of vaudeville in the 1950s, and later still serving as an art-film house. Albany's greatest theater, Harmanus Bleecker Hall, was only a few steps away from Lark Street, where the Avenue began. It existed on the north side of Washington Avenue, next to the Tenth Infantry Armory, just below Lark.

Performing artists of world reputation played the hall regularly after its opening on October 9, 1889: Eleonora Duse in *Camille*; Anna Held, "exclusively engaged for America by Mr. F. Ziegfeld, Jr."; Lew Dockstader "and his great Minstrel Company"; Paderewski; Mary Garden; Lillie Langtry "in her great play, *Agatha Tylden*"; Sousa's Peerless Band; Anna Pavlova and the corps de ballet; Ethel Barrymore in *The Shadow*; Lionel Barrymore and John Drew in *The Mummy and the Hummingbird*; John Barrymore in Edward Sheldon's *The Princess Zim-Zim*.

Barrymore (John, of course—the only Barrymore known by one name) strolled up Central Avenue after one performance to look over the model-train complex of local fame in the backyard of Hausmann's bakery at Central and Northern Boulevard. Created by George J. G. Hausmann, the train tracks zigzagged over miniature bridges and through tunnels and tiny railroad stations, delighting Hausmann's visitor, who did not introduce himself. He did, however, inquire whether Hausmann had ever seen John Barrymore act, and when Hausmann said no, Barrymore unmasked and, with theatrical flourish, presented the trainmaster with two tickets to a Barrymore performance at Harmanus Bleecker Hall.

The Hall prevailed as the city's preeminent theatrical palace for a generation, eventually turning into a movie house run by F. F. Proctor. It was destroyed by fire on May 19, 1940.

Daniel P. Corr, a much-lauded science teacher, grew up on Sherman Street between Quail Street and Lake Avenue, in Cabbagetown (so called for what the early Germans grew there). He remembered seeing skating performances at the hall; also saw a play, *Seven Keys to Baldpate*, when he was maybe ten years old, in 1919. He remembers a lot of action in the play—a mystery, maybe, about who's got the keys. He wasn't sure what Baldpate was—a house, a castle, perhaps? My notes don't tell me, but they reveal that when that show played Albany it was December 4 or 5 of some year and that the play was a "mystery farce" based on a story by Earl Derr Biggers (who invented Charlie Chan) and adapted for the stage by George M. Cohan, a dandy playwright of that era.

Dan Corr remembered more vividly that across the street from the hall, in the Stuyvesant Apartments (still there), lived Dr. John Sampson, a world authority on gynecology who rode in an old Franklin that was guarded by a Doberman pinscher when not in use. Dan also remembered the doctor had a fibroid uterine cancer named for him because of his work in medicine. He remembered such things because he delivered the doctor's newspaper, the *Albany Evening Journal*.

Dan's paper route, begun when he was eight, in 1917, and continued until 1923, began at the *Journal* building at the Plaza, at the foot of State Street. He'd walk the mile and a half from his home to Downtown, pick up his fifty papers (about twelve pages to an issue), and move westward, dropping them off at customers' homes around Lafayette Park, then up Washington Avenue to the home of Dr. Arthur Elting (a famous surgeon and big-game hunter who brought back a hippopotamus head from Africa), over to Civil War General Amasa J. Parker's home on Washington Avenue, where the general, toting his large pocketbook, walked to the edge of the iron fence around his front yard and every day extracted from the purse the two cents Dan required from his customers, though he didn't require them to pay daily—that was only the general's way. Dan would then serve his customers on Lancaster Street, and on Lark Street would leave a paper at Hagaman's bakery, where, if he was flush, he would buy an oversize chocolate éclair for three cents and trek over Lark toward Elk Street, go up Elk through Pluck Hollow, where the Irish lived, all the way to Lexington Avenue, and then over to Central, where he'd deliver a paper to a grocery, Jacob Smith's, and on days when Dan wasn't stuffed with éclair he'd buy one of Jake Smith's dill pickles for a penny, and then, out of papers, he'd head home to Sherman Street, where, with his Irish-German heritage, he'd spend the remaining years of his exceedingly happy childhood (until he moved away in 1927) communicating with his peers through the medium of such games as Red Rover, a touch-and-run game, Johnny Ride the Pony, involving survival on piggyback, and Trigger, a form of baseball played with a "trigger"—a piece of wood about one by one by six inches, which you whacked with a paddle about one by five by fifteen inches. The trigger was numbered Romanly—I, II, III, and IV—on its four sides, and if a player caught the flying trigger, the whacker was out. If it landed, then the number facing upward designated a single, double, etc.

Why a trigger? Why not a baseball?

"Baseballs you had to buy," said Dan.

Dan and his pals swam in Baby Creek, which ran alongside the New York Central tracks north of Livingston Avenue and was famous for its bloodsuckers, which bit into you. Cabbagetown kids also played games dangerous to their health—gang fighting with Pluck Hollow kids, for instance.

"They were hard-boiled, at the lower end of the financial scale," said Dan of the Pluckers. "They'd come up and try their luck against us, and we'd arm ourselves with bricks and bats and cobblestones—no guns, no chains."

Dan was hit on the forehead with a brick during one fight, and the wound never properly healed. He was twenty-seven when a doctor decided it was potentially cancerous, and Pluck Hollow's signature was then removed from Dan's skull by X-radiation.

Pluck Hollow was the area beneath the Northern Boulevard viaduct, just north of the Bowery. When I wrote something about Central Avenue years ago, a woman wrote me about the name's origin in the 1860s, when Christian Rapp operated a slaughterhouse on the north side of the Bowery by the viaduct. "On butchering days," the woman wrote, "the poor people living in the Hollow came up to the slaughterhouse for the plucks—that is, the hearts, livers and lungs which were to have been discarded or sold at a pittance. In those days the great nutritional value of these organs was unknown."

Rapp moved his slaughterhouse out to Washington Avenue and Manning Boulevard, sold out in the 1870s, and retired. This news of his influence in naming a neighborhood comes from the pen of his granddaughter, Charlotte E. Ickert, who heard it from her mother.

Dan Corr knew all sorts of influential people who came from the Bowery and Cabbagetown. He recalled that the son of John Pauly the younger grew up to be a three-star general in the Air Force; Gerald Kelleher, who went to CBA with Dan, became a major general during World War II and fought in Korea, in charge of commandos; Joe Ryan, Dan's playmate, became the Catholic Archbishop of Alaska and is now the U.S. Military Vicar—the top chaplain—of all the armed forces.

The military element was significant to Dan because of his

father, who had served forty-two years in the Army—in the Spanish-American War, World War I and the Mexican Border incident—and who, as a stable sergeant, became state armorer, in charge of the Tenth Infantry Armory at Lark and Washington. His name was Francis J. Corr, Sr., and Dan says, "He was the finest horseman I ever knew, not because he was my dad, but because he was."

Dan also knew people from Cabbagetown who grew up to be civilians: Louis Wolner, for instance, who became president of the New York State High School Principals and was an authority on the Cardiff Giant; Mrs. Mary Bergan, who ran the grocery on Robin Street and raised a son, Francis, who grew up to become a justice of the Court of Appeals; and the Kohn brothers, who became shoe millionaires (Barney and Sam) and lawyers (Reuben and Milton). Another brother, Dave, played par golf on the Shaker Ridge course, using only five clubs.

Renown of a lesser order came to other Cabbagetowners: Peter Kindlon shot a gas station owner in the early 1920s and went to the electric chair for it. The Oley brothers, from Orange Street, and Percy Geary, from Central Avenue, kidnapped John O'Connell in 1933 and they all went to jail, Franny Oley's part in the kidnap a source of confusion still for Dan Corr, who was Franny's classmate and liked him a great deal. (The kidnapping is discussed in the Delaware Avenue section of this book.)

As to Dan Corr himself, he graduated from St. Patrick's grammar school, then Christian Brothers Academy, and went on to State College as a chemistry major. After graduation in 1931 he began thirty-seven years of teaching science in the public schools, and after that spent five years redesigning Albany Academy's science department. The American Chemical Society named him the outstanding chemistry teacher in the eastern U.S. in 1968. In 1969 the New York State Board of Regents named him Teacher of the Year, and State College honored him as one of its 125 most distinguished alumni, living or dead, in the school's 125-year history. Most of his teaching years were at Columbia High School in East Greenbush, where he initiated the idea of teaching earth science to bored ninth-graders, and he spent five years developing the course that spread through the U.S. to Japan and then around the world. He also collaborated with Dr. Curtis Hemenway of Albany's Dudley Observatory on a Skylab project. Dan wrote the handling procedures for Skylab's micrometeorite-particle-collection experiment, which, to the symbolists among us, bears a striking similarity to those flying rocks from Pluck Hollow.

Dan Corr now looks back on his childhood with pleasure, but it was not without its tragic taint. In 1921 the Central Bank was established on the Avenue, with John B. Hauf, president, and William Dawson, who ran a Central Avenue clothing store, vice-president. It occupied the Wendt brothers' saloon at Central and Quail, and boasted of having Albany's first night depository. John Hauf served for four years as a dollar-a-year man, and people on the Avenue like Dan Corr, the newsboy entrepreneur, supported the bank with their savings.

Dan couldn't bank much in the years he went to high school and college. He was working in Stahler's ice-cream parlor in the old Pearl Theater on Central, between Lake and Quail. "I'd dig eleven cans of cream a night," Dan said of the Stahler's job. "I'd say it was the most popular ice-cream parlor in the city."

He turned over all the money he made to his parents, and just let his newsboy fortune accumulate interest. Then one day in 1933 the Central Bank went bust and Dan lost everything: $154, the fruit of seven years' work.

"Bill Dawson lost a lot, too," said Dan. "An honest, gentle man. He was never the same after."

The bank's failure was symptomatic of the decline that hit the Avenue during the Depression. But the merchants resisted decline vigorously and by 1936 had banded together in the Central Avenue Civic and Merchants Association to run promotional campaigns: the Halloween Jamboree for kids, Clean Sweep Day, Ten Percent Day (I remember shopping for shirts and ties with my father in the Snappy Men's Shop on the Avenue, where he always got "ten off" from the manager, Moe Kahn). The 1930s were also the beginning of an innovation—evening shopping— that gave the Avenue an edge over the main commercial center of North Pearl Street, Downtown.

"Small shops and groceries started it," John Hauf remembered, "but it was Woolworth's staying open late that gave it the real impetus."

The Avenue was widened in the 1940s to permit angle parking. Overhead wires were buried and trees disappeared. "When those trees were taken out," said John Zwack, the Central Avenue undertaker, "the heat in the summer was really something we weren't used to up here."

But angle parking didn't forestall doom. First came the competition from the mail-order houses, then in the 1960s the fight with the shopping centers. Central Avenue lost that fight. One by one the merchants moved away or went out of business and the famous Avenue ceased to be the city's second-ranking shopping street. Certain stores survived for a while, like Hauf's, which lasted until 1981. John Hauf died six months after his store closed. Before John Pauly died he sold his bar and hotel to a pair of enterprising young men, Tom Wiltshire and Barry Wallock (son of that noted Albany food distributor, Max the Pickle Man). Wiltshire and Wallock preserved and perpetuated all Paulyness in the place, making it the oldest continuously useful bar in the city, but also giving it a dimension suited to the 1980s.

On a sweltering afternoon in the summer of 1981 I ventured back to the cool oaken interior where I'd talked to John Pauly eighteen years earlier, and sat across the bar from John Wisniewski, thirty, the bartender, who had North End connections: his grandfather was Joe (Fiddler) Whelan, who ran a saloon across from the North Albany carbarns for a generation. We talked about how Pauly's had changed in eighteen years.

"Weekends it's packed out," said John, "old-timers and young kids listening to swing and jazz and blues and honky-tonk piano. Bubbles Nixon played piano awhile here and Doc Scanlon plays with a swing band. The shuffleboard [installed in 1941, one of the first in Albany] gets a lot of action at night and we've got a Happy Hour from eight to nine-thirty in the morning for the night shift—cops and factory workers and nurses, draft beer for twenty cents. By eleven the place is empty. We do some trade during the lunch hour, beers and shots, but it dies after lunch."

What about Central Avenue? What is it like these days?

"During the day it's one way," said Wisniewski, "blue-collar, working-class people and old residents of the neighborhood going about their business. Pauly's is still a hotel, a mix of old-timers and college students. At night the street is pretty wild. You've got Mickey's, which gets a leather crowd, bikers. Same for the Colonial. And J. B. Scott's is a lot of rock music (and some jazz). You got three gay bars, the 369, the Voodoo Lounge, a gay membership club, and one place the cops busted. But it's not a gay strip. It's totally mixed. You get assistant district attorneys and college students, all types in here, and the Hibernian Hall is around the corner."

What about that ethnic mix?

"Still a lot of Irish, Polish, Slavic," he said. "You get black kids, too, at night. The Falcon's Nest is where they hang out.

That was Ticky Burden's bar till he got busted." Ticky was an Albany High School basketball whiz who went on to be an All-American and pro Rookie of the Year and then quickly fizzled. He is now doing eighteen long ones for robbing a Long Island bank.

Any Germans left in the neighborhood?

Some, but John didn't know how many.

"It's like a downtown urban area anywhere," John said. "People shop here because they don't want to drive out to some shopping center in the suburbs."

A year passed before I got around to writing all this, and so I called John Wisniewski for an update. Pauly's was about the same but J. B. Scott's heavy success in bringing rock and jazz to the Avenue (the Ramones, pioneer punk rockers, the Go Goes, Manhattan Transfer, Count Basie, Buddy Rich—who on the *Tonight* show lauded Scott's as "a super club") had also spawned a small musical enclave of equipment and record stores (Drome Sound, Strawberries, others); and then Scott's burned down in the summer of 1982—torched, the fire department thinks. And so, for the time being, the music has died on Central Avenue while the owners of Scott's decide how to regroup.

The Voodoo Lounge had been sold, said John, and turned into a straight disco called the Fat Cat. Dan Hurley's old Irish bar on Quail Street, near Clinton Avenue, had been reopened by two young fellows who were catering to a hip young crowd, as was Pauly's, although in daylight hours old-timers gathered there still, trying to be traditional.

Also, the city had built new brick sidewalks, with planters, along the Avenue, and had also built several parking lots on the sites of expendable buildings. This solved for now, and possibly for the future, the double-parking congestion that was traditional on Central Avenue.

As to crime and trouble, John said, "It's pretty safe despite all the rowdiness on the street. The police do a good job."

And so in the fall of 1982 the street was probably somewhat akin to what it was in the days when the Irish and Germans were beginning to trickle in after the Erie Canal debacle, or when Woolworth's was getting ready to stay open evenings. It's a street with a future—maybe.

Betting people up in Linter's horse room would probably give small odds the street will bloom in a few years. You walk along it between Lark and Northern Boulevard and primitive chic is at work, the street trying to shed its primitivity and start oozing elegance. There, too, stands the old John Hauf furniture store, a large building boarded up and waiting for Godot. My wife had never been in Hauf's, but the sight of it, the knowledge of what it had been and what it had become, a victim of capricious destiny beyond its control, moved her, made her feel she'd lost a friend.

John Hauf's Avenue is as dead as the Turnpike. The Central Avenue of today, that street of mellifluous name (bring back the Bowery, I say), pushes toward the 1890s as a new kind of neighborhood—scraggly, raffish, unloved, unsung, but staying busy even so, trying to tidy up and get it together, like a lot of old friends who never quite made it out of Cabbagetown.

The Gut: Our Boulevard of Bluest Dreams

*D*ongan Avenue is named for Thomas Dongan, Catholic, Irish-born governor of the British province of New York, who on July 22, 1686, sent his greetings to the place that had sometimes been called Beverwyck, sometimes Williamstadt, sometimes Albany. The greetings came in the form of a charter that formalized the rights of the mayor, aldermen, and commonalty of the city of Albany to own, purchase, and hold land in the city's name.

Part of the land mentioned in the charter was "a certain parcel ... commonly called 'The Pasture,' situate, lying and being to the southward of the said town, near the place where the old Fort stood, and extending along Hudson's River till it comes over against the most northerly point of the Island commonly called Martin Gerritsen's Island, having to the east the Hudson River; to the South the Manor of Rensselaerwyck; to the West the highway leading to the town."

The Pasture, sometimes called the Great Pasture, sometimes the Pastures, was a tract of common grazing land that in modern measurement existed between Madison Avenue and Gansevoort Street. On November 1, 1687, the Pasture was sold by the city to the "Reformed Nether Dutch Congregational Dutch Church" for £390, the deed signed by Albany's first mayor, Pieter Schuyler.

The Dutch church dredged and filled the land, and the Pasture became a site for homes. It was from this area that the ferry took travelers across the river to Greenbush, and eventually it would become the city's most populous area.

I traced to its early origins a single house on Dongan Avenue, the street named for Governor Dongan, and before that called Dallius Street, a modified version of the name of Dr. Godfredius Dellius, pastor of the Dutch church when it acquired the Pasture.

The church sold the land to Solomon and Susan Allen of Philadelphia, who sold a plot to Reverend William Allen of Brunswick, Maine. Allen may have built the house on the plot. The land was held by him until his death, and his heirs then sold it to George Canaday, a wealthy Irish American who had large landholdings in the city. Canaday acquired the house in 1868.

On November 17, 1878, the house and other property appear to have been purchased by Samuel Gross, and upon his death it passed to an heir, James Gross, who sold it to Isadore Goldstein but then foreclosed the mortgage on the house. The house passed into a referee's hands and was bought on January 14, 1907, by Bella Gallup, who held it until December 20, 1923, when she conveyed it to Domenico Rappazzo and his wife, Mary. The City Savings Bank of Albany held the mortgage and on May 4, 1934, a referee conveyed the house to Mike Pistilli and Pasquale Micare. On April 1, 1947, the New York State Realty Liquidating Corporation, a firm owned by Sidney Albert and Irving Kirsch, bought the house from Albany County, which had taken it from the Pistilli estate for unpaid water rents and taxes. NYSRLC held it until February 2, 1955, when it sold the house to Ruth Willis. Her heir-at-law, Willard L. Bueford, sold the property on June 12, 1962, to William Sherman, of 171 Colonial Avenue, and Robert Levine, of 273 Tampa Avenue. Sherman owned the house alone when I confronted it in 1965. Its tenants were blacks.

The point of all this is to see this neighborhood, and this street and a particular house, as a fragment of the entire span of American history, from the Dutch to the Yankee clergy to the Irish, the Jews, the Italians, and then the blacks.

William Sherman said that at one point the house had been used for prostitution. Dongan Avenue had had for some years the reputation of being one of the lifelines of the red-light district. It was such a lowly street that in 1965 the city did not even collect its garbage.

■ ■ ■

"The Tenderloin was above Bleecker, up to Beaver Street. They said Albany was second only to Chicago in prostitution. Mother Donohue's was fifty cents. All the boys used to go there, on Union Street, north of Madison Avenue. Across the street were the Creoles. They were more expensive. French Emma's was another place, a cheap one, and then there was Big Bertha. She'd sit in the window and look like the fat woman in the circus. Way down on lower Broadway was the Red Onion. That was two dollars. Thank God I was never in need of any of them places."

That was Thomas [Happy] Evans, seventy-two, talking, a South Ender looking back to the Tenderloin as he recognized it in the first and second decades of the century. His nostalgic pride in Albany's being second only to Chicago is matched in vitriol by Carl H. Stubig, former writer for the *Knickerbocker Press*, who left the city and wrote a comic diatribe in 1913 called *Curses on Albany*, in which he attacked Republican boss Billy Barnes, the Albany newspapers, and a venal merchant class for letting Albany's Tenderloin exist on such a scale.

"On the lowest estimate," wrote Stubig, "there are perhaps 1,200 women in the Tenderloin. Something like 400 of them are known as street walkers." The lowliest got a dollar for their company, double the bottom line in Hap Evans's memory; and the higher types cost five. Stubig said of the latter that they "give as good an imitation of the life in high social circles as one is able to find. High-balls, cigarets and scant attire, prurient stories, high kicking and the bunny hug dances are features. Beer is 25 cents a glass and is invariably a barrier to the shortskate." The company of such a woman for an entire evening, said Stubig, could run about twenty-five dollars.

The Tenderloin, said Stubig, was "not segregated," by which I assume he meant not confined to one section of town. "A red light burns on nearly every thoroughfare Downtown," he added, ". . . around the Union depot, and north to Clinton Avenue, including that notorious hotel called the Windsor." On these blocks, he wrote, students from Union College and RPI come to town to "meet the gang" and to go out to the "great white way." As night wanes, "the dawn of morning brings realization to some virgin youth that he has taken a false step." These young men find themselves "stopped by women who invite [them] to furnished rooms within whispering distance of the Broadway Y.M.C.A., into alleys running around the Sunday Telegram office on Van Tromp Street, or to trysting places within the glimmer of the lights at the Third Precinct Police Station."

This condition persisted, said Stubig, because the Barnes politicians argued, "Look at the money it brings into Albany." Ministers who complained about the Tenderloin were told it was needed to give "some resort" to the legislators. Businessmen argued that "the women of the underworld are their best customers, and pay the highest prices for everything."

So it looked (to one writer) before World War I in Albany. If his count of women seems astronomical now, it is because the city has grown conservative in recent decades. But a similar count, or higher, could have been made during World War II, when Albany was a crossroads for travelers and a wide-open mecca for servicemen. The Tenderloin by then had become The Gut, clearly a loss in poetic allusion, and was highlighted by one street—Green Street—whose name since the 1930s had carried the connotation of the whole red-light district.

Green runs parallel to Dongan Avenue, a block to the west. It had been the street of the Irish (they built St. John's Church on it, the city's oldest Irish parish, founded on Dallius Street in 1837). The Italian neighborhood later wove itself through the old Irish streets (a somewhat reputable Italian doctor inspected the girls weekly to keep down disease), and the girls were of an ethnic mix. After World War II the nightclub business waned, the frenzy of wartime pleasure seeking cooled, Governor Dewey moved his state police into the neighborhood to raid gambling and vice, causing the clientele to grow wary, and the town, for the first time in living memory, decided to lay low.

The ethnic and racial mix vanished in the 1950s and the houses became solidly black. Those occasional Creole places (also called tar shacks) from Happy Evans's time had become the whole game, and whites need not apply. (Well, yes. But if you really needed one, Dixie would send out and get her; for Dixie was a special case. Thin Billy, the Lansing Street pimp, was busted for breaking the rule and putting a white girl to work and would never run a house again, so it was said. Because there's no excuse for a white girl to be a prostitute. And so, Mother Donohue, your day is over.)

We focus now on 1965 and 1966 in the Green Street and Dallius-Dongan neighborhood, when The Gut's scarlet day was in a terminal condition, just flickering pinkly amid the ruins. Yet the pink was still capable of shocking, in its own sluttish way. This

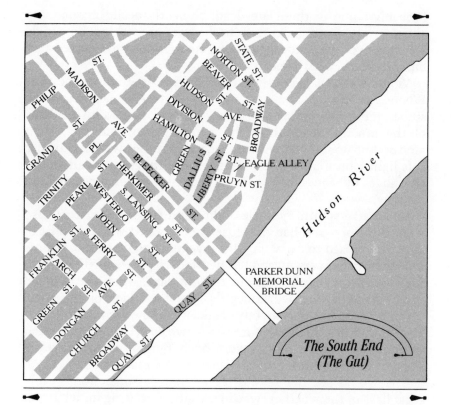

was a time of eschatological woe in the neighborhood, made visible through a look at a handful of residents who refused to believe in the death of the streets, and through three professionals, among the last in a very long line.

The three were Dixie, who ran the busiest place in town; Lucinda, who was personally as well as professionally terminal when we met, but not one to give up without a struggle; and Violet, who was bottoming out, like Lucinda, on Dongan Avenue, the lowliest street in Babylon. Dongan was already half gone, the power turned off in many houses, making space for the new arterial highway and the new Dunn Memorial Bridge over the Hudson that that crazy Rockefeller was building.

Dixie, Lucinda, and Violet are not real names but they are real and verifiable people. I don't know what they're doing now. Maybe they've gone into social work, or computers, and in case they have I harbor no wish to disturb their peace with name naming.

Probably some of them are dead, or nearly dead, or reputably silent, or just resting. On their backs but not working: how nice. Wherever you are, ladies, *pax vobiscum*. That's pronounced *pox*, but you know what I mean.

Violet was the player everyone knew. How could one not? When you turned the car onto Dongan Avenue, there she stood, one of the jazzers, a loner who did business by the light of the moon, the light of the noonday sun, and the rather archaic but nonetheless useful red lamp in her window, whose soft light illuminated the presence of willingness, availability, and love by the clock somewhere in the shadows behind its glow.

Violet had willful qualities. She used to grind her teeth, so went the story, and had one customer arrested when, in a fit of guilt, he refused to carry on with love, extracted himself and his money from her person, and left her flat. Violet charged him with robbery, but it didn't stick. In the old days, when she peopled her house with other working girls, Violet would go on the town, throw $500 across the bar, buy drinks for all the men in the place, lose her roll to a thief, and come back two days later with another roll, just as fat. She ran a tavern once, but for seventeen years she'd been living in her own house on Dongan Avenue.

You would see her in the lee of that personal front porch, regardless of the weather, waiting, waiting, waiting for whatever might come her way. You could pass her in your car, but you would not really pass her, for her afterimage would remain in the frontal lobe: arms folded, feet in ankle socks and loafers, or rain boots, or other seasonal protections, her slim body wrapped in a fashionable shortie coat, her hennaed hair in a snoodlike net, her lips colored with curves of red, all of these quasi-glamorous achievements not only part of her professional equipment but also death-defying tools of the trade that refused to let age subtract the residual evidence of desirable youth. Violet had a small potbelly, and wrinkles—no show stopper. But few others of equal age (fiftyish? sixtyish?—take a guess about Violet, the ageless wonder) could fool the traveler as frequently as did Violet. From the lee of her porch Violet would take one step forward, the only movement on the quiet, empty street, a motion guaranteed to catch the passing eye. And once caught, the eye would look, could not not, and then, in her thrall, the eye would see Violet nod and say "Hi" without sound, see her move her hennaed head so slightly that it could barely be identified as movement, and yet could be nothing but, and whose hithering meaning was unmistakable to any man, or any boy past the age of first knowledge.

It was very late summer and we were talking on the porch of Violet's house, and as I took an occasional note on her remarks, Violet interrupted herself to ask a passerby, "Are you the man's supposed to fix the plumbing in here?"

The passerby shook his head and smiled at Violet.

"You look like him," Violet said, but the man walked on.

"I came down when this was a nice place," Violet said, "and I got trapped here. I bought this house in 1949 and it was a dump. I put eight thousand dollars into it. It's got all hardwood floors and Mansville ceilings, French doors and new walls. Not a thing in this house is old except those old bricks on the walls outside."

Violet's house was furnished with middle-class taste, sturdy, not flashy. The Madonna and Babe gazed down from a tapestry in the front hall, opposite a small print of Notre Dame Cathedral. In the living room against the windows lay a well-worn sofa, its cushions out of shape in a way that indicated a particular, recurring kind of wear. Elsewhere the house was in turmoil, boxes atop boxes, as Violet prepared to leave.

"If I buy the building I'm lookin' at, I'm gonna take seven of my rooms with me," she said. "I got a lot more than that furnished but I'd only take seven. I furnished the whole upstairs but nobody lives in it. It's a nice house and I'm gonna put nothing but welfare people in it 'cause I know I'm gonna get my money. But there's no big rush. The state's good to me, gave me thirty more days to stay here. I got no complaints with nobody. I'm a Democrat and I love it."

Lucinda used to live a few doors up from Violet but she was gone, heavy trouble, and her house was closed down and men from the Niagara Mohawk Power Company were taking down wire that would no longer be needed in all the tenantless houses on the street. Lucinda's house had a bit of a canopy over its porch, and like Violet's house it still had its awning intact, those awnings the trademark, the flag, the high sign of romance, the nighttime substitute for Violet's hithering nod. Across the street the houses were windowless, already in advanced decomposition. Violet's house was really the only one still in use.

"That's right," said Violet, "this is the only decent house down here."

■　■　■

Lucinda left Dongan Avenue under rather different conditions from Violet. She was an early member of a brand-new neighborhood group that called itself Better Homes. When the women of Better Homes took their troubles to Mayor Corning it was Lucinda who broke up the gathering. "The roaches," she said, "they walk right across the street to my house and if you open the refrigerator they beat you into it."

"Excuse me for laughing," Mayor Corning said, "but you paint a marvelous picture of the situation."

But now no one was laughing. The Albany County Welfare Department was withholding Lucinda's welfare check—unfairly, she argued to Olivia Rorie, the president of Better Homes and a source of strength to all members. And so it came to pass that a delegation that included this writer called upon Lucinda in her living room to hear her story. The room had curtains and real and artificial flowers, figurines on the bookcase, a photo of Lucinda's mother on the wall over the TV set, a meticulously clean and well-kept room. Lucinda wore a loose-fitting shift, open-toed slippers too big for her feet, bat-wing spectacles, and a terrible black wig. She was a dark-skinned, fine-featured woman of fifty-eight, but without even any lingeringly attractive elements to either her face or her body. She was sick, and she listed her ailments:

Heart trouble, ulcers, arthritis in the right hip, blood clots in the right leg, poor circulation, a second lump in her neck (the first having been taken out three months earlier), fluid in her legs and feet that prevented her from wearing shoes, back pains, and anemia. "My blood was so low they couldn't hardly find a heartbeat," she said. She'd been in and out of hospitals for back treatment and cobalt treatment; she took heart pills, nerve pills, pain pills.

She'd worked in a coffee shop in 1954, had lifted a pot and something slipped in her back and she couldn't straighten up. She won $1,463 in a lawsuit, and managed to keep it, over the objections of the Welfare Department. She later severed an artery while working and won $1,022 in a court settlement. But she was receiving welfare then, and so the department took all of that. Now the contention with the department had arisen over another settlement—$2,520 for reaggravation of her old back injury. The $2,520 had been sent to Lucinda and had swiftly vanished, and welfare got none of it; so Lucinda's welfare checks stopped coming.

Lucinda explained to our delegation where the money had gone:

She had bought a blue dress for $50, a three-piece suit for $48.98, two robes for $17, a coat for $30 and another coat for $59, a rhinestone necklace for $18, and repairs to her picture tube for $44.80. This left, unaccounted for, a balance of $2,252.22. Oh yes—she'd owed a lawyer $390 and had paid him that. But that still left $1,862.22. Well, maybe so, said Lucinda, but the money's all gone.

During the conversation in her living room Lucinda went to the window twice to shoo away people standing in front of her house. "Old drunks come knockin' on my door all times of night," she said. "One night four men were standing in the hall sayin' they lookin' for action. And three white men come in a black-and-white Plymouth and throw a full can of beer through my front window."

Sick, in pain, put upon by the government, Lucinda was, it turned out, still hustling out of her well-appointed front room. She had also been renting it out to a man called Sunny Boy who used it to perform abortions on white girls. Olivia Rorie discovered these things and also that Lucinda and another woman were working for a pimp named Sam. And about the time Lucinda received her check for $2,520, Sam turned up with a new station wagon.

Lucinda was no longer welcomed at Better Homes' weekly meetings, and Olivia called up the county welfare commissioner and told him she didn't want Better Homes smeared by Lucinda's case.

Lucinda remained in the neighborhood after she left Dongan Avenue and after they tore down the house. She continued to hustle out of an all-night bootlegger's bar at Bleecker and Franklin streets, near Dixie's place. Then one day Dixie called Olivia to tell her some bad news: there was blood all over Bleecker Street. What happened was Lucinda was in a doorway with a twenty-seven-year-old white man from Arbor Hill at four o'clock on an April morning and then Lucinda cut him with a linoleum knife. "Like cuttin' fat off a duck," Olivia later said. Lucinda cut the man on the throat and when he tried to protect himself she kept hacking and cut his left middle finger and left pinkie. The man had bitten Lucinda, which was why she cut him. Now he was running to the bootlegger's bathroom and Lucinda was running after him to get him good, but she stopped when she saw all the blood. Then she went back to the bar and sat down and waited for the police to come.

. . .

Listen to Olivia Rorie talking about the neighborhood.

"There wasn't nothin' workin' right here. I'm living in front of a whorehouse and they're hanging out the windows half-naked. It's hot and you can't sleep and they're laughin' and talkin' at five a.m. And this house got no water in the winter, all froze up. You payin' sixty, seventy dollars a month for gas and you don't feel it. The house was open, like livin' outdoors. You had a roof on your head, that's all. My hot-water tank froze up and busted, the toilet leaked all the time, with a split in it. Every time you called repair service, the landlords they was talkin' junk. I was in that house about five years and every once in a while they'd do a little patch. Somebody'd come in and put a little putty and some tape and go on about their business. My house wasn't under rent control. I tried there first. We had a meetin' with somebody from the state. This cigar-smokin' sapsucker, he leans back with his big cigar and he talked mud shit. And I told him so. I said, 'Somebody is greasin' you palm, honey, and don't deny it.' I tried everywhere, the city, the board of health, and we even called in the underwriters about the electricity. The buildings commissioner of the city came down and I was showin' him the house. He was scared to walk. I was grabbin' him and pullin' him. 'Come on, see it good.' 'I'll take your word,' he says. I says, 'You go on in here where we growin' mushrooms upsides the walls. I want to show you my mushrooms in here.' 'I'll take your word.' I says, 'You gonna see this.' So he told me, 'Don't pay no rent,' but he wouldn't give it to me in writin'. So they all go slow.

"I got active in the PTA and they called me from Trinity Institution and asked if I wanted to be on this South End Advisory Committee. We had the first meeting at the school and I threw out some questions but I never did too much with that. . . . I went to Trinity to complain about this stinkin' house, and dope peddlers on the street, and the wineheads. You wake up in the morning and you got to kick them off the stoop. They drink in the street, scatter wine bottles everywhere, they steal everything that's not nailed down, and the language out of them on the street is ridiculous. You leave clothes on the line, you got to watch 'em or the wineheads will steal them. And all the time my kids are gettin' older, and you got to put a stop to all this. So then Jack Mayer come down here from Trinity and he talked about getting people together. This was his first assignment and it was December and I couldn't get it straight in my mind to accept Jack or throw him out on his ear. Finally I says, 'Okay, Jack, we'll organize,' and in January we had the first meeting in my house. One man lives over on Pearl Street, he was scared. He said, 'Messin' with those whores, they're gonna have all of us killed,' and then we got to talkin' about the city administration and he was scared of that. Lucky was there. The first time he came he was very nice but the next time he's talkin' under people's clothes. He didn't have no respect for nobody. And Shirley and Mamie and Ruth and Grace, all sisters, they were there. We walked all over the neighborhood gettin' organized and talkin' about what we wanted to do. They laughed like hell at us. 'You ain't ever gonna get no playground,' they told us. They were gamblers and prostitutes and dope addicts. Just ignorant. We went to a place over in back where they write numbers and a girl there tried to give Jack some home brew, a typical hoocher. I had to get Jack out of there. She'd of give him a knockout and keep him till he's thinkin' the way they want him to think. Young meat. I've seen too many young girls and boys messed up behind women. You take an older woman. Now Jack's white. He's nice-looking. She'd want him around just like a picture. She'd dress him, feed him, and take him out of town. Pee Wee, why she had it so bad she'd do what she had to do right on the street and now she's got a sixteen-year-old boy and she's got him all dressed up wearing flashy rings. I see one of them women once and this big joker was attacking her on the street and I told him, 'Don't do that, Fishy,' and she told me to mind my own goddamn business. I said, 'Kick her some more, honey.' You see so much goes on down here. One woman was messin' around and her husband caught her and he got two women to hold her and they stretched her legs and he shot her in the tail. That's somethin' else. What me and Jack did was walk the streets rustlin' up people and then some others came along and we got us some action."

Olivia Rorie was a thirty-eight-year-old, 350-pound black woman with nine children, an ailing husband, an eighth-grade education, inexhaustible energy, a politician's gift for organizing, and an irascibly golden tongue. She lived at 99 Herkimer Street in a one-family house owned by Sidney Albert and Irving Kirsch, law partners who operated the largest slum real-estate business in the Albany area—they housed 6,000 people, collected rent from 1,200 families and individuals in 761 buildings, many in the slums, and also owned 6 middle- or upper-class apartment projects. They were multimillionaires who would come to public embarrassment through Better Homes and Olivia.

Olivia's inability to get the landlords to fix her tumbledown house after many phone calls and requests to city agencies for help surfaced in a mimeographed newspaper called *The Voice of Poverty*, and within two months Albert and Kirsch were household names. I wrote a series of articles on Albany's slums and featured their world prominently and enhanced their real-estate reputation slumward. But they survived, prospered, became benefactors to the neighborhood groups, got rid of the worst of their slum junk (so they said), moved into philanthropy and good works, and at Olivia Rorie's testimonial dinner in 1978, not long before her death, Irving Kirsch presented her with a gift of $1,000.

But in 1965 Olivia and the landlords were cat and dog, likewise Olivia and Mayor Corning, and Olivia and Dan O'Connell's Third Ward committeemen, who were barred from Better Homes' meetings. Those meetings came about after Olivia met young Jack Mayer, a community organizer at Trinity Institution, the South End Episcopal settlement house that was headquarters for implementation of John F. Kennedy's antipoverty program.

Jack Mayer's meeting with Olivia was an early milestone in the so-called neighborhood group movement, in which the federal government invested in social change directly, without an intermediary role for cities and counties. Trinity won its federal funds and entered on a collision course with the Mayor by undertaking such a power play; but collision was still a year and a half down the road. Now Trinity, directed by Richard Collins and with Michael Nardolillo as associate director, was sending its agents out to the various South End neighborhoods, and in time a dozen or so groups were formed and even banded together in a short-lived federation. The story of this movement is long and complex and is worth a book of its own. It comes to an end during the administration of Lyndon Johnson, when he dilutes the power of the neighborhoods and strengthens the hand of City Hall.

But before that, Olivia Rorie would become the highly visible matriarch of Albany's poor, vocalizing every Thursday from her chair in the Pilgrim Baptist Church on Franklin Street, where Better Homes held its meetings.

"We hold these truths to be self-evident: That all men are created equal; that they are endowed by their Creator with certain unalienable rights; that among these are life, liberty and the pursuit of happiness" was the motto of Better Homes and was printed on the reverse side of membership cards, available upon payment of one dollar in annual dues.

Membership was initially impressive, forty to fifty at the early meetings, blacks and whites, old and young, Catholic and Protestant. Housing was the prime topic—getting the landlord to make repairs. Rats and roaches were always under discussion, as were trash collections, broken streets, empty houses where winos gathered, whorehouses, day-care centers, playgrounds, and poll watching—the latter a particular sore spot with the neighborhood politicians.

The pols began pressuring members of Better Homes who held city and county jobs, and the group's meetings were defined as enemy territory. White membership dwindled, Catholics fell away, the remainder largely black and Protestant, with a few whites such as Lester Sweet staying on. Significant social work in the neighborhood already was being done by St. John's parish, most notably by Reverend Peter Young, who became one of the best-known and most revered figures in the South End for his work with alcoholics and the indigent. But St. John's did not intersect with Better Homes until a later moment, when Albany's Catholic Bishop-to-be, Howard Hubbard, then fresh from the seminary, was assigned to the South End. He lived at St. John's and worked with Olivia, among others.

Some volunteers with Better Homes were Catholic, some of them nuns and lay teachers from the College of Saint Rose, who even today continue their educational work with slum children of promise, work begun in the era of Better Homes. Novelist and critic Doris Grumbach, author of the novel *Chamber Music* among others, was a volunteer during her teaching days at Saint Rose, and also a close friend of Olivia's. In a later moment Doris would remember the day Olivia decided the city needed a prod in order to start collection of neighborhood garbage, and so Doris and others joined Olivia in making a modest collection and dumping it on the lawn of the Mayor's home.

Another ad hoc volunteer group called itself the Inter-Faith Task Force. It was put together by Reverend Robert C. Lamar, pastor of the First Presbyterian Church, on Willett Street, and Reverend Nellis Tremblay, now the pastor of St. Joseph's Catholic Church, on Ten Broeck Street. Father Tremblay was then the liaison between the Albany Catholic Diocese and the black community. The Task Force numbered among its more enduring members an architect, Carl Baumann; a student (now a lawyer), Jane Schneider; the wife of an Albany neurosurgeon, Dottie Kite; the wife of a maverick black politician, Jacqueline Haith; and a young Franciscan priest from Siena College, Reverend Bonaventure O'Brien, who because of his attacks on local politicians in these months would be silenced by pressure from the Diocese and become the center of a rebellion by local Catholic faithful that would alter the power structure of the church in Albany.

These and other volunteers provided insight, social leverage, transportation, occasional money, and much time that was not otherwise available to the people in Better Homes, but it was the members themselves, not the volunteers, who made the decisions on what to do next: send a delegation to see the Mayor about garbage collection or streetlights, bring in speakers on rent control and child care, and decide on what to do about whorehouses.

Father Bonaventure took Better Homes' list of the whorehouses to a high-level Irish cleric in the Diocese, who read them and said they didn't exist, that Dan O'Connell wouldn't let such things go on. Olivia Rorie called Police Chief John Tuffey and complained about the whores, especially in Dixie's place, "these women hangin' out the window naked . . . and they didn't have no respect for our kids. I told him come on down here, sittin' in my yard he could see it. So anyhow they closed up the houses. I told them first maybe we could go over and talk to the madam and maybe she could make the women have more respect, because when you close up the whorehouses the men gonna run after the kids, which did happen."

Dixie didn't close, she moved—to a part of Dongan Avenue that wasn't being demolished—and while her move cleaned up the view from Mrs. Rorie's backyard, it created brand-new problems, as Dixie explained to Olivia. "She came," Olivia recalled, "and said how come we had her place closed? She said, 'You know the kids aren't gettin' any peace, the men are lookin' for us and they can't find us.' You know they put streetlights up down there, they had a light right in front of one of them whorehouses. And they wasn't much business, even with a big light there, so I said, 'All I want you to do is respect these kids. All day long them cows hangin' out the windows half-naked, this's got to stop.' So she says, 'I'm gonna move back up there,' she says, 'I guarantee you, my whorehouse will respect the kids.' And they have. So far."

Dixie went back to Bleecker Street, but that wasn't the end. Other whores began to worry about Olivia and Better Homes, and word got around they were going to bomb Olivia's house. "This was some prostitutes, the numbers people and the shop-lifters," said Olivia. "They all hang together, 'cause they figure if you close down one of them you gonna hit the other. This all was supposed to scare me and make us stop, but it didn't. I let them know I knew about the bomb. I called the precinct and said I wanted Chief Tuffey's home. They wouldn't give me his home but they told me Chief Tuffey said any time I called to take care of it so I told them and they drove around the block. So the prostitutes seen all them cops out there in the street, they thought twice."

The city was responding. It tore down some old buildings and built a playground on Franklin Street, a block away from Pilgrim Baptist Church, and Lester Sweet became assistant, without pay, to the custodian (paid by the city). Everyone in Better Homes called him Mr. Sweet and he never missed a meeting. He was fifty-four, retired, he said, from the railroad on an $88-a-month pension. He wore his shoes half-laced, his trousers with tattered cuffs dragging on the ground, his suitcoat hanging on him like a double-breasted poncho, his hair invariably rumpled, and even after a shave his beard showing indelibly black under the skin.

Dottie Kite summed up his role at the playground: "He treated the kids like some of my old uncles do. He kept the big kids off the swings to let the little ones on. The kids followed him. He's a pied piper, always giving them ice cream. They begged him. He has no money, and he doesn't have any because he does this sort of thing. He also buys grown-ups secondhand iceboxes and furniture when they get burned out. He's a nut, an eccentric, he's got a bigger heart than anybody I know. He worked the Salvation Army kettles for several years and when it rained they came from the Salvation Army with rain capes. But Mr. Sweet never wore one because, he said, 'I look so pitiful when I'm wet I get more money than anybody else.' "

He lived on South Pearl Street in an apartment that was a storehouse for rummage, a museum for his collection. "You may have heard of me," he said at a Better Homes meeting to a new-comer, "I'm the fellow collected four thousand bottles for the Girl Scouts." His bottles dominated his apartment, a garden of Pepsi stalks, half a dozen layers of dead Cokes, Bud, Schlitz, Miller, and the rest that Mr. Sweet collected over the weeks in alleys and vacant lots so the Scouts could make a trip to the Kennedy Memorial Library exhibit. He also solved Better Homes' security problem when it had seven station wagons full of old clothes donated for its rummage sale. Mr. Sweet moved the lot into his apartment. He continued collecting clothing for people in need even after the sale netted $300. He gave George Marbley (Better Homes' vice-president) a suit and George didn't even need it.

The legend of his altruism gathered even greater force as Better Homes grew into a cohesive family organization. And so it came as a shock when a neighborhood woman placed charges against him and the police took him to court and booked him as a vagrant while they explored the situation for more precise evidence of crime by Mr. Sweet. The woman, a young mother of two, had become hysterical when she arrived at the playground and found her five-year-old daughter gone. Police were called and an anguished twenty minutes passed before the child returned in the company of Mr. Sweet.

"It's preposterous, it's fantastic," said Mr. Sweet describing his arrest and detention, which lasted from Saturday noon to the following Friday morning. "It's absolutely out of order. They picked me up and took me to the precinct, giving me a so-called trump charge. I had to saw off the lock to the gate to let the kids into the playground. There were no keys available and I did it on the city's recommendation. A policeman's. Then I went to buy a lock and the child came with me. I stopped for coffee and bought her a hot chocolate."

"He took her out of the playground and to the street and back without my permission," the child's mother said. "Boy oh boy, thank God nothing happened. They told me if I wanted to press any complaints to be there at nine o'clock Sunday morning, which I was. The judge asked what happened and I told him and he said, 'We'll give him a mental test.'"

Better Homes people viewed the arrest as an attempt to smear the organization because of its public criticism of the city. It had picketed City Hall to get the playground, and the members specifically blamed John Tucker, a cool and dapper black man who had been acting Democratic committeeman in the Third Ward for a year. He denied telling the child's mother to press charges and said he only told her she could if she wanted to.

The arrest brought to light a black mark on Mr. Sweet's record:

a morals charge lodged two years before, for which he was still on probation. It was not for molestation but what a psychiatrist interpreted as an immature sexual impulse. And thus was new meaning given to Mr. Sweet's altruism and such remarks by the mother as "He used to pick up kids and kiss them. My daughter told me one day, 'Mommy, that man wouldn't let us leave the playground.' "

Mr. Sweet's friends boggled momentarily under the weight of implied evil, but only momentarily. For as he began his movement through the justice machinery, there, behind the railing in police court, stood Olivia Rorie, Dottie Kite, Carl Baumann, and Jane Schneider, quadrumvirate of concern for the bottle collector.

Mr. Sweet filed in with the drunks and speeders and vagrants and assorted flotsam of the morning lineup, and when it came his turn he said he wanted a lawyer, which the judge took as a statement of nonguilt. He was allowed one phone call and the Better Homes delegation met him in the hallway outside court. A young policeman said to Mr. Sweet, you must be a nice guy, you've got a lot of friends. And Mr. Sweet said, they're my people, I belong to them and they belong to me, and the quadrumvirate chorused, You're right, Mr. Sweet, you said it, absolutely, and gave him a dime and the phone number of a young lawyer who had already agreed to take his case and awaited only Mr. Sweet's formal invitation. Mr. Sweet stood by the phone booth with dime in hand and said he didn't trust local lawyers, they were all corrupt, all afraid of the local political machine, and he wanted a New York City lawyer. The quadrumvirate groaned at Mr. Sweet's thickness at such a thin moment and pushed him into the phone booth, but an older policeman ordered them back and not to talk to the prisoner. At length, and with the poise of the truly secure, Mr. Sweet called the Albany lawyer, asked him to take the case, was told yes, hung up, and went off to jail for a week.

At his next court appearance the Better Homes delegation had grown to eight. Olivia had bought him a suit and shoes in a secondhand shop so he would look more presentable, and he did, but he still looked frowsy after a week in jail, his eyes wild and wandering. Mr. Sweet was released on bail after a conference in chambers, and then the Better Homes group went to the county probation officer, who reported that the psychiatrist found Mr. Sweet not senile, of normal IQ and intellect, with childish sexual impulses, and not dangerous, but since he was still on probation from the original morals charge he shouldn't be around children.

And so the crisis was over, but still to come was the formal dedication of the Franklin Street playground, attended first by fifty, then a hundred and fifty, then an uncountable swarm of children. Parents and neighbors were there. John Tucker was there as emissary of the Mayor, but because of his role in Mr. Sweet's case, Better Homes people wanted nothing to do with him. The fact that he provided eighty-four pounds of hot dogs for the kids cut no mustard with Better Homes.

The mother was there and so was Olivia and all the Task Force clergy and volunteers and some newsmen who reported on the speakers. "Because you kids didn't have no place to play, you got this," said Olivia. "Now no bad language or broken bottles." Reverend William Roland, pastor of Pilgrim Baptist Church, said to the people, "In the South End you feel forsaken. You are dirt at times. But Better Homes went out to get the place cleaned up and the Mayor is one hundred percent with you." He blessed the playground in the name of Jesus and then Olivia screamed for somebody to get the mustard and on came the hot dogs, the cheese bits, and the Mitey Bite ice cream. "You can be a jitterbug but not a litterbug," Reverend Roland told the children.

Across the playground the mother was saying about the absent Mr. Sweet, "They didn't investigate him. He shouldn't have been placed here. They said if I see him around here to call the police right away."

"You mean he can't walk the streets?" Olivia asked.

The mother shrugged.

Six days after his release on bail, Mr. Sweet sat in a pew at Pilgrim Baptist Church, listening to a discussion of the playground. It wasn't open long enough. When little kids who didn't go to school wanted it, it wasn't available. Twenty-eight people in the room listened as Olivia addressed the gathering. There was Jesse Johnson, who would soon be ninety, and his son, Leroy, a spiffy dresser but a wino, and LeRoy's frail wife, Mary (also a wino), the little echo lady who repeated everything, and Mr. White, the elderly gentleman who wanted an assignment to visit the sick and reported that somebody had called the Better Homes people a bunch of communists. Mr. Sweet was in his double-breasted poncho and his half-laced shoes as Olivia spoke.

"Why is it when you get old they shove you in the corner and let you stay there?" she was saying. "We should love one another all the time, not some of the time. How many older people are living in this area, shut-ins? We got to figure how much we're gonna spend on the kids and on each old person for the holidays. We gonna make a canvass and the kids we're lookin' for is the unfortunate children. We want to have a Christmas party with gifts for all the children and oodles of baskets for the people to take home, and we want to have a play that night. We'll have a big spread, a big feast. We will need money. We can raise the money for this. I'm gonna ask for donations and have budgets made up and go around and solicit. We'll get it 'cause when you're gonna do good you're always gonna have help. We want to have a hundred and fifty kids and fifty to seventy-five older people."

The smiling little echo lady, who had been yea-yeaing and nodding, spoke up and told Olivia, "Mr. Sweet smiled when you said Christmas party. That's what he's longing for."

Discussion followed then of the fund-raising raffle for the party. Mr. Sweet was put on the raffle committee. The party would be held in the gymnasium at Trinity Institution. Also, said Olivia, darling Mr. Sweet can be Santa Claus and give the kids and grown-ups their gifts.

Mr. Sweet nodded approvingly and the meeting continued with other business.

Olivia Rorie died of cancer on September 28, 1978, at the age of fifty. Her Herkimer Street home had partially burned in 1969, and in time she moved into a new home of her own in Kenwood, with front and back yards. Some of her children live there now. Bishop Howard Hubbard said of her when she died, "I considered her to be one of the foremost influences on my life and ministry. She displayed great love and compassion for others and tremendous courage in fighting injustice."

The city withdrew its financial support from Trinity Institution in November 1965, after election. As peaceful times returned to the South End, some of the money was restored, but never again to the original level. The whorehouses moved elsewhere. Violet retired and became a part-time baby-sitter. Dixie, who carried a gun and rode in a white Cadillac, retired and closed her house and considered having her breasts lifted. Father Bonaventure O'Brien was removed from his teaching position at Siena College by his Franciscan superiors and assigned to hear confessions in service parishes, first in Providence, then in New York

City. He eventually left the priesthood to work at rehabilitating alcoholics. During the protests, the teach-ins, the prayer meetings, and the debates that exploded throughout the city after his silencing, his role was compared to that of Saint Francis of Assisi. The two monsignors responsible for his punishment, which had so openly linked the church to politics, were, in time, removed from positions of diocesan authority and assigned to pastorates.

Albany Bishop Edward Maginn created Providence House in the South End with an endowment of $100,000 to benefit all the city's poor and put the young Howard Hubbard in charge. The latter's levelheaded intelligence and humanitarianism would be so widely recognized that in a dozen years he would himself be Bishop, the most popular in local memory.

The Task Force faded away as the era of civil rights became the era of black power and whites were no longer welcomed in the slums. At Better Homes, Jesse Johnson married the echo lady. One of the group's female officers went briefly to work for Dixie as an administrative assistant, and was removed from office. The Pilgrim Baptist Church was torn down, as were many houses in the neighborhood, Dixie's among them. LeRoy and Mary Johnson both died as alcoholics. Mr. Sweet died a natural death without becoming involved in any moral turpitude (as far as is known).

The Gut is no longer The Gut. There is no Gut anymore. It is now known as the Pastures, as it was in the beginning. The section of Dongan Avenue where Violet and Lucinda lived no longer exists as a street. Olivia's house still stands on Herkimer Street and will probably be restored. There are about a hundred houses and no people left in this once-populous area. The houses are all empty, boarded up, and numbered in white paint. Saplings with small leaves were growing on these old streets in the fall of 1982, a city crew was at work building brick sidewalks on Green Street, and also along Green another crew was installing a series of sculptures by artist Dan George that would create a small controversy: for the sculptures were of a very feminine design—a pair of legs, a shape that might be construed as a naked breast, and another shape, very like an O. Did all this mean the prostitutes were back on Green Street? one reporter wondered. The city father's weren't confirming that, but it did seem very like art remembering life, did it not?

Old-fashioned black streetlamps were being installed to light up the evening, houses were being auctioned off to lower-, middle-, and upper-income buyers, mini-parks were being built, and shaded blocks and walkways were taking shape. Who could remember when the area looked so pretty? Perhaps in all its years it never did. Millions were being spent to create these streets as the Pastures, the city's newest and oldest and most ironic neighborhood.

COMMON PLACES

*N*otable, some would say
even improbable, billboard. Need we say more!

UNCOMMON FACES

*E*rastus Corning: the first Erastus of many, first president of the New York Central Railroad, and, at mid-nineteenth century, the city's richest man.

2

*T*his toll gate has long been identified as being on Western Turnpike, the way west out of Albany. But real estate man Bob Fivey says he and his father, the gate-keeper, are in the photo, and the gate was on the New Scotland plank road, not on Western Turnpike.

3

4

*T*he New York Central Railroad shops in West Albany: with some early steam engines that could, and did.

5

*R*abbi Isaac Mayer Wise:
at age thirty-five in 1854,
the year he left Albany after
having firmly established
Reform Judaism in the city
and the nation.

*A*lbany's premier
nineteenth-century banker,
Thomas Olcott,
captured from life in 1878
by the artist Walter Launt
Palmer while reading in the
library of his home, Arbor
Hill, the mansion that gave
the neighborhood its name.

6

7

*H*anging out at William
Bauer's German meat
market at Washington and
Lake avenues in the 1880s
are assorted carcasses,
horses, goat, and people,
including two butchers and
one meat cleaver.

8

*Y*es, there was an Albany Sonntags Journal and here's the proof. But you can't find any editions of it anymore. They disappeared after World War I.

*P*eter Kinnear, man with beard at center, posing with his employees in 1860. Kinnear took over John Wesley Hyatt's invention, celluloid, a pioneer version of plastic, and made billiard balls from it.

*T*he piles of lumber at Kibbee's were among hundreds of such stacks in more than forty-six lumberyards in North Albany, the white-pine center of the world.

11

A hundred years ago these men handled the lumber in Kibbee's lumberyard in North Albany. One day they paused long enough to let us take a good look at their faces, their mustaches, and their splendid assortment of hats.

12

The horsecar was replaced in the 1890s by the electric trolley car, but not in North Albany. This car ran into the Lumber District until about 1920.

13

Cutaway coats for everyday wear were all the rage around J. F. Toohey's saloon at 39 South Pearl Street before the century turned. Bar towels were also de rigueur, and men without hats could not be served unless accompanied by money.

14

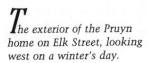

*A*hhhh. Huybertie Pruyn as an elegant eighteen-year-old debutante in 1892.

*T*he exterior of the Pruyn home on Elk Street, looking west on a winter's day.

15

16

*T*his is the main dining table, modestly set for four, in the home of J. V. L. Pruyn (Huybertie's father) at 19 Elk Street. The Pruyns were social leaders in the latter decades of the nineteenth century.

17

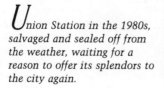

*H*uybertie in 1942:
still elegant at sixty-eight.

*U*nion Station's interior, a
glorious place when built in
1900, was crumbling in the
late 1970s, long after the
golden age of railroading had
passed. Time and vandals were
wrecking the old, abandoned
corpus, and almost did it in.

18

19

*U*nion Station in the 1980s,
salvaged and sealed off from
the weather, waiting for a
reason to offer its splendors to
the city again.

*T*his is Broadway in 1913, during a flood. The river rose up often and brought out the rowboat crowd until flood control was created at Sacandaga.

*F*armers gathered daily at the Albany Public Market, shown here in 1915. Corner at top center is where Lodge, Beaver, and Grand streets meet. Grand was a main artery in the Italian neighborhood.

*S*tate and Pearl streets intersect here. Pearl is neither North nor South when you are halfway across, and at that point you are in the center of the city's heart and soul. This is the way it was in 1917.

The "Dance L'Enticement," by Mollie Williams, was a sight to see at the Empire burlesque house on State Street (south side, above Pearl). Note the enticing costume at right.

23

24

Safety first—don't play ball in the gutter—was the warning of this newspaper photo, taken October 23, 1935, on Madison Avenue, with St. Anthony's Church in background. Ballplayers are Isador Harnoff and Pasquale Lombardo, residents of this Jewish-Italian neighborhood.

25

The area around Union Station, here about 1917, was a center for social high jinks for a century. The Monte Carlo, a gambling house run by politicians, was upstairs over the trolley car in foreground.

*B*eer baron Dutch Schultz, bosom
pal and archenemy of Jack Diamond,
was barred from Albany by Dan
O'Connell. Schultz went to Cohoes
instead, there killed Jules Martin, his
own henchman.

*J*ack (Legs) Diamond, looking every
inch the movie gangster, was
photographed in a Catskill courtroom
in 1931 after being arrested for
kidnapping and torture of a trucker.

*A*lbany Police Chief William
Fitzpatrick, who was murdered by
one of his detectives in January 1945.
Did he send Legs Diamond bye-bye?

*J*ack Diamond nearing the end,
December 1931, on his way to court
with his attorney, Daniel H. Prior
(center). Jack's wife, Alice (left), was
superimposed by a newspaper artist,
a commonplace way that editors
improved on reality in the 1930s.

31

*T*he O'Connell brothers: Patrick,
the state patronage connection; John,
called Solly, the mainspring of
Nighttown; Dan in 1937, looking
tough, which he was; Edward,
the lawyer and political brain,
shown in 1938, the year before
he died.

33

34

*E*dwin Corning: a full partner with
the O'Connell brothers in
establishing the modern Democratic
party in the years 1919 to 1921.

35

*T*his is Keeler's, Albany's greatest restaurant, waiting for the crowds to arrive, the waiters all at the ready, as they were for most of a century.

36

*T*he crowd has arrived and Keeler's is in full sway, with a tray of its sublime food balanced deftly at right on a waiter's palm. This was perhaps in the 1950s.

37

*W*hen the red light changed at South Pearl Street and Hudson Avenue in 1934, you could gather a crowd, for the city was busy with life. Naughty Marietta was playing at the Leland Theater at left.

38

39

*O*livia Rorie: charismatic
spokeswoman for the city's poor
during the 1960s.

*H*oward Hubbard at age thirty-
eight in 1977. He would become
Albany's most popular Catholic
Bishop in memory.

*L*eon Van Dyke: one of the most
famous Brothers, in front of the
group's North Pearl Street
headquarters in 1968, when the place
was being relentlessly damaged by
vandals.

*S*am McDowell: firebrand member
of The Brothers, seen during one of his
many political speeches, this one on
the Capitol steps in 1971.

40

41

*R*obert F. Kennedy with ex-Congressman Leo O'Brien. Bobby accused the O'Connells of spreading the word to the party faithful not to vote for him. Leo said that wasn't true, even though they didn't like him.

42

*G*ene Robb: publisher of the two Albany daily newspapers, who engaged in warfare with the Albany political Machine and changed history.

44

43

*C*ity Hall: designed by H. H. Richardson and adjudged the seventh most beautiful building in America in an 1885 poll of readers of the American Architect and Building News.

45

*T*he Capitol: the most expensive
building on the American continent
when finished in 1898, also ranked as
ninth most beautiful in America.
H. H. Richardson was one of its four
architects; the others: Thomas Fuller,
Leopold Eidlitz, and Isaac Perry.

46

*T*he South Mall under construction:
the tower dwarfs the tallest structure
on Albany's nineteenth-century
skyline, the Catholic Cathedral of the
Immaculate Conception.

47

*T*he South Mall completed:
seen from the air in 1979. Odd
white circle next to the tower
is the Egg; Capitol is at
bottom.

*T*his is the South Mall looking north from Madison Avenue. The lone man is in front of the Motor Vehicles building, which is a quarter of a mile long.

48

*T*he South Mall is mostly lines. The sculpture in front of it, a work by Alexander Calder, is mostly angles. The Mall is really a museum of modern art, because of Nelson Rockefeller's interest in contemporary art works.

49

*C*ivil War General Philip Sheridan, perhaps Albany-born, rides permanently in front of the Capitol.

50

51

*elson Rockefeller:
striking a pose that
characterized his
attitude toward the
state constitution, the
public, and the
received political
morality of the
nation.*

52

53

*R*ocky and Erastus: no longer
at each other's throats over the
South Mall. The two were
social friends in their early
years, during their summers in
Maine.

*R*obinson Square is what the sign
says. But this block, before becoming
the ultimate in Albany gentrification,
used to be merely Hamilton Street, a
latter-day slum until the South Mall
sent real estate values through the roof.

*T*he Mayor as matinee idol: here in February 1942, early in his first term in office. He remained a star performer for another four decades.

54

55

*E*rastus at the flood: in full dress with complete smile, an unbeatable candidate.

PART

3

NIGHTTOWN

*State and Pearl streets at night, 1922. It wasn't Times Square,
but if you couldn't find the action within a block of here,
you'd never find it in Times Square either.*

Sports and Swells

A friend of mine was talking about the sadness of an ex-millionaire, a pal of his who had gone broke and was wandering around the city looking shabby and lost. The man had behaved foolishly in business, had gambled some, and spent lavishly on an assortment of woman companions, only one of whom remained to give solace to his busted days.

"But you know," said my friend, "what he misses most is the good restaurants. He loved to eat and drink in the best places and then pick up the check."

My friend's friend had thought of himself as a swell, but he was really a sport. Swells tend not to go broke. Sports are broke as often as they're flush. Swells tend to pick up only their own checks, and they hate to lose. Sports think like Nick the Greek, who said that after gambling and winning, the thing he liked most in the world was gambling and losing.

Swells and sports traveled the same streets, frequented the same places in Albany, and the focus here is on a few of these places: Keeler's Restaurant and Keeler's Hotel, the Kenmore Hotel and the Kenmore's Rain-Bo Room, the Delavan House and the city's Nighttown.

If you were a Damon Runyon sort of sport, up until the

1940s you'd have hung out in the center of Nighttown, which was Broadway—a block long, between Steuben and Columbia streets—directly across from Union Station. The block was home to some famous places, including the Famous Lunch, the American Tavern (which had been Schlitz's Hotel), Brockley's Grill, the Cadillac Hotel, Swift Mead's saloon, Rinaldi's fruit store for when you needed a banana, and Joe Preiss's pawnshop for when you went broke. The night world sprawled outward from Union Station's block—down Broadway and up State Street and over Eagle Street and up Hudson Avenue, up Columbia to North Pearl, up Broadway into Little Harlem, down Green Street into an assortment of back alleys and shadowy streets where you could make your fortune for the week in a blind-pig card game, or lose your virginity or your dignity with Big Betty, or if she wasn't how you wanted to lose whatever it was you needed to lose, you could try Madge Burns's house, or Little Read's, or Davenport's, which was the expensive place, five dollars a shot. So they say.

The pleasure houses were around the corner from the cabarets or, as with places like Big Charlie's, they *were* the cabarets. At Yudel's, on Hudson Avenue, Big Marie was famous for her rendition of "Ace in the Hole," and on Columbia Street Grover Mahoney sang like a thrush in Butch O'Hagan's Silver Slipper. For more formal entertainment there were the theaters along South and North Pearl and the burlesque houses: the Gayety, the Capitol, the Majestic, and the last big one, the Empire, on State Street, where you suffered through Snuffy the Cab Man or Sliding Billy Watson while you waited for Mollie Williams to do the hula-hula and the Dance of Enticement. Ladies were invited to the Empire, and some, they say, really went. But were they ladies?

Headquarters for the gamblers was the Monte Carlo, across the street from Union Station. It was the political Machine's place and the Machine's main man in Nighttown was John (Solly) O'Connell. In one era the Monte Carlo was administered by Charlie Fry, who believed some of America's smartest horseplayers were in Albany, even if he did beat them regularly. Upstairs at the Monte Carlo you played roulette, craps, the bird cage, or the horses. Policy and clearinghouse—the numbers—were written downstairs, and just about everyplace else in town.

McGrane's crap game at 18 Green Street catered to legislators, and in Little Harlem, Dugan's crap game catered to players with money. On Arch Street an entrepreneur named Bimbo, who ran a place called Bimbo's, operated a peaceful crap game until somebody threw an ax through the window. In Moonlight Murphy's horseroom a crapshooter put a pistol on the table and four players faded him.

Pete McDonald, my gambling uncle, remembered Albany from the 1920s to the 1940s with superlatives. "It was the best town in the country," he said. "There were slot machines in every grocery store, nickel machines, numbers, gambling houses, card games—everything went. Nothing was legal but it was all wide open. They'd pay you off right out in the street. There was always more action than you could handle. One of the greatest towns in the world."

Red the Barber, whose straight name was Romildo Bottari, agreed. "They were great days. You could go broke ten times a day and still go home winners, ten or fifteen dollars in your pocket, staked by somebody who hit a big one. That's how they used to run this block. I win, I support you. You win, you support me."

Red was on Broadway forty-three years. He started in the Ross Barbershop facing on Broadway, run by Nick Massino (known as Nick Ross) in the days when it had fourteen chairs and rivaled Paladino's at State and Pearl for being the city's busiest shop. He later became the manager of the Kenmore's barbershop and ran it for years. Then he moved to Columbia Street and stayed there till they knocked the block down around him.

"Why I'd make ten, fifteen a day just putting hot towels on guys who wanted to feel good," Red said.

Jimmy Liuzzi shined shoes for years in Red's barbershop and had similarly fond memories. "We used to have one hell of a clientele," he said, "from penny-ante guys to millionaires. I shined Senator Billy Byrne's shoes once and Solly O'Connell's and Chief Humphrey's [the chief was a private detective], who was a very good friend of Al Smith's. I never shined Al Smith's shoes."

Pete McDonald rememberd how it was on a given midnight Downtown in the 1930s. "The Knights of Columbus would close at one a.m., the shows would be out and the dances over, and guys would be breaking out of poker games and speakeasies. You'd always go for something to eat, down at the Waldorf on Broadway or the Morris Lunch on James Street. Generally we went to the Grand Lunch on Clinton Avenue, next to the Grand Theater. Dan Shugrue ran it and Jack Malarkey, his counterman, took over when Dan died. It was the place to go, and open twenty-four hours a day."

Nighttown was a famous place even a century ago, though it was never called by that name, and its precise center has shifted with the changing moods of the city's streets. But the corner where Union Station stands has a very long history of notable action. The Delavan House, built in 1850, became a temperance house and was host to such notables as P. T. Barnum and Charles Dickens, later turning into an intemperate palace of political wheeling, where Boss Tweed held forth when he came to town to buy the legislature, and where swinish swells drank champagne from the slippers of scarlet actresses. The Delavan was mostly destroyed by fire in 1894, and the part that remained functional for a few years was torn down to make way for the station, which centered the attention of millions on the block until it closed in 1968.

In later ages the DeWitt Clinton and Ten Eyck hotels were the main places of expensive transience, and down the block at the foot of State and Broadway there was the Hampton. The latter was noted in the 1920s for its roof garden, which offered a romantic view of the city and the river until George Douglas Miller, an eccentric man of means, put up a building next door that blocked the view. George expected the Hampton's owners to buy him out and reclaim their vista; but instead, the Hampton added a story to itself. So did George. And then the Hampton closed its roof and turned it into guest rooms. George's building, never finished, with no stairs to its upper stories, became a home for pigeons, unused for a generation, a monument to perversity known as "the Spite Building."

A few doors up from the Hampton stood the formidable Keeler's Restaurant, and its fame was far more than local. It had its origin in an oyster bar at 85 Green Street, established in 1864 by the brothers William and John Keeler. In 1871 William went into Albany politics, became an alderman, street commissioner, and sheriff. People called him Sheriff Bill. John continued as a restaurateur, and in 1884 the brothers opened, at 56 State, the restaurant that would become world famous.

The partnership didn't last, and Bill, in 1886, opened his own restaurant at 26 Maiden Lane. His business grew, took over eight buildings, in time occupying half the block as Keeler's Hotel, For Men Only, with entrances on Maiden Lane and Broadway. It catered to the sporting crowd, had a bowling alley and pool and billiard parlors on the main floor—the Keeler bowling league had its origin there—and dining rooms, but no bedrooms, for women.

Sheriff Bill's success was such that he expanded across the street to an annex run by his son, Rufus.

On State Street, meanwhile, John Keeler was creating a quality restaurant that was gaining cachet with the hefty politicians, and with the crowd that rode the *Twentieth Century* and spent August at the Grand Union Hotel in Saratoga: Lillian Russell, John Philip Sousa, Mary Garden, Grover Cleveland. Geniuses Charles Steinmetz and Thomas Edison came for breakfast, and beer baron Augustus Busch would make the trip in from Cooperstown to have dinner.

John Keeler's sons, John and William, took control of the restaurant in 1891. Gaynor Keeler, son of this latter-day William, took over in 1930 and ran it until 1955, when he leased it to a New York man. Gaynor had his own barber chair in the restaurant, and also a private entrance to shield him from the crowds. It was William Keeler who told Al Smith he ought to wear a brown derby. Smith said he would if Keeler bought it, and he did, and Smith wore it ever after as his trademark, the original hat and replacements always bought in London. William fancied the artwork of Walter Dendy Sadler when he saw it in London, and decorated his room and bar with several score Sadler prints, many now owned by the Albany Institute of History and Art.

The main point of Keeler's, of course, was its extraordinary food. At its peak, 1,500 patrons were served daily by 178 employees—48 waiters, 6 busboys on every shift, 27 cooks and assistant cooks: fry cooks, broil cooks, sauce cooks, roast cooks, fish cooks, vegetable cooks, oystermen, pantrymen, a meat butcher, a fish butcher, bread chefs, pastry chefs, topped off by the head chef, bottomed off by the potwasher and dishwasher. There were 14 dining rooms, a laundry on the third floor to handle table linen by the ton, a full-time seamstress to repair rent linen, a complete bakery, a printing plant for the daily menus and souvenir postcards, a machine shop, and a carpentry shop.

Keeler's bought crabs from New Orleans, shrimp from Georgia, and in a late era was buying $5,000 worth of meat weekly from five locations in the Northeast. It had 14 walk-in coolers for meat and produce, one just for ice, a walk-in humidor for 6,000 cigars, and its own name on the best whiskeys.

Fred LeBrun, restaurant critic for the *Albany Times-Union*, quoted John Gustafson, Keeler's general manager in its late years, as saying, "Every day Foley's seafood truck left the dock at Boston at five a.m. with two hundred lobsters and two thousand dollars' worth of seafood. If there were more than four stiffs in a barrel, it all went back." Keeler's last head chef, Anthony Padula, told LeBrun, "We used a case of butter a day, which we clarified, of course, just to serve our lobsters."

Said Gustafson, "What we threw away every day was staggering. Every morning two guys from a pig farm . . . came to take away the garbage, all the fish, pastries, breads, sauces. Everything. We started all over again every day."

The customer, of course, was always right, even when he was wrong. John Gustafson told me a story of his recurring conversation with Monsignor John J. Gaffigan, pastor of Sacred Heart Church in North Albany. "First he'd holler at the waiter and complain about the lobster, 'This is not very good.' " John would then intervene and take the blame: "It's my fault." The priest would recant and say, "No, it's me. It's my responsibility. I didn't put the order in right." John would say, "No, no, no, Monsignor, it's not your fault."

John remembered another way of satisfying a regular customer, Mrs. Louise Corning, mother of Albany's all-powerful Mayor Erastus Corning. She came in religiously at eleven-forty-five every Wednesday to have lunch with the Mayor, and always gave John two dimes to put in the parking meter so her son's policemen would not give her a ticket.

Probably more than any person, place, or thing in modern Albany history, Keeler's is mourned by the people who knew it. I remember it from my earliest time. My mother loved the lobster patty, the potatoes au gratin, and the ladyfingers; my father, the liver and bacon and the pound cake. I had my first taste of venison there, and learned how great waiters waited tables (rapidly, with imperious courtesy, wearing black jackets and white aprons down to their shoetops). The main dining room was a hall of mirrors and chandeliers, with three long rows of tables and two aisles, oak paneling, shiny brass rails in the bar, narrow stairs to the upstairs dining rooms, and the odor of culinary sanctity pervading every corner of that wondrous set of rooms. What you had when you went to Keeler's was not a meal but an encounter with gastronomic history.

Albany had another legendary pleasure palace in the Kenmore Hotel, a famous place from the time Adam Blake, a black man, opened it in 1878, until the time of World War II, when it went into a slow, thirty-year decline. The hotel, at Columbia and North Pearl streets, is a shell now, maybe with a future, maybe not.

There were efforts made in the early 1980s to restore it for apartment use, but they have come to nothing so far.

Andy Bekerian, who took care of the place when its furnishings were being sold, gave me a tour of the bar, the kitchen, the nightclub, and the only thing I've ever seen that was more dismal was an abandoned house where winos slept. The Rain-Bo room, a center of good and great music and swanky high jinks for a generation, was falling in on itself from water leaks, broken plaster. An old piano in the room still functioned and Andy played a few bars of a song I don't remember. Maybe it was Legs Diamond's favorite tune, "Happy Days and Lonely Nights." Diamond had requested it often in that room, whose reputation was made slightly notorious by his frequent presence in 1930 and 1931.

Jack Burns (a pal of Pete McDonald's), whose introduction to sporting circles was as a pin boy in the K. of C. alleys, and who was a young man about town in the 1930s, remembered Jack Diamond's presence: "He had one section of the Rain-Bo Room. Nobody sat there but him and about six bodyguards and his girl, Kiki Roberts. Nobody ever gave him trouble. And he paid. And did he get service."

When Adam Blake closed down his first hotel, Congress Hall, on Capitol Hill, and opened the Kenmore, it became instantly posh, the place where proper young gentlemen stayed when they came to visit proper young ladies of the town for a weekend gala. Adam Blake died in 1881 and his widow ran the hotel. Later the Rockwell family from Glens Falls bought the place and ran it successfully until about 1900, when Robert Murphy bought it. When he died in 1922, his son, also Robert, took over and it was under the son's management that the place became a celebrated nightclub.

When the Ten Eyck and the DeWitt Clinton hotels were built, they took away the Kenmore's fancier trade, but its nightclub kept it busy and the sporting crowd stayed on. The management of the Albany Senators booked transients and visiting teams there until Bob Murphy backed the wrong political candidate in the early 1930s, fell from favor with the O'Connells, and found that the Senators no longer saw fit to use his premises. You're out, Murphy.

I talked with Bob Murphy in a late moment, when the hotel was catering to welfare clients, people at the dead end of their days, looking for a place to lie down. He had hopes of reopening the Rain-Bo Room (which his father had named), but that was really an effort in nostalgic futility. He couldn't forget the hotel's great age, when it was the mecca for big bands and headline performers.

Murphy took credit for obtaining a direct wire to WGY, Schenectady, one of the pioneer radio stations in the U.S. and owned until 1983 by General Electric. The wire enabled the bands to broadcast from the Rain-Bo Room on a national hookup. Bandleaders clamored to get booked into the place, and music publishers paid handsomely to get a song played on the air.

Business boomed, even with $1 cover, from 1922 to 1929. Then, in 1929, said Murphy, he reacted to complaints, removed the cover charge, and instituted what he claims to have been the first minimum check charge—$2.50—established in the U.S. He advertised "never a cover" and business boomed anew.

The parade of bands reads like a Who's Who of popular music— Kay Kyser, Tommy Dorsey with Frank Sinatra, Guy Lombardo, Vincent Lopez, Rudy Vallee, Ben Pollack with Benny Goodman as his clarinetist, Red Nichols and the Five Pennies, Ben Bernie and All the Lads, Duke Ellington, Cab Calloway, Fletcher Henderson, Sophie Tucker, Jack (and Charlie) Teagarden, Bix Beiderbecke before anybody knew him. Two bands stayed in residence for long periods: Phil Romano, who was the first to broadcast over the radio and remained six years, and Doc Peyton, who lasted from 1929 to 1932.

People came to dance at all hours, even for lunch. On a typical Saturday night, say around 1935, you couldn't get in without a reservation.

"Most people wore evening clothes," said Murphy. "I had four hundred in the Tavern, which had the longest bar in Albany [four hundred feet], and another five hundred in the Rain-Bo Room. I'd serve nine hundred lunches in the Rain-Bo Room and the band would play for luncheon, dinner, and supper." The latter was from ten p.m. to closing at three a.m. Filet mignon with mushroom caps cost $3.25 in about 1935.

While Murphy and I chatted, a few quiet drunks were talking at the bar, and a young couple danced to the only remaining music in the place, the jukebox. Murphy had just come up from fixing the boiler, which was being temperamental, and was eating a late supper behind the bar while we talked. He was full of memories of political days—of John Dunnigan, leader of the State Senate, and of Al Smith's son, young Al, who lived at the Kenmore when his father was governor.

"I made plenty of bands," Murphy said. "The Kenmore was their good-luck charm. Kay Kyser got his first break here. I gave him that thought about the professor of musical knowledge." He also said Ruth Lowe wrote the 1939 hit song "I'll Never Smile Again" at the Kenmore.

He reserved his fondest memory for Dan Prior, Albany's famous criminal lawyer: "He had the voice and face of a Caesar, and he was my buddy." Murphy said he acquired Bunny Berigan's trumpet after Berigan died, and he then gave it to Prior. Berigan was a heavy drinker, and I wonder now whether he didn't give Murphy his horn in payment for a bar bill he couldn't otherwise handle.

No answer on that one now. All gone: Berigan, Murphy, Prior; Broadway and the gamblers also gone; both Keelers gone. And at the end of the Rain-Bo there wasn't even a pot. Bob Murphy remembered that the federal government slapped a 20 percent excise tax on entertainment after World War II. The Big Band Era was fading; rising union scales sent music costs soaring. "People resented the tax," Murphy said. "Then money got short and television came in." Nobody came to the Kenmore, and in 1947 Albany's greatest nightclub closed its gate on history.

Down on Broadway, things went bad about the same time. Governor Dewey moved against gambling and cut the wire that brought horse-racing information into Broadway, putting horserooms out of business.

"Half a dozen guys were making handbook after the war," Pete McDonald remembered. "They had sheets on the table, or on the wall, but when they cut off the information it went bad. They had to scrounge around for the results. They were calling Troy and getting past-posted time and time again. Pretty soon they started paying off the next day, instead of after every race. Whatever the papers said, that's what you got paid."

It wasn't the same on Broadway anymore.

Keeler's Hotel was long gone by then, destroyed by fire in 1917. Keeler's Restaurant carried on into the 1950s, undaunted by change. In 1954 Orange County Assemblyman Wilson C. Van Duzer introduced a resolution into the State Assembly extolling Keeler's virtues. It passed unanimously. That same year Gaynor Keeler denied Keeler's was for sale. But the next year he sold it to Simon

Adler of New York City. Local Keeler's fanatics praised Adler in coming years for maintaining the high standards of his predecessors.

But the city itself was in decline now, and by the mid-1960s Downtown's commerce would be terminally ill. The theaters were shutting down, nobody rode the trains, Broadway was gone, North Pearl Street forlorn with vacated shops. Adler leased Keeler's to a catering company that put up a sign that was in egregious bad taste, aesthetically and historically. KEELER'S STEAK & GOBLET, said the sign, and the motto of the place was "All the draft beer you can drink and all the salad you can eat."

That was 1966. On November 17, 1969, a sign appeared on Keeler's door. CLOSED, it said.

Sports and swells everywhere cried in their beer.

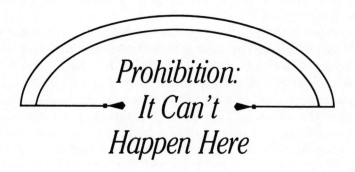

Prohibition:
It Can't
Happen Here

*T*here were eras when the city
was a single neighborhood, when community was not compart-
mentalized by ethnic lines or gullies or bridges or railroad tracks,
and the 1920s was such an age. It was Prohibition, when beer
was where you found it, booze was expensive and sometimes
deadly, and the bootlegger was a social outlaw and universal hero.
Neighborhoods had their own speakeasies, to be sure, but men
from Arbor Hill came up to the North End to slake their thirst,
everybody went to O'Connor's on Beaver Street, and you hung
out in Ames O'Brien's Parody Club on Hudson Avenue so you
could bump into Jack (Legs) Diamond at the bar (or you didn't
hang out there because you might).

Prohibition in Albany was a contradiction in terms. Very little
was ever prohibited in this city, which has always had a mind
to do what it wanted to do and never mind the civil law, or the
moral law, either. Albany was always a place where you could
restore your spirit or smudge your soul. One notes as far back as
1760, when certain Albanians thought the theater was a scandal
and a shame, that a troupe of performers came here to give the
city a month of Thomas Otway's play *Venice Preserved*, which
concerned English military officers. The Dominie of Albany's
Dutch Church, a man named Theodorus Freylinghausen,

found the play and players to be the embodiment of evil and said so in a sermon. He woke up to find menace on his doorstep—a crust of bread, a piece of money, and a pair of old shoes, all shaped in the design of a club. The Dominie took the hint and also took the next boat back to the Netherlands. For the show, as we all know, must go on.

The show in the 1920s was wetness—home brew, bathtub gin, bootlegged whiskey. The stage was the speakeasy, the place where you achieved wetness. It was all illegal, for the Volstead Act, which took effect in 1920, prohibited intoxicating beverages— anything more than one half of one percent alcohol—which is less than the alcoholic content of sauerkraut. A plate of sauer- kraut could get you higher than a barrel of near beer could— which was all that the breweries were permitted to make until 1933, when real beer came back and the Volstead Act was re- pealed. In Albany it was the Dobler Brewing Company that made near beer, and in North Troy it was Quant's brewery. The late Bob Murphy, proprietor of the Kenmore Hotel, handled near beer for his guests and told me in conversation, "People used to drink a whole lot of that stuff and think they were getting drunk."

Drinking exploded ridiculously in the 1920s when people were told they couldn't drink. People who didn't drink at all, drank a little bit. In Albany the drinking was the same old show. As early as 1653, a century before Dominie Freylinghausen, the Dutch settlers were already noted for their antiabstemiousness. A Dutch poet named Nicasius deSille wrote in that year: "They all drink here, from the moment they are able to lick a spoon."

The pattern carried forward into the day when the Irish re- placed the Dutch as the controlling power in this town. And an old Irish uncle of mine, perpetuating the stereotype, told me rather proudly one day, "The last time I refused a drink I didn't understand the question."

The lore of drinking in the Prohibition Era is well known to us from films, from novels, from television—Jimmy Cagney making bathtub gin, Humphrey Bogart hijacking booze on the highway, running a boatload of whiskey in from Rum Row—that notable line of ships that stood just outside the three-mile limit, waiting for couriers to carry their illicit cargo to parched Amer- ican customers. The gangster as the assuager of thirst was an important man to American society in the 1920s, and Albany knew him well. So did Troy, Fort Edward, Saratoga, Catskill, Kingston, and so on. Dutch Schultz, Waxey Gordon, Vincent

Coll, Fats McCarthy, Lucky Luciano, and numerous lesser-known hoodlums—they all played roles on our local stage. Legs Diamond's noted contribution to the local scene is documented elsewhere in this book, as is the manner in which Albany remained a local protectorate in this age, forbidding gangsters to gain a foothold in the city. But there is an overlapping story about Dutch Schultz, told to me by Dan O'Connell in 1974, which is relevant here because Schultz is relevant.

Dan said Jimmy Hines, the Tammany Hall leader, called him one day in the early 1930s to ask a favor. "Good fella, Jimmy was," said Dan. "Called me up and asked me could Dutch Schultz come up and stay awhile in Albany. But I didn't want him around town and I said no. Jimmy understood."

Hines did four years in jail for his hoodlum connections not long after this. Charlie Ryan, Dan's associate, confirmed the Hines-Schultz story for me and said Schultz was already on the way to Albany when Hines called Dan. Dan then sent Tony Dean, one of the more truculent detectives on the Albany police force, to meet Schultz's train at Union Station. And Schultz did not get off the train, or so goes the story.

Schultz was a major figure in beer distribution in New York City, Yonkers, New Jersey, and also in Troy, and had ties to the north country. There was a well-known brewery in Troy that closed down when Prohibition began, but didn't close all the way. It produced both beer and alcohol, the latter at a still of considerable proportions. Schultz, I was told by a man who as a youth had worked with an owner of the brewery, was involved in Troy and also involved in another brewery in Fort Edward, which was a major supply house in the dry age. Schultz distinguished himself locally by murdering one of his associates, Jules Martin, putting a pistol in Martin's mouth and pulling the trigger after Martin admitted stealing between $20,000 and $70,000 from him.

The murder was done in 1935 at the Harmony Hotel in Cohoes. Martin's body, full of ice-pick stabbings and stuffed into a trunk, was dumped near Oakwood Cemetery in Troy.

Beer came to Albany from New Jersey and Pennsylvania, the main supply sources. It came in on freight cars and trucks, in half barrels, and was unloaded not in the city but in an outlying town to the south where there were fewer citizens to rubberneck at what was going on. It was unloaded, then reloaded onto local trucks and shepherded into the city in a convoy for redistribution to speakeasies.

The New Jersey supplier, at least for part of the era, was Waxey Gordon, who became Public Enemy Number One. An underworld figure and another source within the Albany Machine both confirmed this to my satisfaction, though they prefer not to be quoted.

Naming names becomes tricky, for there are descendants of bootleggers who live straight lives and do not want their reputations besmirched by their rum-running ancestors; and there are also some ancestors still alive capable of stern reprisal for besmirchment.

But the facts herein are handed on with confidence, if occasionally with anonymity. I believe them up to the point I believe any stories filtered through sixty years of talk.

But to return to that convoy that was approaching the city a minute ago—one beer truck and two cars in front of it, two cars behind it (they never sent two trucks anywhere at the same time). I was a young police reporter when I first heard a story about that. A veteran Albany detective was reminiscing that he was on duty one night in the 1920s when a call came in that a truck loaded with beer had gotten a flat tire that couldn't be fixed. And so the police dispatched a repair crew with new tires and a wheel and got the truck back on the road.

This is known as civic cooperation.

Without civic cooperation, Albany would have had the gang wars common to other cities and would not have been the relatively peaceful city it was throughout Prohibition. This was the consequence of the control of the alcohol traffic by the Albany political powers; for if Dan O'Connell kept the gangsters out of Albany, then who ran the beer and booze that kept Albany's thirst abated for thirteen years? One need not strain for the answer. Men who gave allegiance to the O'Connells all their lives were the kingpins. Even Dan himself owned a truck garage at South Pearl Street and Fourth Avenue during Prohibition.

But the relatively peaceable kingdom did have its moments of violence. Assassins tried to kill Mush Trackner, a notable trafficker in beer, in a struggle for control. The Oley brothers were linked to Legs Diamond in the beer traffic at one point, but allegiances were brief and Diamond fell out with that crowd. John Oley was one of the men who took Joey Green for a ride to Loudonville, shot him full of holes, and left him for dead, as a consequence of Green's hijacking a load of booze en route to Albany. Green didn't die and Oley and others were arrested but not prosecuted. Green, whom a friend remembered as a likable young hoodlum, recovered from his wounds and lived two more years before being shot dead in a roadhouse near Saratoga.

Also, a Madison Avenue speakeasy owner shot a federal dry agent after the agent tried to shake him down twice in two weeks. The agent died and the owner went to Italy forever.

The role of the federal agents in Prohibition was absurd and implausible. Walter Winchell reported that one agent scrimped and saved and put away $180,000 in one year. Even the less shrewd agents pocketed $1,000 a week for looking the other way and not enforcing what was really an unenforceable law. In Manhattan the federals couldn't get near Owney Madden's gigantic brewery, which produced 300,000 gallons of beer daily, for it was too closely guarded by New York City police.

There were 1,700 dry officers employed by the federal government in 1924, an insufficient number. In 1925 the government added 200 more, and that did the trick, or so said a man named Robert A. Corradini, the research secretary of the World League Against Alcoholism. Corradini counted only 463 speakeasies in New York City, only 15 on all of Broadway from the Battery to Yonkers. Apart from the decline in drinking, there was also less profanity, Corradini said, since people tended not to curse and swear outside saloons.

The actual speakeasy count was rather higher. By 1929, said the New York police commissioner, there were 32,000 in the city, or twice as many as the saloon and blind-pig count before Prohibition.

All you needed to create a speakeasy was two bottles and a room, and Albany had hundreds. The largest was O'Connor's, on the south side of Beaver Street near the old Odd Fellows Hall. It had one of the biggest and most elaborate bars in town (that bar eventually ended up in Smith's Restaurant in Cohoes). It was strictly a speakeasy and it was always crowded, so recalls an old South End man who was a frequent customer. The O'Connor brothers opened an all-new restaurant on the opposite side of Beaver Street after Repeal, and later moved the business to State Street above Pearl and made it one of the city's best restaurants.

The other major speakeasy was the Parody Club, run by Ames O'Brien, on Hudson Avenue below South Pearl, next to the firehouse. There was a nightclub upstairs and some people remember the night Jack Diamond turned up as a customer and insisted on hearing Pat Panza sing a song. Pat Panza, who in the 1950s operated the 21 Club on Elk Street, was running his own place at the time, the Cretonne Club, at 22 Norton Street, but that didn't matter. He was sent for and he came and he sang what Diamond wanted to hear that night: "You Made Me Love You." The speakeasy was a money machine. One man told me he went into Tom McCaffery's place on Maiden Lane: "I asked McCaffery to give me two tens for a five. And he did."

Jack McEneny, Albany's human resources commissioner, in his history of the city, records some of the speakeasies and their proprietors, and I quote from his list: Big Charlie's, at Green and Division streets; Swift Mead's and Brockley's, both on Broadway near the railroad station; Gallogly's, in Sheridan Hollow; Mullen's and O'Malley's, at Northern Boulevard and First Street; Eddie Cahill's, at 4 New Scotland Avenue; George Linter's, at Sherman and Quail streets; Pauly's (still in business), on Central Avenue; King Brady's, at North Street and Broadway in North Albany—which McEneny suggests was a "particularly wet neighborhood." As a former North Ender, I don't know whether to take this as a slur on the place or as a badge of social courage in resisting a fatuous law with superior numbers.

McEneny mentions Tom Prime's and Hugh Diamond's and Jack Jennings's as well as King Brady's in the North End, but that was only the tip of the iceberg. One he left out was Blue Heaven, which was built long before Prohibition and run as a Lumber District saloon by my great-grandfather, an eccentric man everybody called Big Jim Carroll. Big Jim had the reputation of throwing boiled potatoes at your head if you disagreed with him during dinner. The saloon he ran became a speakeasy during Prohibition—Big Jim was long dead—and I talked to a banker who remembered going there as a young man. It had a potbelly stove, said the banker, and only the back end of the place was used, with room for only about ten people. Whoever made the home brew (the only drink sold in the place) was not much of a home brewer. It had in it what the banker called "the mother"—that cloudy element common in cider.

Home brew did not have such a mother when it was made by serious homebrewmasters. I talked to one man who ran a speakeasy in his garage for ten years. His system was to make only three or four half-barrels at a time, boil it, ferment it four or five days, let it stand two weeks "to have it decent," and then sell it at five cents a glass. It was clear, like the beer of today. Or so goes his story.

This now-elderly entrepreneur recalled that most speakeasies in the city sold only beer. Whiskey, he said, was more difficult to get away with. Even in the best of the speakeasies the choice of whiskeys was not abundant, for proprietors worked on the principle that if they were raided they would lose their stock to the dry agents; and it was more important to have stock than to have an abundant back bar as a showcase.

The dry agents, when they did raid a speakeasy—and in Albany it was usually because of complaints of excessive drunkenness or violence—had to have a warrant. If you were convicted three times of violating the law, you did a year and a day in the Atlanta Penitentiary (so said my informant, who was raided once but not prosecuted—his manager took the fall).

The speakeasies ran wide-open in some places, usually with a doorman to keep out undesirables. Speakeasy cards, common in big cities as a form of membership, were not used here, or at least were not in common use. Some places had steel doors as a precaution (Pauly's still has one), and when the raiders did enter they spilled out the booze, or confiscated it, and knocked the bungs out of the beer barrels. One woman proprietor, whose dress had been wet by the abundant spillage, pulled the light cord in her basement and was electrocuted, illuminating for us all the wages of wetness.

Jack McEneny reports in his book that several barrels of whiskey confiscated in a saloon on Judson Street were sent to the Fifth Precinct, on Central Avenue, where a miracle took place. "Overnight," he writes, "inside the police station every barrel's contents had turned to water."

That story, as I heard it, began when a pair of well-known federal dry agents turned up a store of booze in an uptown bowling alley, fifteen or twenty fifty-gallon barrels of liquor. The agents then turned this over to police in the Fifth Precinct. Well-connected entrepreneurs who knew what might profitably be done with such a haul convinced the precinct captain to leave the station house unguarded for a time, went in with a team, and rescued the booze from useless captivity. The two federal agents were also in on the steal, said my source.

Booze came to Albany from Canada, or up from New York City. One ex–booze hauler, later a taxi driver, recalled that he drove regularly to Albany from Chestertown, in Warren County, the site of a garage where cars and trucks were switched and serviced in Pony Express tradition. The run to Albany sometimes terminated in the Albany Garage on Lodge and Howard streets, Downtown—a more central location hard to imagine.

The value of these shipments was enormous, and so hijacking was most common, and practiced with great success by Jack Diamond. When FDR's state troopers confiscated his property and traced all his holdings in mid-1931, they found booze, wine, champagne, and cordials that had a total street value of $10 million. Most of this, said a man who knew Diamond, had been hijacked.

Bathtub gin was a commonplace and one source remembered a local man who had the exclusive contract on Gordon's gin—importing it from Canada and selling it to the Albany gentry in abundance. But it was merely bathtub gin—made in a Cohoes bedroom, actually—with the Gordon label added. His scheme collapsed when one of his wealthy customers found a label inside a bottle.

My banker acquaintance recalled that as a child he would be sent to a bootlegger at the corner of Northern Boulevard and Elk Street to buy a pint of gin for seventy-five cents. "You poured it on the curbstone and lit it," he said, "and if it turned blue you drank it. If it turned yellow you threw it away or took the risk of going blind." He doesn't recall anybody throwing away any gin.

I looked through a bound volume of the old *Knickerbocker Press* for a week in April 1925 as a way of focusing in on some particulars of the local and national scene that would give a feeling of the age apart from all this received mythology. It wasn't really *all that wacko*, was it? Well, judge for yourself.

Timothy J. Quillinan, the district attorney of Rensselaer County, made a speech to social welfare workers at the Troy YMCA and told them the "automobile was the greatest asset for the commission of crime which has ever been brought forth by civilization. . . . You will find," he added, "that in practically every criminal case the automobile has been used in some way." He also suggested that the "jazzmanian" problems of the day (a coinage I'd never come across before) could be solved only in the home.

At Proctor's (later the Grand Theater) Norma Shearer and John Gilbert were starring in *The Snob*, a story of a jazz cabaret, a moonlight ride, a shooting in a gay roadhouse. The Leland Theater was playing *Isn't Life Wonderful*, a D. W. Griffith film said to be "a simple romance of love and potatoes." The Capitol Theater was presenting burlesque that was "clean, swift, smart, jolly, mammoth, merry, musical, and girly."

Calvin Coolidge broke a world record by shaking 1,040 hands in sixteen minutes, or one a second, and tourist agencies were advertising the presidential handshake as a Washington attraction. The ocean liner *Mauretania* of the Cunard Line hit a small boat in the Ambrose Channel off New York and sank it, but rescued three men and several cases of whiskey. The sailors on the Navy dirigible *Los Angeles*, before landing at Lakehurst, New Jersey, hovered over Rum Row on the way into port and dropped a number of cases of whiskey to the ships waiting below.

A judge named Charlie W. Boote in Yonkers had before him a man who had beaten his wife the previous month. Charlie had put the man on probation and here he came again for beating his mother. Charlie let him go free this time because "I don't want my probation officers associating with the likes of you."

A German archaeologist said he had found the lost continent of Atlantis and it was in Spain. The writer Hilaire Belloc was arguing that there was too much teaching of literature and what was needed was more instruction in the mechanical arts. And Rear Admiral Bradley Fiske (Retired) said women were the chief cause of war. Women were working for peace societies and trying to raise the standard of living, and this, said the admiral, obstructed military preparedness. "The best way to prevent war," he said, "is not to keep raising the standard of living but to lower it."

Also, intoxication was said by State Motor Vehicle Commissioner Charles A. Harnett to be the chief cause of people's losing their driver's licenses. There had been 226 such losses in New York City, and second to that—ahead of Buffalo, Rochester, and Syracuse, the state's next-biggest cities—was Albany, with 58. Little old wide-open Albany.

The night beer came back in April 1933 Albanians went out hunting for some. Brewery spokesmen told the *Knickerbocker Press* (which was then refusing to accept beer ads) there would be no legal beer until May 10. Little hilarity was noted in the city, two people were arrested for being drunk, and a diehard Anti-Saloon League preacher in Schoharie said people were deluded if they thought the fight against John Barleycorn was dead. "The war against alcoholic beverages will go on and will be won," he said.

Dan O'Connell didn't believe him. He opened up Hedrick's

Brewery almost immediately, having perceived quite close up the city's fondness for Waxey Gordon's product, and before long was selling his own brew in amazing abundance. He undersold his competitors—"two dollars less a half barrel, and a good glass of beer," said one informed citizen. And by the end of the 1930s, as Governor Thomas E. Dewey would note in his campaign to break the O'Connell Machine, Hedrick's was sold on draft in 200 of the city's 259 barrooms. Proprietors stacked it up in the cellar rather than offend Dan, and by way of reciprocation, Dan's authorities looked the other way when these proprietors extended their drinking hours beyond legal limits.

Prohibition was notable for the moral havoc it wreaked in America: creating a new race of drinkers, advancing women and children into a new libertinism, establishing the exchequer that would finance organized crime on into the drug age, making mythic figures out of hoodlums who slaked the public thirst. Why do people relish the memory that they were putting mustard on their hot dog when Legs Diamond walked into the roadside diner? Why did Albany Mayor William S. Hackett, in 1924, close two hundred soft-drink saloons on the ground they were surreptitiously violating dry laws, while Albany speakeasies were egregiously violating the same laws with the consent of the police? Morality, this suggests, was selective and pragmatic in Albany, and, in ways wondrous to behold, this allowed the political power to be held, and held, and held.

Bugs Baer, the witty columnist for the Hearst papers, was fond of celebrating New York City as the greatest of towns. "After you leave New York," he said, "everyplace else is Bridgeport."

Obviously, Bugs Baer overlooked Albany, a hot town, a crazy town, a town with a smudged soul, to be sure, but a town with a soul to besmudge.

The Death of Legs Diamond

*J*ack (Legs) Diamond, the most visible, most maligned, and most glamorous criminal in the East throughout the latter years of Prohibition, was Albany's preeminent underworld celebrity. He came here early on as a rumrunner, bringing spirits down from Canada. As a hijacker, he preyed upon truckers on upstate highways, one of the pioneers in this field; and he relaxed and played in Albany, most particularly, as has been noted elsewhere in this book, in the Kenmore Hotel, which is inseparable from his legend.

He was a complex figure, and the world's response to him was equally complex. I gave several years of my life to exploring all that when I was writing a novel about his life and times, a novel that is historical in outline. I set out to write a meticulously documented piece of fiction, for most of the gangster books I'd ever read were cavalier about facts. But as I went along I understood one reason that was so. Almost every book that carries information about Jack Diamond is contradicted somewhere by another book, or they are both contradicted by accounts in the newspapers, which in turn contradict one another, even on such matters as his age and his name.

As to the spoken word, he spawned any number of liars of notable substance. I talked to one bar owner who said Jack Diamond was a nice fellow and when he came in regularly to drink you'd never know he was a gangster. I asked when this was and the owner said he opened for business in 1935, which was four years after Jack died.

What I came to eventually was a plan to assimilate all the truth, all the lies, all the fudged areas in between, and reinvent Jack (after three years we were on a first-name basis) as a brand-new fictional character; and so while the novel's historical outline is accurate as to fact, the daily specifics of Jack, his wife, Alice, his girl friend, Marion (Kiki) Roberts, and his gangland cronies and enemies are products of one man's imagination.

My wife had a dream, just about the time that *Legs* was published, and in it she met Jack as he was rolling on our front lawn, kicking his legs in the air in obvious excitement. He said he'd just read my book, and he added, "Bill got it just right." The dream was contradicted later by a story someone told me about Kiki Roberts: that she was in a rest home out West, someone brought a copy of my novel to her, she read a little of it and said it wasn't factually correct. But of course it wasn't. It was a novel. Kiki also told that person that Jack was meaner than most people realized, that he didn't mind torturing and shooting people, which was hardly news to me. His cruelty pervades my book. A local hoodlum who ran with Jack in his last years told me he and Jack stopped at a roadside restaurant, where the owner's dog was bothering them. Jack took serious affront and offered a suggestion to his companion: "You bang the dog and I'll bang the owner." My friend the hoodlum talked Jack out of this; they kept their pistols cool and went elsewhere to eat.

This is a true story and so are all the other facts in these pages. Nothing is fictional. What is here is based on press reports and on interviews with people who were close to the events. Some details of Jack's death are reported here for the first time, I do believe.

His momentous period in Albany was the latter half of 1931. Earlier that year at Catskill he had kidnapped and tortured a trucker named Grover Parks, who was hauling twenty-six barrels of hard cider and wouldn't say where he was taking them. Jack assumed they were bound for an applejack still, and the still wasn't his, and he thought it should be.

When the kidnapping became known, Jack suddenly felt the full weight of the state government on his body and soul. Franklin Roosevelt became the first governor in the land to use his power against a gangland figure. He moved the state police and the attorney general and his staff into the Catskills, destroyed the booze, beer, and racketeering empire Jack had been building for two years, and scattered his gang.

Jack was jailed, bailed, then almost killed in the fourth known assassination try against him, this one at the Aratoga Inn, near Cairo, in Greene County. He was hit by two shotgun blasts but didn't die, and recovered in Albany Hospital. In time he came to Albany to stay and flopped in at the Kenmore to await trial in Rensselaer County Court, in Troy. His lawyer, Daniel H. Prior, a former Albany City Court judge and the most famous criminal lawyer of his time in this area, had won a change of venue from Catskill to Troy; and so Jack became an impious presence in the city.

His legal maneuverings and social doings were in the Albany papers every day, and we were also frequently aswarm with out-of-town newsmen, particularly the New York tabloid crowd, which claimed Jack as its own and regularly gave him pages of space in order to deplore his depredations. A serious effort at deploring Jack was as good for circulation as a kinky Hollywood sex murder.

Jack was known everywhere and involved in just about every-thing illegal in Prohibition, a notable local tie being his interest in the biggest still in upstate New York—it was on the Mechan-icville-Stillwater road. A man who made his living as a card thief—a genius at that, really—told me the still was the biggest thing he'd ever seen, bigger than a rum-manufacturing plant he'd visited in Cuba. "It had three huge vats and pissed a barrel of alcohol an hour," said the card man.

Diamond's connection to it during its rather long life was ap-parently crucial, for after he was killed the still was raided by federal agents and destroyed. During his late years Diamond had a charmed life, insofar as federal crime went. He had been arrested in connection with a dope-smuggling ring (the stuff was hidden inside bowling pins) but never prosecuted, and gangland histo-rians ascribe this to his close ties to Arnold Rothstein, the finan-cier of the 1920s underworld, who had influence at high levels in Washington.

Before his empire toppled, Jack had been making beer (with a Canadian label) at a Kingston, New York, brewery. "It was lousy," said an Albany speakeasy operator whose taste for beer sounds as though it may have been impeccable. When Jack came to Albany and took a good look around, he decided he would go into business here, a decision that may have contributed to his sudden demise at the age of thirty-four.

The men who killed him were never identified, though they were heard, probably seen, their car definitely seen, the pistols they used found in the neighborhood. The instant assumption was, and has continued to be, that it was a gangland killing; and Dutch Schultz, well known as a Diamond enemy (though they had a reconciliation, or at least a summit conference, in Jack's Kenmore suite in the summer of 1931), was said to be the man who ordered it. Lucky Luciano was also assigned a role, for the burgeoning young Mafia was in these months methodically ridding its target territories of competition: murdering the old Mustache Petes of the Black Hand, wiping out the Irish and Jewish gangleaders, then moving into the vacuum. Schultz and Luciano had tenuous ties but they didn't trust each other, and who can blame them?

Salvatore Spitale, a former Diamond gang member who was responsible for Jack's presence in the town of Acra in the Catskills, and who in a later moment won small fame as an underworld emissary in the Lindbergh kidnap case, was long considered a part of the murder conspiracy. So was Dutch Schultz's number-one gun, Bo Weinberg, who was said to have bragged that he and a fellow killer held Jack by the ears when they shot him.

Fats McCarthy (real name Edward Popke), one of Jack's late-blooming allies (along with Vincent Coll, a psychopathic Irishman), was a principal suspect in the killing, for he was living near Albany and had friendly access to Jack. McCarthy and Coll were in this area, on the run from New York City police who wanted them for several killings. A man who ran with both their gangs at different times said, "They were just thieves," a pejorative comparison to Jack, whom he viewed as an underworld whizbang.

This man, who lived to a respectable old age, said Coll and McCarthy, when working for Dutch Schultz, had been assigned to kill Diamond and tracked him around Manhattan from one speakeasy and nightclub to another. They found him so well liked, so congenial, so unlike Schultz, that they joined with Diamond and became Schultz's most feared enemies in the gang war that ensued.

The confusion over who killed Diamond was compounded in later years when Spitale, convicted on another charge, had his jail term increased by a judge because of a probation report that said he had been involved in the Diamond killing. And then, about 1939, New York City Police Commissioner Lewis Valentine said Jack was killed by Fats McCarthy, who himself had been shot to death by state police in Albany's Pine Bush early in 1932, a few months after Diamond died.

My source, who was in McCarthy's gang, and who missed being at the shoot-out with state police only because he was visiting a girl friend, told me McCarthy was absolutely not involved in Jack's killing and was surprised when he heard about it. Naturally, you couldn't believe my source, but I tend to.

Finally, late in 1981, six years after I published my novel about Diamond, I received a call from a man who said he knew all about the killing of Diamond and who had done it, and so I went to see him. He told me that *he* had done it—that when he was four years old he was playing with somebody's gun in a speakeasy-brothel, pointed it at Diamond, and shot him through his undershirt. The grown-ups with him scrambled madly to get away, and when they heard the police were looking for the family car they hid it in an empty lot and left it there forever. The man said he shot Diamond in the chest. I pointed out that the autopsy proved Diamond had been shot three times in the head and not at all in the chest. "Well, maybe it wasn't him," said the man, reluctantly, "but I shot somebody."

A persistent rumor in Albany about Diamond's killing was that a death squad from the Albany Police Department did him in. I always thought that unlikely—why would Albany bother? But then again, Jack's acquittal in Troy meant he had beaten the state's best case against him. He did have a federal conviction for beer possession hanging over him (a four-year sentence), but he also had that noted charm when it came to fixing federal charges. And then there was his avowed intention of going into business in Albany.

This was confirmed by former *Knickerbocker News* managing editor Robert G. Fichenberg in a talk with Dan O'Connell in January 1967. The talk came during Dan's reclusive period. He was not yet the media celebrity he would become a few years later. Fichenberg kept the talk all off the record until Dan died in 1977, and then he quoted Dan as saying this:

"You hear about the Mafia and the rackets moving into other cities, but you won't hear about it in Albany. You know why? We kept them out from the start. You've got to have a good police department and we have one. In order for the Mafia to move in, they have to have protection, and they know they'll never get it in this town. We settled that years ago. Legs Diamond . . . called up one day and said he wanted to go into the 'insurance' business here. We knew what he had in mind. He was going to sell strong-arm 'protection' to the merchants. I sent word to him that he wasn't going to do any business in Albany and we didn't expect to see him in town the next morning. He never started anything here."

The insurance business was only one of Jack's proposed ventures. Beer was the other. He was adept at both pursuits and may have been considering pairing them. The Catskills had become no-man's-land for him. A new mob (Joe Rock's) had moved in down there and Jack's gang members were either in jail or in hiding. What Albany offered was the comfort of familiarity, and the attitudes and opportunities that go with a wide-open city.

But having Diamond as a frequent visitor would not have been the same as having him as a permanent addition to the citizenry, and so for any number of easily imagined reasons, competition in beer among them, he wasn't wanted. In 1974 I talked with Dan O'Connell about Jack (Dan called him Legs) and he was unusually candid. He spoke of three men: Dan Prior, who was Jack's friend as well as his lawyer; Dave Smurl, Albany's chief of police in 1931; and William J. Fitzpatrick, a cop who would become head of Albany's night squad of detectives, and who would eventually replace Smurl as chief.

About Legs, Dan said, "Prior brought him around here . . . but he brought him around once too often. Fitzpatrick finished Legs. Dave Smurl was afraid of Prior. He [Smurl] went on the force too old. But Fitzpatrick wasn't afraid."

Dan mentioned Diamond's being "over in Troy on some business," which I took as a reference to the Diamond trial, and he added that Fitzpatrick and Diamond were "sitting in the same room and [Fitzpatrick] followed him out. Fitzpatrick told him he'd kill him if he didn't keep going."

Another man, very close to the bootlegging power in the 1920s in Albany, told me a parallel story, with some different specifics. I apologize for being unable to name this person. Let him be Mr. B. (for bootleg).

"Diamond was mixed up with the Oleys," Mr. B. told me, meaning John and Francis Oley, the two Albany criminals who would later be involved in kidnapping Dan O'Connell's nephew, "and they were going to try to take over. The Oleys were peddling some beer and it looked like Legs was going in with them. And he could get more beer for them."

When Mr. B. says "take over" I do believe he means from himself and his associates, who were not the only people running beer into the city but certainly among the most significant. During this time Jack Diamond sent out word he wanted to meet with Mr. B., but in the interest of health Mr. B. declined.

Diamond, in a later month of his life, was arrested on a minor charge in a rooming house on State Street, but nothing came of the arrest. The point, said Mr. B., was that "the authorities"—his euphemism for Dan—"didn't want him in Albany." He was put out of the rooming house by police and told not to come back. "Then," Mr. B. added, "when Prior beat the case [in Troy], Diamond came back to Albany, to a rooming house on Dove Street."

The rooming house was at 67 Dove and Mrs. Laura Woods was the landlady. Jack had been there about a week with his wife, Alice, and his dead brother's wife, and his brother's young son, Johnny, all of whom had been part of Jack's humanizing entourage during the Troy trial. The rooms were ten dollars a week and Jack took them under the name of Kelly.

He went to a celebration party at Freddie Young's speakeasy across from Union Station following his acquittal, a large festive gathering. He left it all to go to an apartment at 21 Ten Broeck Street where he was keeping Kiki Roberts. He was drunk and with her he became drunker. Did he stay with Kiki three hours, or did he stay only fifteen minutes, as she later insisted? You take your choice. He left Ten Broeck Street in his hired taxi, John Storer driving the cab, and rode to 67 Dove. There are more points of view on all this, and more people to take into account, but none of it matters here. While the party raged at the speakeasy, Jack, euphorically, drunkenly acquitted, fell into bed, alone, and in his underwear.

At five-thirty in the morning of December 18, 1931, Mrs. Woods heard two visitors arrive, heard them talking. Mr. B. remembered that the landlady heard Jack pleading for his life. She also heard one visitor reject mercy and tell Jack, "Others pleaded with *you*." Then, as is historically known, she heard several shots, of which three went into Jack's head, the rest into the walls. The assassins moved to the doorway, paused to reconsider. One of them said, according to Mrs. Woods, "We waited too long to miss on this," and the other said, "Oh hell, that was enough." And then they went out and rode off into anonymous eternity in a red Packard.

I was sitting in the Kenmore bar in the early 1960s, interviewing Bob Murphy, the owner. He was talking about December 1931 and how he had testified at Jack's trial, giving evidence Jack was really in Albany having dinner, hobnobbing, being socially benign, when Grover Parks was being viciously tortured by someone like Jack in Jack's garage behind Jack's house in Acra. Perhaps Murphy's testimony helped Jack go free, or perhaps it was Dan Prior's superior powers of persuasion in court, or perhaps it was the threats that circulated among the jurors. Whatever it was, Jack was freed and Murphy was remembering the day fondly.

Ray O'Connor, retired night city editor of the *Times-Union*, was sitting beside me at the bar, muttering and interjecting his view into the discussion, and reasonably so; for he had a major claim on any conversation about Jack, whose doings in the Catskills he'd covered for months in 1931; and also he'd had a very privileged, close-up look at Jack Diamond dead.

Ray ran the night desk when I came to work on cityside for the first time, and he taught me how you covered the police beat by telephone. He cared about little else. He was a sad and lonely man, a generous and likable grump with almost no teeth and a bad foot, or maybe two, and he believed in the full moon: that it drew the crazies out of their lairs and drove them to phone up the *Times-Union* city desk and ask irrational questions.

At the Kenmore bar, Ray kept repeating the phrase "I got out before the bulls came in and I saw him dead." He said it six or seven times in a matter of minutes, unwilling to let Bob Murphy's tales of trial testimony distract from the main event, which for Ray was Jack's corpse.

Ray and Joe O'Heaney were both police reporters for the *Times-Union*, and both were tipped by someone to the fact that Jack was dead, both went to the Dove Street rooming house and glimpsed the body before it became official, before the bulls, as he put it, turned up. There is much more to this also, as you might expect, but none of it matters here. What matters, if it matters, is how Ray and Joe were told of the killing. Anybody in Albany might have told them, but it was the historical custom of the police to rouse Joe, who lived next door to police headquarters, when something of import was happening. Did some Albany detective alert Ray and Joe to Jack's passing?

Ray wasn't saying.

"He still won't tell who," said Murphy, nodding his head at Ray.

Sitting next to Ray was an obstreperous drunk who kept interrupting me as I tried to cajole Ray into revealing whatever it was he wanted to reveal.

"Tell him nothin'," the drunk advised Ray, over and over. "A guy like you with the information you got, it's worth twenty-five thousand. Where I come from they tell 'em nothin'. If I was you I'd tell him nothin'."

"I got out before the bulls came in and I saw him dead," Ray explained.

All the years I knew Ray, he never told me what he knew. The implication was always there that the police had something to do with it. I asked John Maguire, who was new to the paper as a reporter when I was new, if Ray ever talked about it. John remembered that whenever Ray was talking about Diamond and John moved into range, Ray stopped talking. Ray had a conspiratorial mind. He trusted few people in life. He once accused me of being a Republican.

Ray O'Connor is dead and Joe O'Heaney is dead, and so I will never know with any certainty what they said about Jack's death. (But in 1974 Leo O'Brien told me it was the police who tipped Joe that Jack was dead.) William J. Fitzpatrick is also dead, shot through the head in 1945 by Albany Detective Jack McElveney, his pal, while he was sitting in his office at police headquarters, seven or eight blocks down the street from where Jack Diamond took it, also in the head. There was even a Jack Diamond connection to Fitzpatrick's death. Bob Parr, widely known as a friend of Jack's, was in the chief's office, visiting, and was the lone witness to the killing. Parr may have been talking to the chief about the revocation of the liquor license of his bar, the Klub Eagle, up the street from headquarters. The license had been lifted for sales to drunks, and sales off premises and after hours.

Albany County District Attorney Julian B. Erway told the press that a month before the killing, Fitzpatrick and McElveney had gotten into a playful scuffle that turned serious. (An Albany gambler told me Fitzpatrick was planning to raid a Chapel Street crap game but his raiders found no game. Fitzpatrick blamed McElveney for tipping the proprietor that the raid was coming, and swore he'd break him. The two policemen then fought.) McElveney was punched in the mouth and his jaw was damaged.

Another report said he had to have teeth extracted and that during the extraction a jawbone splintered. Dental surgery then became necessary, all this at a very high financial cost. McElveney went on sick leave.

Erway said McElveney wanted Fitzpatrick to pay the dental bills but he refused and denied he had caused the injury. Fitzpatrick had the reputation of being a practical joker. One reporter of that age recalled that Fitzpatrick (before he became chief) playfully locked a young reporter inside Fitzgerald's saloon to keep him from meeting his sisters, who were arriving from out of town. Fitzpatrick urged the reporter to drink—just one more, one more—and the reporter, who did not know how to get out of this situation, kept drinking. Fitzpatrick eventually had two burly policemen hand-carry the reporter, very swozzled, to meet his sisters.

Fitzpatrick, apart from jokes, was a very tough cop, exactly the kind Dan O'Connell valued. "Dan organized the night squad [of detectives]," Leo O'Brien told me, "and thought he did everything they did." Fitzpatrick went on the force at the age of twenty-seven in 1925, became a sergeant in 1928, a lieutenant in 1932—less than two months after the death of Jack Diamond—and was named assistant chief and head of the night squad in 1934. He became chief in April 1940, after the death of David Smurl. He was widely known and well liked by other policemen, who called him Fitz, or sometimes Doc—titles he preferred to Chief. "Doc" came from his frequent remark to people who brought problems to him: "I'm the doctor. Why didn't you come to me sooner?"

At 3:00 p.m. on January 5, 1945, the Doc's best pal, his drinking buddy, his confidant for special assignments, Detective John W. McElveney, forty-eight, walked into Fitzpatrick's office with his problem, and angry words ensued. Among other things, McElveney talked about his broken jaw. Then at 3:10 he took his .38 out of his pocket and, according to Erway, told Fitzpatrick, who was sitting at his desk, "I'll break your jaw." He meant to shoot Fitzpatrick in the jaw, he is said to have confessed to police, but he missed and shot the chief through the head. He then walked to the front desk and handed his gun to a policeman, saying only, "Here." *Knickerbocker News* reporter Freddie Martin was by the desk and he heard McElveney say, "I did it." Another report said McElveney added, "He ruined my life."

Charlie Ryan, one of Dan O'Connell's closest associates for four and a half decades, said Fitzpatrick had called McElveney at home and told him he was finished as a cop, and to turn in his badge. But he didn't mean it. This was another of Fitzpatrick's little jokes on McElveney, said Charlie, one of many. The bullet in Fitzpatrick's brain was the punch line.

At his death the *Knickerbocker News* said in an editorial that Fitzpatrick had the reputation for "fairness, efficiency and absolute courage." It said also: "Fitzpatrick had come up in a hard school of training. It included that chaotic period when Albany was on the direct route with the rum runners, in the heyday of the racketeer, when the only police protection was a hard and vigorous hand."

McElveney tried to plead guilty to first-degree murder, despite a family-appointed attorney's efforts to enter a plea of not guilty by reason of insanity. He was jailed, didn't eat, almost died of malnutrition, but survived to plead guilty to second-degree murder. He was sentenced to twenty years, did eleven, some in a medium-security prison, was pardoned in 1957 by Governor Averell Harriman, and died of cancer in 1968. Bob Parr's Klub Eagle license was permanently revoked.

It is quite neat, for purposes of this report, that both Jack Diamond and William Fitzpatrick died of bullet wounds to the brain. Jack, too, might have accused Fitzpatrick of ruining his life, if it was, in fact, Fitzpatrick who shot him. I asked Leo O'Brien, who was a very busy Albany newsman in 1931, what he thought about such a possibility, and I mentioned Dan's words to me on the matter. "I never heard that," Leo said, "but I'd be inclined to believe it."

I spoke also with a man who was involved with the political Machine from its early days in the 1920s, and when I quoted Dan as saying Fitzpatrick had something to do with finishing Diamond, this man nodded and said, "He had everything to do with it." And he added that there were three men, all police, who went into Diamond's room and shot him, and that one of the shooters was McElveney.

Another man who was close to the Oley brothers before and during this period was listening to our conversation, and he was surprised. "I always thought John Oley killed Diamond," he said. This has been a theory for years, as has the notion that one of the Oley gang told the police the address of the rooming house where Diamond was staying in Albany. One of Diamond's friends told me years ago that Diamond thought he was safe and that no one but the family knew where he was living. This helps to explain Alice Diamond's hysterical outburst when she saw her husband's corpse in the bed. "I didn't do it," she kept saying to the dead Jack of Diamonds—didn't tell anybody where he was staying, that is.

All of this hardly closes the case on who shot Jack, but what it does do is give equal time to the police. For it wasn't backroom gossip among reporters, politicians, and old-time hoodlums that brought this skeleton out of the closet. It was Dan the man.

"Fitzpatrick finished Legs" is what he said.

Twelve men, ten steins, nine mustaches—a group of Germans at Schutzen Park at the turn of the century. Man at left front is said to be Herr Picard, owner of Picard's Grove. Bald man (front, right) is (perhaps) Noodle Fritz Ehrhardt, a Bowery notable.

PART
4

SOME
OF THE
PEOPLE

Jews

*O*n November 29, 1655, Peter Stuyvesant, director-general of the colony of New Netherland, received a petition from three Jews in which they asked permission for themselves and "others of the Jewish nation" to trade throughout the colony, which included Fort Orange, the settlement that was to become Albany and that after New Amsterdam was the colony's second most important center of trade—principally in furs.

Stuyvesant promptly denied the request and warned the Jews not to dare to try to trade at Fort Orange. The Jews, who'd come from Amsterdam in February with permission from the directors of the Dutch West India Company to trade in the colony, re-petitioned Stuyvesant and were swiftly re-rejected.

Stuyvesant feared a weakening of Dutch supremacy in the New World. He not only disliked the presence of Jews but was equally xenophobic about Quakers, Mennonites, and Lutherans, whom he shunted elsewhere whenever they turned up—undesirable aliens all. At least twenty-three other Jews, expelled from the Dutch settlement in Brazil in 1654 when the Portuguese took over, had arrived in the colony on a British ship. And so Jews were now a special concern.

Dominie (cleric) Johannes Megapolensis, who had been in

Fort Orange, Greenbush (Rensselaer), and New Amsterdam since 1642, joined Stuyvesant in alerting the West India Company's directors to the grave dangers all these intruders presented to the colony. He supported their recall to Amsterdam, for he saw a Babel in the making. The salvo he fired at the Jews was traditional: "These people have no other God than the Mammon of unrighteousness and no other aim than to get possession of Christian property."

"Both Governor and Dominie knocked at the wrong door," write Henri and Barbara van der Zee in their book on the New York Dutch, *A Sweet and Alien Land*. "The company in Amsterdam had no intention of recalling the Jews, seeing their immigration as a valuable contribution to the population of New Amsterdam." Also, the company itself, "struggling to stay afloat, needed Jewish money badly and would at no cost insult at least four per cent of their investors by boycotting any Jewish trader who might wish to go to New Netherland." The directors told Stuyvesant to let the Jews alone.

But he would not. He continued harassing them, and when the Jews made yet another appeal to Amsterdam, Stuyvesant found himself reprimanded. Jews were to be allowed to live and trade, said the directors, but with certain limitations: they could hold no jobs in public service, could open no retail shops. They could not build a synagogue, but could "exercise in all quietness their religion within their houses, for which end they must without doubt endeavor to build their houses close together in a convenient place." This last quotation is from a document cited by Louis Silver in a richly documented article, "The Jews in Albany, N.Y. (1655–1914)," published in the *American Jewish Historical Quarterly*.

The directors consoled Stuyvesant with the insight that, after all, the Dutch Reformed Church was, "as we all of course know," the only true church, and sooner or later all people would see the light. "Now, unfortunately, many of them still persist in their errors but if we treat them with harshness, they will persist all the more obstinately. . . . Wherefore, suppose we try kindness and mildness! Suppose we show them by our example the superior virtues of the Dutch Reformed, the only true religion!"

And so, amid Stuyvesantean mildness, did the Jews trade and worship. And in time they prospered, but in the light of their own religion, not the Dutch Reformed. The most triumphant among the Jews was a man named Asser Levy, who was said to have come to New Netherland from Jamaica, but seems to have arrived with those Jews expelled from Brazil and then jailed as debtors in New Amsterdam. Levy not only paid his way out of debt; he became, says Silver, one of the "most respected and wealthy" men in the colony, though not necessarily its most loyal. Upon its conquest by the British in 1664, Levy was "among the first to swear allegiance to the British monarch." He had residences in both New Amsterdam and Fort Orange, and it was on his land that the first synagogue in America was built—on Mill Street, in New York. He also advanced money to the Lutherans—companions to the Jews as victims of New World religious persecution—for the building of the first Lutheran church in America, in 1671.

So while we cannot look to New Netherland as a shrine of religious tolerance, we can look to its Jews as survivors, as pioneers of civil and religious rights in the new nation. Silver says the Jewish community in Albany came to an end at the close of the seventeenth century, when the fur trade disappeared, valuable fur-bearing animals having been all but exterminated.

Silver cites the role of individual Jews as merchants in the eighteenth century, but says there was no Jewish community in Albany. But by the early nineteenth century, as Jews were finding haven here from persecution in Europe, the community began to grow. In the October 4, 1825, issue of the *Albany Daily Advertiser*, a letter appears signed by three Jews, Leopold Zunz, M. Moser, and Eduard Gans. The writers declare European Jewry has but one means of escape from "endless slavery and oppression"— America, where all can enjoy "public freedom [and] general happiness."

By 1838, German Jews (notably emigrants from Bavaria, where anti-Jewish restrictions were rigidly enforced) had established in Albany a Jewish society for mutual aid and communal prayer. They bought 166 Bassett Street, in the city's South End, a former private home, and made it a meeting place. The congregation grew and in 1841, for $2,500, the society bought a small church at 76 Herkimer Street (between Franklin and Green streets) from the Hibernian Benevolent Society. The building was situated on a plot owned by the Dutch Reformed Church, and so the Jewish congregation was still in Dutch hands, but only minimally—they paid an annual rent of $10. The Jews repainted the building and on September 2, 1841, the eve of Rosh Hashanah, they dedicated it as the Bethel (originally Beth El) Synagogue, the first in Albany.

Five years would pass before the synagogue would have a rabbi—this in the person of Isaac Mayer Wise (1819–1900), a most willful man who came to America from Bohemia at the age of twenty-seven and transformed American Jewry. He assumed his post in Albany in December 1846, being paid $250 a year as rabbi. He also established the Jewish Academy of Albany and taught pupils Hebrew, religion, English, arithmetic, history, and geography, earning $9 per pupil per year. There were only five other such schools in America—three in New York, one in Baltimore, and one in Cincinnati.

The Albany Jewish community into which Wise entered was growing steadily, almost all newly arrived Jews in the city joining this congregation, some of them having fled Germany imbued with the fervor to change the old ways of life, the old forms of religion. Reform Jewry began in Germany and Wise brought it with him to the New World and found his followers among his fellow immigrants. Many Jews began their lives in this city as peddlers, and Wise, in his *Reminiscences*, reports on their types:

"The basket peddler—he is as yet altogether dumb and homeless . . . the trunk carrier, who stammers some little English and hopes for better times . . . the pack-carrier who carries from 100 to 150 pounds upon his back and indulges the thought that he will become a businessman some day. . . . In addition to these there is the aristocracy. . . . The wagon-baron, who peddles through the country with a one or two-horse team . . . the jewelry-count, who carries a stock of watches and jewelry in a small trunk, and is considered a rich man even now . . . the store-prince, who has a shop, and sells goods in it. At first one is the slave of the basket or the pack; then the lackey of the horse, in order to become finally the servant of the shop."

In Albany in 1840 there were 250 licensed peddlers, of whom 58 were Jews. (I am indebted to a paper by State University history student Sharon R. Kolodny for these data.) By 1845 there were 163, of whom 121 were Jews; and then the high point in 1847: 269 peddlers, of whom 166 were Jews. In 1855 a census recorded 772 Jews in the city. By 1857 there were 95 city peddlers, only 21 of them Jews; and by 1870, 65 peddlers, only 5 of them Jews.

Peddling led to the store, as Rabbi Wise noted, and by 1875 Jews operated 14 of the city's 30 clothing stores, 15 of the 34 dry-goods stores, 6 of the 9 millinery shops, 18 of the 55 tailor shops, and so on.

Jews were little understood in this Christian land when they first began to arrive in sizable numbers. Louis Silver says some farmers came into the city just to see what a Jew looked like. Yet anti-Jewish behavior was not tolerated. A lawyer who said in court that "Jews cannot be trusted" had to apologize abjectly in the press, and a Baptist cleric who attacked Jews from his pulpit was forced to leave Albany.

Rabbi Wise, meanwhile, was stirring up considerable animosity toward himself, not from Gentiles but from Orthodox Jews. At synagogue he introduced a mixed male and female choir and mixed seating, both of which struck at the traditional segregation of the sexes. He replaced traditional prayers with hymns and music, denounced the congregation's ritual slaughterer, performed confirmations instead of bar mitzvahs, fought with two Jewish butchers, and emphatically denied belief in a personal Messiah and bodily resurrection.

The traditionalists, led by the richest Jew in Albany, Louis Spanier, brought seven charges against Wise, citing in particular his denial of the Messiah and resurrection, and also said Wise had been seen writing on Rosh Hashanah and seesawing on the Sabbath (*geschwungen ein Schwung*). The congregation met on the morning of the eve of Rosh Hashanah, September 7, 1850, and declared Wise's contract as rabbi null and void. Wise said he didn't recognize the validity of this decision, said he'd continue to perform all rabbinical functions.

That evening the synagogue was overflowing with loyalists of both camps when Wise entered. His seat had been taken; his official robes were gone. What happened next, Wise later reported in his own words: "I stepped before the ark to take out the scrolls of the law as usual and to offer prayer. Spanier steps in my way and without saying a word smites me with his fist so that my cap falls from my head. This was the signal for an uproar . . . the people acted like furies."

Police were called and some among the furies were arrested, Wise accused of being ringleader of a rebellious mob at a public service. Wise told Spanier he would appeal, and later quoted what he said was Spanier's reply: "I have a hundred thousand dollars more than you. I do not fear the law. I will ruin you."

The Wise faction almost immediately split off from Bethel and formed its own congregation, Anshe Emeth, holding services in a house at Madison Avenue and South Pearl, a year later purchasing for its synagogue the Baptist church on Herkimer Street where the anti-Semitic cleric had preached against Jews.

Wise's trial on the ringleader charges took place on May 7, 1851, the judge finding in Wise's favor and ruling that Spanier, for insulting a clergyman in the presence of the congregation, had to pay $1,000 damages and court costs. Wise refused the award, relishing the moral victory. Spanier resigned as president of the Bethel congregation.

Anshe Emeth added members, reaching 80 by 1852, and it instituted changes in the reading of the Torah that many congregations elsewhere adopted as a new form of "American Judaism," as it came to be called. Rabbi Wise left Albany on April 19, 1854, to assume rabbinical duties in Cincinnati. Congregation Bethel remained Orthodox but in time instituted so many reforms it no longer differed from Anshe Emeth, and in 1885 they merged to form Temple Beth Emeth, with a combined congregation of two hundred families. For the dedication of the new $200,000 temple at Lancaster and South Swan streets in 1889, Isaac Mayer Wise returned to Albany at age seventy, having become the revered leader of the movement that had established Reform temples throughout America.

Relative harmony prevailed among the Albany Jews after the Orthodox-Reform war ended, but there would be continuing tensions, most of them growing out of European origins. Jews from Poland had been in the city for a decade or more, and when they first found themselves looked down upon by the German Jews, they formed their own congregation, Bethel Jacob, in 1841, five years before the arrival of Isaac Mayer Wise. They remained militantly Orthodox and thought Wise's Reform movement a tragedy for Judaism that could lead only to conversion to Christianity.

A new and far more enduring form of anguish would descend upon Albany Jewry in the early 1880s, for on March 1, 1881, revolutionary terrorists would assassinate Russia's Czar Alexander II, and the ascendancy of his son as Czar Alexander III would begin an era of butchery and destruction that would send millions of Jews into a flight for their lives. Some two million European Jews would come to America beginning in the 1880s.

In 1886 the Jewish population of Albany totaled 3,000, and by 1900 it was 4,000—of whom 2,500 had come from Russia and Poland. From the first, the Russian Jews went their own way, affiliating neither with the Germans nor with the Poles of Bethel Jacob. They established an Orthodox group, Khevre Bnei Jacob, which after four years was solvent enough to purchase a former

Reform temple, and they changed the congregation's name to Bnei Abraham, continuing the Orthodox line.

But country of origin alone did not cause all the tension among Jews. Much of it rose out of differences in economic and social status. By 1902 many newly arrived Orthodox Jews from Russia who sought to associate with Russians in Bnei Abraham found themselves slighted and referred to as "ash-men," according to Silver, because of their poverty and "peddling of the poorest kind." They formed yet another splinter group, Agudath Achim, bought their own cemetery in 1906, and in 1911 built their own synagogue across Ferry Street from Bnei Abraham, an act of "insolence" according to the latter congregation, whose members called the new building the "Cossack's synagogue."

The situation—a rivalry of classes within an ethnic structure—was not unlike that which would prevail in the city when the established life of Old-Albany blacks was overturned in the decades following World War I by a wave of Southern agrarian black migrants (discussed elsewhere in this book). The difference would be that well-to-do blacks would find no easy haven in the city, for, with token exceptions, most white neighborhoods would be closed to them as the black neighborhoods became impacted.

The elite Jews of Albany, the Germans, were of a different order, people of money and growing power and repute in industry, business, the law and other professions, and they were already conducting their lives on elite streets—Madison Avenue, Grand, Lancaster, State, Willett—and they could and did hold themselves socially and geographically aloof when the hordes of newcomers arrived.

Irving Howe described those newcomers in his book *The World of Our Fathers*. They left behind them, he said, "a good portion of their culture and religion. The rabbis, the learned institutions, the political leaders, the burial societies, the intellectuals, the wealthy: almost all the figures of moral authority remained in the old country . . . those who came were the dispossessed, the wanderers, the surplus population of the decomposing *shtetl*, those without a place in the old home or those whose homes had been destroyed . . . men without skills in search of elemental survival; or fugitives from the Czar's armies."

Of the quarter of a million entrenched and prospering German Jews in America, Howe inquired: "What benefit could they foresee, what but certain embarrassment and probable burden, from a descent of thousands of penniless Jews whom they supposed to be steeped in medieval superstition when not possessed by wild radicalism?"

Nevertheless, Howe reports further that the American German Jews not only systematically helped the newcomers but also engaged in a subterranean struggle against efforts to restrict further immigration. "Their sense of solidarity, their moderate but firm liberal principles, their growing ease in America—whatever the reason, they were now committed . . . to supporting the masses of Jews pouring in from Eastern Europe."

Ira Zimmerman, in a paper on twentieth-century Jews and anti-Semitism in Albany, interviewed, in 1975, a woman of German-Jewish background, Cora Livingston Marx, who recalled such an instance of ambivalence toward the Russians: while the German Jews in Albany contributed money to help the indigent newcomers, they also practiced exclusion at the Pinecliff camp, which accepted only German-Jewish children.

One of the earliest Russian arrivals after the assassination of Czar Alexander II was a tailor named Aaron Allen, who, in 1881, with his brother Solomon, left Vilna, a province in the Pale of Settlement, that vast region between the Baltic and Black seas where 94 percent of Russia's Jews were forced to live.

Allen's daughter, Anna Allen Strisower, who was 95 when we talked, remembered how it was in Vilna for the Jews: her grandparents taken from their home and jailed because her grandfather's license to work as a tailor had expired; Jewish children whipped by police on horseback for running into the street during a parade for the governor of the province; one of her father's brothers, not yet ten years old, kidnapped and probably forcibly conscripted into the Czar's army as a Christian, and never heard from again. (Alexander Herzen, the nineteenth-century Russian radical, wrote in his memoirs of such children: "It was one of the most awful sights I have ever seen, those poor poor children! Boys of 12 or 13 might somehow have survived it, but little fellows of eight and ten. . . . Pale, exhausted, with frightened faces, they stood in thick, clumsy, soldier's overcoats with stand-up collars, fixing helpless, pitiful eyes on the garrison soldiers who were roughly getting them into ranks. . . . And these sick children, without care or kindness, exposed to the icy wind that blows unobstructed from the Arctic Ocean, were going to their graves.")

And then on that baleful night in 1881, Anna Allen Strisower remembered, the lights of Vilna were all ablaze for a holiday, and then suddenly there was darkness. "They said the Czar was hurt."

But he was dead. And the pogroms began with a new savagery that had not existed under the assassinated Czar, whose reign would now be remembered as a time of liberal attitudes toward Jews in Russia. The persecuted Jews took flight. Aaron and Solomon Allen came to Albany in that year of 1881 and started work as tailors—for another man named Alexander, an English Jew. In time the brothers would open their own tailor shop, at 47 Hudson Avenue, and Solomon would run a clothing store at 88 Green Street. But in the beginning the task was servitude, self-denial, and saving money. By 1882 Aaron Allen had accumulated enough to bring his wife and daughter, Anna, to Albany.

They were able to leave Vilna by having a friend bribe border guards, and then they traveled two days to Hamburg, Germany. There they stayed at a hotel while waiting—endlessly, it seemed—for the ship that would take them to America. When it came, the landlady told them she would have to hold their belongings because they could not pay their suddenly increased bill.

"There was very little shortage," Mrs. Strisower remembered.

The landlady said her son in New York would eventually be sent their package and they could pay him and get it. When they arrived in Albany they received a letter from the son saying the package had been delivered but because it cost so much, $54, he hadn't accepted it.

Everything the Allens owned was in it—bedding, blankets, "Grandma's silver candlesticks," the samovar. They never saw any of it again.

En route to Albany from Hamburg they were thirteen days on a ship; they landed at Philadelphia, encountered no immigration inspection ("just walked off"), took a train to Albany, and then sat in the station all day, waiting for Aaron Allen to come for them. While she waited, Anna Allen, age eleven, ate a banana, her first: a new taste, a new life. She liked both. "Everybody said America was so good," Anna said. But it was hard, and her mother wanted to go back to Europe.

They stayed, and at age seventeen Anna married Maurice Strisower, whose father came from Austria, and they raised a son, Sidney, and two daughters, Hilda and Helen, who were both present when I spoke with Mrs. Strisower. Her daughters grew up, without oppression, in a section of the city shaped by their family and friends. The main stem of the Jewish neighborhood was South Pearl Street, and life wasn't quite so hard anymore.

"Everybody got work," said Helen Strisower. "I never heard

anybody not getting work on account of their religion. You never thought of yourself as being poor. You just went along. We never wanted for anything. We didn't have central heating, but nobody else did, either. We had coal stoves. We were lucky, we had indoor plumbing."

Her father, Maurice, opened a grocery on the street and ran it until he retired in 1913. "Everything was on South Pearl," she said, "the fish market, the meat markets, the bakeries."

There were Bryer's, Bookstein's, and Strauss's—all kosher meat markets; Zimmerman's and Blumberg's kosher delicatessens; Simon's and Schenkel's and Brown's and Zuckman's bakeries; Kessler's and Naumoff's drugstores. There were Jewish newsrooms where Jews bought the *Daily Forward*, the *Tagblatt*, the *Day*, the *Amerikaner*; and in the same store they bought prayer books and prayer shawls. There was Teitelbaum's glass store, Alexander's crockery shop, Boochever's furs, and Waldman's department store. Harry Hellman opened the Fairyland Theater and later the Royal, and Samuel Sucknow showed silent movies at the White Way at South Pearl and Herkimer streets, with his daughter, Naomi, playing piano until business picked up, and then he'd hire a regular pianist.

So remembered David Silberg, an Albany funeral director, when we talked. Silberg was raised on South Pearl, he said, "with a golden spoon in my mouth . . . I didn't know any hardships." His father, Aaron Silberg, had come from Vilna with his bride, Bessie, on their honeymoon, and had gone to work as a peddler, always with the image of his uncle Solomon Allen as a model of success. In time Aaron Silberg matched his uncle Solomon and opened his own clothing store at 188 South Pearl, selling to police and firemen who bought their clothes on the installment plan—fifty cents a week. And Aaron Silberg prospered.

David Silberg and his cousins, the Strisower girls, grew up in a world freighted with sorrowful history but leavened by high and low culture—Shakespeare in Yiddish, vaudeville performances, and plays with the great actors of the Yiddish theater— Boris Thomashevsky, Jacob Adler, David Kessler. Jews came from as far away as Pittsfield and Amsterdam to find romance at the Sunday night dances at the Albany Yacht Club sponsored by the Young Men's Hebrew Association.

The YMHA and YWHA both began at the Hebrew Educational Institute at 60 Franklin Street, where Jewish children pursued a Hebrew education and studied the Old Testament and the Talmud after school. Hilda Strisower remembered a high point of her time there as a member of Puellae, the high-school girls' club: a public debate by the club at Beauman's Hall on State Street about 1916 in which the topic was "Should the Philippines Be Given Their Independence?" Puellae sold tickets, gave a dance afterward, and packed the hall for a singular success. One must also note what happened thereafter: on July 4, 1946, the Philippines were given their independence.

On Saturday night on South Pearl Street it was a Jewish convention, especially for women. Housewives even came over from Troy to shop. "Everybody kept the Sabbath," said Helen Strisower, "except the ones who were in business. People had no refrigeration then and couldn't buy food ahead, and they came down to buy their meat on Saturday night. At Thomas's fish market they bought carp live and put it in the bathtub and let it swim until they wanted to eat it and then they killed it. I never liked carp. But that was really socializing when all the housewives got together at the butcher's."

Gatherings of a different sort were taking place at the corner of South Pearl and Division streets, where the Adelphi Literary Association had its room. Established by the German Jews on January 26, 1873, this would be one of the most enduring Jewish organizations in the city. By 1886, one historian noted, "its elegant balls given here are prominent among the fashionable and pleasing entertainments which give the capital city its distinguished social reputation."

It was exclusively Jewish, and existed at several South End locations before moving to 134 State Street, later the site of the Raleigh Hotel. Its annual stag dinner, to which each of the one hundred and fifty or so members brought a guest, attracted the elite of Albany political, professional, and cultural life. In 1912, an era when country-club living had already captivated the city's gentry—but in an exclusionary way: no Jews allowed—the Jews of the Adelphi Club established one of their own, the Colonie Country Club, which existed for fifty-two years on Central Avenue. The members kept both the country place and the Adelphi until 1928, when they closed the Downtown club. The country club moved to Voorheesville in 1964 to make way for Colonie Center, the shopping mall.

As the German Jews found it a problem penetrating the world of the nativist elite, so did East European Jews find it a problem penetrating the elite world of the German Jews. The Colonie

Country Club, with a nine-hole golf course, was a desirable social goal, but limited in the membership it could and would take.

Dr. A. I. Milstein, a retired dentist and businessman, recalled that the people who couldn't get into Colonie were mostly Orthodox and Conservative Jews—Colonie members were mostly Reform Jews. And so the outsiders in 1930 bought 325 acres of land and an old farmhouse from the Shaker colony near the Albany Airport and established a country club of their own, Shaker Ridge. It now has a twenty-seven-hole golf course. The president and organizer was Joseph A. Fields, a Schenectady businessman. Dr. Milstein was club president from 1949 to 1951, and when we talked in 1982 he was the only charter member still active in the club.

The same social pattern held for fraternal organizations. In 1844 the German Jews had founded Albany's first, the Albany Jewish Association for Brotherly Aid. In time they established B'nai B'rith, Gideon Lodge, and others. As in the case of Colonie, Yiddish-speaking Russian and Polish Jews were not welcomed fraternally by the German Jews, and so they formed their own groups. Among these were the Hebrew Tailors' Society (each member contributed five cents to join), the Independent Order Brith Abraham, and the Assembly of Israel, among others.

The prominent social clubs in the city were closed to all Jews for more than half a century, notably the University Club and the Fort Orange Club, although Jews are members of both today. (Jews also now belong to the Albany Country Club, and Gentiles are members of the Colonie Country Club, but not in large measure in either case. No Jews belonged to Wolfert's Roost, the predominantly Irish-Catholic club, until the mid-1960s, when civil rights pressures seem to have changed everybody's exclusivity patterns.)

Fort Orange's relationship to Jews, curiously familial, was reported to me in 1982 by Albert Hessberg II, a lawyer and fifth-generation Albanian whose first ancestor here came from Germany in the early 1840s. Another Hessberg ancestor by marriage, Simon Rosendale, was one of the founders of the Fort Orange Club in 1880.

Rosendale, a most prominent Jew, became assistant district attorney in Albany during the Civil War, later city recorder and corporation counsel, and in 1891 state attorney general under Grover Cleveland. He served on the board of directors of the National Commercial Bank and the National Savings Bank, and in 1897 his wife stood in the receiving line to celebrate Albany's one-hundredth anniversary as the capital city of the state.

But in the subsequent years of Fort Orange even Jews of Rosendale's standing ceased to be welcomed as members (Governor Herbert H. Lehman was one exception). Rosendale lived until 1937 but had little to do with the club in his late years. Fort Orange, often under attack for exclusionary policies, sought change in the mid-1960s.

"Two of Albany's prominent citizens came to me then," Hessberg recalled. The two were the club president, Storrs Bishop, head of Niagara Mohawk Power Company, and Mayor Erastus Corning, vice-president.

"They said, 'We don't like the policy, and will you be the first to join?'" Hessberg recalled. "I said yes and I was elected. Following me, nothing happened for six months, and then two more were elected. And since then it's been a steady dribble." He said the Jewish membership now is a "reasonable number—more than a token."

Rabbi Bernard J. Bamberger, of Congregation Beth Emeth, in recalling his fifteen years in Albany—1929–44—wrote: "Jews for the most part took a self-reliant, but not truculent attitude. Though they were excluded from a few clubs, they mingled socially with gentiles to a greater extent than in most places. . . . There was no evidence of significant organized anti-Semitism."

Anti-Semitism was abroad in the land during the 1930s, when homegrown fascists were dredging up the Protocols of the Elders of Zion, that hoary fabrication about a Jewish conspiracy. Gerald L. K. Smith, Father Coughlin, the Ku Klux Klan, the German-American Bund were taking strength from the European fascist movements, and this created a new cohesion among Jews.

"During the resurgence of nativism in the 1920s," writes Ira Zimmerman in an article on this subject, "Albany's B'nai B'rith had been inactive. But with Hitler's rise to power B'nai B'rith and other Jewish groups began to attract new members. The growing concern over the problem of local anti-Semitism resulted in the formation of the Albany Jewish War Veterans in 1935, and the Albany Jewish Community Council in 1938."

Zimmerman's article, titled "The Jewish Leadership's Fight Against Anti-Semitism in Albany, New York, 1933–1945," reports on how these two organizations coped with threats. The Jewish Veterans marched on a Bund meeting in Troy and forced the police to close it down. They persuaded the owner of an

Albany meeting hall to cancel another Bund meeting that was to celebrate Germany's annexation of Austria.

The Jewish Community Council, representing twenty-six local Jewish organizations, was headed by Samuel E. Aronowitz, whom Zimmerman describes as "the leading Jewish figure in Albany." He also gives major attention to Sol Rubenstein. Both men were lawyers and both extremely intimate with local politics. Aronowitz was the law partner of Edward O'Connell, one of the founders of the modern Albany Democratic party. Rubenstein entered politics in the late 1920s and became city recorder and later City Court judge.

Aronowitz and Rubenstein as council leaders sought to keep anti-Semitic incidents out of the public eye whenever possible. Because of their political weight they were able to effect change merely through persuasion. When hate ads appeared in the *Albany Times-Union*, a conversation led to the newspaper's agreement not to run any more. Aronowitz talked with a local college's board of trustees, and anti-Semitic remarks from an athletic coach ceased. Critics of this approach to the problem said its quietness covered up the council's lack of substantive action. But Zimmerman argues that the two men, and the council, were effective in making change. He adds anti-Semitism in Albany was never rabid, usually unorganized, and random.

Steven Windmueller, director of the Greater Albany Jewish Federation, the present-day successor to the council, said that with about 13,500 Jews in the city in 1982 there is almost no overt anti-Semitism and exclusion has all but disappeared as a practice. In October 1981 some swastikas were pasted on the door of a synagogue, but Windmueller says police know who did this—"a couple of kids . . . young adults"—and that when they were identified the defacement stopped. The last heavy wave of anti-Semitism, he said, dates to the 1940s, and from Zimmerman's conclusion, that would mean the war years, when Hitler was still in power.

After the war the South End Jewish neighborhood began its final decline. The Italians had superimposed their neighborhood on the old Jewish blocks and Southern blacks were beginning to do the same. The Russian Jews by now had gained economic leverage and many were moving uptown. The old neighborhood had really been dominated throughout its existence by a single street, South Pearl. From the 1840s it was sandwiched between the Irish, east of Pearl, and the Germans, west of Pearl.

A German resident of the South End once described South Pearl to me as "the Gulf" between the two, more sprawling neighborhoods (although all three overlapped), and I don't know whether this was his personal coinage or an actual nickname now fallen into disuse. I've never found anyone else who heard it called that.

Howard Simons, who grew up at 203 Madison Avenue (at Eagle Street) from 1929 to 1947, remembered a boundary line of a different sort: Lark Street as an abstract meridian that separated South End Jews from their uptown kinsmen. Howard's Jewish ancestors came from Poland and Lithuania, and I asked him if he was talking about the separation of German Jews from such others.

"The German Jews were way beyond what I'm talking about," he said.

What he had in mind were the arrivistes from Russia, Poland, and elsewhere who earned enough to buy an uptown house and then developed instant elevation above the neighbors they left behind.

"It was frowned upon, dating across the line," Howard recalled. "Being a South Ender meant you went to Philip Schuyler [high school] and not Albany High or Albany Academy. People who lived above the line had made it—though not by much, I've found. People downtown developed a scrappy 'We'll beat the world because the world is beating on us' attitude. It was embodied in Schuyler, an elementary school converted to a high school. Six-footers had to bend double to get a drink out of the little water fountains. It was a very tough place, a stepson school. My graduating class had a hundred and twenty-five kids, and six of us went into college, and three or four, maybe five, finished."

Schuyler students, he said, were mostly Jewish and Italian, and some were black. After Schuyler, Howard went on to Union College, finished, and wended his way into journalism. The world does what it can to beat on him still, as it does with the rest of us. Howard did what he could to beat back, and wound up the managing editor of *The Washington Post*. His trip from the South End of Albany to Fifteenth Street Northwest in Washington, D.C. is without doubt a line worth tracking. Trackers are herewith advised the line begins just back from the curbstone on the frowned-upon side of Lark Street.

When the Jewish neighborhood began to fade, the Jews did not move anywhere else as a group, for there was no need; no suburb or city neighborhood was closed to them. Today, however, there is a heavy concentration in the area bounded by Academy Road on the east, New Scotland Avenue on the north, Krumkill Road on the west, and Whitehall Road on the south. The Jewish Community Center and several synagogues exist in this middle- and upper-middle-class area, which is really too large to be considered a neighborhood.

So, then, if the life of modern Albany Jews is not perfect, it is at least better than it ever has been since this New World set eyes on its first Jew. Poverty barely exists among the Jews today, except with the aged, and even that is limited. Discrimination, if not dead, is at least in a coma. Jews are everywhere and prospering.

What is fading with the atomizing of the old era, the old neighborhood, is the intensity of the Jewishness that was. Albany architect Harris Sanders, fifty-five, third-generation Jew in America, sees himself diluted by time and distance from the past to the point where his friends might even remark, "I didn't know the guy was Jewish." He grew up in a kosher house on Philip Street and he did go to Hebrew school two hours daily, but Philip Street was by then an Italian neighborhood.

"I thought I was Italian until I went into the service," Harry said with his Borscht Belt syntax. "I remember when the bells rang at St. Anthony's, the Italian church, you put your head down. I still do it today when I hear bells, and people look at me funny."

Harry Sanders is part of the classic progression of Russian Jews, a witty part. His grandfather, David Sanders, came here about 1885 from a town near Kiev and went to work for German Jews—Mendleson's potash factory on Fourth Avenue, the firm that in 1917 took over the B. T. Babbitt Company and made the scouring powder Bab-O. David brought a dozen relatives to Albany from Russia and Europe, got them homes and jobs, some in politics. He was a well-connected Republican in the era when Billy Barnes bossed this city, and when President McKinley was shot David draped his store with black. (Grandson Harry is a well-connected Democrat who has designed several city buildings, the nifty Albany Public Library among them.) After years of struggle, David opened a store to sell stoves, then taught his son, Andrew (Harry's father), to install them. Andrew eventually developed into a heating and plumbing contractor and became known as Andy the Singing Plumber.

"He was brought up on he backs of immigrants," Harry said of his father. "He was the bridge between the Old Country and the New. He was the American and they were looking to him. He was about fourteen when he met my great-uncle at the train station in Albany and he wanted to show how American he was. 'Show your uncle things in Albany,' his mother told him, and so he took the old uncle to the Gayety on Green Street, a burlesque joint. When he came home his mother says to the uncle, 'Did he show you Albany?' And the uncle says, 'He showed me these naked women.' My father thought that's what everybody was interested in—South End kids grew up fast back then. My father liked to run, sort of an athlete. He could really run fast and he ran up on Arbor Hill. You ever see a Jew in Arbor Hill? They had to run fast in those days to outrun the Irishmen who were chasing them. We never really fought with the Irish. Only in spelling bees. We were more runners than fighters and we spelled better than the Italians. I ran away from home once but I didn't get too far because I took a belt-line trolley. My father was a funny guy. A woman called him up once and said she had a leaky pipe. 'Put your finger on it,' he told her. Another time he's leaving this place and a woman says, 'Oh, don't go, I got a leak in the bathtub.' 'Go ahead,' says my father. He used to do plumbing in one of those hot-mattress hotels up around Eagle Street. The bill came to a hundred and twenty dollars and they paid him all in five-dollar bills. He went to a meeting once in the synagogue and a guy was running a meeting with the Roberts Rules of Order and somebody says, 'I make a motion,' and they say, 'You're not in new business yet.' So they get to new business and he says, 'I make a motion that the congregation buy a chandelier.' The motion is seconded and the fellow says, 'Is there any discussion?' and a man gets up and says, 'I don't think it's a good idea to buy a chandelier, nobody here can play one.' Those old days I barely remember. The Jewish section was breaking up when I was young. I remember some things—the guy around Franklin Street: you'd bring in your live chicken and hand it to the guy [the shochet, or ritual slaughterer] and he'd kill it. I only saw that a couple of times. It was in the era before me. And I saw my mother buy fresh fish and put it in the tub and you couldn't use the tub until the fish was killed. This was frustrating for me and my rubber ducky. I never had any really strong experience in the old neighborhood—carrying groceries home once in a while, maybe. I never encountered much anti-Semitism. I knew Italians who were refused entrance into medical school and country clubs, but that kind of thing never happend to me. Anti-Semitism wasn't organized. Jews had enemies all over. Guy'd call me a dirty Jew and the next minute we'd be the best of friends. After the fight's over it's gone. Nothing like the blacks got in the South. I just remember how it was down there in the South End—it was a good life. All you had to remember was, when you're in trouble, get a Jewish lawyer."

Italians

*I*t was approaching noon on a late-summer day in 1981 in Lombardo's Restaurant on Madison Avenue, and Charlie Lombardo was getting the place in shape for lunch. He was in his shirtsleeves, mopping the floor's white tiles, which probably needed it by Charlie's standards, though, as I wrote somewhere else, the only thing Lombardo's doesn't have is dirt. Charlie used to have solid black hair with a natural streak of pure silver down the middle. Now he has no hair to speak of but he seems to have all his teeth and he hasn't really changed a whole lot since we went to school together thirty-five years ago. I am maybe one of three people in the world who call him Charlie. Everybody else calls him Bill nowadays. But since he hasn't changed and his restaurant hasn't changed, who am I to be trendy?

While he was mopping, a scurvy, scraggly leftover in a 1960s costume came in, lugging a bag of somebody's cast-off junk, and tried to sell Charlie an old box of Spic and Span and a rusty can of Drāno. "Like new," he said.

"Not buying," said Charlie.

"I'm practically giving it away," said the scurv.

"Out," Charlie told him, and he left. "Neighborhood isn't what it used to be," Charlie explained.

I had an appointment here with Mike Nardolillo, executive director of Trinity Institution, who was born and raised in this neighborhood, and when he came in to talk he said the same thing: "It isn't really Italian anymore. There's nothing below South Pearl at all." All that was left, he said, was Cardona's grocery on Grand Street, the Grand Cash Market, Pellegrino's for Italian food imports, the Madison Grill for pizza (though that had just been sold), Len Gaspary's bar for more pizza, maybe another few places, and Lombardo's. Even the Sons of Italy were gone from their hall across the street, the hall taken over by a black Masonic lodge.

Lombardo's then, still vital, always busy, is an anomalous monument to the lost age, a place that looks very much as it did thirty-five or forty years ago. Charlie's father, Charles, started it as a saloon in 1916, turned it into a speakeasy during Prohibition, then into a first-class restaurant and bar when beer came back. He acquired the place next door and expanded into what is now the bar, and it positively reverberates with the spiritual history of an almost exclusively Italian street.

Madison below South Pearl Street, even as late as 1941, could have been a street in Italy: Calsolaro's barbershop, John Virgilio's tailor shop, Leonardo Derenzo's grocery, Stefano Giacoppe's meat market, Orazio Milazzo's shoe-repair shop, Rocco Padula's beverage depot, and dozens of families with similar names.

In 1880 the census reported a total of 77 Italian-born residents in Albany. By 1920 there were 3,403, comprising the largest foreign-born group in the city. By 1925 the racist "national origins" law had been in effect four years and had all but curtailed immigration from Italy, which was one of its purposes. Yet in 1925 international travel was still important. The Albany Italian Exchange, steamship agents, was up the block at 141 Madison, and Germano P. Bacelli, the Italian consul, had his office in the same building.

Mike Nardolillo, "venerable," or leader, of the Sons of Italy when I first talked with him back in 1963, estimated then that the great wave of immigration that brought 4 million Italians here from 1887 to 1916 (2.1 million of them from 1906 to 1916) eventually swelled Albany's Italian-American population to between 20,000 and 30,000. Mike, now fifty-three, after eighteen years out of office was again "venerable" in 1982. He suggested the Italian-American population of the city, including West Albany, might now be as high as 40,000.

When the early wave of immigrants came and settled in Albany's Little Italy, they clung together defensively. John Virgilio, who came in 1904 and established himself as a tailor, talked candidly about what it was like to be a new Italian here. In an interview with Patrick Bulgaro, a native of the neighborhood who became a teacher and now is an executive in the New York State Department of Civil Service, Virgilio said, "You got used to people calling you 'guinea,' 'wop,' 'banana-boat,' or 'Sicilian.' You got used to it because you couldn't fight everybody, and you got used to it most of all because you had to feed your family."

Italians found work in abundance—back work. In 1907 they constituted 44 percent of the U.S. construction labor force and 15 percent of all steam railroad workers ("Where do you worka, John? On the Delaware Lackawan' "). Work was harder to come by in local businesses, especially the smaller ones. But the newcomers overcame this prejudice and proved themselves attractive to employers, their docility a marked contrast to the truculence common among Irish immigrant laborers. Some local firms specialized in hiring Italians—Liberty Union Laundry on Dallius Street for one, Forchini's Produce Company for another.

Produce, like the church, had been dominated by the Irish. In 1925 it was Brady and Donohue and Doyle and Dugan and McMahon and Mahar and Murphy and Willie Ryan who were the source of all potatoes. In 1941 the Irish were all but out of it (though Willie Ryan the younger is still in business in Colonie), and it was Aiello and Caruso and Rinella and Battaglia and Ciccolella and Pepicelli and Scarlata who now knew their onions.

The center of the Italian neighborhood was at Grand and Madison, and the centerpiece was St. Anthony's Church, established in 1908 by Reverend Francis Buono in a basement, the rest of the church coming along in the century's second decade. Father Buono was wildly popular and had the reputation of scheming to get his church built. He talked Enrico Caruso into coming to Albany, had tickets printed and sold, but the great tenor failed to appear because of illness. Was he really sick? Did he know Albany existed? Heaven knows.

The Italians, so numerous, so churchgoing, found their religion in this country, in this city, to be in the hands of the Irish prelates. But they pushed and pleaded for their own church, and in time the Irish ecclesiarchs who ran the Albany Catholic Diocese created St. Anthony's as a "national parish," with jurisdiction exclusively over Italians. But in wondrously chauvinistic fashion, they named an Irishman pastor, Reverend Emmett A. O'Connor.

Was he liked?

Andrew Viglucci, a newspaperman who was born in the Italian neighborhood and grew up going to St. Anthony's, had an answer: "It wasn't a case of liking him. He was it. He gave two sermons at mass, one in Italian and then one in English. You went to him with all your problems. He was it."

Father O'Connor remained pastor for forty years, and when he fell ill, Reverend Anthony Sidoti, an assistant, took over and in time became pastor. By 1963 St. Anthony's was fading as a parish, the Italians having moved to West Albany, to Western Avenue in the vicinity of Russell Road, and, most heavily of all, to the Delaware Avenue neighborhood. St. Anthony's closed in 1973, and Father Sidoti became pastor of St. James's, on Delaware Avenue.

Most Italian social life in 1982 is focused in the Italian-American Community Center on Washington Avenue Extension, and the streets that once teemed with the Italian language and the odors of Italian cooking (it was called "the Garlic Core") are now all but empty of Italians. Mike Nardolillo estimated that along Grand, Van Zandt, South Lansing, Jefferson, Elm, and Hamilton streets, along Park, Myrtle, and lower Morton avenues, and on Madison Avenue from Philip Street to Broadway, there are no more than two hundred Italians still in residence.

Mike remembered the neighborhood when it was bursting with life, when Johnny Sherley's market at Church and Madison was one of the largest and busiest groceries in the city. Roc Tarzi ran La Bella Napoli restaurant, first at Van Zandt and South Pearl, later on Grand near Beaver Street (it's still in business, on Beaver west of Grand).

"Those were the days when Albany was a vibrant place," Mike said. "I'm getting that feeling of how it was when I talk about it. I'm getting those tingles. When you went into La Bella Napoli in the forties it was really something."

Italians displayed little interest in politics but showed great talent for serving food and drink and for generating music and the festive life. There was a guitar on the wall or in the back room of almost every Italian barbershop. The Italian talent shaped itself in musicals and plays, some put on at St. Anthony's, some at Harmanus Bleecker Hall, Albany's premier theater. The Sons of Italy held its dances in German Hall on Beaver Street or at

Odd Fellows Hall, long gone from the southeast corner of State and Lodge streets. Music was by Rufus and Rocco Zita, one of the most famous orchestras in town, and by Frank Laudis and Peter Fraziade, and later by Petey Emma and Joe and Mike Pantone (Mike taught me how to play the banjo and also umpired our baseball games on the days I took my lesson), and later still by Tommy Ippolito and Johnny Costas and Joe Cosco.

Two or three bands would come up annually from New York to play for the early-August celebration in honor of Our Lady of Grace, a religious event that was also a three-day Albany feast, with dancing in the decorated streets, and vendors from New York selling fancy pastries and pizza and nuts and candies from pushcarts.

Phil Romano's orchestra played at the Sons of Italy hall on January 12, 1927, for an unusual event, the "annual cabaret and ball of the Thomas J. B. Dyke Association." Tommy Dyke, at that time, was probably the best-known Italian in Albany, the most influential, the most flamboyant, with connections to major names in show business as well as in the city's Nighttown. He manufactured the Dyke cigar and owned the Club Petite at 512 Broadway, at whose opening $15,000 worth of booze and champagne was consumed, so they said, at $25 and $50 a bottle. Advertisements in the program for his 1927 annual cabaret and ball came from Eddie Cantor, Vincent Lopez, Texas Guinan, Abe Attell, Jimmy Durante, and such local notables as John (Solly) O'Connell, Ames O'Brien, Morris (Mush) Trackner, Harry Berman, Eddie Valion, Tommy Hen, among many. Membership in the association read like a Who's Who of the Red-Hot 1920s.

Another well-known man in the Italian neighborhood, quite the opposite of Tommy Dyke, was Frank Ruggeri, who came here in 1914, worked thirty-five years on the railroad, and then became a familiar figure through his second career—as a door-to-door John Hancock insurance man. In 1916 he helped organize a different kind of association from Tommy Dyke's: the Young Men's Italian Association.

"We were young and we wanted a literary club and sports, things like that," he said when we talked. The YMIA urged immigrants to attend night school, won its fight to get merchants to wrap bread and cover macaroni, plumped for neighborhood cleanup, and campaigned against an image the members felt degraded all Italians—the organ grinder as beggar.

The YMIA had a bill introduced into the state legislature to prohibit men from playing publicly any "street piano, hand organ or music box unless such person is incapacitated for labor on account of some physical condition or deformity." I haven't consulted my attorney, but the bill seems unconstitutional on the grounds that it prohibits the pursuit of happiness. In any case it did not pass and the organ grinder continued to pump away at his monkey business until his organ finally broke down, or maybe the radio drowned him out. But he died a natural death, unmourned by Albany Italians.

Charlie Lombardo knew I was going to write about the old neighborhood, and so when he saw Carmen Treffiletti come into the restaurant for lunch he sent him over to talk. Carmen's father, Joseph, had run a grocery on Madison Avenue, and today Carmen and his brothers, John and Tony, run a wholesale grocery business. Their parents came from Italy, their father in 1909, when he was twenty-three, their mother, Adrienne Siculia, in 1903, at age four.

"Like most of the Italians," said Carmen, "they started in Little Italy in New York and then moved upstate. My mother came to Albany in 1908."

Carmen's father started a grocery at 105 Green Street in 1914 and the building remains part of the Pastures, an ambitious urban-renewal project that will restore the old houses. Joseph Treffiletti and Adrienne Siculia were married in 1920 in St. Anthony's Church. They went back to Italy in 1922 and stayed ten years. Their son Tony was born there. They came back and opened another grocery in 1932 at 104 Madison, just east of South Pearl.

"The building is there," said Carmen, "and they say the ovens where my father used to make macaroni are still in the cellar. There was a lot to be said for city living in that time versus our living today in suburbia. My mother was entertained by getting a change of clothes and sitting on the stoop. 'Hi ya, Mrs. Triff,' people'd say, and she'd spend three, four hours out there.

"I can picture things as they were. I can name every family on the block and know everything that happened to them and reflect that those were great days because life was sweeter. You'd go to Candido's, the pharmacy, to Angelo Femia's on South Pearl to buy meat, go to the bank across the street, to Panetta's to buy fish, to the Public View bakery to buy fresh baked goods, you'd go to Saint Anthony's to church, two blocks. There was the Regent, the Leland, and the Ritz theaters, all nearby. To do all this now where I live you need ten gallons of gas."

Pressure built up in the family to move off Madison Avenue, but Adrienne resisted. "I'm living in little Paris," she told her children. "Why do I want to go anywhere else?"

But they moved in 1955. Eight years later Adrienne, sixty-three, died—"a young woman," her son said. By that time lower Madison had turned into a hangout for derelicts and the north side of the street was about to become a vacant lot. Governor Rockefeller had expropriated ninety-eight acres to make way for his South Mall, and nine thousand residents were being removed from their homes, half of them from the Italian neighborhood. On Adrienne's block the houses turned to hovels, rubble and dust, or into shells, boarded up to await creative restorationists. Despite all that, Carmen Treffiletti is sorry he moved his mother away.

"It was a mistake," he said.

Andy Viglucci's memory of the same age is very different, far less idyllic than Carmen's. Andy is editor of the *San Juan Star*, the English-language daily in Puerto Rico (and he was, during 1966–67, managing editor of the *Albany Times-Union*). He was born in 1927 on Grand Street, son of Helen Fitzgerald and Carmine (Jinx) Viglucci, and grew up a denizen of Little Italy. His father was born in Italy, the family coming from Bellona, near Naples, all of peasant stock. Andy's Irish grandfather was Tim Fitzgerald, a Van Woert Streeter.

Andy went to Public School 8 on Madison, just down from Pellegrino's. "It was a school that succeeded the way public schools were supposed to succeed," he said when we talked in 1982; and he meant the school was a leveler, a democratic mix of Jews and Irish and Italians and blacks and Greeks. "The only thing we weren't exposed to were Protestants," he said.

We are talking now about the years between 1933 and 1940, when School 8 was run by Irish spinsters—Miss Casey and Miss Roach and Miss Mary Delaney, the principal, who was the sister of John T. Delaney, Albany's district attorney. It was the Depression, and Andy remembers his mother's giving a bottle to the baby after heating it on the kitchen stove on a winter night, and in the morning what was left in the bottle was frozen for want of heat in the house.

"All kids were put out to work at an early age," Andy said. "My father started to work at age six, selling papers at Union Station. The older paperboys didn't like him and named him Jinx, this cute little kid selling papers. People would ignore the big kids and buy his papers and give him a fifty-cent piece."

Andy remembers young people running away from home to get away from their families. He remembers kids with d.a. haircuts standing outside Candido's Pharmacy, razzing one another. "But if you weren't home at nine-thirty you were locked out. Kids had to produce—money—or get out. Guys took up boxing to get away. And I know one who started packing guns and turned into a Mafioso. I know whole families of girls who ran away from their parents—stupid people. They'd shake out the kids' shoes to find pennies they'd hid. The family across the street from me had a padlock on the breadbox so the kids couldn't eat between meals."

The drive for money, he said, "screwed up my father. He burned out. He told my mother when they got married, 'If my mother or father offer you anything, don't take it. There's a catch to it.' " That was in 1924, on the day after their marriage. Jinx's mother came to visit soon thereafter and gave her son's new wife $100 for herself. " 'She bought you' " is what Andy remembers as his father's historical response to that. " 'That was a bribe. You're an American girl and she wants you to keep a good house and not to stay home and eat chocolates all day.' "

Andy has vivid memories of his Italian grandmother, whom he positions in an Italian matriarchy of peasant women who became well off by investing in property. "They were something, these women, all in black, setting out in the morning, first to church and then to the marketplace with their black leather bags. They went out and picked dandelions for salad and soup and for wine. Their husbands had winepresses in their cellars. The women came back from the market with vegetables and fruits, and once or twice a week a live chicken, especially for Sunday.

"To kill a chicken, my grandmother'd grab it by the head and twirl it and then slit its throat—in the kitchen. I never saw her in anything but black all my life—in mourning for relatives, for kids who didn't make it over from Italy, for everybody she knew. The dead were more important than the living."

Andy's memory of communication with his grandmother is one-dimensional: "Howsa you? Andrew, eat. No makea skinny, makea fat. Shut up, eat." When she died, he said, she left $30,000 in the house, which somebody got to and kept. Andy was bequeathed $600 in the woman's will.

Charlie Lombardo said he knew an old-time resident of lower Madison Avenue who is thinking of buying the old house his family used to live in—it's part of the Pastures project—and maybe opening it as a store.

Andy Viglucci has no plans in that direction.

Germans

*W*e know how sappy it is to believe that the old days were the best, life was easier, people loved more, knew more about how to be happy, etc. All that is dismal malarkey because it is linked to our most idealized memories of childhood; also, it's nostalgia for an age in which homegrown pleasure was necessary because the automobile wasn't around yet and people were rooted to the neighborhood.

Nevertheless, Herb Roos could say, "I think life was better. It was slower. You don't see no picnics anymore."

And Larry Ehrhardt could remember dances, and music, and riding a hay barge—being towed down the Hudson for an outing. "And when the singing societies rehearsed," he said, "they were heard all over the area, and the neighbors would stop to listen."

Slow motion and the element of song: "That, they say, was Bonafettle." Or *Bohne Viertel*, which, they also say, is how it began, those words translating from the German as "Bean Quarter," the place that spread in the city's deep South End like a patch of beans in a hausfrau's yard, with its arbitrary boundaries being South Pearl and Elizabeth streets, and Second and Fourth avenues.

The Germans came to America in great numbers in the nineteenth century. In the early 1830s, 10,000 a year were arriving; by 1837 it was 24,000. The numbers increased during the liberal revolution that swept through the German Confederation in 1848, and when the revolution was overthrown there was another sweep, so that between 1852 and 1854 half a million German refugees arrived in the U.S.

In Albany in 1880 they numbered 6,648, or about 7 percent of the city's total population. They settled in the South End, mostly to the west of South Pearl Street (the Irish—14 percent of the city's population in 1880—were dominant east of Pearl). Heavily German sections also developed along Central Avenue (called the Bowery) and Cabbagetown, to the north of the Bowery. This story, in part, concerns the people of those neighborhoods, too, for the entire German-American community bears deep scars on its soul, wounded spiritually when the Kaiser declared war on Russia, France, and Belgium, and England and America declared war on the Kaiser, and wounded again in the age of Adolf Hitler. Both eras altered the life of Germans in this country.

In 1852 there were enough of them in Albany to support a German-language daily newspaper, the *Albany Freie Blaetter.* Then came another, the *Albany Daily Herold*, plus a Sunday paper, the *Albany Sonntags Journal.* The immigrants established German Hall, the Deutscher Club, a Masonic lodge (Guttenburg, Number 737, Otto Scholz, master), the Wohltaetigkeit Verein (a welfare society, one of many), a German veteran society, and all the locally renowned singing societies: the Mannerchor, the Eintracht, the Harugari Saengerbund, the Liederkranz, the Apollo, the Caecilia, the Harmonia.

They built their first Catholic church, Holy Cross, at Hamilton and Philip streets, and then Our Lady Help of Christians on lower Second Avenue. They built three South End Protestant churches: the German Evangelical and Trinity Evangelical Lutheran, both on Alexander Street; and St. Matthew's First German Evangelical Lutheran, at the top of the hill on Delaware Avenue, between Clinton and Elizabeth streets. And in the area of the Bowery several more German churches flourished, Catholic and Lutheran.

Out of the South End's German community came one of the most significant scientists of nineteenth-century America. Born on Alexander Street in 1859 was Theobald Smith (né Schmidt). He worked his way through Cornell playing an organ, earned his M.D. from Albany Medical College, and as a pathologist taught at Harvard; but he made his mark with the discovery (announced in 1892) that a cattle disease called Texas fever was transmitted by the cattle tick. The notion that insects could transmit disease was brand new and would, in time, set other scientists on similar quests—men such as Walter Reed, who tracked the mosquito as the carrier of yellow fever.

Smith also differentiated between human and bovine tuberculosis and, in all, contributed greatly to preventive medicine. In 1937 Albany Medical College dedicated one of its buildings as the Theobald Smith Memorial Laboratory. Smith died in 1934.

About the time Smith's immigrant parents were doting on the hero-to-be as a toddler, Carl Rappe's grandfather was establishing a butcher shop at Clinton Street and Third Avenue in the middle of Bonafettle. Carl was running the same shop a century later (it's now closed) when I talked with him; and on one of its walls was a photo of a horse and wagon rigged out for the parade on August 14, 1905—German-American Day in Albany. A sign on the wagon, in which Carl's brother and grandfather were sitting, offerd a $10,000 reward to anyone who could find better bologna than that made in Rappe's back room.

"In those days down here," said Carl, "there was a Dutchman's meat market on every corner. And they all did business. Gus Metz had a grocery across the street with a cellar full of sauerkraut. It cost about one cent for a head of cabbage in those days and you'd get a big glass of mustard for two cents. It was all Germans down here."

The Germans ran bakeries, too—Legler's, Buehler's, Harlfinger's, Deiseroth's, Roessler's. There was Shultz's apothecary and Schifferdecker's coalyard. Machwirth and Greb ran groceries and Zimmerman a lumberyard. Simon Rissig had a carriage works, and down at Weber's bottling works on Third Avenue *weissbier* originated—"what the old Germans drank during Lent when they'd go on the rock," Herb Roos recalled. "But that'd knock your hat off, same as the regular stuff."

Doc Pitts was the neighborhood physician and would pull your tooth at home for half a dollar. "When my grandfather broke his leg," Carl remembered, "Doc Pitts came over with a saw and a board to make a splint."

Men could find work in the neighborhood. There was the tar works on Broad Street, there were the potash works and the Albany Chemical Works next door to that. There were the Delaware and Hudson freight sheds along the canal slip, the Townsend Furnace and Machine Company on Broadway, Pappalau's icehouse along the river, and Wilpers' icehouse at Kenwood. And there was the powerhouse at Pearl and Gansevoort streets, where the flywheel would sometimes let go. "On more than one occasion," said Larry Ehrhardt, "it went through the roof and landed a couple of blocks up the street at Third Avenue."

The good old days.

Ehrhardt, city comptroller for forty years, remembered also from those days the outings that seem gone forever now. "A good many churches would have picnics or river rides. We kids would gather at the church with a shoebox of sandwiches and fruit and with change tied in a knot in a handkerchief. We'd walk, headed by a snare drum and fife, from the church west to a picnic grove whose name changed many times—Marshall's Grove, Colling's Grove, Dobler Park."

Herb Roos, who with his brother, Adam, was running the plumbing business their father, also Adam, started in the 1880s, remembered that other nostalgic staple, baseball; remembered particularly the Welches (Tommy Welch was the manager)—a half-Irish, half-German team—playing their games in Beaver (later Lincoln) Park. "There'd be a fight at every game," said Herb, "and your heart'd be broke if your team got beat. I used to sell the pears out of our backyard at the games. Make five, six dollars on a Sunday."

"Games were played between rival corners on old brickyard grounds," Larry Ehrhardt said. "The men'd bring kegs of beer and they'd bet. Even the kids'd put up eleven cents apiece, and older brothers and uncles put up a dollar a man."

Football was another unifier of the Germans and the Irish, the Delphians being the most famous team and the O'Connell brothers, Dan and Ed, being the team's most famous alumni. Herb Roos remembered getting a dime for holding their coats during a game at Maple Ridge Park. One annual Delphian game was with the enlisted men's team from West Point, and the rumor persisted that the team was studded with ringers from the Army varsity eleven. But that made little difference, even if true. In a later year of his life Dan O'Connell told a reporter the Delphians never lost a game and that when he quit playing the team disbanded.

The Germans in Bonafettle shared all manner of common ground with other South Enders: landmarks such as the milk depot on

Alexander Street (four cents a pint and beware of the flies) and the communal water pumps, where people went for a pail of water in the days before we all got used to having a faucet in every room.

There were nickel shows in the neighborhood: the Fairyland, run by Neil Hellman's father, Harry; the White Way; the Unique; the Star; and next to the Leland, on South Pearl, the Majestic, where an ex-cop, hired to keep order, let kids in for a nickel (a ticket was fifteen cents) to see the vaudeville and a movie, but was fired when the balcony turned up full and there was no money in the box office.

There was also the unifying lunch fork in Dick Leahy's saloon, shared by one and all. "Talk about sanitation," Herb Roos said. "After you'd use it you'd put it back in a glass of water that was so greasy you couldn't see the fork."

The saloons were shared territory for the Irish and the Germans. The Irish drank as regularly at Groelz's and Hausman's and Henzel's as the Germans drank at Leahy's and Fleming's and John (Black Jack) O'Connell's, he the father of Dan and Ed. That saloon was at Fourth and South Pearl, and Black Jack was as fluent in German as his sons were to become in politics. The saloon closed in 1919 upon the arrival of Prohibition, but someone ran it as an ice-cream shop for a time, and then another O'Connell son, Patrick, ran it as a tire store. Eventually Dan turned it into Democratic party headquarters—Little City Hall, it was called—and it functioned as that until 1971, when it closed forever. Dan then had it torn down, rather than rent it or sell it to strangers.

Jack O'Connell and his son John (Solly) were both associated with the Republican boss of the city, Billy Barnes, as ward politicians; and the majority of German Americans in the city also gave allegiance to Barnes. Writing about him in the *Times-Union*, C. R. (Tip) Roseberry said these Germans, "coming into their second generation and acquiring some prosperity after a bitter struggle . . . gravitated to the Republican banner against what they felt was an oppression."

The oppression politically might have come from the Irish, who resented the German incursion into their South End turf, and who were traditionally associated with the Democratic party. Irish-German tensions seem to have been largely a matter of ethnic distance, for they really had much in common—a love of song and strong drink, and many also shared the Catholic religion. What friction there was seems to have lacked the venom that perpetuated other ethnic animosities for generations.

By identifying with Barnes, the Germans went with a winner in 1899, for he elected a mayor, John Henry Blessing. And he did not let go of City Hall until the O'Connells (no longer Republicans), in company with Edwin Corning, established Democratic hegemony over the city and in 1921 sent Billy Barnes into the political wings.

The element of song that the Germans and Irish shared was real, but the Germans had a formal musical tradition the Irish lacked; and so, though singing was apt to erupt in any saloon, the back rooms in the German bars came to be used by the singing societies for rehearsals. In Gustav Wickert's saloon at 371–73 South Pearl, for instance, there was an assembly hall where the Eintracht Singing Society was spawned in 1868. It grew to be one of the largest, with a membership in 1886 of 38 active, 175 passive, and 3 honorary members. It ran picnics at Dobler Park—all the food and beer you could swallow for a dollar, all day long. The Apollo, a disgruntled spin-off of sixteen Eintrachts, numbered 375 in 1886.

The Gogglewood Singing Society, of which Larry Ehrhardt was a member, met at Groelz's saloon at the southeast corner of Fourth Avenue and Broad Street, a place especially noted for its draft beer. I can remember going there in the 1950s on someone's recommendation that Henry Groelz served the best glass of beer in Albany. I tended to agree with that assessment on grounds that the beer was full-bodied, with a firm head, and yet it was Hedrick's, Dan O'Connell's beer, which was okay but hardly the best brew this side of Bavaria. In some bars Hedrick's tasted as if it'd been sitting out in the yard all night. The difference, I was always told, lay in the way it was piped. But I have since come across a column by Edgar S. Van Olinda, who wrote about Old Albany much of his life for the *Times-Union*, and he said of Groelz's beer: "It was drawn 'from the wood' through a highly polished brass spigot only a few feet distant from the keg." Was it the brass spigot that did the trick? Was it the way Henry washed his glassware? Was it German magic? Was it something other than Hedrick's?

Ed Van Olinda, a splendid old gentleman who also wrote music and film criticism (though that's the wrong word—he liked everything, criticized almost nothing), went to Groelz's after his own rehearsals with the Mendelssohn Club, a singing society. You went to Groelz's to drink, yes, but also to continue your singing, for members of the Eintracht and the Liederkranz singing societies also turned up there, and for the Gogglewoods it was headquarters.

Singing in those times was a male pursuit, and no women were allowed into the saloon. They could come in the side door—the family entrance—and go upstairs to Groelz's restaurant for a plate of ham and sauerkraut, and rye bread from Harlfinger's bakery. But even though they were denied entry downstairs, they could be sure no words would drift up from below to scandalize them, for Henry Groelz allowed no profanity on the premises and the utterers of same were asked to leave.

The joy of all the Germanic songs that had floated so wondrously through the air of the South End faded into inaudibility when World War I came. Germans suddenly found themselves the Enemy to some neighbors. One Delaware Avenue storeowner, who had a German flag on the side of his establishment for years, became a traitor in the eyes of young men who saw it for the first time, and he was attacked. Albany High School stopped teaching German and so did the Catholic schools where German students dominated, such as Our Lady of Angels, the parish the Germans had established on Central Avenue in 1868. And down at Schlitz's Tavern on Broadway, across from Union Station, the sauerkraut was suddenly called Liberty Cabbage.

Jane Schneider, an assistant state attorney general, is German and Irish, a classic product of the deep South End. Her father, John M. Schneider, was from Teunis Street in Bonafettle, and she remembers that when the war broke out he left Albany Law School, just as he was about to graduate, in order to enlist in the U.S. Army. Jane remembers his being praised in the family for his patriotism and idealism, and reasonably so. When we talked she wondered how much impetus for the enlistment of such young men of that age came from their desire not to be considered inimical Germans.

Jane's aunt is Ethel Scheiberling, widow of the man who became John Schneider's law partner, Edward N. Scheiberling. Ed Scheiberling also enlisted in the Army, went to officers' training school, and became an adjutant to the colonel of the 312th Infantry in France. He came out of the Army a captain and in private life became an Albany City Court judge. But his fame was as a war veteran. He became New York State commander of the American Legion in 1935, and in September 1944 he became national commander. He thus presided over the Legion during the victory celebrations on V-E and V-J days in 1945.

On the day after V-J Day, Mrs. Scheiberling recalled, she and her husband, he in his role as national commander, paid a call on President Truman at the Oval Office. She remembers Truman's affability and the card he wrote to the Scheiberlings' son, Nicky. "Regards, from Harry S. Truman," it said.

The patriotism of such men as John Schneider and Ed Scheiberling was the positive side of German-American loyalty. The other side was recalled by Tip Roseberry, who was a columnist on the *Knickerbocker News* in the late 1930s and early 1940s, and who in 1982 recalled that he was notably anti-Nazi in his attitudes. He aired such local controversies as the appearance here of Fritz Kuhn, head of the German-American Bund, the major pro-Nazi organization in America. Kuhn spoke to a rally in Schutzen Park, off Fuller Road, where the Mannerchor singing society had moved its headquarters after it left Bonafettle. The rally created a furor when reported, and intensified the anti-German sentiment in the patriotic Albanian's breast.

Tip also, with some information from Treasury agents (T-men, who in those days were almost as alphabetically important as G-men), wrote about the control of chemical plants in Rensselaer by the I. G. Farbenindustrie (German Dye Trust), a fundamental part of Nazi Germany's industrial empire. In 1941 U.S. Secretary of the Treasury Henry Morgenthau, Jr., took control of General Aniline and Film Corporation and suspended five executives. Numerous cartels formed by Farbenindustrie were revealed here and elsewhere. Sterling Products and subsidiaries, the Bayer Company among them, were enjoined for antitrust violations in 1942, as a way of curtailing German influence. Winthrop Chemical was investigated in 1942 in regard to what the U.S. government said was a monopoly on the German patent for a substitute for quinine, the malaria drug, then in short supply. It was argued at the time that the fall of Bataan, its loss to the Japanese, happened in part because of a lack of quinine.

Tip's articles put the chemical manufacturers so much on the defensive that he was invited in to see the research on the quinine substitute, called Atabrine. It proved to be superior to quinine, said Tip, and so he had a world scoop out of his anti-Nazism.

Because of his public stance, Tip wound up in naval intelligence during the war, communing with figures from the European underground and such notable exiles as Aleksandr Kerenski, who was living in Manhattan's East Sixties, and Jan Masaryk, the Czech foreign minister in exile, who was later defenestrated in Prague by the Communists after the war had been won. Tip also was assigned to track a Mata Hari at the Barbizon Plaza—she'd been traced to the sinking of several ships by German U-boats, the source of her information being naval officers susceptible to her charms.

What did the antipathy generated by two wars do to Albany Germans?

The same as it did to Germans everywhere in America: it brought on a repression of Germanic life. People Anglicized their names, or transferred their ancestry to Holland (*Deutsch*men became "Dutchmen"), or they turned into purebred American Wasps (Braun became Brown) and faded into the floral spectrum of the American fabric. Schlitz's Hotel became the American Hotel.

A more significant loss was the disappearance of the German newspapers that had chronicled the life of Germans in the city from the beginning of the immigration. Margaret Conners Harrigan, a North Ender and daughter of Assemblyman Richard J. Conners, did her doctorate at Harvard on the Irish and Germans in Albany between 1850 and 1915, and when she went to explore the German papers they weren't there. She turned up a few issues—three days in 1875, 1877, and 1886, in the files of the American Antiquarian Society in Worcester, Massachusetts, and a few more fragments in the New York State Library in Albany. But no more than that.

She advertised in an Albany newspaper for information on the papers and on the German community in general, and received a few responses but no information on the papers. Spokesmen for the German club at Schutzen Park told her they'd never heard of the *Freie Blaetter* or the *Herold* or the *Sonntags Journal*.

Harrigan theorizes the Germans of the war years were so sensitive to rising prejudice that they chose to discontinue the papers. The *Sonntags Journal* had already fallen by the wayside when the other two merged in 1913. The merged paper continued publishing until about 1917 and then it ceased. None of the papers appears in the 1918 *City Directory*.

This recasting of identities and the vanished record of life suggest a mystery: Did the Germans really destroy all records of their history, or did they merely place them in a time capsule somewhere, to be opened in another, less vulnerable era? The question also imposes on Bonafettle's history a mystical condition very like that of the history of Oz, that other idealized crucible, where real men suddenly turned to tin and straw, and the Wicked Witch vanished with a *poof.*

Blacks

"*T*he Slums of Albany" was the name of the series I was writing, a heavily documented muckrake of Albany's slumdwellers and slumlords, not a pretty picture. "The slums of Albany are a horror" was the opening line, and things went from there down to rat level. Because the subjects of the articles were mainly the exploited black poor, I was getting a great deal of hate mail from white bigots; but then a woman caller identified herself as Negro and screamed her anger at me for ten minutes.

She was, she said at the top of her voice, sick of reading about "former maids and dishwashers." Her home in Livingston Village, a middle-class housing project in Albany, was like Mayfair, she said, it was so well furnished. Her husband was a minister; she was a schoolteacher, educated in "ten universities." She said instead of focusing on the slums I should explore the days when many Negroes had built their own homes. I should go out and interview some "first-class Negroes," she said, and lay off the lowlife.

I had a second call from an elderly woman who gave her views less hysterically but also said, "I am a Negro," and told me I misunderstood the situation in the slums.

"I don't feel sorry for the people there," she said. "If they asked me for a dollar I wouldn't give it to them. When I went around the corner they'd spit at me, and you, too. They won't thank you for what you write about them. They must get up. They must pull themselves up far enough for us to reach them. We're not going to dig them up from the gutter.

"My family were slaves. My great-grandmother was beaten till the walls were bloody. A woman in my family had to sit on hot coals, and I have seen a man hanged in North Carolina. But I can't dwell on that. I can't destroy myself by hating your race. If they can look down on you and make it stick that's your fault. Years ago white people couldn't look down on us. Our society was much more refined than the Negro society is today. Society is cracked up now. That's why I moved out of Albany. Thirty years ago the Negro in Albany had property and kept it, too. . . . People of the 1930s and 1940s had a society that they were proud of, a certain amount of social life with white people. My family and my husband's family helped to build the Arbor Hill Community Center, but now those people are forgotten."

It is true those days are gone, most of those people all but forgotten. I spoke with two of them in 1963 before I began writing about the black slums, and found their nostalgia like that of most other ethnic groups—a harkening back to peaceful times, prettier days. Race prejudice marred that halcyon age, but in light of the tortured days to come in the 1960s and beyond, those were looked back on as days of tolerable bigotry.

Negroes, sometimes coloreds—so they shall be called for this piece only—had been in the city almost since the beginning. The West India Company sold a slave in Albany in 1650. By 1790 there were 572 slaves in the city—one sixth of the population (3,498). They were freed in New York State in 1827, and those who stayed became part of the Albany community. Howell and Tenney's history of the city through 1886 noted that "they often achieve comfortable positions in life, and are, as a class, honest, industrious and law-abiding. They have not to contend against the race prejudice that exists in some cities."

One ex-slave recalled in that history that the first church to serve Negroes (1815) was across from the Dutch Reformed Church on North Pearl Street. The Methodist church in that era was significant for its embrace of Negroes, who comprised 10 percent of its congregation (16 of 153), also in 1815. Methodism had had difficult times in Albany since it arrived in the person of a British lay preacher in 1765. Half a century later, Methodists were still considered intruders—"uneducated in the classics."

In 1829 the Methodist church's trustees decided to charge rent for pews, and this caused an uproar among the 400 members. Most of the 25 Negroes, plus 150 whites, withdrew. The whites formed a new congregation; the Negroes went to the African Methodist church, which was all their own. A struggle persisted on into the 1830s within the main body of Methodism in the city over the slavery issue, and many Abolitionists were driven out.

The first school for Negro children, the Wilberforce School, began as an adjunct to a church on Hamilton Street, with an Irishman named McCabe as the first teacher. Wilberforce was the name given to School 16 in the late 1850s. It was at 201 Hudson Avenue and was part of the public school system, but was segregated, with room for 143 pupils. Segregation ended with a Civil Rights Act in the early 1870s and Negro pupils were admitted with equal privileges to all city schools.

In 1886, Howell and Tenney noted, there were 1,300 Negroes in the entire county of Albany, but they did not specify how many were in the city. They mention that one ex-slave in Albany, Stephen Meyers, had helped "thousands of slaves" to reach Canada through his participation in the Underground Railroad. Of that the historians say: "No modern railway ever had so many lines, so many trains, so many stations, or so many agents or conductors. It was very exclusive, for its passengers were all colored people. It started anywhere and everywhere in the Slave States and always ended in Canada. No through route ever had such a signal light, for it ran its trains by the north star. Every genuine lover of liberty was a stockholder, and every stockholder was a minute-man. Of course every true black man was a charter member."

One freed slave in Albany, Adam Blake, was body servant to the Patroon, Stephen Van Rensselaer III. Blake was born a slave in 1770, died a freedman in 1864. He was known as the Beau Brummel of his day and served as master of ceremonies for the annual Pinksterfest—a weeklong celebration on Capitol Hill (where the pinkster flowers grew) by Albany's Negro population. It began the Monday following Whitsunday and was, say Howell and Tenney, "the Carnival of the African race, in which they indulged in unrestrained merriment and revelry."

Blake's son, also Adam, became the best-known and most affluent Negro in nineteenth-century Albany. He was born in 1838 and grew up on Third Street in Arbor Hill when the area was part of the Patroon's demesne. The boy became a waiter, then headwaiter, at the Delavan House, and in 1859 opened his own establishment, the McArdle House, at 6 James Street. He moved to State Street, became steward at the posh Albany Club, then in 1866 became proprietor of the Congress Hall Hotel on Capitol Hill, a famous place and Albany's leading hotel in its prime.

Blake rejuvenated the establishment, which was widely used by legislators until it was bought by the state—for $190,000— to make way for the new Capitol. The building was demolished in 1878 and Blake opened the Averill Park Hotel at Sand Lake— a crossroads community that is now the village of Averill Park, twelve miles east of Albany—but the place didn't last. Back in Albany, he opened the Kenmore Hotel, expanded it between 1879 and 1880, and in these years it was, along with the Delavan, one of the city's two principal hotels.

Blake died in 1881, leaving an estate valued between $100,000 and $500,000, including parcels of real estate on First Street in Arbor Hill.

The Blakes were part of Arbor Hill from early on, not isolated. With the slaves who stayed in Albany after being freed, with an influx of more from the South after the Civil War, there still was no such thing as a Negro neighborhood.

"There wasn't no more than three hundred colored families in Albany when I was a boy," said Charles Van Buren, who was seventy when we talked. "They was scattered all over—Delaware Avenue, Orange Street, Madison Avenue, Hamilton above Lark, Hawk, old Lafayette Street." Van Buren was born on Orange above Lark but lived in the South End from age six, when he peddled the *Albany Evening Journal* to make twelve cents a day.

His grandmother, he said, was a full-blooded Iroquois, and her family had been in Albany since it was called Fort Orange. His father was Professor Charles Van Buren, who taught dramatic arts, elocution, and music, and acted the role of Othello at Harmanus Bleecker Hall. The family members were communicants of All Saints Episcopal Cathedral.

Young Charles, growing up in the South End in the century's teens, said he "went around to dances with white people, went on excursions with them." He chose not to talk of Negro life exclusively, but of the general life of Albanians of that day. He remembered the speed with which the Albany–Susquehanna trolley rocketed you out of Albany, across the river, and down to Electric Park on Kinderhook Lake; the fireworks on the Fourth of July in Beaver Park; the annual Italian street festival; the vaudeville he saw for a dime; the burlesque that was packed from September through May; the showing of *The Great Train Robbery*, "a great, outstanding movie."

Mrs. Hattie Lewis Van Vranken, seventy-three when we talked, had lived on Lafayette Street on Capitol Hill when she went to Albany High School. That street, mixed Negro and white, disappeared when the State Education Building was put up in 1912. Congress Street, nearby, one block long and all Negro (the aristocrats who originally built the houses on Congress Street abandoned them to the Negroes when livery stables moved onto the block), disappeared when the park west of the Capitol was built.

Some of those displaced went to Arbor Hill, Mrs. Van Vranken recalled, and this movement, along with the influx of Southern Negroes after World War I, fixed Arbor Hill as the main Negro neighborhood of the city. Mrs. Van Vranken, who became Albany's first Negro teacher in the public school system, remembered Arbor Hill just before that time—the first decade of the century—as a racially harmonious place: "I can't remember two Negro families living next door to one another. As children then you wouldn't feel the prejudice like the children feel it today. It wasn't until the girl-boy age that you got away from your young [white] companions. But there was prejudice shown for getting employment. There were those who broke through the color line [Mrs. Van Vranken's father, Charles Lewis, broke it at the post office and became Albany's first Negro mailman] and got along very well, but there were a lot more who didn't."

Her Arbor Hill was "a beautiful section, streets lined with elms and chestnuts, even narrow Third Street. Some of the homes had small front yards and beautiful backyards, well kept." She lived at 54 Lark Street, with the Delmars and the McMahons as her neighbors. The area was mostly Irish. She remembered Dillon's and Lynch's groceries, Delaney's bakery, and McAllister's notion store, run by Mrs. Roseboom. Among the Negro families on the hill were the Simpsons, pillars of the Concord Baptist Church on Second Street; Mamie Dorsey, who taught music; Mrs. Fussmore, on First Street, who mended and laundered fine lace curtains; John Chapman, the head bookkeeper at Brandow's printshop; Dr. Elting, who did tooth extractions and sold patent medicines; the four Van Vranken brothers: Charles (her late husband's father), Ed, a barber, Frank and Fred, tailors—all with mostly white clienteles; and Tom Campbell and Pete Lawrence, Republican politicians.

(John Boos, an Albany history buff raised on Arbor Hill, remembered Pete Lawrence's saloon on Third Street above Lark. "He gave the biggest pail of beer for a nickel on Arbor Hill," Boos said, "and he ran annual picnics at Shafer's Grove. There was always an ashwagon race at the picnic that all the ashmen in Albany and their spavined horses would enter. It was one of the outstanding events of the city.")

"The standard of living of the Negro on Arbor Hill," said Mrs. Van Vranken, "was equal to and in some cases superior to the standard of the whites, even though their income was much less. I've always contended the Negro has always had to live beyond his means to maintain a good standard.

"The fraternal organizations did what good was done in the Negro community, helping each other—the Odd Fellows, the Masons, the Knights of Pythias, and the Female Lundys, which was founded in 1822 and which cared for the sick and buried the dead. That was really a mother-and-daughter affair, a social organization way back. The fraternal organizations were a major factor as social groups until the First World War."

She remembered fairs and socials: "The Israel AME Church was where many went, although some belonged to the white churches—probably there weren't more than half a dozen Catholics. And a dozen families were Episcopalian. But the large majority were Methodist and Baptist. It was in the churches where speakers from out of town were heard. Back in those days it was against church rules to indulge in dancing or cardplaying, so there were few programs set up to interest the youth. One minister opposed a girls' basketball team at the church on grounds that girls shouldn't wear bloomers. . . .

"The Negro group was class-minded, as were the whites. They had social groups . . . on the basis of things such as position, money, family background. As a child I always found that with white parents who subscribed to a community of social and cultural equals, we were thought of as a better class. There was a woman up the street who had one daughter, and the only child she played with was my son. When I was young my mother wouldn't let us play with the trash. . . .

"From around 1915 on, you really saw the Negroes getting together, organizing for the betterment of the group, and the stimulus came mainly from older men and women"—men such as her father and Abe Myers, who worked as a porter, and William H. Johnson, who was a barber. "Those men had been very active in the Underground Railroad and they continued to fight for Negro rights and press the young people to get an education."

Johnson, the acknowledged leader of the Negro community, published a weekly newspaper, *The Albany Capitol*, $1 a year, adding a local voice to other such newspapers of the era—the *Boston Guardian*, the *New York Age*, and later the *Chicago Defender*.

The Negro was frequently an object of ridicule for the sake of comedy, as Mrs. Van Vranken recalled. "That sort of thing was accepted by our group in those days, but there was always a feeling against it. The Negro has always been pushing for the progress of the group and what we have today is the result of step-by-step progress, the hard work of intelligent, diligent Negroes."

Mrs. Van Vranken became a teacher in 1911, taught at School 6, on Arbor Hill, and other schools, and was automatically dismissed when she married in 1915. She eventually turned to social work and was employed by the State Department of Social Welfare until she retired in 1958, the same year her husband retired as head of the printing bureau of the State Department of Audit and Control.

"I have met with prejudice," she said, "but it has never been strong enough to deter me from getting ahead and getting my rights. I've met prejudice in schools—children who wouldn't have anything to do with you—and the same in church. Also, when I was young it was considered that Negroes, to get any kind of job, would have to leave the city. I felt when I finished school I would get a position in Albany, and I was not rebuffed. If you just make up your mind that you're going to do it, you do it."

After World War I the large influx of poor rural Southern Negroes changed the world for longtime residents. Because the newcomers settled in the South End, Arbor Hill became a desirable place for the Negro elite and those with upward mobility. The Arbor Hill Community Center, whose forerunner was established in 1928, became the liaison between the Negro and white communities. The Negro population of the city had gone from 1,239 in 1920 to an estimated 2,100 in 1930, and a sizable Negro neighborhood had been created in the South End. The Reverend John Johnson, in 1963 pastor of Franklin Street's Church of God in Christ, remembered the neighborhood's being below South Pearl Street, from Hudson Avenue to Schuyler Street, although Irish and Italians and Jews also occupied the same areas.

"That was the Depression," he remembered, "and they could

only rent the cheapest kind of houses. Then the work started picking up, and more and more came in. During the war they flooded in like water."

The effect newcomers had on Old-Albany Negroes began to be noted as early as 1927, in a report by the Urban League: "The old population is a very staid and conservative one, typical of the historical spirit of Albany. This group in the main, until recently, held itself apart from the newer population element in every respect. Evidences of this aloofness are noted in membership in churches composed chiefly of white persons and an insatiable pride expressed in being 'native Albanians.' "

The report added that the old residents gave little aid to newcomers in search of housing, causing progressive Negroes "to resent the satisfied or 'laissez-faire' attitude of the native born."

In 1950 a report by the Albany Council of Community Services pointed out that children recently arrived from the South found it "difficult to function at an inter-racial meeting. Moreover they resent the fact that Albany Negroes 'act like white people' by participating as fully as possible in school activities—speaking in assembly, running for office, etc."

Schools in the 1920s felt the impact of the newcomers. Negroes in one public school increased from 5 to 45 in one year. The Catholic Diocese alleviated the overcrowding by building a new school. The following notice was read at Sunday mass in St. Mary's Church: "St. Mary's parish will build a parish school for the Colored Children of the city. The building will be of tapestry brick, stone trimmings, and fire-proof. It will contain basement, first and second floors, three classrooms on each floor. In time a third floor may be added, giving nine rooms to the finished school building. The site will be at South Swan and Sheridan Park." The school, known as St. Philip's School for the Colored Children of Albany, opened in September 1931. Forty pupils attended in 1931, 55 in 1932.

In the mid-1950s, following the U.S. Supreme Court's ruling against segregation in public schools, St. Philip's role was questioned—not legally, since it was a private school, but morally. On April 13, 1962, the Catholic Diocese announced the school was closing as of June 1963 because of popular opposition to segregated schools. The Diocese said the school had been founded "not with racialist but with charitable intent." When it closed it had 68 students, some white, very few Catholic.

By 1950 the number of Negroes in Albany was clocked at 5,759 by the census, almost five times the number present in 1920. That 1950 figure would almost double by 1960—and by then the transformation of Arbor Hill from white to black would be all but complete. The white exodus had begun after World War II, and by 1962 only 46 percent of Arbor Hill would be white. By the mid-1960s the white population would be considerably smaller, maybe 25 percent of the total. The new and growing Negro middle class, many state professional workers in its ranks, was also outwardly mobile, but only insofar as space was available in the suburbs or in Albany's lily-white neighborhoods. By October 1965 the city's population of Negroes was estimated at 15,000 people, of whom only about 80 families lived outside the two Negro neighborhoods, Arbor Hill and the South End, both of which were just beginning to be referred to as ghettos.

An estimate by knowledgeable Negroes of that time was that another 400 Negro families with money and mobility were slum-locked owing to the absence of reasonably priced housing and the usual discrimination. As of 1965 not one Negro family had penetrated the Pine Hills neighborhood. One man, an attorney named John Jennings, with the personal backing of Mayor Corning, had bought a home on its fringes—on Marsdale Street, near Pine Tree Lane, off New Scotland Avenue—but the house burned to the ground before he could move into it; although the fire was officially listed as "accidental," Jennings's family and friends all were convinced it was arson. The fire started on the ground floor, and footprints were found leading away from the house.

Causing a further impaction of Arbor Hill beyond the influx from the South was the displacement of Negroes from the 98.5 acres expropriated by the state in 1962 for Nelson Rockefeller's South Mall. Some 9,000 people were relocated, of whom 1,500 were Negroes. Housing became scarce for everybody in Albany, but incredibly so for the Negro househunter. Arbor Hill landlords restructured their buildings, jammed three families into one-family houses, and turned two-family flats into apartment houses.

By the mid-1960s the fight between the conservative Old-Albany Negroes and the newcomers was passé. A new battle was developing between the activists in the civil rights movement and those in the middle class who were finding their way out of Arbor Hill and into the newly developed suburbs.

The activists accused the outwardly mobile of abandoning the group struggle and thinking only of themselves. "I got mine, now you get yours" was how one activist, left behind, summed up the phenomenon. To be sure, there were some in the departing group who continued to fight the good fight in the NAACP, the Urban League, on school boards, and elsewhere. But with rare exceptions what they did had scant effect on Arbor Hill.

The poor and working class there found their avenue out of squalor, or trouble, either through solitary struggle or through the usual Albany political channels—the ward leader, city alderman, or county supervisor. In the main, these people felt herded, exploited, and forgotten in a neighborhood that was spiraling rapidly into the lower depths.

The neighborhood group movement of the mid-1960s, discussed elsewhere in this book, had brought forth a chorale of articulate and feisty matriarchs who roused the poor, picketed City Hall, and tidied up their blocks. Malcolm X, Stokely Carmichael, Martin Luther King, Jr., Eldridge Cleaver, and Elijah Muhammad were also a chorus—not in harmony, to be sure—and the maleness of their cries aroused something new in young black men, and in Albany that arousal gave birth to a group that called itself The Brothers.

They were between the ages of eighteen and thirty, and they opened headquarters in a storefront at 170 North Pearl Street, just north of the Palace Theater. The press referred to them as militants, a buzzword of that age that implied toughness, not revolution. But The Brothers made no secret of their fondness for the Black Panthers, whose trademark was a machine gun, and for Malcolm, who was saying white men were devils; and so their image was, early on, cast in the bronze of violent rhetoric.

They picketed South Mall construction sites and the Laborers Union over the scarcity of jobs for black men—and *black* was now the operative word, *Negro* was as passé as Old Albany. They pushed for an Arbor Hill trash pickup by the city (as had the neighborhood groups) and they eventually looked back on this as one of the few fights they won. They staffed a health center with volunteer doctors until they couldn't pay the rent any longer. They took on politically hot issues—police brutality and the five-dollar vote. They were shot at anonymously; their storefront windows were broken repeatedly. At least fifteen members were arrested, and with each defeat, each new harassment, they seemed to become more militant. They dropped a bag of live cockroaches on the desk of a slumlord, ran candidates against the Machine on the Liberal party line, feuded with the NAACP.

Who were they? Young construction workers, in large measure, who got some of their original impetus from George Bunch, a maverick black professor and social worker who ran Albany's federally funded poverty program for a time. But he was only the starting gun. The men were Gordon Van Ness and Pete Jones and Sam McDowell and Leon Van Dyke and Michael Dunn and Maurice Newton and Earl Thorpe and Robert Gene Dobbs and John (Bo) Foulks and Moses Thomas, and more who came and went.

The harassment by police, the arrests that grew out of their militant stance, drained their meager finances for bail; the pressure from enemies never ceased; they had trouble agreeing among themselves on what they were or how to become something else; their social life, their many nights out, began wearing down the goodwill of their wives; and then one day in 1969 The Brothers realized they were no longer much of a group.

"We said we were a violent nonviolent group, that we'd retaliate if treated violently," said Gordon Van Ness. "This scared a hell of a lot of people."

Leon added, "Maybe our rhetoric destroyed us. What we had—and maybe we'll never get it again in Albany—was a group of real strong men with strong ideas, guys into Black Is Beautiful and teaching black people how to love themselves."

Leon was broke, hanging out in Belardo's bar on Clinton Square, and editing a biweekly black radical newspaper, *The Liberator*, when I looked him up in 1971 and walked through Arbor Hill with him to get a Brother's response to what the neighborhood had become. Pushers eyed him when we walked by them, for they knew he was involved with an antidrug campaign. A once-timid woman whose son The Brothers had helped out of trouble with the police stopped Leon and asked where he'd been that afternoon. "Why weren't you down marchin' with us for welfare rights?" she wondered. "They brought the cops in on us."

A black man crossed the street to talk to Leon. In his late forties, he reminisced about the Arbor Hill of his childhood—in the late 1920s, the same era when Mrs. Van Vranken was already seeing *her* childhood neighborhood being destroyed.

"People cared," the man told Leon. "Then they cut down all our trees and blacktopped the sidewalks." The man led us over to Ludlow Alley, wide and deep in garbage and trash, no street-lights because the kids broke them so often the city no longer replaced them, and the alley itself caving in where old sewers used to function. The man feared a major cave-in or a sewer-gas explosion. He really didn't know what he feared. He just hated Ludlow Alley.

Down the street a black man said he was afraid to go out at night to buy a bottle of liquor, afraid of young hoodlums robbing him. "Change a twenty-dollar bill in a liquor store? Sheeee."

Leon talked with a young boy just out of jail. "I got busted for narc," the kid said. "I was really dealin', man, had a car, a woman, and you know who turned me in? A brother." He meant a black man, not a Brother.

We walked along Ten Broeck Street, the street of the lumber barons and their elegant brownstones. The facade of elegance was still there, all but indestructible, but behind the facade were warrens of poor, stacked in their misery. The street was now called the Shooting Gallery.

"Our young are on drugs and alcohol and the elders are selling it," said Leon. "It's a death camp. I come down here to pass out *The Liberator* and it's like walking through a concentration camp." He estimated the ratio now was 90 percent black to 10 percent white on Arbor Hill.

"It's getting very close," he said, "that the spirit to resist is dead. People have almost accepted that there's no hope. That decay in spirit, it can't help but affect you. You want to escape to save your own self."

Pete Jones was running a restaurant, Our Place, next door to the old Brothers' headquarters, serving hot lunches free to poor children. Gordon Van Ness had founded a community referral service for the neighborhood and had organized a program with seventy-three college students, each of them tutoring a neighborhood child. Leon was fighting for more jobs for blacks and was running the paper, but was mostly on his uppers. He was, nevertheless, in demand as a speaker because of the fame he had achieved as a Brother.

Speakers' committees, he said, eventually got to the point where they said, "We need a black militant who's starving to death." And then they'd call up Leon and ask him to lunch.

Leon in 1982 was living on Orange Street and doing well in an affirmative-action position in the State Education Department. He'd gotten his master's at State University and finished the course work for his doctorate. Gordon Van Ness was the affirmative-action officer for the State Health Department. He was also local president and state vice-president of the Association of Black Social Workers, and local president and regional coordinator of the Albany Client Council, which monitors how legal-service agencies spend the money they're supposed to use for the poor. Clearly there is a continuity in the lives of Van Ness and Van Dyke, a pair of black men with Dutch names (like Van Vranken and Van Buren) right out of Old Albany.

And the other Brothers? Earl Thorpe was still working in construction in Albany; Maurice Newton was still a glazier but had gone to Florida because he couldn't get work locally. Michael Dunn was working with the State Division for Youth's Tryon School in Johnstown. Robert Gene Dobbs and Bo Foulks both went to California to work. Pete Jones is dead, so is Moses Thomas, both from natural causes. Sam McDowell, who was doing community relations work at a prison in Coxsackie, New York, died by his own hand after killing the woman he lived with.

People were afraid of Arbor Hill in the 1970s, and some, blacks as well as whites, fear it still. The Arbor Hill Community Center in early 1982 was in steep decline compared to its social role in past eras. There are no Downtown movie theaters in Albany anymore, not only because of the flight to the suburbs but because people feared black violence. There was a mini-riot on Pearl Street during one of the hot summer nights of 1967, and forty-four young blacks were arrested after a spree of storefront destruction. And the demise of Albany's main Downtown theater, the Palace, followed closely upon the racial killing of a white youth there in 1969. (The city eventually took the Palace over and it is now used for symphony and rock concerts and theater.) A lawyer friend of mine wouldn't drive across Northern Boulevard, a main Arbor Hill thoroughfare, in those days, and he delighted in the advent of the superhighways that ringed the city and allowed him to enter Downtown without going anywhere near Arbor Hill.

During the 1970s the city implemented its long-awaited urban-renewal plan for the area, renovated 169 acres, displaced 572 families, 316 of them black, built the new Arbor Hill Elementary School, bulldozed the Van Woert Street ravine, and rerouted Van Woert in such a way that erstwhile residents like my father would never again recognize it. Some 385 houses were knocked over and 105 rehabilitated. Two private apartment complexes for low- and middle-income families were built: Ten Eyck Manor and Dudley Park Apartments; and on North Pearl between Livingston and Van Woert the city built 350 public housing units, low- and high-rise, for families and senior citizens. Part of the high-rise obliterated lower Colonie Street, and the area where my family once lived disappeared from the world.

This whole urban-renewal thrust was a major upgrading, and improved the quality of life for thousands. But a swath of the southern sector of Arbor Hill, bounded by Clinton Avenue, Northern Boulevard, Third Street, and Swan Street, despite the presence of some well-kept buildings, was, in 1982, in galloping decay. First Street, in particular from Lark to Swan, was, with the exception of a few solid houses, really just a vast vacant lot. More than half the houses were gone, and those that remained were swayback buildings—boarded up, gutted by fire, or merely uninhabitable.

The nicest thing that can be said about present-day Arbor Hill is that it is "in transition," and I heard this repeatedly from those who know it. On the positive side there is rehabilitation of buildings afoot, and more about that presently. Gordon Van Ness and Leon Van Dyke, however, have the grimmest of visions of the place. "Unemployment," said Leon, "is worse than it was in the sixties, and drugs are just rampant. Fifteen, twenty years ago we had about two drug addicts in the whole city and everybody knew them. Now I'm amazed at the number of people busted for drugs."

"With crime and drugs," said Gordon, "the problem has gotten worse. You even see kids in the preteens involved. They've gone from the normal drugs and now they're popping pills and into alcohol. Basically, if you had to measure it, compared to when the Brothers were around, we've gone backwards."

"In almost everything I could point to," said Leon, "things are worse."

One major agent of change now is the rehabilitation of houses bought from either the city or the county. "Own a piece of the block" is the city slogan that drew home buyers to bid on these properties.

Ward DeWitt, a thirty-four-year-old black South Ender who went to Philip Schuyler High School and on to Wesleyan for an anthropology degree, became director of the State Correction Commission after serving as an adviser to Governor Hugh Carey on criminal justice. With his salary, his position, he could probably buy a home in the suburb of his choice (in 1980 there were 1,411 blacks living in the town of Colonie, 374 in Guilderland, 350 in Bethlehem).

But DeWitt chose a house on Hall Place, facing Ten Broeck

Street, next to the Ten Broeck Mansion. He bought it from the city for $7,000, and with a twenty-year mortgage of $166,000 at 3 percent interest he gutted the building and restored it, put his mother, a senior citizen, into the top floor, and occupied the rest of the house with his wife and three children.

Why did he choose Arbor Hill? He wanted to put roots down in his native Albany, he said; the city auction offered him the opportunity to buy "sturdy housing stock" at a reasonable price; and for what he's paying he has a third more house than some of his co-workers, plus ready access to state offices, services, and transportation.

He has heard few complaints about the drug traffic on the block that was called the Shooting Gallery. There was a rash of burglaries in the summer of 1981, but he nevertheless sees his part of the neighborhood as "a pastoral setting . . . pleasant, a mix of ethnic groups and professionals and nonprofessionals, a healthy mix if it can be maintained."

Others like DeWitt are restoring houses on lower First, Second, and Third streets, St. Joseph's Terrace, Ten Broeck itself, and a few other streets of Arbor Hill. A similar rehabilitation plan was designed by Albany for Clinton Avenue, and many houses there are boarded up, "stabilized," waiting for investors. County Executive James Coyne estimated in mid-1982 that through city and county foreclosures, the county owned about 200 houses on Arbor Hill (maybe 350 in the entire city).

Rehabilitation of such houses awaits purchase by investors. But few are leaping to restore houses these days; low-interest federal money has become scarce because of recent cutbacks by the Reagan administration. So the houses sit there with blinded window sockets, waiting for the light of yet another morning.

The future of Arbor Hill, then, is again problematical, as it was when the creation of Washington Park drained it of its elite status and when the arrival of Southern agrarian blacks hastened the departure of its Old-Albany Negroes. But every new fire that brings in the bulldozer, every evacuation of a low-income family to make way for another rehabber, looks very like a quixotic design of the Urban Fates to purge Arbor Hill of poverty and to restore the sunny and tree-lined garden that existed when the world was young and beautiful.

*The presence of Dan O'Connell, Albany's political boss,
towered over Albany for fifty-six years. No photo ever caught
his power and menace quite like this one by Bernie Kolenberg
of the* Albany Times-Union, *taken about 1965.*

PART

5

LONG-RUN
POLITICS:
WIZARDRY UNBOUND

They Bury
the Boss:
Dan Ex-Machina

*D*an O'Connell died a happy
death, as they say, when he stopped breathing in his sleep on
February 28, 1977, at the age of ninety-one. "You're not finished
till you're dead," he once said. Now he was finished.

There was no wake—half the city might've shown up, and
how could the family have coped with that? What followed in
lieu of a wake was a tidal wave of words and pictures in the press
so we could all privately recapitulate his life, cheer, weep, or
wonder at his passing, and contemplate what next.

Without a wake his funeral became the point of farewell to
the man who had controlled the political destiny of the city and
county of Albany for so long that only if you were seventy-nine
years old on the day of the funeral could you have voted for a
Democratic candidate for mayor of Albany who hadn't been of
Dan's choosing.

That meant you had voted in 1919, and it meant also that
perhaps you voted for Dan himself, for that was the year he
squeaked into a city assessor's post by 145 votes and proved he
could do something Patrick (Packy) McCabe, the Democratic
leader since the turn of the century, couldn't.

"Packy was quite a scholar," Dan said when we talked in 1974.
"He could write a good letter but he could never elect

anybody. I probably gave him more money than he ever had in his life after things got going good."

By "going good" Dan meant after he and his brother Edward, the lawyer, and Edwin Corning, the young aristocrat with the Old-Albany name, pooled their formidable political talents following Dan's victory, and structured a new wing of the Democratic party. In 1920 they were so prepared for a primary fight with the ineffectual McCabe that McCabe withdrew from the fray. The new Democrats that year elected a congressman, Peter G. Ten Eyck, and an assemblyman, John T. (Cap) Merrigan, and for the first time since 1898 they carried the city for a Democratic candidate for governor, Alfred E. Smith. Then, in 1921, they ran William S. Hackett, a banker friend of Corning's, for mayor of Albany, and elected him.

This put an end to the age of William (Billy) Barnes, "the Boy Leader" from Harvard who in 1891 had taken over Albany's wallflower Republican organization and vitalized it. He bought the *Albany Morning Express*, took control of the *Albany Evening Journal*, which his maternal grandfather, Thurlow Weed, had established; and in 1899 Barnes elected a mayor of Albany, John Henry Blessing.

Barnes became a state power in the Republican party, and in time became known as "the President Maker"—he won a second presidential nomination for Taft, helped nominate Harding. He sued Teddy Roosevelt for libel (over a slur about Barnes being a "boss") and lost, and he opposed two principal issues of his day: woman suffrage and Prohibition. His bossism may have seemed Tammanyesque, but his style did not. At a legislative correspondents' dinner he made an arrogant speech that credited himself and his allies with electing Charles Evans Hughes governor. Hughes wagged an angry finger at Barnes and said, "You are the representative of an effete oligarchy."

When the Democrats took power in the state legislature, Packy McCabe became clerk of the Senate and brought about an investigation of Barnes (later Republican administrations would do the same to Dan O'Connell). The probers discovered Albany was not observing the law on public bidding on city contracts, was levying tribute on saloons, and that in the Tenderloin prostitution was "openly carried on, without molestation on the part of the police or other officials of the city." The Barnes Machine survived the investigation in notable good health.

Barnes believed "the equipped few" should lead the masses, a view that peaked on Lincoln's Birthday, 1921, when, in the midst of a citywide trolley strike, Barnes told a dinner audience, "The labor of a human being is a commodity." He derided the theory "that a human life brought into this world deserves a living."

The working class in the city did not warm to these notions. Also, Martin H. Glynn—who with Packy McCabe's backing had been a congressman, state comptroller, and then lieutenant governor (he also served as governor for a short time after the impeachment and removal from office of William Sulzer)—was now the feisty editor of the *Times-Union*; and he was publishing a most partisan array of news stories: MACHINE CASTS EVIL SHADOW ON THE CITY—PORKHEAD POLITICS COST YOU $32,000. Then a coal scandal turned up: accusations that $18,000 worth of city coal had been diverted to Barnes's underlings. ("Why, there was no coal stealing," Dan said candidly in a later year. "Those damn newspapers distorted the whole picture.")

The distortion, if such it was, piled on top of both Barnes's political idiocies and a factional fight within the Republican party, helped win the day and the decade for Hackett and the O'Connell ticket, and out went Billy. "Ignorance has had its day in court," he wrote in his *Journal*. Crowed Glynn, "Triumph of the people."

Barnes went broke eventually and sold the *Journal* in 1925, but before that, Dan prevented foreclosure on the *Journal* building by lending Barnes $10,000. Dan talked about the loan to Barnes when we chatted, and others confirmed it. Barnes paid the money back, and lived on until 1930, in time to see the decade end with the O'Connell Machine's supporting a citywide printers' strike. Barnes, a Classical scholar, faded away parsing Cicero, and passed into history, like Packy McCabe, an unwitting adjunct to the O'Connell monomyth.

Dan was an unlikely candidate for mythic status. He went to Public Schools 15 and 17 but quit in the sixth, or maybe the fifth, grade (he seemed unsure which). "I wasn't much of a scholar," he told me. "I wouldn't go to school for anybody." What did he do after he quit?

"Nothin'."

He was born on Friday the 13th of November, 1885, the year Grant died and Cleveland was inaugurated. He was a kid around politics, "workin' the wards," as he put it, growing up in the middle of Irish and German neighborhoods, working in a brickyard, maturing into a bartender in his father's (Black Jack O'Connell's) saloon, at Fourth Avenue and South Pearl Street, before joining the Navy in World War I. Black Jack served so many German customers (only one drink on payday—Thursdays—then get home with that paycheck) that he became fluent in German, and so, said one of his intimates, did Dan.

Dan's parents married across from the saloon, in St. Ann's, one of two Irish churches in the South End, and there also, on March 3, 1977, Dan would silently suffer his final celebration. The church was half full at 10:10 a.m., fifty minutes before the funeral mass was to begin. Teddy Kennedy was coming, so went the rumor from City Hall, and Averell Harriman was to be Jimmy Carter's representative. Governor Hugh Carey (Dan supported him early on) would be here, and so would Congressman Sam Stratton (Dan annexed him) and ex-Congressman Leo O'Brien (Dan created him out of a crackerjack newspaperman) and Mayor Erastus Corning ("I idolize him," Dan said), and several state legislators, and all of the current and ex–district attorneys and judges who were such an indispensable arm of Dan's power, and all the lawyers: Young Turks in three-piece suits, cadaverous old men getting ready to cross the bar themselves. Then, too, came the patronage swarm—the ward bosses and committeemen and foot-sloggers who formed the basic metal of Dan's Machine. Three quarters of the people in the church were men over fifty (half of those were over sixty-five). There were some women: wives and sisters and nuns and workers for the party and two handsomely tanned figures who had flown home from Miami Beach for the occasion. Dan had one woman, Mary Marcy, a longtime friend and campaigner, as vice-chairman of the party, but otherwise he involved women only at low levels. "They're all right in the kitchen," was his view.

"Are you taking names?" a man asked Kathy Powers, a *Troy Times-Record* reporter who was standing at the back of the church making notes on arrivals. "I forgot my card. I didn't know you'd be taking names."

The man was told that nobody was taking names, and he smiled his disappointment and slithered into a pew.

By 10:40 a.m. the firemen standing guard duty closed the church doors, opening them only to let Dan come in, feet first, wheeled along on a velvet-covered, chrome-plated dolly by the undertaker, and followed by the honorary bearers (among them Dan's driver, his barber, and a man he helped become a judge of the Court of Appeals—New York's highest), by the family (no children, his wife and three brothers long dead), and by the longtime hangers-on whose loss of Dan would be fatal to their political futures, all standing in solemn line behind the coffin.

Among the mourners were Jimmy and Charlie Ryan, twin brothers, very close to Dan (about them, more later); and what Dan really thought of all these politicians who had come to see him off, Charlie would report when we talked: "Dan said he'd never trust a politician with anything, but would trust a chicken-fighter with his life."

"Yeah," Dan told me in 1974, "I always fought chickens. My father fought 'em, Solly [Dan's brother] fought 'em. I had five hundred chickens at a time, probably the best in the world. I beat Gus Melick out of sixty-five thousand dollars in a night, up in Foley's, in Troy. I beat him, seven to three."

Charlie also remembered, "One time I brought Joe Kennedy out to see Dan in the Helderbergs [the Albany County mountains where Dan had his summer camp], and Dan was fooling around with the chickens. He was in a T-shirt and had a chicken under one arm and his shoes were full of chickenshit, and Joe Kennedy didn't believe it was Dan. He thought I was kidding him."

What Joe Kennedy was looking for was Albany's backing for Jack Kennedy at the 1960 Democratic National Convention, and he got it. Charlie Ryan said Lyndon Johnson sent a representative to see Dan on the same question, and this fellow was a chicken-fighter. Charlie remembered what Dan told the man: "You should've got here before Joe Kennedy did, and I'd have gone with you. But if Kennedy doesn't get it by the third ballot, we'll switch."

Switching proved unnecessary, and the Kennedys were grate-ful. Joe Kennedy said later that Dan was the only leader he'd gone to who hadn't asked him for money. And Jack called Dan from the DeWitt Clinton Hotel after he campaigned on Albany's Cap-itol steps, to thank him for his support. Leo O'Brien recalled that moment: "Jack talked to Dan and then hung up, grinning from ear to ear, and he says, 'I might become the President of the United States, but you know what he just said to me? "I didn't do it for you, I did it for your old man." ' "

Teddy Kennedy didn't turn up at the funeral. Maybe he was never really expected. Or maybe he'd heard what Dan had said about his brother Bobby ("a stiff, a louse") or about Teddy's own presidential candidacy ("I'd rather not see him run. On account of drowning that girl. You can't get drunk and drown a girl and run for president and win. I don't think. But that doesn't make any difference to me. I'd support him every day of the week").

Word came that Jimmy Carter had sent a personal message of condolence to Dan's survivors, but neither Harriman nor anyone else from Washington would turn up at St. Ann's. The higher courts of power to which Dan gave allegiance were better represented: eight priests and a monsignor suited up as celebrants of Dan's mass, the principal celebrant being the Bishop of the Albany Diocese, Howard J. Hubbard.

The church always has the last word if you give it credence, and Dan did. He not only kept his rosary beads next to his telephone and coffee cup, but had holy-water fonts mounted in both his Albany home and his summer camp. Reverend John J. Fearey, a former North Ender who became pastor emeritus of St. Ann's, had described Dan to me in 1964 as "a good, solid, American, Christian man, a humble man who sits down with others, anyplace at all. He's one of the most generous of men and he wants no praise or jubilee."

Generosity had endeared Dan to the Diocese for generations—gifts of money, land, moral stricture (Dan's district attorneys went to court against such "lewd, lascivious and obscene" celebrity villains as novelist John O'Hara), plus gifts of special services, such as paving, snowplowing, and sewer work, whose like did not necessarily accrue to other denominations. Also the public school system (in which teachers were often political appointees) was not much of a challenge to the city's Catholic schools in terms of scholarship and special education. This kept costs down for Dan, and enrollment up for the parochial schools, which in the 1960s, before Catholic education began its nose dive, counted half the city's student population in their enrollments.

In its turn, the Diocese had favored Dan and his Machine: pressuring the Franciscan order to silence a radical priest who kept pillorying Albany politicians in the newspapers; giving communion in a body (i.e., as a group) to Dan's police force (which the patsy press usually covered with a page of pictures), but denying the same kind of communion to George Harder and his friends, maverick Catholic Democrats challenging Dan for various public offices. Dan's pastor in his uptown parish (the priest who did the denying) denounced from the pulpit such Johnny-come-latelys as Harder, and praised Dan for installing the new traffic light in front of the church. Harder took to calling Dan "Saint Daniel."

Father Fearey was up on St. Ann's ceremonial altar for Dan; so was Monsignor James Hart, whose father was a chicken-fighter;

so was Father Joseph R. Romano, the new pastor of St. Ann's, who in 1972, as chaplain of the Albany firemen, had sided with the firemen publicly in their strike for better wages. Dan told the Diocese to keep its nose out of city business and then denounced Father Romano as a "dago son of a bitch."

Ethnic slurs were commonplace with Dan, an Archie Bunker with clout. "Don't call me Mister," he told *Times-Union* reporter Bill O'Brien in 1963 during a rare interview. "The only ones I want calling me Mister are niggers and Jews." This didn't get into the paper, of course. Dan had always been smart enough not to say such things publicly, or for the record, smarter still not to give many interviews. Then came the slur on Father Romano, on tape, during a phone chat with a WOKO radio reporter; and the city erupted in a horselaugh: Ho, ho, ho, Dan has gone bananas at last.

Two years after the insult, Father Romano was named pastor of St. Ann's, a deft retaliatory stroke by the Diocese, for Dan was still a trustee of his old church, even though he'd long ago moved up to Whitehall Road, in St. James's parish. Father Romano went up to Dan's home to present him with his appointment letter, and Dan asked him, "Are you mad?" Father Romano said he wasn't, and Dan apologized, calling his remark a mistake. "I never meant in my whole life any disrespect for any priest," Father Romano quoted Dan as saying. "Forget it," said the priest.

The incident was symptomatic of Dan's behavior, as recalled by Charlie Ryan: "Dan wouldn't hold a grudge. You'd have a fight with him today and then when you wouldn't come around he'd ask why you didn't. 'Because of the fight,' somebody'd tell him. And Dan'd say, 'What kind of an Irishman can you be if you can't have a fight with somebody once in a while?'"

"I bless you, Daniel, with the holy water which recalls the day of your baptism."

So intoned the soft-voiced, boyish-looking, tough-minded Bishop Hubbard, standing over the flag-draped coffin of the no-longer-contentious leader at the rear of the church. Howard Hubbard was a wildly popular Bishop, part of his reputation as a progressive and humanitarian directly attributable to Dan's resistance to the social changes of the 1960s.

When the federal antipoverty programs were being established everywhere—money and power being parceled out to the poor so they could lift themselves by their rotting bootstraps—Dan resisted. He didn't want City Hall bypassed, and these programs were doing just that. He had always shunned federal money, for it meant federal snooping into what you did with it. He told *Times-Union* reporter Tom Wilkinson (off the record) that the poverty programs were "a lot of horseshit." And so Albany was the last major city in the United States to accept one; and by then City Hall had everything its own way.

In the fighting that went on in the 1960s (and which is discussed elsewhere in this book) the Catholic church in Albany emerged as corporately ruthless, unfeeling, and politically partisan; and also, because of young men like Howard Hubbard, productive of individually splendid figures. Bishop Edward Maginn reversed the church's negative image by putting Father Hubbard, then a fledgling priest only two years at work in the slums, in charge of the church's first public tie to the black, non-Catholic poor: a storefront outreach program called Providence House, a few blocks up from where Jack O'Connell's saloon had stood. Now, a decade later, Father Hubbard was Bishop, throwing holy sprinkles at Dan, yesterday's villain.

Dan was always somebody's villain. In 1923 insurgent Republican candidate for mayor Dr. James N. Vander Veer viewed the City Hall incumbency this way: "To the rogues and rascals of the town, the gang with the itching palm, two years in power was sufficient to sustain them for the future. They traveled a coarse, rough alley, which reeks with the indecencies of life, with its thugs and bullies, its addicts and harlots, yes, and lower than all—that poor, miserable person who lives off the infamy of the unfortunate creature of the street."

Reducing Dan and Company to consorts of pimps did not win the day for Vander Veer. Hackett thrashed him soundly.

But similar accusations dogged the O'Connell Machine on into the 1940s, when the state police finally closed down Albany's open gambling. Most of its elaborate network of vice also faded away, though neither pastime left town entirely.

The Machine had always permitted a night world to function, and had profited from it, city detectives sometimes doubling as bagmen to collect weekly dues from politically established gamblers. One high-level detective sat guard duty for Jack (Legs) Diamond when Diamond stayed at the Kenmore Hotel, the purpose, presumably, to keep the peace; but the detective was also on Diamond's payroll during that period. Dan described his police, in later years, as "the first line of defense. I don't think the country'd stand up without a well-organized local police." One of the Machine's first actions upon assuming power in 1921 had been to raise police salaries. When I was covering the police in the 1950s, John Tuffey was chief, and he made daily visits to Dan, wherever he was, to keep him in touch with what was going on in the city. The cops were Dan's army.

Dan's role in the night world was well known in the 1920s but became a matter of vagueness in later decades as he evolved into the aging eminence. But he clearly knew, or could find out if it interested him, when every sparrow lost two dollars on a horse. His brother John, known as Solly, was the more visible power figure, to whom a series of lesser chieftains, their turf divided geographically (Green Street, State Street, Broadway, etc.), gave immediate allegiance.

In 1936 a reformer named George Drew Egbert, pastor of a Congregational church in Flushing, New York, and president of the Society for the Prevention of Crime, called attention to the situation once again when he called on Governor Herbert Lehman to remove Dan's district attorney, John T. Delaney, "for failure to prosecute houses of prostitution and gambling." Egbert said Delaney's "nonenforcement" was the result of his ties to the O'Connell brothers. Lehman, a Democrat enthusiastically supported by Dan, could find no pressing reasons to bother Delaney, who stayed in office for another decade.

In 1930 the Machine's tax-assessment practices became the subject of an investigation by a state legislative committee, which found that enemies of the organization were "threatened with increased assessments," but if they promised to vote Democratic their assessments went down. The investigation snagged a few small fish in the city treasurer's office and they were lightly fried, but the Machine remained untouched and the assessment practices continued in the same way Dan and Company had learned them from the Barnes Machine.

An assessment case was traced for me in 1974 by Theresa Cooke, a pert young woman watchdog (Dan liked her looks, and Mayor Corning, in response to a columnist's question, picked her as the person he'd like to spend two weeks with) who almost became city comptroller. The building involved was at 54 North Pearl Street, and it was assessed at $120,000. The owners went to the New York State Supreme Court, and on January 18, 1971, the court reduced the assessment to $25,000. The following July the assessment was back to $120,000. Legal maneuvering again lowered it to $25,000. In July 1973 it went back to $120,000.

This sort of action not only kept the Machine's enemies in a state of economic anguish; it also provided work for the Machine's favorite lawyers, whom you hired, perhaps even on a retainer basis, to have assessments expeditiously lowered. A rough estimate is that half a million dollars in legal fees were spread selectively across the bar in the mid-1970s by this method of promoting Democratic happiness.

The assessment system also worked another way, as the *Knickerbocker News* reported in November 1965. The case involved the Town House Motor Hotel, assessed by the city at $300,000, but appraised by the State Board of Equalization and Assessment at $1.7 million. In other words, it was assessed at less than 18 percent of its value, whereas the city average was supposed to be 53 percent. It was revealed that the owner of the Town House was Donald Lynch, executive secretary of the Albany County Democratic Committee, who was married to Dan's niece.

The only investigation that nailed Dan to his political cross was begun by one of Dan's friends, Governor Al Smith, who, Dan said in later years, was the greatest governor the state ever had. Smith, on April 29, 1925, wrote to Albany County Sheriff Claude Tibbits, and noted that what had once been looked on as "an innocent feature of the annual baseball season has grown to be a well-known lottery and as far east as the City of Boston, people are talking about 'The Albany Pool.' " Smith opined that it was violating the law and ordered the sheriff to stop it. Nothing was done.

By 1926 the federal government had taken charge of the investigation, on grounds the pool's tickets were shipped as a lottery in interstate commerce, a violation of the U.S. Criminal Code. Dan was one of thirty-six indicted and was fined $750 in 1927. Solly O'Connell was also indicted, but the charge was dismissed. Ten defendants pleaded guilty and drew fines and jail terms of a year, the jail terms suspended. One man drew an eighteen-month sentence, plus a $5,000 fine, and because of a prior conviction he was jailed.

In 1929 another federal investigation of the pool was begun. Dan was subpoenaed, but refused to answer questions before a grand jury. He was indicted for perjury, but ultimately the charge was dropped when he pleaded guilty to a contempt charge that stemmed from his refusal to answer questions. The plea bargaining avoided open confrontation with a thrice-indicted founder of the pool, William F. (Cooch) Buchanan, who was a witness for the prosecution in a related case.

In November 1929, in New York City, Buchanan testified at the federal perjury trial of James Otto, who was said to be an O'Connell associate in the pool. Buchanan said that Dan and his brother Ed had crowded him out of the pool. He also said the brothers had threatened another man, James W. Wright, owner and originator of the Capital City Pool, with jail unless he paid them $2\frac{1}{2}$ percent of his pool's gross receipts. Buchanan said the O'Connell share in 1927 amounted to $820,000. Buchanan also said an Albany police captain assigned policemen to accompany members of the pool when they transferred large sums of money.

Buchanan testified that Dan had directed that the money coming into Albany's coffers from the pool be divided five ways: "Otto, yourself, Ed and I, and Ed Corning." The prosecutor did not seek to identify Corning further, but the press quizzed Edwin Corning about the matter later in the day. "Not worthy of comment," he said in Albany. "There is not a word of truth in it." Nothing further came of the accusation.

The government made a case that the pool was rigged, that a "dummy-player" operation, said to be directed by Dan O'Connell, assured the pool's operators of winning anything they chose to win; anybody else won only if they were lucky. Romildo (Red) Bottari, a former barber of mine, told me that as a youth he'd cut the hair of a pool director, and when he complained to the man he'd never won in the pool, the man said he'd put him down as a winner for an upcoming week. That week the federals closed the pool with their investigation, and Red was spared what he felt would be certain riches.

Dan, in 1965, was asked by an interviewer what his connection to the pool had been. "No connection at all," he said. "My problem was that I knew the fellows who were running it. I did them a few favors, but that was all." But Dan was being coy. Leo O'Brien recollected that the $820,000 was not an unreasonable figure for the Machine to cull from the game. "But none of it stuck to Dan," Leo said with characteristic loyalty. "He put his share back into the organization."

Nevertheless, Dan did time. Of sorts.

Charlie Ryan told me a bit more of the story than I'd ever heard before. The perennial Dan-in-jail story is that Charlie's father was Dan's benevolent jailer, but that is wrong. James Ryan, Sr., said his son, was actually a stockbroker who had known Dan for years and had contributed to the 1921 campaign in Albany. The Ryan family lived near 242nd Street in the Riverdale section of New York City, and Ryan was so well connected in New York politics that he arranged for special jailhouse treatment for Dan.

That meant, said Charlie, that Dan would be picked up in the morning, by car, in front of the Federal House of Detention, and be driven up to the Ryan home in Riverdale, where he would spend the day. At night the car would carry him back to jail.

Dan was so pleased with these accommodations that he told the elder Ryan he'd take care of his sons if anything ever happened to him. Ryan died the same year, 1930. "Dan told my mother to move the kids to Albany," Charlie said. And she did.

"The kids" were Charlie, who was going to Manhattan College, and his brothers, James and John. John became a federal bankruptcy referee in Albany; Jimmy and Charlie became heavyweights in Albany Democratic politics, Jimmy as county purchasing agent and later party executive secretary, and Charlie as party treasurer. Jimmy died of cancer in Florida in 1979. Charlie, still alive in 1983, lost a bitter battle with Mayor Corning for control of the party in the years following Dan's death, and at that point, for the first time in the history of the Machine, control of both party and City Hall centered in one man, Erastus.

From the beginning the leadership had been split. The principal decision-making was shared by Edwin Corning and Dan's youngest brother, Ed, the lawyer, establishing the pattern of a Catholic-Protestant division of power. When Edwin Corning died in 1934, the main financial decisions about the city and county government fell to Ed O'Connell. But his associations from early on were with men of power and wealth in the Protestant establishment—epitomized by the membership of the elite Fort Orange Club. In his fledging years as a lawyer, Ed worked in the law office of Neile F. Towner, a man associated with great fortunes, and who is credited with having articulated the doctrine that the mayor should always be a Protestant. This was followed religiously in Albany after the O'Connell-Corning takeover: the Irish Catholics running the party, the Protestant power in control of the city government.

Such divisions are hardly clear cut. Dan always had a say in city business; and an old-time Democratic committeeman remembered Towner's political clout: "The party [i.e., Dan] put up George Foy to run for the State Senate. Towner was in Europe but when he heard about it he said no, for he'd promised that job to [Julian B.] Erway. We had all our petitions signed for Foy when we had to change them all at midnight for Erway." Erway, Towner's law partner, was Albany County district attorney from 1945 to 1953, served in the Senate from 1942 to 1944, and again from 1957 to 1968.

Towner himself, from 1936 until he died in 1962, was president of the Board of Education, another office traditionally held by a Protestant.

Dan's personal areas of power in the early years were patronage and police; his brother Solly ruled over Nighttown, the sporting world. Patrick (Packy), Dan's oldest brother, was leader of the First Ward and patronage conduit to the state legislature as clerk of the State Senate the year he died, 1933.

Parker Corning, brother of Edwin, was one of the party's early financial backers and served in Congress from 1923 to 1936, at which point he was shunted back into private life by the O'Connells for party disloyalty. (The Corning family is discussed at greater length in the chapter on Erastus.) Edwin suffered a debilitating heart attack in 1928 and lingered until August 1934, when he died of arteriosclerosis at the age of fifty. The O'Connell brothers then took control of the party.

Because of the extraordinary early success of this oddball oligarchy, the potential for political influence beyond Albany was clearly recognized. At three moments in history the Machine almost elected one of its own as governor.

The first was Mayor Hackett, who from his election in 1921 was a possible choice; and after 1923 and 1925, when his pluralities fattened, he became, said the *New York World* in his obituary, the logical candidate for governor if Al Smith refused to be drafted as the nominee in 1928. Hackett, too poor to go to college, was a self-made lawyer and banker whose popularity as Albany's mayor was extraordinary. The Albany Democratic organization insured his life for $100,000 during the 1925 mayoral campaign. He was a Baptist, a bachelor, and a Mason, the latter element especially important to Smith, who was moving toward a presidential candidacy. Leo O'Brien recalled it: "Hackett was a thirty-third-degree Mason, and very active. And here was Smith, a Catholic, handing him the governorship. It would have been a national coup."

Then, on February 16, 1926, Hackett was riding in a car in Havana with two Albany men and a Cuban racing-car driver.

Their slow-moving automobile hit a construction ditch and over-turned. Hackett was thrown from the car, struck his head, was hospitalized, developed erysipelas, and died March 4.

The second gubernatorial near-miss was Edwin Corning, who was credited with managing Hackett's successful campaign, and who became a figure of major significance in the state. He was named Democratic state chairman in 1925, and in 1926 was elected lieutenant governor under Al Smith, who asked him to become the gubernatorial candidate in 1928. Corning was too ill to accept and the nomination went to Franklin Roosevelt.

The third chance centered on John Boyd Thacher II, who suc-ceeded Hackett as mayor. His grandfather (John Boyd I) and great-grandfather (George) had been Albany mayors before him. He was Princeton '04, well-to-do, and had been in politics from early on. He declined to run for district attorney in 1919, when the McCabe faction offered it, but ran and won the city comptroller's post with the O'Connell-Corning group in 1921. He won fame as an orator and in 1925 became president of the Common Council, which put him in line for Hackett's job.

He was the Albany crowd's bright prospect for governor in 1932 and a group of state Democratic leaders backed him as their candidate to succeed FDR, who was stumping for president. FDR wanted his lieutenant governor, Herbert H. Lehman, to succeed him, and a fight ensued during the September convention in Albany's Tenth Infantry Armory.

Leo O'Brien covered it and recalled what happened:

"The convention sat in recess all day while a group of leaders met in the DeWitt Clinton Hotel and fought it out. There was Dan and Ed O'Connell, and Al Smith, and John Curry, the leader of Tammany, and John McCooey, the leader of Brooklyn, and others. FDR was putting all kinds of pressure on and they'd all have to deal with him if he didn't make it to the presidency and came back as governor.

"Al Smith quit first, and then McCooey surrendered. Curry stuck. It was a nasty meeting. Ed O'Connell laid his tongue to McCooey particularly for running out, but McCooey only said, 'Go 'way, I'm an old man, I'm tired.' Al Smith quit, maybe for financial problems. He didn't leave the [governor's] mansion with very much money and the Lehman supporters had a great deal of it—not bribes, but things he could do. McCooey ran out be-cause he was afraid of the Jewish vote. They all offered Thacher every other state office, but the O'Connells refused. It was all or nothing.

"I was there till eight o'clock at night in the lobby, and then Dan came down and told me what happened and asked me would I go up to the armory and tell Thacher it was no. I can remember Gil [Gilbert V.] Schenck [a Supreme Court judge] was sitting next to Thacher, and I said to him, 'I haven't got the heart. Will you tell him?' And he did. And an hour and a half later Thacher was up there seconding the nomination of Lehman."

Such loyalty to the party's choice was not unusual; it was Albany dogma. In 1972 when the volunteer campaigners for George McGovern's presidential candidacy were working miracles in primaries around the country, bringing out the student and youth vote, they descended on Albany, ready for another blitz, only to find Dan hostile to their plans. "I'm running the campaign with our own organization," he said, "and we don't want any separate campaign here."

The McGovern crowd persisted, and so Dan put himself on the primary ballot as the head of an uncommitted delegation; for Dan preferred Hubert Humphrey or Scoop Jackson. It will come as no surprise that Dan and his folks won and went to the convention uncommitted, and Albany was the only city in the state that didn't elect a McGovern delegate. But when McGovern won the nomination, Albany cranked out 33,000 votes for him, compared to Nixon's 21,000, making Albany the only city in the state McGovern carried.

In 1942 loyalty had taken another shape. John J. Bennett—a former attorney general under Lehman who had conducted a more hostile investigation of Albany vote fraud than seemed to befit a Democrat investigating other Democrats—ran for governor against Thomas E. Dewey. Dewey had been nosed out by Lehman in the 1938 gubernatorial election, but it was Dewey's accusations against the O'Connells that had forced Lehman to unleash Bennett against his old friends.

The smart money in New York City knew Dan's crowd would never forgive Bennett—he won 174 convictions against them, mostly for double to quadruple voting—and they were betting Albany would cut him (i.e., spread the word not to vote for him). The New Yorkers offered heavy money, said to be about $100,000 eventually, that Bennett wouldn't carry Albany County by 20,000 votes. (Lehman had carried Albany County by almost that in

1938 against Dewey—19,923; Lehman's victory in the whole state was only by a slim 64,000 votes, which no doubt contributed to his decision not to run again in 1942.) Dan's advisers, so the story goes, wanted to take the bet, but Dan resisted, saying if we wait they'll lower the figure; and he was right. The gamblers came down to 15,000 votes, at which time, said Leo O'Brien, who was privy to the event, "Dan shot the works." That is, he turned out the folks to vote for Bennett, who carried Albany County by 20,010 votes.

Dan won the bet. Bennett lost the election.

Dewey, having captured the Capitol, pursued his attack on the Albany Machine. Between August 1943 and February 1946 he spent half a million dollars in formal appropriations trying to break Dan's power, though the total cost of his investigation, including his use of state services, workers, and police, was said to be $1.5 million.

The Bennett investigation had turned up so many voting illegalities that Dewey, in his campaigning, charged that "the Tammany Machine braves are pikers by comparison with this Machine when it comes to vote frauds. . . . They have registered 82,000 people in Albany, and that's 3,000 more than the *City Directory* could find."

One city water inspector was arrested passing out envelopes to voters at a polling place, and when searched he had 45 envelopes in his pocket, each containing $4. This looked rather like a man purchasing votes. But he said he was contributing to a charity fund to buy food and shoes for needy folks and the polling place was the best spot to find them. He was released, probably because such ingenuity could not go unrewarded.

Dan's wizardry with elections, fabled for several decades, was recollected in 1982 by Governor Mario Cuomo, who told the story of Dan's being marooned on an island with another man, with only one coconut between them. They decided to take a vote on who should eat it, and when the vote was counted, Dan had won, 110 to 1.

Governor Dewey, in 1943, set out to put an end to such maneuvering and imposed two hundred state troopers on city polling places, plus a team of special deputy attorneys general. The Machine prepared its loyalists for the assault with full-page ads in the papers, warning them to be on guard against "terrorism . . . foreign-inspired methods . . . the New Gestapo . . . a cheap burlesque for the sole purpose of terrorizing a few state employees and cleaning women."

Thus warned, the folks trod lightly. The humbling result for Dewey: four arrests for vote buying and repeat voting.

Dewey also put twenty investigators to work on City Hall's books, and he did find some illegal manipulation of funds, but nothing came of this. His people also indicted John J. Murphy, Dan's closest associate in the party, for misappropriating $45,000 in party funds; indicted Cohoes political boss Mike Smith, Dan's longtime ally, for conspiracy; indicted Daniel H. Prior, defense attorney for several of Dan's indicted minions, for income tax evasion; caught Judge Gilbert Schenck in a compromising conversation with Dan about a court case in process, which resulted in Schenck's being censured by the state legislature.

The charges and countercharges were dubbed "the Battle of Albany" by the press, which treated them with only slightly less importance than the real wartime battles going on in Europe and the South Pacific. Mayor Corning (who had replaced Thacher in 1941) charged Dewey with trying to "ride to the White House upon the backs of decent people in one small community. . . . Does Dewey think the attack on the Albany County Democratic organization will be the measure of a world leader?"

In 1944 Corning was drafted into the Army as a buck private, gaining enormous sympathy for the Democrats. Just as Corning was about to leave for the war, Dewey's wiretappers caught Dan in conversation with his top attorney, Robert E. Whalen (Dan called him "Sir Robert"). Dan's brother Ed had died at fifty-one in 1939, and Dan at that point put his nephew, John O'Connell, Jr., the victim of a 1933 kidnapping, in as figurehead chairman of the party, replacing Ed. Now Dan was having second thoughts:

"Now listen here, I was thinking this. Johnny never had any taste for politics, and it was a damned shame to put him in there as a figurehead. And in addition to that, he's in the brewery [Hedrick's, the O'Connell family business], and it is a good way to raise his family. . . . Couldn't very well withdraw him except under one condition, and that is to make myself county chairman."

"Why, hell," said Sir Robert, "that's the way it ought to be."

"I'll be the wartime premier," Dan said, "and I'll let the boys and girls know that I'm going to carry on the duties until Erastus is back out of the Army."

This plan wasn't followed. Sir Robert feared Dan would become an irresistible new target for Dewey's investigators if he took the chairmanship, that he'd be subpoenaed and of course would have to refuse to testify, and so it seemed like a bad idea.

Dan had another plan: appoint John J. Murphy, under indictment for misappropriating party funds, as party chairman. This was both a gob of spit in Mr. Dewey's eye and a vote of confidence for Jack Murphy. And so it went. Murphy died a few months later, and Dan did take over the chairmanship at last, his first visible, public role since his 1919 assessorship. At the party meeting, Dan's name was put in nomination by Mike Smith, who was also under indictment. Another gob for you, Mr. Dewey.

Corning came back from the European Theater a private first class and a local hero, and won emotional points for the beleaguered Albany crowd. But by then the investigation was winding down and ultimately it died, for reasons I'll get into.

The results: fifty-two indictments by Dewey's probers; thirty-eight guilty pleas, mostly to election-law violations; no jury convictions (Dan's folks controlled the empaneling of grand and trial juries). All indictments of major figures were thrown out of court either by juries or on appeals, or died for want of prosecution. A few lesser figures went to jail.

The reason always given for Dewey's failure to nail Dan, or anybody important, has been that Dan retaliated with his own investigation of the legislature (which sits in Albany County's jurisdiction). Well, yes. But a story goes with it.

In 1943 District Attorney Delaney did summon a grand jury to investigate how money had been disbursed by the legislature over the previous eight years, and he subpoenaed state officials. The legislature squawked and sqwooked, and Dewey quickly superseded Delaney with not one but two special investigators: one to investigate Albany, one to investigate his own legislature. The former was George P. Monaghan, assistant district attorney of New York County, who as special prosecutor turned up the aforesaid fifty-two indictments against Albany; the latter was Hiram C. Todd, a New York lawyer whose real job was to do nothing, and he did it extremely well. His investigation of the legislature resulted in one indictment of a senator, who was acquitted, and a contempt charge against the Democratic minority leader of the Senate, Irwin Steingut, for evasive answers. Steingut was convicted but the conviction was reversed on appeal.

Dan's investigators did rather better, and the story of that was told to me by Charlie Ryan, who had a key role in the events. Charlie had been working in the state comptroller's office and became privy to the fact that some top Republicans (also a top Democrat) in the legislature were receiving checks from a western New York firm that was performing contract services for the comptroller. Charlie became privy because he was delivering the checks. The people who were getting the checks, said Charlie, did not always live or work where they said they lived or worked; and sometimes names of relatives such as children were on the checks.

The man for whom Charlie had been working was later indicted on another matter entirely and went for help to his powerful legislative friends, who'd been getting their checks through him. "He asked them," Charlie recalled, "to come up with some money. And they were reneging a bit. So he had me go to where the canceled checks were and make photostats. I kept a set for myself, two suitcases full, over at the house."

What happened to Charlie's indicted friend is not important here. But keep your eye on those checks. They come into play sometime later, when Dewey starts to investigate the O'Connell Machine. Charlie is over at Dan's house with Dan's district attorney, John Delaney, and as Charlie recalls it, "I said, 'Imagine those phony bastards trying to do this to us when they're doing the same thing themselves.' " And he told Dan and Delaney the story of the checks. Dan immediately sent him home to get them, and he came right back with the two suitcases.

"Delaney fell off the seat when he saw the checks," said Charlie, so powerful were the signatures they bore. And at that point a counterthrust was born: Charlie, as Dan's emissary, went to Washington with an associate of Delaney's to see the head of the company that had written all the lovely checks. The man in question, said Charlie, was at work in Washington on an international project.

"We all had dinner in the Mayflower Hotel," Charlie remembered, "and in the middle of it I told him, 'I don't want to be a rat, but this fellow here is an assistant district attorney and he's got a subpoena for you. All those guys you put on the payroll . . .'" The man was rather taken aback and argued that he only did it for Charlie's old boss in the comptroller's office; but he got the subpoena anyway.

Back in Albany, Charlie reported these events to Dan, and Dan told him, "Go home and call me up and tell me the whole story."

Knowing his phone was tapped, Dan understood this was the quickest way to get a message to Governor Dewey. Charlie went home and called Dan, and he remembered Dan's then saying, "Jesus, we'll fix those phony bastards. We'll start an investigation of the legislature next week. We'll get all their bank records . . ." And so on.

Charlie said that very soon thereafter, Dewey, being friendly with Leo O'Brien, told him to tell Dan that if he called off the legislative investigation, he, Dewey, would call off his own investigation of Albany.

"And he did," said Charlie.

Leo O'Brien has a somewhat different memory of the events. He was the Capitol Hill columnist and correspondent for the *Times-Union*, the *New York Journal-American*, and Hearst's International News Service, plus half a dozen more newspapers, and was certainly the best-known and best-connected Albany newsman of that era. He lived next door to Jim Hagerty, press secretary for Dewey (and later for President Eisenhower), and by covering Dewey as a newsman, and being close to Hagerty, O'Brien came to like Dewey. Of course, he'd also been close to Dan for twenty years.

"The worst thing you can imagine," Leo recalled in March 1982, "is two people you think a lot of, out to crucify one another. And then to find yourself in the middle is not a happy situation. But it got to a point, at the most delicate time, they had to have somebody both sides would trust, and I happened to be the guy. I wanted the damned investigations ended, not only of the O'Connells but of people on the other side.

"I got a call from Charles Breitel, counsel to the Governor, that Dewey wanted to see me in Pawling [where Dewey lived]. He hinted what it was about and also hinted Dewey could have gotten O'Connell if he'd had more time. I rode like hell in a state car, and when I got there, Dewey sent his guard of troopers to wait outside the house. Mrs. Dewey and the kids were already at a movie in Pawling. Dewey emphasized to me how secret the whole thing was.

"I hadn't even talked to Dan. It was an awkward position, speaking for someone who wasn't there, especially being a newspaperman—you're not supposed to do those things. We went into [Dewey's] library and he said he wanted to end the investigation on condition that Mike Smith and Jack Murphy plead guilty and take suspended sentences. I argued that Murphy had cancer of the throat—and why put a sick man in that position?—and that the O'Connells didn't control Smith. 'He thinks they're whippersnappers,' I told Dewey." Leo said he also argued that Dan was aware that one of Dewey's own investigators of the moment had held a no-show job when he was in law school.

What Dewey said, according to Leo, was " 'I don't want to drop one investigation and have another one pick up.' He was naturally suspicious. I told him, 'That won't happen.' I took a chance. I thought I was making a pretty good deal. When I got back to Albany I called Dan and asked him to meet me on the steps of the Elks Club, and I told him, 'The investigation is over—provided, if the one is closed you won't keep the other one going.' And Dan said, 'That's easy enough.' "

The bare-bones story of this deal, which Leo says took place late in 1945, wasn't made public until after Dewey died. Dan, in an interview with Ernie Tetrault of WRGB-TV in 1971, put it this way: "O'Brien came in after the investigation with the proposal that if I got some of 'em to plead guilty . . . he'd close the whole thing up. I said I wouldn't ask anybody to plead guilty to anything. We're not guilty of it anyway. So Dewey said . . . if I didn't back into his legislature with my district attorney he'd drop the whole matter. Get Monaghan out . . . let him try a case or two and try to convict 'em . . . but he wouldn't. I said that's all right with me. I ain't got no ax to grind with the legislature or anybody else. So we got along fine from then on."

As to those notable checks, Charlie Ryan says they ended the investigation. Leo thinks they surfaced well before the end of the investigation, and that, while they remained Dan's trump card, they alone didn't cause Dewey to quit.

"Dewey wasn't frightened out of that investigation," Leo said. "He decided it had gone on long enough and produced too little. He came up with zero. I had a feeling he was getting fed up with it. There was no flock of Jimmy Hineses [Hines was a discredited Tammany Hall leader] up here as he expected. He was running for president and his advisers were telling him, 'You're riding a pretty tired horse.' One of Dewey's associates was drinking a great deal and on the [tapped] phone Dan quoted some of his indiscretions."

Dan, like Dewey, was suspicious that, despite the truce, Dewey would reopen the investigation or begin a new one. In 1974 I asked Dan what he thought about Dewey. "He's a tough little bastard," Dan said, as if Dewey were still lurking down there in the corridors of the Capitol. Dan told Ernie Tetrault, "I never met him, but I know the last four years he was the best governor we ever had. He made an agreement with me."

Dan later revised his estimate of Dewey downward, but continued to respect the fact that he kept his word. Dan, too, kept his side of the agreement. One of the state's topmost Republicans, very close to Dewey, and against whom Dan held presumably damning evidence, was planning a subsequent run for high office, but he feared Dan would play his trump. Said Charlie Ryan, "Dan told him, 'Go ahead and run and nobody will know a thing.' " And nobody did.

When the Dewey investigation ended, Dan issued a statement of vindication: "If the city wasn't well administered they would have shouted it—but they found nothing." He predicted Erastus would be reelected mayor in 1945 with a plurality of 35,000. The official tally was 36,122.

The Machine remained a target for investigation in later decades, most notably in 1972 when Governor Rockefeller's State Investigation Commission looked into Albany County purchasing practices and found such things as a 500 percent markup on one item, a dealer's charging $232,000 above list price during a three-year period, and $700,000 spent with one dealer without public bidding. Vehemently castigated was county purchasing agent Jimmy Ryan. "The worst-run county in America," said one investigator.

Ryan's tenure as purchasing agent ran out just after the probe ended. Dan instantly reappointed him (a gob for you, Mr. Rockefeller) and proceeded to investigate himself with his own district attorney, using the evidence the SIC had accumulated. Dan's investigators exonerated Dan in general, Ryan in particular, and indicted three vendors for shortweighting the county.

The question after all this—and this is hardly all—is: Why didn't the people of Albany ever rise up against the Machine? Why, even now in 1983, after sixty-two consecutive years in power, is the Machine still in good health and likely to continue even with Erastus now gone?

As to the people, we'll get to that. As to the Machine, a pair of moments in Dan's life come to mind as a way of exploring the foundation of this longevity. The first was in his living room when we were talking about governors and I asked about his relationship to Franklin Roosevelt. "We were all right," he said, and paused. Then he added, "I didn't like him. He didn't like Tammany Hall. He had no reason to hate Tammany Hall."

"What did you think of Tammany?"

"Everything. They were the only thing in the world for me. My kind of people. Murphy was in there when I came up. I met him several times in New York. He was the last leader New York had. In 'twenty-four he died, wasn't it?"

Yes, it was. Charlie Murphy led Tammany from 1903 until his death in 1924. He was the successor to Boss Tweed and Richard Croker and, like them, became a millionaire swiftly from political graft. He was a baseball player, a saloon owner, an uneducated, taciturn conservative, devoid of ideology. Dan's model.

The second moment was recalled by Carl Touhey, a businessman who ran for mayor against Erastus in 1973 and lost by only 3,000 votes, the closest call Erastus ever had. Touhey told me he met Dan once and asked him the secret of his political success.

"Money," Dan said.

Not jobs? Or getting out the vote? Or campaigning hard?

"No," said Dan, socking his palm with his fist. "Money. Get the money!"

Tammany and money: a winning combination. All of the Tammany tricks and traits were adapted to Albany by the Machine through the years: largesse to the poor; the establishment of a party organization more powerful than the local government; padded public payrolls (John McLoughlin, an enterprising Albany newsman, discovered that while the Empire State Building employed 60 janitors for 102 floors, Dan's Court House had 72 for 6); control of the night world; open gambling; what state investigators called "incomparable gouging and overcharging and the waste of public funds"; and the manipulation of elections. Charlie Murphy's men threw ballot boxes into the East River in 1905 and successfully reversed William Randolph Hearst's election as mayor of New York City. In Albany, it was rumored, even the dead voted, early and often. And vote buying? Dan called it "street money" and said Billy Barnes openly admitted buying votes with such money. As to himself? "There was no vote buying in my whole career that I know of," he told Ernie Tetrault. "I never knew a vote to be for sale."

Yes, well . . .

Back in the 1950s, when John Maguire, a first-rate Albany newsman and a very funny fellow, voted in the city for the first time, a North End Democrat pressed two five-dollar bills into his hand at the polls. John wanted to give it back. His wife said that would only cause problems, and she took the money and kept it. The next time he went to the polls he walked up to another Albany Democrat he knew and said, "How come nobody gave me ten bucks this year?"

"John," said the man, "I just lit my last cigar and I already licked it, but you can have that if you want it."

The last major uproar over vote buying came in 1966, after citizens' groups raised the issue. One of Dan's grand juries investigated the practice and found it did not exist. Dan's district attorney, John T. Garry, made a pronouncement at that time that helps us all understand why it didn't exist. If anyone produced evidence of vote buying, Garry said, he would prosecute "the giver *and the receiver*." He pointed out that a conviction carried up to five years in prison. All Dan said to the press after he left the grand jury was "So long, boys."

The money that passed hands on all those election days in the city came in part from the people who were already benefiting from being Democrats—city and county employees. The *Knickerbocker News* reported in 1973 that the party collected $25,000 from such employees in the final weeks before the 1972 election. Contributions ranged from $25 each from sanitation workers to $200 from a city housing director.

The tithe, for years, was collected in part by one of Dan's closest aides, Leo Quinn, who accepted contributions at his perch in the Elks Club. Other contributors gave at the office. Charlie Ryan, party treasurer in 1973, denied the party solicited funds from city employees; and when the *Knickerbocker News* reporter pointed out that sanitation workers made donations alphabetically, A through J, all on October 13 and 20, Charlie laughed and said, "It must be coincidence."

The money came to Dan's coffers from everywhere, and on Election Day a good deal of it was put back into circulation among the same people.

"Dan spent a quarter of a million at every election," Charlie Ryan said when we talked in 1980. "It went to the ward leaders and on down, and they all got a piece of the action. When it got down there, some of it stuck to the fingers of people along the way, and they'd turn up with a new car or a new boat. And Dan would say, 'That's okay. Now they got something to look forward to next year.' "

How much of it stuck to Dan? When he died in 1977 he left

an estate of "between $50,000 and $100,000," according to news reports when his will was filed for probate. Neither figure is very large, even considering only his nonpolitical income from the successful family business he oversaw for almost four decades, Hedrick's Brewery. The legacy went to Leta Lynch Boyle (grand-niece of his late wife), who was said to be like a daughter to him. Either sum is modest compared with Tweed's millions of a century earlier (Tweed did not enjoy them long and died in jail) or with Murphy's quick fortune or that of Croker, who died on his English estate in 1922 and left $5 million to his third wife.

Millions, no doubt incalculable now, if they were ever calculable, passed through Dan's hands, much of it in cash, enriching many, perpetuating what Dan called his "Democracy"—"There was no Democracy in Albany when I started," he told me.

Despite Dan's access to millions, Charlie Ryan insists, "Money didn't mean anything to him. He gave away more money. He never signed a note for anyone. He did when he was young and he got stuck. He'd just give out five hundred dollars instead of signing a note for a thousand, and then say, 'I just made five hundred.' "

Leo O'Brien shared this view of Dan: "He had no interest in money, in having a big house, or in women—all the things that have tripped up others. Another thing that protected him, he was always very scrupulous about income taxes."

Dan took nightly walks through the city with his cronies in his heyday, stopping to see special friends along the way, and clusters of people often trailed him, for the same reason they waited for him outside church on Sundays—a handout. Leo remembered Ed O'Connell's saying in the Elks Club one night in the 1930s, "I don't even have a dime in my pocket. Dan gave away all his own money and then he gave away mine."

Dan tipped the waiters at Keeler's Restaurant fifty dollars for dinner, and cabbies fought for the right to take him home from Downtown, a guaranteed ten-dollar bill. He summed up his contempt for the tinseled flashiness of latter-day Tammany leaders in a single phrase: "Sireens and ten-cent tips."

His summer home in the Helderbergs, with its pool and its majestic view of Albany, may have summoned up a vision of sumptuous living, but not to anyone who went there. Edward L. (Ned) Pattison, who served two terms as a Democratic congressman, visited Dan there in 1970 and was disabused of his expectations of splendor.

"It was not a bad place at all," he said, "but just ordinary. Wallboard with studs exposed. Charlie Ryan was cooking a meat loaf in the oven. There was nothing in the place you wouldn't find at your average rummage sale. And the view of Albany— the place wasn't sited for it. You had to work to find the view. It was magnificent when you found it, but you almost didn't know it was there. If a plumber was living in the place, you'd say he wasn't living over his head."

Dan's home on Whitehall Road had a comparable effect on me. It was like a hundred other overfilled, middle-class homes I'd been in and out of all my life in Albany: lace tablecloth, over-stuffed furniture, wall-to-wall carpet, framed prints of old paint-ings without much quality. What made it Dan's place were the particulars: the photo on the piano of his wife, the former Leta Burnside, who died in 1963; the Civil War books ("It's the only war you could get interested in," he once said); the color TV playing a game show and then a soap opera while we talked; books on the Old West, on boxing, guns, and horses, along with *A Tale of Two Cities* and Thackeray's *Vanity Fair* ("Pick that up anyplace and enjoy it," he said); tapes of Wayne King, Glenn Miller, Johnny Cash; and, in the place of honor over the fireplace, a portrait of Harry Truman.

"Did Truman really say you could have the doorknobs off the White House?" I inquired.

"No, but he was friendly," Dan said. "Very."

When Jimmy Roosevelt and Bill O'Dwyer started a dump-Truman movement in 1948, Leo O'Brien called Dan up for a quotable response. Dan said he thought they were "rats deserting what they think is a sinking ship." Leo put the interview on the news wire and Truman read it. After he was elected he told New York's Democratic chairman, Paul Fitzpatrick (so said Leo), "I want to make sure those fellows up in Albany get anything they want." Truman later said Dan was a great leader. Dan said Tru-man was the best president since Jefferson.

Just before he died, Leo told me the story of how he leaped out of newspapering into the halls of Congress. When Parker Corning was eased out of Congress in 1936, Leo wanted his job and asked Ed O'Connell for it. Ed thought it could work out, but Dan didn't agree. Dan, Leo said, wanted to get rid of State Senator Billy Byrne to make room for Erastus Corning in the Senate. So Byrne was kicked upstairs into Congress (about which Dan cared very little),

Erastus became a state senator, and Leo carried on as a newsman, slowly consolidating his position as correspondent for numerous newspapers, and so he was sitting pretty, financially, from all this when Billy Byrne died in 1952. And then Dan, remembering Leo had once wanted the job Byrne got, called Leo up and said, "The nomination is yours."

"I wanted it like a hole in the head," said Leo.

But he took it because he revered Dan, and he stood for election and became ridiculously popular, far beyond what was necessary. But before he took the job, Leo asked Erastus, who was then mayor, whether Erastus wanted the job for himself, or for his brother, Edwin. The answer was no on both counts, and so the newspaperman became the congressman.

"I invested fifteen years in it," Leo said, "because I didn't have the courage to say no."

Now it was 1974 and Dan was almost eighty-nine and fading, sitting in a stationary mechanical chair, white-haired, scrubbed pink, his beltless black trousers softly girding his large stomach, brown sport shirt open at the collar, feet resting in brown high-top shoes, and a knitted woolen quilt over his lap. Two handsome Irish wolfhounds, Tara and Siobhan, and a brown-and-white mongrel named Mac raged and barked and sniffed as we talked, a Celtic strain in all the room's wildlife, including the parrot, which was green. Dan's housekeeper said people called the parrot Polly, or Pol, which, as we all know, is short for polly-tician. The bird seemed to be saying "Bye, now," which I took as a cultivated hint not to overstay. But the housekeeper said Pol was really saying "I know it" and "Get to work," a pair of phrases to live by. Dan said his cousin Walter Doyle had given him the parrot four years before. "Walter had it forty years," Dan said, "but he's very sick or dead now, the last I heard of him."

Dan was sick now also, with emphysema, the seventy cigarettes a day having touched him at last. He quit them, quit drinking, too, long before that, except for a couple of Old Overholts and milk before bed. He didn't approve of whiskey after he'd finally quit it, and down at the Elks Club, when they saw him coming, they'd sweep the whiskey glasses off the bar just to keep his mind off it. "Let him catch you with your hand in the till," said a cousin of mine who worked in City Hall, "and he suspends you for two weeks. But come to work drunk and you're all through." When Dan was drinking he'd wake up in the middle of the night, Leo said, remembering things he'd done when he had the load on. And he'd kick the bedpost.

A special news report interrupted our game show with word that Federal Judge John Sirica had ordered Richard Nixon to turn over sixty-four of his White House tapes to Watergate investigator Leon Jaworski.

"That Sirica's a tough guy," Dan said. And Nixon? "He's unaccountable in all directions. If it wasn't for Ford pardoning him, he'd have went to jail. What the hell did he want all those records around for? Any records of the job'd be in my possession, nobody else's. Funny fellow, that Nixon. Hasn't got the character most of the presidents had."

We talked an hour and a half, and much of what he said has been used where it seemed to fit, elsewhere in these pages. But there were some points of history worth reporting here, one being the matter of his campaigning in his sailor suit for the 1919 assessorship, a rather surreal headnote to the myth. Dan served on the USS *Prairie*, a supply ship that crossed the Atlantic several times in World War I with a crew of thirty. In later years the crew proved to be infinitely expandable, as veterans wanting to bask in Dan's glory reassigned themselves to the *Prairie* as his shipmates (Willie Quinn, a real shipmate, turned up at Dan's funeral, on furlough in a wheelchair from the Veterans Hospital).

"No," Dan said about campaigning in the sailor suit. "They had a banner with a picture of me in the suit. Simp Quinlan put that up over South Pearl Street, just above Bassett Street, next to Victor Kenel's saloon. Simp Quinlan was a roofer, and he and Jimmy Quinn, a little short fella, a hell of a guy, a real ballplayer in his early days, they elected me if anybody did. They elected me as sure as you're born."

"How?"

"Organizing and working."

"What happened to them?"

"They were always around me, and friendly. They were around till they died."

Dan had always fought chickens, but I wondered: Had he ever fought dogs?

"No, I never had any fighting dogs. Tobin had a hell of a dog. Had a place on Hudson and Green. He was a game dog and a good dog. Bulldogs, always bulldogs, different colors. I seen a dogfight once, lasted four hours. Every so often they'd break them and wash them up and scratch them. There was quite a lot of dog-fighting. I wasn't into politics then."

And I wondered about a story I'd heard years ago from an Albany policeman: that because some witnesses from Albany saw a woman electrocuted at Sing Sing, and because she exploded when the current hit her, there had never been any capital punishment in Albany since.

"It was me," Dan said. "I wouldn't stand for it. We never had a first-degree [murder prosecution] for thirty years. Not since that little woman [who murdered her husband]. Delaney executed her. Lehman would have commuted that. There were probably half a dozen who would've gone to the chair, but I wouldn't let them. And they won't try them now."

Dan's Democracy was always like that: more dictatorial than democratic. For anyone dealing with Albany this created, at worst, a feeling of fear, at best a respect for unleashable power; for Dan's power was indeed supreme and pervasive of every level of life, and he would not hesitate to exercise it to perpetuate his rule or to convert an enemy, whether it meant hiking an assessment to change a voter's mind or starting an investigation to quell a rambunctious governor. With all the judges, all the district attorneys, the entire jury system, and all local lawmaking falling under one man's control, then the independent individual or group was all but certain to run second in any contest with the Machine's interests.

Did this mean there was no hunger for justice in Albany?

There were reformers, uplift movements, outspoken clergymen, good-government goo-goos, outraged taxpayers, outraged moralists, courageous liberals, militant blacks, and all their campaigns for office, or for change, often transformed the consciousness of their days a notch or two. A Citizens party movement took over the city of Cohoes in 1963, ousting Dan's allies, who were leftovers from Mike Smith's rule; and a crusading newspaper editor, Daniel E. Button, snatched away Dan's congressional seat when Leo O'Brien decided not to run again in 1966, and held the seat for two terms. But these hiatuses in Dan's control were really aberrations, and in time Dan took back Congress from Dan Button, and the Democrats took back Cohoes from the Citizens.

And so in answer to the question about justice, no, there really has been no hunger for it, not as it is conventionally understood; for the Irish Americans who gave Dan his power base always understood it in a different light. Politics was justice itself, and sufficient unto itself; and vast numbers of the Irish considered themselves political, even when all they did was take five for voting, pass out election cards, and hobnob with the committeeman at the saloon. Politics was justice in the form of benevolence from Dan's poke, and probably two or three city jobs somewhere in the family. You pursued justice with the help of your ward leader.

Harry Staley, a professor of English at State University at Albany, recalled that his Irish grandfather was a police captain in Brooklyn, and when an envelope with bribe money turned up on his desk he sent it back to its source. When he told his wife what he'd done she was appalled. "Who are you," she howled, "not to take a bribe?"

Comparably, the graft by which Dan's Machine maintained itself carried no more moral stigma with this electorate than did chronic overtime parking. What's more, both were fixable.

But it wasn't only the Irish who permitted Dan to prevail. The whole city voted for him, with the enduring exception of about 15,000 intractable Republicans; and what this suggests to some is a congenital set of traits in the Albany makeup: a predilection for a strongman at the top, a love of continuity, a firm belief that whoever took power would carry on with the same chicanery. A clergyman in the late 1960s called this "the Patroon psychology," as if Albanians never quite got over what the Dutch feudal barons did for them in the seventeenth and eighteenth centuries.

Also, part of Dan's longevity flowed from the personal charisma that charmed the voters and that came not only from his fame, his power, and his generosity but from something personal that even his brother Ed is said to have lacked. "Ed," said Charlie Ryan, "was good with lawyers, but he wasn't like Dan. Ed wasn't good with the common people. Dan knew how to talk to ordinary people."

There is disagreement on this. I spoke with two longtime Democrats who both trace their party histories as far back as Dan's and who saw a different side to the man. Neither wanted to be quoted by name. Said one, "Ed O'Connell was a grand man. Dan, you couldn't believe him from here across the street." This man told me a long story of Dan's political duplicity and concluded, "This was the kind of a son of a bitch Dan was, may he rest in peace."

The second man told me, "Dan hated every one of his brothers till their dying day. Hated them. I never seen a man so bitter. He hated Ed's wife, and she was a wonderful and beautiful woman. Packy's wife, Dan put her in headquarters for a while and got rid of her."

These negative qualities, however visible in the 1930s, were transfigured by the mid-1950s, when Dan was the only one left, when all things O'Connellistic seemed now to have had their origin in himself. All the favors, the charisma, the power, the belief that Dan was a man of golden qualities, generated a loyalty in his followers that often reached absurd heights. The notes and files the *Times-Union* kept on him, for instance, kept disappearing in his best interest, even news clippings, and, most notably, anything that carried negative news. It was not possible to research anything about his jail term or about the baseball pool in the files. History had been burglarized and the cupboard was bare.

We all thought we knew the loyalist who was doing the light-fingering, but who could prove it? It went on for years and climaxed when John Maguire was assigned to write an advance obituary on Dan—anticipating that he might eventually die—and filed it in Dan's folder.

Death, of course, is considered negative news by some, and the obit disappeared. With the collusion of a few editors, John then filed a second copy, not under Dan's name, but under Air Pollution; and it was from this folder that the obit was safely retrieved and published when Dan reluctantly died.

Assemblyman Richard J. Conners said he once asked Dan why he had never told his own story of his long reign by writing his memoirs. Dan's answer: "When I die I want to die all over."

He was a private, imperious man, and yet he also had a quality that two of the politicans closest to him, Erastus Corning and Leo O'Brien, found singularly important. Erastus, who visited him every day, said Dan was the one person he knew to whom you went when you were feeling low, and just by talking to him you felt good. Leo concurred, seeing Dan as a man without anguish, a man suited utterly to his life's work.

"He got more sheer joy out of being a successful politician than anyone I ever met," Leo said, "and I include national people like Jim Farley. He loved to make the wheels turn, to constantly see people. He got joy out of that, and out of the fact that he was a boss. He took the investigations in stride, knowing you pay a price for being in politics. He thought of his life as a championship chess game. He didn't feel it was a cardinal sin to speak well of a Republican. They were playing the game, too, an exciting game.

"You'd go out to see him with something bothering you a little bit, and when you'd walk away your step was a little higher and quicker from talking to a nice guy, a guy who knew. You felt you were close to a form of royalty, the ruling family. And you were in."

Not everybody got so close, for Dan insulated himself from emotional involvements with his loyalists.

"He believed," said Leo, "in visiting the sick and burying the dead, but he never did it himself."

Jack Kennedy called Dan when his father had his stroke, and wanted to send up his plane, the *Caroline*, to carry Dan over to Hyannis to visit for a few hours. (The story went that Joe Kennedy offered to help Dan with money during the Dewey investigation, and Dan never forgot that.) But Dan's fear of flying overcame his good feeling for an old friend, and he didn't go. Also, he hated to be around people who were sick, and he didn't go to funerals.

"The only funeral I ever saw him at was Ed's," said Leo. "He didn't even go to Solly's."

But there he was at his own, flat on his back, dead to the world while his mass moved along. Chief Judge James T. Foley, lector for the second reading, was quoting from the Book of Revelation: "And I heard a voice from heaven saying, 'Write: Blessed are the dead who die in the Lord henceforth. Yes, says the Spirit, let them rest from their labors, for their works follow them.' "

Indeed they do.

And their followers follow them as well—all those faces from the North, South, and West ends of the city that I remembered from my childhood and that had grown aged in the reign of Dan, who outlived his enemies but not his friends: who now looked out into the cold morning at St. Ann's, their feisty faces tough even in solemnity.

And then it was Father Romano talking, giving the homily, saying Dan was a great politician, a great human being of "curious humility—curious because in our society one who possessed the ability to do what Dan has done with his life is not expected to be humble."

Willie Quinn of the *Prairie* took leave of his shipmate for the last time and was wheeled out at the Holy, Holy, Holy. And then people went to communion—the family first, and then several dozen others, many of them women, and some of them party

celebrities: County Judge John Clyne, of whose harsh jail sentences Dan didn't entirely approve and said so in print; and Leo
O'Brien; and State Senator Howard Nolan, who promised Dan
he wouldn't give Erastus a primary fight for the mayoralty, but
did—the same year Dan died—and lost.

Bishop Howard Hubbard had the last word—that Dan "never
forgot from whence he came, or where he was going. And with
what he achieved nationally, his life-style never changed. I think
it will be for this that he will be remembered."

Curious humility, yet again.

It was an odd epitaph indeed for a man who had arced through
his long day's journey at such a height. And yet that epitaph
suited him, for he understood limitations better than most men.
("You won't get any votes," he told one would-be governor.) If
his life was long, his language was to the point and without
pretension: "I know it. . . . Get to work," said his parrot. "You're
not finished till you're dead," said himself. Now he was truly
finished. Dan was all done. Dead all over. And so they wheeled
him out of St. Ann's and rode him up to St. Agnes Cemetery and
they buried him.

So long, boys.

The South Mall: Everything Everybody Ever Wanted

*I*saac Bashevis Singer had come to town to speak at State University about writing, and after the visit a friend asked would I take Mr. Singer to the train. We had a spare hour, so I took him to the Marketplace, a watering hole on Grand Street that looks up the hill at the South Mall. He ordered two fried eggs and a cup of tea, and while we talked we gazed up the hill at the Mall's Egg, the performing arts center that is officially called the Egg since it is shaped like half a boiled egg (from some angles it looks like an avocado) cut on the bias.

"It could look like an egg," said Mr. Singer, "it could look like a *blintz*." He concluded the design was forced originality and left me with two thoughts: "When a bird builds a nest he doesn't care about material, he cares about a nest" and "Tolstoy never made an effort to be original."

Nelson Rockefeller, who built the Mall, and who authorized that truncated egg, was not Tolstoy, but he was an original in his use of money and power to feed his compulsion to be extraordinary. And so because the seat of his governorship humiliated him, because he had to drive Queen Juliana of the Netherlands through the slumminess and decrepitude of Albany's South End in order to reach the executive mansion, he undertook in 1962 what is said to be the largest marble project in the history of the world (a claim I am fond of but can't prove), a complex of massive buildings and skyscrapers built on a platform five levels deep, which, if stood on its end, would be 112 stories high, taller than Manhattan's World Trade Center, in which Rockefeller also had a hand.

The moment of conception of the Mall was described by Joseph E. Persico in his book *The Imperial Rockefeller*. He quotes the Governor on his discomfort the day Queen Juliana visited Albany to celebrate the anniversary of the city's founding as Fort Orange: "The Queen was riding with Mayor Corning and myself. . . . I could see the way the city was running down and what this lady might think. Here was a great Dutch city built in the New World, and then she comes to look at it, never having seen it before. My God!"

Thus inspired, the Governor went ahead to build what he said, in a fit of modesty, would be "the most spectacularly beautiful seat of government in the world," a project that could prove to be "the greatest thing to happen to this country in a hundred years."

"When we look at the marble-faced buildings of the Mall," wrote Carole Herselle Krinsky in an article contained in the book *Art, the Ape of Nature*, "we know that we are in no ordinary part of the city, but rather in a ceremonial place. The separateness of this complex is made clearer by its elevation on a platform, which differentiates the ground level here from that of the rest of Albany."

That platform was Rocky's own doing, early designs having proved unacceptable to him. In an airplane with Wallace Harrison, the principal architect of the Mall (also of Rockefeller Center in Manhattan, and adjudged by Rockefeller to be "the greatest architect in the twentieth century"), the Governor sketched on the back of an envelope a plan inspired by one of the extraordinary capitals of the world: the palace of the Dalai Lama at Lhasa, Tibet. He later told Ms. Krinsky he "always admired" that palace. She added:

"He remembered that at Lhasa there was an approach across a low plain to the hilltop palace and to the cliff supporting the palace, and that one could enter that complex at the base of the cliff through a portal within a high wall."

This is precisely how the South Mall was conceived. An early plan situated it on a Helderberg mountain cliff, fifteen miles south of Albany. Today, one enters it by car from the east, through an artificial cliff: that five-level platform, atop which sits $1 or $2 billion worth of buildings (the final tally is not yet in), among them a marble trapezoid that alone cost $90 million, that Egg ($42 million), a low-slung marble structure a quarter of a mile long, four twenty-three-story matching buildings, a forty-four-story tower that is the tallest building in New York State outside Manhattan, and more.

Wolf Von Eckardt spoke for an army of naysayers when he evaluated the Mall architecture for *New York* magazine and called it an "ugly anachronism—the City Beautiful's last erection." Former Assembly Minority Leader Stanley Steingut called it Rockefeller's last erection. Rockefeller said it might be the last but it certainly was going to be a beaut.

Is it really a beaut?

Scores of writers, scholars, and critics have had their say about it and the saying is far from over. The early raves for Harrison's bold design have been buried by a tidal wave of diatribes, which seem aesthetically justified. The Mall itself is an awesome nonesuch, but the individual buildings (apart from the Egg) seem derivative in a tradition of monumental minimalism and feckless grandiosity. The Capitol, completed in 1898, sits alongside the Mall, far more fascinating to look at, and to be in, and with its own grandiose history—the most expensive building on the American continent in its day ($25 million); and just down the block stands Albany City Hall, designed by H. H. Richardson, one of the most sublime structures ever built for the aggrandizement of politicians.

The Mall's epic blandness invites smears, the most widely seen being one by Robert Hughes, *Time* magazine art critic, who during his 1981 Public Television series, *The Shock of the New*, compared the Mall to the architecture of the Italian Fascists, the Nazis, and the Russian Communists. "One could see any building at Albany Mall with an eagle on top, or a swastika, or a hammer and sickle; it makes no difference to the building." He saw it as having been designed to express the centralization of power—"an architecture of coercion."

Rockefeller would probably agree. He was a coercive sort. But he was functioning in a democracy, one he could never coerce or cajole into making him its president, and thus he was czar only of his own imagination and his localized political willpower. If, then, we consider the Mall as the consequence of one man's

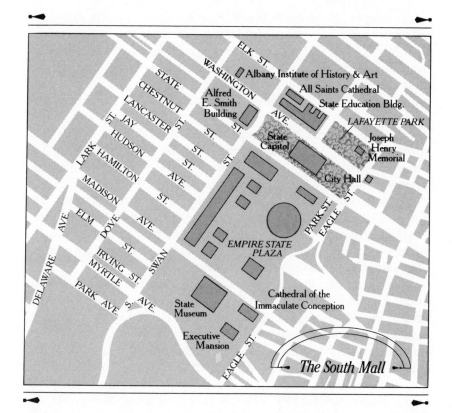

The South Mall

political will, imposed upon our time and space in spite of its
incredible cost, in spite of the arrogant wastry and duplicity that
marked the manipulation of public money, in spite of the many
construction scandals, underworld intrusions, and colossal thievery that went not only unpunished but uninvestigated; if we
consider further the brilliant stroke by which the city's political
leaders took the Mall away from Rockefeller even before he had
begun to build it, and if, most important, we consider the tran-
substantiation the Mall effected in Albany, turning a slug of a
town into a handsome and prancing dude—then I think we may
safely agree with Rockefeller that it is indeed a beaut.

Rockefeller burst his bombshell on Albany in March 1962,
when he suddenly expropriated 98.5 acres in the city center and
asked the legislature for $20 million to buy the land and existing
buildings. It meant destruction of 1,150 structures, most of them
private dwellings, and the displacement of 3,600 households—

9,000 people, 17 percent black, many Italians and Jews, many old, many poor. The loss of annual tax revenue to the city amounted to $650,000, but the potential loss of all those votes in a time of declining population was an even more serious blow to the Albany Democratic Machine. The rooming-house district had done noble work for years. When Governor Thomas E. Dewey was trying to break the O'Connell Machine in the early 1940s, one of his investigators turned up one house where 78 voters presumably lived. When the investigator found only 22 cots, the proprietor explained that the voters slept in eight-hour shifts. That still left 12 who had to sleep standing up.

Mayor Corning called the expropriation "a ruthless takeover" and said the Mall would prove to be a "sterile monument." Boss Dan O'Connell put the displacement of so many of his people in a literary context. "It's a good thing Longfellow isn't alive today," Dan said. "He'd have written a poem about it."

What kind of a neighborhood was it that the Mall displaced and Dan bemoaned? J. Richard Williams, a lawyer with a practice on Elk Street just a few doors down from the old Pruyn mansion, was a precocious teenage bellhop at the DeWitt Clinton Hotel during the early 1940s, when the neighborhood was what it had long since become and would continue to be up to the time of the Ruthless Takeover.

In this incarnation it was the city's rooming-house district, cut through with westering tentacles of The Gut—principally Hudson Avenue, along which you could find song, solace, and some sin in two dozen gin mills between Dove and Green streets. Some solid families still endured in the erstwhile residential neighborhood, but in declining numbers. And as soon as they moved out, their town houses and railroad flats became warrens of commerce and comfort. One might describe the denizens of these furnished and unfurnished rooms as being of moderate to insufficient means, often elderly or crippled, incurably transient (usually in a downward direction), and no more questions, mister. It was the bedroom community for a generation of solitaires: family outcasts, night-shift nurses, semiaffluent winos, motherless gays, dishwashers aspiring to be short-order cooks, horseplayers doing their level best to die broke, closet hookers, and other functionaries and free-lancers of Nighttown who got around to putting their heads on their greasy pillows just as the sun was coming up. It was home to assorted burglars, flakes, flukes, runaways—rocks, the generic term by which this branch of humanity was known to the police—who in their totality cast a cold eye on tomorrow because there was never enough heat in the joint tonight. A famous line, which mentioned a single street but spoke for the whole neighborhood, echoed in Dick Williams's memory: "Are you married, or do you live on Jay Street?"

Williams remembered that three women were considered the real-estate doyennes of the neighborhood—Ma Pierce, Mame Hershberger, and Mae Carlsen. Mae was the best known. She was in her nineties—though she declined to tell her age—when we talked in her most modest basement apartment on Lancaster Street in August 1982. She lay on her sofa, chain-smoking Camels, and recapitulated some of her early days, when she owned thirty or thirty-five houses—she couldn't remember how many—and had maybe three hundred people living in them.

She was closely allied with the city government, and often took welfare clients. Her "Welfare Stew," made with chicken wings (a big bag for fifty cents), was so significant the Welfare Department asked her to teach its clients how to make it. Mae (maiden name Quinn, Irish in all directions) was staunchly Catholic, staunchly Democrat, and was noted for getting out the vote on Election Day—getting it out of her tenants, that is.

Bob Fabbricatore, a close friend of Mae's who was visiting her when we spoke and who is the Democratic committeeman from the Third District of the Sixth Ward, said it took him several years to earn Mae's trust. Her tenants, he said, used to check in with her to be sure of how to vote, especially in primaries when there was a choice of Democrats.

"Nobody got away," said Bob. "They responded to Mae. And this went on for thirty or forty years before I got here."

There are stories that on Election Day people picked up their voting money at Mae's place, that they cashed their paychecks at Mae's place, and that nobody got any money of any sort until they'd proved they'd voted—Democratic. One man told Mae he was going to vote for Dewey and Mae screamed so loudly the police came and asked what he was doing to her. Mae told me she answered, "Ask him what he just said to me." The man explained that he'd said he was going to vote for Dewey. Mae declined to accept this explanation, and so the man was jailed. At 9:05 p.m., when the polls were closed and he no longer could vote for Dewey, Mae withdrew her complaint and let the fellow out of jail.

Mae's style was singular: She was a workhorse and a loner ("I don't go out and I don't neighbor") who used to fix her own roofs and would get up at 2:00 a.m. in midwinter to bank the fires in her dozen or so rooming houses, carrying the coal herself, trusting no one else to do it because they never did it right and the fire would go out.

The Welfare Department frequently called Mae when it had an emergency and needed a place to put people. Albany Police Chief William Fitzpatrick called her one day in the 1930s and asked would she take in a fourteen-year-old boy who'd run away from a home for boys in Massachusetts. Mae not only took him in, she raised him and he called her Mother for the rest of her life. She took into her own home, by her own rough count, fourteen or sixteen people over the years, and some were still with her when we spoke. She also took in a blind man's Seeing Eye dog when the man was hospitalized, and when one elderly woman was so sick in Mae's house that she couldn't stand the smell of cooking, Mae went next door and cooked.

She was a rare bird—she died in December 1982 at (maybe) ninety-six, worth more than half a million dollars—made rarer today by the absence of rooming-house streets like Jay and Lancaster that could produce another like her. When Rockefeller expropriated his midtown acres, Mae yielded up sixteen of her houses, and not with any bitterness.

"They wanted it," she said, "and I knew they weren't going to hurt the place any. I guess they got it going"—she meant the Mall. "I never went down to see what it looks like." It is half a block from her house.

And she had no animosity toward Rockefeller, either: "The only thing wrong with Rockefeller was he was a Republican." She was, in fact, angry with Governor Hugh Carey for not closing down the state government for Rockefeller's funeral.

In the heyday of Mae's era, Jay and Lancaster streets were a little like lower Madison Avenue, and a little like Swan and Dove and High and Hawk streets also; and you found music on lots of streets—tinny tunes from tacky trios, or a racially mixed jazz band at the Melody Inn on upper Hudson Avenue, or barroom bathos from the Embassy Club pianoman, or a continuing card game (a dollar to sit in—"Pay a bean to see the scene," the dealer told you) to piano tunes at Rabbit's, way down on Division Street, where Jody Bolden played before he moved up to his own spot, the noble Kerry Blue, across from police headquarters on Eagle Street. The Kerry Blue was a gem of a place, run by Jean Garrison with her friend Jody, who played the best jazz piano Albany ever called its own.

Jody was Jody in Albany in his later years, but as a kid, when he was learning stride piano as a protégé of Fats Waller, and being Billie Holiday's first accompanist, he used his straight name, Bobby Henderson. He played first for Billie during Prohibition at Jerry's Log Cabin, on 133rd Street in Harlem. Billie took him on after he played "Sweet Sue" for her and knocked her out. At the Kerry Blue in the mid-1950s the racial mix was total, not token, and that was rare. But it was music and not color that mattered, and visiting jazzmen like Roy Eldridge and Omer Simeon and Trummy Young and Hot Lips Page fell by just to listen. Jody finally made some records, having been rediscovered in his late years by John Hammond of Columbia Records, and recorded by Marian McPartland and Hank O'Neal. The music preserved is Jody (or Bobby, if you like) past his prime, but it is music that is still worth a lot of your attention if you can find any of it.

Another element to the neighborhood that was not terribly egregious but exceedingly well perceived in the 1940s was the scatter of scarlet houses, two to four girls, all white, to a house: white prostitution's last wide-open era in Albany. Females of a slightly different order were also available in some of the neighborhood's gin mills, their presence even advertised in the Saturday-morning newspaper as part of the honky-tonk scene. They were called B-girls and they kept you company at the bar as long as you kept their glass filled with seventy-five-cent whiskey, which, if you made the deflating mistake of tasting, you would discover was cold tea or watery sarsaparilla. One of the neighborhood madams kept a pornographic lending library—five dollars a week to borrow a book. And upstairs at the One-Two-Three Club, if you knew the right people, you could see private strippers go all the way and then a little bit farther—with a cigarette. This was not advertised, for stripping within city limits was not permitted—a genuflection, I always thought, to the Albany Catholic Diocese, which disapproved of sex. However, across the Albany city line in the town of Colonie, morally overseen by the same Catholic Albany County district attorney who oversaw city morals, you could see the strippers every night at the Hawaii Klub on Central Avenue, because Colonie was run by Protestant Republican politicians, and everybody knows how casual they are about godless sex. It was a matter of connections, and at Bob Parr's Klub Eagle, across from the DeWitt Clinton, you could connect twenty-four hours a day, and just what is it you need this afternoon, sir?

Jack (Legs) Diamond, a friend of Bob Parr's, was killed in this neighborhood, shot through the brains on December 18, 1931, upstairs in Laura Woods's rooming house at 67 Dove Street, an event commemorated by a plaque, placed there by the Historic Albany Foundation, a development Jack would like.

While I was writing a novel on Jack, Fred Fontaine of the Albany County Department of Social Services told me he had Diamond's widow as a client. This was a surprise, since the widow, Alice Kenny, had been murdered in Brooklyn in 1933.

Fred introduced me not to Alice but to a woman named Lil Pfaffenbach, who was sixty-one and dying in Albany Medical Center of five or six kinds of disease when we met. We got on well and she asked was I married—life in the old girl yet. I bought her a pink negligee as a favor to Jack—even though I wasn't sure how well she knew him—because she said she didn't have anything to make her look good for visitors.

She changed her stories about where and when she met Jack, where they lived, and she'd never heard of Alice, which made everything suspect, because Alice was almost as much of a celebrity as Jack. But I came to believe Lil knew something about him, had probably, as an uninquisitive teenager, been kept by him. She perked up when I asked if she had ever heard him mention a writer named Rabelais. "Oh, he was nuts about Rabba-lee," she said immediately, accenting the first syllable. It was bad literary pronunciation but a correct historical response to the question, for it was a very little known fact that Diamond mystified his friends by giving them copies of *Gargantua and Pantagruel*. And so I believed Lil had something to tell me about him, which she did, and when she left the hospital I visited her a few times in her hovel on Hamilton Street.

Her apartment was a damp basement in a house ripe for condemnation on a street begging for demolishment. The neighborhood was rot city, full of derelicts and wipeouts. Lil had a Latin houseboy who stayed with her on and off, and she was visited while I was there by a woman bloated in odd places, a grotesque junkie from across the street who came in to eat some of Lil's sugar with a teaspoon. I think Lil had operated secretly, for a time, as a low-level madam while on welfare. She volunteered that she could have been a superior madam if she'd only put her mind to it. People had robbed her while she was in the hospital, but she didn't have much worth stealing, and Freddy Fontaine kept the checks coming, so life went on until one day it didn't.

Backward go we now for a bit to Rockefeller's expropriation in 1962, which was swiftly followed by a lawsuit to stop it, brought by the city of Albany. The suit failed and land acquisition by the state continued. The problem facing Rockefeller was the financing of his project.

The constitutional procedure was to go through the legislature for approval and then put the matter to the voters as a bond issue. But no one in his right mind believed New Yorkers would ever subsidize a pipe dream like this in, of all places, the slums of Albany. Momentum slackened, things were taking longer than expected, and costs were going up. Originally the Mall was foreseen as a four-year project costing $250 million. By 1964 the State Office of General Services estimated the cost at $400 million. Five months later the estimate was $480 million. How was Rockefeller ever going to finance this monster?

Mayor Corning had an idea.

With his Municipal Magic Set the Mayor conjured a new version of a plan he had offered to Governor Dewey in 1946, when Dewey was trying to finance his campus office building complex in the West End of the city. Dewey, who had tried to break the O'Connell Machine in the early 1940s, viewed the offer as political leprosy and spurned it. Nelson Rockefeller didn't spurn it. But neither did he understand it when the Mayor first proposed it to him, according to Samuel E. Bleecker in his book, *The Politics of Architecture.*

The Mayor, writes Bleecker, "ebullient that he had devised the bootstrap means" through which the Mall could be built, outlined the plan to Rockefeller. "Rockefeller did not respond to what had been suggested, and in his characteristic manner," says Bleecker, "politely ushered the Mayor to the door, patted him on the back, and thanked him for his interest."

A month went by, says Bleecker, and Erastus, hearing no word, became convinced Nelson hadn't grasped the idea. So he met with him a second time. Bleecker writes: " 'Oh, is that what you meant,' Corning reported the Governor as saying. Corning added that Nelson then 'went after the scheme like a trout for a fly.' "

In Nelson's own version of his response to Erastus he comes off as being more alacritous: "This was a magnificent concept. I mean, this was new, it was fresh. I went for it right away."

What the Mayor proposed was that the state transfer to Albany

County the ownership of the Mall property it had acquired. The county would then sell bonds to finance the Mall's construction. The state would build the Mall as agent for the county. Under a lease-purchase arrangement that would continue until December 31, 2004, the state would buy the land back from the county. Normally a county could not incur a debt so large as the sale of the bonds represented. What Corning knew was that it was all legal if the bonds financed self-supporting projects. The lease-purchase arrangement called for the state to pay the county rent on the Mall equal to the county's cost of meeting interest and principal payments on the bonds. Also, the state would make payments to both the city and county, in lieu of taxes, on the confiscated real estate.

The money to be paid to the county between the signing of the agreement, which took place on May 11, 1965, and the agreement's termination date in 2004 would amount to as much as $35 million. Also, the state would have to pay at least $44.2 million more in interest than it would have paid had the project been approved in a voter referendum. But with a voter referendum there would almost certainly have been no Mall at all, and so the interest represents reality, and the savings through the referendum an unlikely hypothesis.

Mall construction moved ahead, much to the disapproval of State Comptroller Arthur Levitt, who found the whole plan "a circumvention of normal constitutional procedures." He pointed out in 1971 that the Office of General Services estimated the total cost of the Mall would be $850 million. Levitt wrote: "This estimate does not include the cost of the state's share of new arterials and related streets running through or connecting with the Mall. In our opinion, the total Mall costs, including the cost of arterials and financing charges, will be well in excess of $1.5 billion." (In 1982 the OGS estimated the total cost at $1.9 billion, and construction costs alone at $1.7 billion.)

The Mall-financing scheme was extraordinarily complex, and negotiations in 1964 and 1965 dragged on and on as Albany's brain trust fought for the most lucrative provisions possible. Albany County Treasurer Eugene Devine represented Albany in the negotiations, and William L. Pfeiffer, then president of the Albany Savings Bank, represented Rockefeller.

Devine told a story (to somebody I can't mention) that illustrates Rockefeller's frustration. After Devine and Pfeiffer met with the Governor in the executive chamber, Rockefeller asked

Devine to stay on, poured him a drink, and took him to a window that looked out on the site of the stalled construction, much of it still raw earth. "Gene," says the Governor in this story, as he puts his arm on Devine's shoulder and gestures toward the Mall, "I want you to tell my friend Erastus he's got to help me fill that goddamn hole."

But Dan O'Connell's view of the stalemate was firm. Let grass grow in the streets, he said. An ultimatum came from the Governor through Pfeiffer. Erastus, during an interview in his office, recalled conveying the ultimatum to Dan as he sat on the sofa in the same office. Dan considered the situation, said the Mayor, then decided the appropriate response to Mr. Pfeiffer was to "tell him to go fuck himself."

Samuel Bleecker says in his book that Albany threatened to sabotage the deal unless the state substantially upped the benefits to the city. Rockefeller was outraged, says Bleecker, and wrote a public letter threatening to consider the deal dead if Albany didn't ratify the agreement already reached. He says this move spurred Erastus ("shamefaced and defeated") to action within a week.

Four more months of negotiations followed but finally the deal was concluded. History indicates the Mayor was neither as shamed nor as defeated as Bleecker suggests. Erastus's public response was that the Mall was now "a magnificent and breathtaking reality" and, furthermore, "the greatest single governmental complex history has ever known."

Good fortune also started to dog the Mayor personally under the new arrangement. The *Wall Street Journal* pointed out that his insurance company, Albany Associates, plus two Albany banks with which he was closely associated, stood to profit from Mall-related boons. The insurance company wrote two $5-million policies on one of its clients, which had a $12.8-million contract to do plumbing and heating work on the Mall. And as much as a billion was perhaps about to pass through the National Commercial Bank and Trust Company, which was named as depository of cash from Mall bond sales. Erastus was a director of the bank. In the State Bank of Albany, where Erastus admitted he and his mother were shareholders and his mother had a "substantial" account, two Mall-related accounts were opened by the State.

Wall Street Journal reporter Richard Stone asked the Mayor why the National Commercial Bank had been chosen as depository and the Mayor answered testily, "I haven't the slightest idea." As to the State Bank, the Mayor said, "It is absolutely untrue in every single possible way" that he sought to steer bond funds or rentals to the bank.

The Mayor's leverage with the state legislature also took an upward turn after the city became the landlord of the Mall, most notably after March 1971, when Albany suddenly and mysteriously canceled the sale of $70 million in Mall bonds, thus stalling payment by the state of the ongoing construction. The Mayor, County Attorney John Clyne, and other officials refused to give any explanation for the cancellation.

The explanation lay in the city's quest to gain state help in solving some local problems, particularly those related to a loathsome new state law that abolished the Mayor's power to appoint the city school board and made it an elected board, which meant his potential loss of control over the $17-million school budget. This was not the only issue. One official in the Office of General Services told me the city had come in with "a laundry list" of grievances, from which it wanted the kind of relief only the state could provide.

When that relief wasn't forthcoming, the county suddenly canceled the $70-million Mall bond sale. Two months later a case of Strange Bedfellowism surfaced in the State Senate. Majority Leader Earl Brydges, the state's third most powerful Republican, clandestinely introduced into the Senate Rules Committee—and without the knowledge of Albany's maverick Republican senator, Walter Langley, a political enemy of the Mayor's—a bill that would have repealed Albany's elected-school-board law and given control back to Erastus.

This curious maneuver, a top Republican bypassing a fellow Republican to secretly create law benefiting the Albany Democrats—could hardly have happened without pressure from the Governor. And, in fact, Langley accused Nelson and Brydges of yielding to "crude political blackmail" by Erastus and Dan. The school bill eventually passed the Senate, despite Langley's protests, but was killed in the Assembly after another Albany Republican, Fred Field, spoke against it. The law remained in effect and Albany's school board is still elected, but without any depreciation in its loyalty to the wishes of City Hall.

Five months after Albany County mysteriously canceled the sale of the Mall bonds, it just as mysteriously reoffered them for sale. The delay cost state taxpayers an additional $6 million in interest payments.

■   ■   ■

The hole in the ground remained formidable for years. It looked like a deserted Worlds' Fair project when the workday ended, lights erratically blinking in the middle floors of the tower building, which was not yet marbled or topped out, lights twinkling on a dozen motionless cranes that looked like surreal giraffes on watch over this vast pit, with its piles and piles of sand, its dozens of pools of stagnant water, its colorful cartilage thrusting upward—red I-beams, gray reinforcing rods, yellow columns.

Some 1,500 to 2,500 men were at work in the pit at various stages of its development, employed by 63 prime contractors and 200 subcontractors. A reporter for the *Albany Knickerbocker News–Union Star*, Scott Christianson, turned his attention to all their goings-on and showed that the place was chockablock with thievery, no-shows, ridiculous featherbedding, gambling, and a rather spectacular record of arson.

Thievery, for instance, meant the disappearance of half a million dollars' worth of steel rods, $78,000 worth of plywood, unmeasurable amounts of marble. A dozen bookies had a special turf they worked within the Mall site, and their annual take was estimated in the millions. Four men from various labor unions were assigned to monitor a single heater switch in the Justice building, their only function to flip it off if the heater acted up. Their pay ranged from $25 to $35 an hour, and if you play that on your calculator you discover the taxpayers paid $4,000 to $5,000 a week to monitor that switch.

State officials told Christianson there had been seventeen fires at the Mall and gave him dates. The dates were all wrong and he found out there had been sixty fires, some clearly labeled arson by fire investigators—one in a tower building, for instance, causing $2.4 million in damage and setting construction back by months. Christianson's sources suggested motives for the fires: to cover up thefts, to prolong construction, to take vengeance for labor trouble. In eight years, he discovered, there had been no arrests for arson, theft, or gambling.

Senator Earl Brydges's response to Christianson's articles was "I have not heard these things," and he told a television interviewer, "If you hear of anything, let me know."

It was a grab-bag society at the Mall, unfettered by state or city law enforcement. The government's blindfold was Nelson's way of freeing contractors and labor unions of cumbersome moral and legal obligations, and getting on with the task at hand.

Scott Christianson was offered jobs by several contractors, and by a detective agency working the Mall, in obvious efforts to divert him from his investigations. He was also bugged, burgled, tax-audited, followed. A car tried to run his car off a bridge, and a woman he didn't know approached him with sexual overtures, which he evaluated as an effort at scandalous entrapment, though he says he could never prove it.

None of these efforts worked and Christianson kept writing. But the writing produced only a public awareness, no change. Grand juries investigated the allegations without returning a single indictment, district attorneys snubbed the crime wave, and the Mayor and the Governor pointed to each other as jurisdictionally responsible. The fires and thievery continued uninterrupted, the Mall proving to be one of the most perfectly designed perpetual-opportunity machines in the history of boondogglery.

Apart from his willing the Mall on Albany, Governor Rockefeller also willed into existence in the mid-1960s the State University of New York at Albany, which now brings 16,000 students to the city annually. He imposed a residential-commercial-hotel project, created by his Urban Development Corporation, on the downtown site of Albany's old Ten Eyck Hotel. The Albany Hilton (cost: $30 million) opened there in 1982 with 392 rooms, a sleek disco called Cahoots, and a restaurant called Truffles, bringing a cosmopolitan chic and a dining elegance (Luxembourg china, tuxedoed waiters) that overnight returned the lush look of money to Downtown.

Further, in 1978 State University refurbished and occupied for its central administrative offices the former Delaware and Hudson Railroad building, commonly called the Plaza building, which was in a severe decline. It is a majestic structure that is a copy of the Clothmakers Guild Hall in Ypres, Belgium. It was designed by Albany's greatest twentieth-century architect, Marcus T. Reynolds, and brought about by Albany Republican boss Billy Barnes, in conjunction with the D and H, before and during World War I. It is a gift of beauty to the city, and when completed in 1916 gave great impetus to cleaning up Albany's abominable waterfront. Barnes built his own lavish offices in the southern segment of the building, and made it the home of his *Albany Evening Journal*. SUNY Central now occupies also the neighboring old post office at State Street and Broadway.

Further yet under Rockefeller, the state acquired from the Penn Central Railroad the grand corpus of Union Station, through which the last train passed on December 29, 1968. After its closing, the building was scavenged quickly for its copper roofing; and from consequent leaks, decay sprouted. The station sat there in a deepening gray funk, turning into a target for the wrecker's ball, until Governor Hugh Carey, at a cost of $1 million, tidied it up to preserve it for a new era. A high-rise office and hotel project, with the station as a centerpiece, almost became reality in 1982, but faltered. Yet the area seems destined for glory eventually—waterfront living, a heady adjunct to Downtown, being a new possibility in the next decade.

All these developments, though they occurred in isolation, have added cumulatively to the city-center renaissance initiated by the Mall. Washington Avenue, then North Pearl Street, then the Plaza area, began to blossom with new banks, restaurants, shops. The Rosenblatt brothers, Sam and Fred, zapped up a modest skyscraper, the Twin Towers, at South Swan and Washington, shaming the Mall's builders in terms of speed, economy, and efficient use of space. The wise guys in town snapped up houses on the streets bordering the Mall site—Jay, Lancaster, Chestnut, Madison, and the rest.

And on Hamilton Street, where Lil lived, the row of old dogs was marked for extinction by developer Joseph Gerrity, who planned to build new residential and commercial projects, including a high-rise hotel. Neighbors who wanted to preserve the traditional qualities of the row-house neighborhood feared this, as they also feared a proposed McDonald's hamburger parlor with golden arches. In the summer of 1973 demolition began on the south side of Hamilton between Swan and Dove, and several old houses were bulldozed away.

Jane Ramos, an independent candidate for alderman, found out the city had issued even more demolition permits to Gerrity and that contracts had been signed with Becker the Wrecker to knock down houses on the north side. She called a press conference, and a number of activists joined the fight and picketed in front of the buildings to be razed.

The house at 315 Hamilton—five doors from where Lil had lived, and one of a long line of abandoned buildings—became headquarters for the protest. One night the pickets camped inside 315, anticipating the bulldozers' arrival on a nighttime foray. Jane Ramos and the strikers took their case to Mayor Corning, and the Mayor surprised them by rescinding the demolition permits.

The Hudson/Park (named for two streets, not for a park) Neigh-

borhood Association was then formed. Gregg Bell, a neighborhood activist, recalled running its early meetings, chosen by Jane
Ramos to do so because he was the only person in the group with
a necktie. He became Hudson/Park's first president. The Historic
Albany Foundation was formed the following year, 1974, and it
joined the fight to preserve the old houses. Gerrity yielded and
renovated the buildings, turning the block into Robinson Square,
now the quintessentially gentrificated section of the city. Jane
Ramos, preservationist without honor in her ward, lost her fight
to be an alderman and left town soon afterward.

Today, Robinson (Ramos?) Square is a row of chic boutiques
in the basements and on the first floors of the long line of reconstituted buildings, which are generally 100 percent occupied;
and there is a long waiting list for apartment space upstairs.
Harriet Langley, who ran the Papagallo store at 307 Hamilton
until March 1983, when she moved to Stuyvesant Plaza, uptown,
prospered from her business connection to the street's revival;
but she also found the new commerciality along Hamilton, Lark,
and other streets so unsettling that she moved her home to Delmar in search of trees and birds. Harriet and her late husband,
Walter, the state senator, had lived in the neighborhood since
1964, a time when the middle and upper-middle classes had not
yet rediscovered it. But when the Mall's influence began to be
felt, Harriet, unlike most people in the city, saw the influx of
affluence as a form of decline, an elite form of blockbusting.
"What happened to the elderly people living in a room somewhere
on these streets?" she wondered.

Many longtime residents asked the same question, but little
was done until five residents of the neighborhood formed Albany
Area Housing Opportunities, a nonprofit corporation aimed at
making housing available to low-income people. AAHO had no
money, but it sought and got donations from neighborhood
churches, enough for a down payment on the purchase of 143
Lancaster Street. The owner agreed to hold a fifteen-year mortgage at 15 percent. AAHO also persuaded the city's Urban Renewal Agency to commit $105,000 in loans and grants to renovate
the old structure, and won a rent subsidy from the Albany Housing Authority.

The result in the summer of 1982 was that the seven families
and individuals who would have been evicted were only temporarily displaced by the renovation, but would in time return
to the building, at the same rent, and now have a say in how the

building is managed. Among the tenants, two are elderly, one is a blind woman, one a heart-attack victim.

The effect is the anomalous preservation of a bit of living history and a symbolic resistance to the gentrification of Lancaster Street. AAHO hopes to take on a second house.

"None of us are idealizing poor people," Shirley Nelson, a novelist and one of AAHO's founders, said. "But none of us had any taste for the block becoming totally middle class. That's boring, and not a healthy thing economically or socially, to say nothing of being unjust."

Life is so nifty that the Center Square Neighborhood Association, which monitors many of these blocks, now finds itself with a vanishing membership for want of a "unifying problem" to keep folks interested. Most of the association's wars have been won—saving Washington Park from disfiguration by a superhighway, closing rowdy bars, diminishing the number of burglaries and muggings—although the fight with the city on zoning ordinances continues.

During a segment of TV's *Hour Magazine* in March 1982, host Gary Collins was interviewing the author of a book on where people are choosing to live these days, why certain cities attract certain people—accessibility to culture and nature, for instance, or a low crime rate: in short, a high quality of life. The author said, "Now, you take Albany, New York," and Collins said, "No, you take Albany, New York," which got him a laugh, for that is the classic response when Albany's name comes up: one of the ten bottom places of the earth, right? Wrong, said the author, and he began to explain Albany's virtues. That Albany turnaround—from being an object of ridicule to being a city of quality—is a phenomenon attributable in large measure to one man: New York State's all-time master builder, Nelson Rockefeller. And how are we to assess that?

Only a mother, and an uncommonly saintly mother at that, could love Nelson Rockefeller unequivocally. He was loathed by the political left and the political right; he was a Vietnam War hawk, a militant missile-gap and bomb-shelter cold warrior; he was cold-blooded in the exercise of power, as demonstrated in the Attica prison revolt; his contempt for the law and the state constitution when they stood in the way of his plans was never more visible than in the history of the Mall.

And so on.

You can make up your own diatribe against the man, thousands have, but it would only roll off him. His money armor-plated his ego against assault while he was alive, just as it shields him from gratitude now that he's dead. How could any sensible person thank Rockefeller for what he did? Would we thank Cheops for his pyramid (which only took fourteen acres)? But consider what Cheops did for Egyptian tourism.

In Albany the statistics are formidable. Half a million people pass annually through the museum in the trapezoidal cultural center; 405,000 used the facilities of the convention center in the Mall in calendar 1981—proms, graduations, trade shows mainly; but that is changing now with the presence of the Hilton, and the figure is going up. Upwards of 60,000 people came to the Youth Theater's productions in the Egg, and another 60,000 came to see the national dance and drama touring companies that performed there. Also, 98,757 visitors took the guided tour of the Capitol and the Mall, and another 50,000 or so guided themselves through the same marbled halls. Some 40,000 people annually jam together around the reflecting pool for Fourth of July fireworks. Anywhere from 500 to 2,000 use the same place twice a week for a summer-long series of ethnic festivals. A recent festival for blacks was expected to draw 5,000 but 20,000 turned up. And some 80,000 came out for an all-day music festival in the fall of 1980, probably the largest crowd the city has seen since V-J Day.

Erastus's role as an adversarial godfather of the Mall ended oddly in March 1983, when Governor Mario Cuomo signed into law legislation naming Nelson's forty-four-story skyscraper after the Mayor, who was very ill in a Boston hospital. And so the most visible element of Nelson's erection will henceforth be known as Erastus Corning Tower.

The Mall will still be Nelson's, of course, for it was his vision that it would be a great success and a boon to the city, and he said so repeatedly to his critics. Because he was right in his appraisal of what the future would bring, Albany enthusiasts are forced to speak ambiloquently about the man, who has confused us all. Consider, for instance, how he confused Erastus, who was invited to be present when the Mall agreement between city and state was announced by the Governor. Nelson, Erastus told me, wasn't sure what he should reveal about Erastus's role in inventing the financial arrangements, the implication being that the Governor would like to take credit for it himself, at least for the moment. He asked the Mayor what he should say about this.

"I told him," said Erastus, "that I've always made it a practice to tell the truth whenever I can."

Nelson said all right, and when he met the press he credited Erastus with inventing the plan. Then he inscribed to him a large photo of himself superimposed on the Mall. In the inscription he credited Erastus's contribution to making the Mall possible, except that he wrote it "South Maul." This pleased the Mayor so much he took the photo to his summer place in Maine, tacked it on the wall of his outhouse, and had a photo taken of himself seated therein, admiring the Maul photo. But after many solitary moments of admiration he decided it was too rare an item to stay where it was, and so he brought it back to City Hall and filed it in his desk drawer, from which he extracted it to prove to me he was telling the truth.

At this revelation we must take our leave of the curious South Mall, and of the curiouser Nelson Rockefeller, that pharaonic redeemer who, four months after he witnessed the Mall's name being changed from the Empire State Plaza to the Governor Nelson A. Rockefeller Empire State Plaza (that was October 6, 1978), fell out of life's lovely water bed and died, with as much flash, fanfare, ambiguity, deception, and aftershock as he had lived, but leaving a legacy that makes him both truly remarkable and rewardingly kickable. We wore out several pairs of shoes kicking Richard Nixon around, but with Nelson our shoes will last longer, for we cannot help but pause in our footwork to gape at the wonder of all that marble, and to revel in the way the city's old corpus is sitting up and sipping whiskey—because of Nelson. In the spring of 1982, at ten o'clock one evening, there were no parking spaces on State Street below Eagle, or on North Pearl Street and Broadway north of State, or even on Washington Avenue near the Capitol. Cars were double-parked and people were in line to get into Cahoots; others were walking the streets, barhopping under new streetlamps, enticed by the proliferation of lively pubs Downtown. On April 15, 1982, to counter the woes of paying income tax, the Downtown pub and restaurant owners opened their bars and poured free drinks—"anything you want"—for an hour, a moment of magnanimity that created a crush like nothing seen Downtown in two decades.

All this pleasure, all this sensuality, all this money growing out of the Mall, is the basis for a morality play without any morals; and who better to comment upon it than H. L. Mencken, who in 1922, in his *On Being an American*, not only foresaw it all but also dictated the logical response to it:

"And here, more than anywhere else that I know of or have heard of, the daily panorama of human existence, of private and communal folly—the unending procession of governmental extortions and chicaneries, of commercial brigandages and throat-slittings, of theological buffooneries, of aesthetic ribaldries, of legal swindles and harlotries, of miscellaneous rogueries, villainies, imbecilities, grotesqueries, and extravagances—is so inordinately gross and preposterous, so perfectly brought up to the highest conceivable amperage, so steadily enriched with an almost fabulous daring and originality, that only the man who was born with a petrified diaphragm can fail to laugh himself to sleep every night, and to awake every morning with all the eager, unflagging expectations of a Sunday-school superintendent touring the Paris peep-shows."

Yes. Oh yes.

And so to bed.

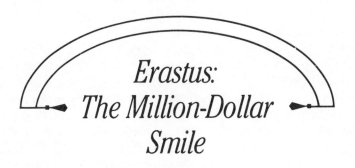

Erastus: The Million-Dollar Smile

*T*he caller at the other end of the phone said, "Mayor Corning would like to speak with you," and that was a surprise, for the Mayor had gone out of his way not to speak to me some years earlier when I was writing stories that complicated his life. But those years had passed, people had mellowed, and now here he came with notable goodwill, saying he'd been reading what I'd written about Albany and liked it.

I had just published my third novel, *Billy Phelan's Greatest Game*, which concerns Albany's Nighttown in 1938 at a moment when politics invades the evening. I'd also written a piece about why I usually write about Albany. I'd mentioned the Mayor by name in that one, for he'd been saying publicly that his ninth consecutive four-year term, which he was then serving, would be his last. I said I doubted it, that he'd probably live to be 287 years of age and still be running the city when it was crowded with intergalactic snowmobiles.

That was a bum joke and I'm ashamed of it. But the point was at least on the way to being prophetic, for the Mayor had entered his tenth consecutive four-year term—he was first elected in 1941—and would go on to his eleventh in 1981. Until he fell ill in the summer of 1982 with debilitating bronchitis and emphysema, he had been a political workhorse, a phenomenon who belonged in the *Guinness Book of World Records* as America's longest-running mayor: 1983 was his forty-second year in office, no one else was close. *Guinness* wasn't paying attention to Albany, but Ripley was. For his eleven-term achievement the Mayor, on July 11, 1982, wound up in the funny sheets next to nineteen wingwalkers and a chicken that laid eggs for 448 straight days, believe it or not.

As we talked on the phone the Mayor said people kept telling him he should write his memoirs; and what did I think of collaborating on such a project? He also told me a story Alben Barkley, Harry Truman's vice-president, had told him during a political convention years ago. Barkley went to an Arab soothsayer, said the Mayor, and the soothsayer told him, "You're a lucky man. You're going to live to be a thousand years old." And Barkley told the Mayor, "You know, I believed him. And it's the first time I ever believed anything an Arab said."

I took the story not as a revelation of Barkley's distrust of Arabs but as a clue that the Mayor had changed his opinion of me, that in accepting my view of Albany he especially believed my line about his living to be 287, and that it was the first time he ever believed anything I wrote.

And so we did explore the possibility of a book, not a formal biography, which I had no interest in doing, but a work of journalism about his life and times, in which I would say whatever I felt like saying, and then he would read it and expand upon it, or rebut it, in his own words. The format was his idea. I'd never heard of a book like it before, and I'm not sure such a work could come into existence without the collaborators ending up in a duel to the last drop of psychic blood and brain fluid. Two fruitful sessions at his office in 1979 did come of it.

The office looked out on Pine and Eagle streets from the cubicle designed by H. H. Richardson. The Mayor sat where he always sat, behind his orderly desk, beneath the portrait of Pieter Schuyler, Albany's first mayor, amid the dark wood paneling and red drapes and carpeting, dressed in a single-breasted gray pinstriped suit, white shirt, and striped tie, salty in his language when I took notes, desalinated when I turned on the tape recorder.

Three years later I took him to lunch (to get a change of scenery) at Quackenbush House, Albany's oldest building (1732), now a restaurant, and handsomely restored, as is the adjacent old city waterworks, where Hudson River water was filtered in the nineteenth century.

At Quackenbush House in early March 1982 he appeared fit, on the way back from a hip ailment that had sidelined him, but on the way to the hacking cough that would plague him the rest of his days ("this lousy laryngitis"). He had grown more gaunt since the talk in his office, a bit looser in the jowls. But his personality had always lived in his face, and in his smile, which had charmed, by this time, millions of voters.

He was a witty raconteur when he chose to be, with a benign quality in his voice that had nothing whatever to do with what was going on in his brain. He would have lost most shouting matches, but I couldn't imagine his getting into one. He stood tall: six-two and well-built; no longer with the outdoorsman's physique or the athletic bounce in his step, but presenting a moving image that was recognizable at fifty yards, so ubiquitous had it been for most of everybody's lifetime. Equally well known was the nomenclature that went with the physique: Mayor Corning. Jack McEneny said most people thought his first name was Mayor.

And so we talked, but our book project was eventually shelved, not for reasons of conflict but for reasons of time commitments of all concerned. I was working for money, and this project would have produced none of the instant. His duties kept his time at a premium. And so no book was produced.

While I was waiting to talk to an old Democratic pol in a Downtown law office in 1980, another lawyer hanging out presumed I was looking for the villainous secrets perennially linked to the Machine, especially during the 1920s, and he said to me, "The old-timers will never give you the real story." Not true. They'll give you more stories than you can possibly use. The problem is how to separate their truths from their lies, or their distortions, and then how to get it into print without libeling anybody. Nobody on the inside of the Machine ever wrote a memoir, although Jimmy McGuinness, the city corporation counsel, who had a falling-out with the powers, was making noises in the late 1950s about a confessional history. But he died before doing anything about it.

Revenge of that sort would hardly have motivated Erastus to write his memoirs, but he was ready to let the History Department at State University of Albany tape his recollections of his life. But after only one taping session he was hospitalized; and so his record went largely unspoken. What he clearly hoped to do with that now-lost verbal memoir was to shape his own image of his life and times for posterity; for when longtime Democratic party boss Daniel P. O'Connell was alive, Erastus was inevitably viewed as "Dan's Mayor."

The two mayors who preceded Erastus, William S. Hackett (1921–26) and John Boyd Thacher II (1926–41), were, like Erastus, popular vote-getters, able administrators, and men of wealth and elevated social position. Also, both had come extraordinarily close to being governor.

But, however eminent, none of the mayors had independent leverage in party workings while Dan was boss. None could have challenged Dan and survived the battle.

But Dan began to fade, had less and less to say about what went on, and in this way he allowed Erastus time to consolidate political power in his own right. And so, when Dan died in 1977, the Mayor took over the party machinery, gaining such total control of all government, and all politics, in both the city and the county, that he became answerable only to the electorate, which had never asked him a question he couldn't answer or deftly evade. Two books were written about the Machine and he liked neither. He wanted to set the record straight, which is why I was in his office.

The Corning name, says one genealogy, comes from the French De Cornu, meaning "horn of the hunter." Some De Cornus went from France to England, where the name was changed to Corning. Certain of its bearers supported Oliver Cromwell in the Protectorate in the seventeenth century, and then fled to America after the return of the monarchy, settling in Beverly, Massachusetts, about 1641.

The Corning tie to Albany came through the first Erastus, a sixth-generation Corning in America, who was born in Norwich, Connecticut, in 1794. His father, Bliss Corning, a Continental Army soldier of no particular distinction, and his mother, Lucinda Smith, of an old American family, gave Erastus an education in a private school run by recent graduates of Yale, which remained the family school into the twentieth century.

The Cornings migrated to Chatham, in Columbia County, about 1806, and a year later Erastus went to work, at age thirteen, for his uncle, Benjamin Smith, a successful hardware merchant in Troy. Smith was Jeffersonian in his politics, and eventually left Erastus his fortune, thus shaping both the family's destiny for business and wealth and its enduring ties to political democracy.

Erastus proved to be a businessman of singular talent. He became a hardware merchant in his own right, eventually owning the Albany Iron Works (in Troy), a formidable firm that, among other achievements, built the *Monitor*. He led the consolidation of several railroads into the New York Central system, and served as the corporation's president for eleven years. He was president of the company that built the St. Marie's Falls Ship Canal, was mayor of Albany from 1834 to 1837, state senator, congressman, a member of the Albany Regency, and an eightfold millionaire, which made him the richest citizen in Albany, in his day the second city in the state.

A common question when the Corning name comes up in conversation is this: "Corning. Any connection to Corning Glass?" It turns out there are no Cornings in Corning Glass, which takes its name from the city of Corning, New York, named for Erastus Corning, the celebrity figure in an 1835 land speculation deal that was to connect the state's southern tier to the Eastern Seaboard by way of the Chemung Canal.

Erastus Corning died in 1872, but his name lived on. The name, a Latinized version of the Greek *erastos*, meaning "beloved," became talismanic in the family, and since him there have been six others. The line, with the numberings all my own for the sake of clarifying this confounding history, was this:

Erastus I begat Erastus II who begat Erastus III who begat Erastus IV who begat Erastus V, none of whom is our Erastus.

Our Erastus came into the light through a second marriage of Erastus II (who was called Erastus, Jr.). Having begat Erastus III, Erastus II remarried and begat Edwin (who in union with the O'Connell brothers would give headbirth to the Albany political Machine). It was Edwin who begat the object of our attention, whom, for the sake of rounding out this numerology, we might as well call Erastus VI. He, in turn, begat Erastus VII.

Our Erastus was born October 7, 1909, and is called Erastus Corning 2nd—he liked the Arabic—since he was one of two Erasti begat through Erastus II.

Erastus I was the great-grandfather of our Erastus.

Erastus II, grandfather of our Erastus, was born 1827, died 1897, and succeeded his father as president of the Albany Iron Works. Though an ardent Democrat, as almost all Cornings have been, he had little connection with politics, his lone public office having been that of city alderman. He is better remembered as a breeder of Hereford cattle and Thoroughbred racehorses, and for his vast collection of flowers. "His orchid collection was the best in the country," our Erastus recalled when we spoke in March 1982. "He sold it to somebody in Philadelphia in the 1890s, and it's still there, I'm sure. You know, orchids live forever."

Our Erastus (henceforth merely Erastus) recalled that his grandfather also loved chickenfighting, a pastime he shared with South End saloon owner Black Jack O'Connell, father of Dan O'Connell. There is a portrait of Grandfather Corning at a chickenfight, which Erastus inherited and gave to Dan. Dan took Erastus to the fights when he was a young man, but when Erastus was elected mayor, Dan decided it was unsuitable entertainment for the city's leader, and he wouldn't take him anymore.

"There were a whole bunch of characters in the South End," Erastus recalled, "and one was a well-known dog thief. My grandfather complained to Dan's father, on behalf of a friend whose dog had been stolen, and Dan's father went to the thief and asked, 'Why did you steal that dog?' And the thief said, 'I didn't know the dog was a friend of yours.'"

The Corning and O'Connell children grew up together, hunted together; Edwin (Erastus's father) and Dan were only two years apart in age (Edwin born 1883, Dan born 1885), and so their eventual union in politics was really an extension of a long friendship. Erastus's earliest political memory is from the teens of the century when he was a small boy and saw a group of Democrats, Dan among them, come to the Corning home on Washington Avenue to meet with his father, a prelude to political union.

The O'Connells—Dan and his brothers Ed, John (Solly), and Patrick—had grown up in the city's South End before and during the supremacy of William (Billy) Barnes, a Republican boss with national power in his party, who ran Albany from 1899 to 1921 the way the Tammany bosses ran New York City. Dan's father and his brother Solly were both ward workers for Barnes, and Dan was also working the wards from the time he quit school in the fifth grade. You could say that at the outset all the O'Connells knew how the game was played.

What they needed was the money and the players, and these were furnished by the Cornings—Edwin and his brother, Parker, who were part of the Albany Democratic Machine from the first. It was the Cornings, for instance, who talked Hackett into heading the 1921 ticket that made Albany safe for Democracy—ever, it would seem, after.

As to the Corning money, it had seen some extremely lean

years, but the family was again flush. The leanness had become visible at the death of Erastus II in 1897, the estate overextended through borrowing, presumably to save the Corning ironworks, and, according to papers at the Albany Institute of History and Art, the estate was insolvent.

Perhaps the Cornings, then, lived with more frugality than theretofore; but it wasn't exactly hard times. Edwin and Parker, for instance, both went to Yale. Two years after graduation, in 1908, Edwin married Louise Maxwell of Washington, D.C. (she'd been born in India, her father a missionary, her mother, Ellen Maxwell, a novelist, author of *The Bishop's Conversion* and *Three Old Maids in Hawaii*). The union produced four children: Erastus, the eldest; two daughters, Louise, who died in March 1954, and Harriet, who died in February 1966; and another son, Edwin, who died in 1964 of injuries suffered in a car accident in 1959.

The Cornings moved into Brides Row on Chestnut Street, a handsome row of look-alike yellow-brick houses below Lark Street and a traditional starting point for affluent newlyweds. Erastus was born there, and during the rehabilitation of the property years later, when he was the street's most famous alumnus, he visited the new occupants of his birthplace. A reporter present to do a story asked the Mayor, "Were you really born in this house?"

"Yes, I was," the Mayor recalled saying. And, he added, "The reporter looked at me again and asked, 'Did your mother live here?' I never knew whether I should have hit him or not. I think he thought it was kind of a half-baked promotion."

The Cornings moved from Chestnut Street to a bigger house when Erastus was four or five. This was on Washington Avenue, across from the Fort Orange Club. Then, with a return to serious affluence, they decided to build. The affluence came during World War I, when Edwin and Parker owned major shares in the Ludlum Steel Company, a long-held family interest, plus shares in the Albany Felt Company. Ludlum was said to be making $200,000 a year through government contracts, and the Felt Company was doing $1 million a year.

The Corning family had long owned property south of the city along route 144, in the area now known as Corning Hill. Erastus I had bought land there and built a mansion on it in the 1830s, and Edwin did the same. And so, as the 1920s approached, Edwin Corning, the modern squire of Corning Hill, formed his union with the O'Connell brothers and gave shape to a new political era. After being divided and moribund—bought out, really, by

Billy Barnes—Albany Democrats found new strength, and in 1919 elected four supervisors, three aldermen, and an assessor (Dan O'Connell himself). Also they almost elected a mayor (Reynolds King Townsend), losing by only 1,500 votes (Democrats usually lost by 10,000) and carrying eleven of the city's nineteen wards.

With this new power to sway the voters, they went on to even more vigorous campaigning in 1921, and Hackett won by 7,153 votes. They also swept the city and most of the county. Erastus did not remember much of the early days when we talked, but he did recall the torchlight parades for Hackett, and a moment of modest violence during his father's involvement in that year's campaigning.

The Republican county chairman, Frank Wiswall, Erastus said, "accused my father of throwing a potato and hitting him in the head. My father said he didn't do it but wished he had." The next day Albany produce dealer Willie Ryan took an ad in the paper to say that he didn't know who threw the potato but he knew where they bought it.

Erastus was not involved in any politicking of the 1920s. He went off to Groton at the age of twelve, and thereafter to Yale, and was gone from 1922 to 1932, spending little of his childhood in Albany. He became a denizen of the natural world instead of politics.

"When I was about eight," he said, "my father, a heavy and sedentary man, decided I should not be like him, and so he hired Pete Scharff of Glenmont to teach me about wildlife and how to hunt and trap and fish." This was done mostly in the summer in Maine, which was a traditional resort for the Corning family from the time of Erastus I. Erastus II built a home in Northeast Harbor in the 1870s, and Edwin and family summered at Ellsworth, Hancock County, where Erastus established his summer place at Webb's Pond.

While he was being tutored by Scharff in the ways of nature, his father was functioning as chairman of the Albany County Democratic Committee. He managed Hackett's reelection campaigns in 1923 and 1925, which, because of their success—unprecedented among Democrats upstate—made Hackett the prime candidate for governor should Al Smith have faltered or retired. Corning's stock was also high with the party—he became its state chairman. Then, in 1926, Hackett was killed in Cuba in an auto accident. Corning, in 1927, became lieutenant governor under Smith and the next heir apparent to the governorship. Smith did offer it to him in 1928, but Edwin declined.

"My father was very much interested in politics, loved it as a game," Erastus said, "but he didn't like public office much. He was taken sick [a heart attack] in August of 1928, and so then the nomination was offered to Roosevelt."

Edwin had arteriosclerosis. A surgeon who was a close friend amputated one of his legs in an operation at New Haven. He remained ill from 1928 until a second leg amputation was done in Maine in August 1934. He died on the operating table, said his son. Edwin was only fifty years old, and his fortunes as well as his health had been in decline. In 1928, the year of his heart attack, he was replaced as president of Ludlum Steel by Hiland D. Batcheller; and in 1934, when his will was admitted to probate, his real and personal property, left to his widow, was valued at something more than $20,000, the fortune gone.

Leo O'Brien recalled a visit with Mrs. Louise Corning, the widow, not long thereafter. Erastus had just been elected to the State Assembly, and he called Leo, then on the *Times-Union*, and asked if Leo would do a story on the wedding of his sister, Harriet.

"So I interviewed Mrs. Corning about it," said Leo, "and made the usual silly remark that 'I suppose you're pleased your son has been elected to the Assembly,' and she said, 'No, I'm not. When my husband got out of college he said he was going to have a million dollars by the time he was thirty, and he did. But now, because of politics, I have neither a husband nor a million dollars.' "

That proved not to be an enduring condition. When Louise Corning died on May 24, 1976, at age ninety-one, her will disclosed that a rather broadly uncertain bequest of between $500,000, and $990,000 went to Erastus, her only surviving child. This amount was one third of her total estate.

The monied Brahmins of Albany had never approved of Louise's husband's politicking with the O'Connells; and Erastus recalled that in the Machine's early days, a commonplace insult found its way into a newspaper headline that gave grievous offense to his mother:

CORNING CARRYING CORN
TO O'CONNELL'S HOGS

The same attitude prevailed into Erastus's day. I recall one Republican politician's telling me in the late 1960s, "I never forgave Erastus for tying in with them."

Many of the social and power elite did forgive, however—those, for instance, who found it pleasant to do business with the city, or with the banks or law firms to which the city gave allegiance. Many of Erastus's peers found his politics merely an amusing aberration in an otherwise splendid man. His fellows at the Fort Orange Club tended to view him as an overarching figure to whom not only respect but also homage was due. A mention to certain of these clubmen that you were writing about him would evoke sanctifying eulogies; and you would be warned against saying anything negative about this apotheosis of the silver spoon, the silver crown, the silver tongue, and don't forget the silver fist.

The fact is, if Erastus functioned as Dan's captive most of his political life (Democratic maverick George Harder used to say Erastus was Dan's Charlie McCarthy), it was because he wanted it that way. He had a filial devotion to Dan, and if Dan's Tammanyesque, pork-barrel bossism wasn't the kind of life and image he wanted for himself, then why did he run the city with Dan for thirty-six years?

Erastus did have an image of his own—one that was a product of the Hemingway age: the hard-drinking (vodka and tonic) outdoorsman who was good at whooping it up with the boys. But when Erastus doffed his shooting togs he could also turn into Cary Grant, standing tall, tailored, and totally at ease as he sipped the Chablis and discussed the lilacs and the lusterware with Albany matrons.

Such duality is hardly abnormal. What was fascinating about the latter-day Erastus was the emergence of the whole (well, maybe not that much) man, the fuller man, once he ceased to be a prisoner of Dan and began manufacturing a party line of his own. But first things first: how did it all begin?

In 1981 there appeared a book called *The Politics of Architecture*, by Samuel Bleecker, and the Mayor cited a chapter on the South Mall in which the author says Edwin Corning was bankrupted by the Crash of 1929's aftermath and the O'Connells bailed him out; and as an obligation for that rescue, Erastus ran for mayor.

True?

"A pack of lies," said the Mayor when we talked. "My father was sick from 'twenty-eight to 'thirty-four and I didn't even think of going into politics until after he died."

Erastus's actual entrance into politics came in 1935, three years after he graduated, Phi Beta Kappa, from Yale, with a dual major in history and English. Three days after graduation he married Elizabeth Norris Platt of Philadelphia and went to work in his own insurance company (his brother, Edwin, became his partner at a later moment).

"I had just started in business as a kid of twenty-two," Erastus recalled. "I knew Ed and Dan [O'Connell] and I was able to get some insurance business—some from the state, some from the county. I was out to see Dan, and he asked me if I'd like to be a delegate to the 1934 state [Democratic] convention in place of my father. So I went out to Buffalo and got to know a lot of people better than I had known them, and Dan said at that time, 'We'd like to have you think about whether you want to run for the Assembly in 1935.' "

Erastus said he'd love it. For years he'd been hearing about politics from his father. "I don't know whether he thought I was a better listener than my mother," Erastus told a reporter in June 1981, "but whenever I was home through the years, ever since I was a kid, he always talked politics to me."

Erastus ran for the Assembly and, of course, he won. The following year, 1936, he ran for the State Senate when Dan picked Senator William T. Byrne to fill the vacancy created by the retirement of Parker Corning from Congress, where he had served since 1923. Parker's retirement was not entirely voluntary.

"He was an economic royalist, a Bourbon," Erastus told me. "He was opposed to the income tax and couldn't stand Roosevelt. He wasn't in the mainstream of Democratic thought by a damn sight." Parker was eased out of office and lived a nonpublic life until he died in 1943.

Erastus remained in the State Senate for five years and remembered how it was for a legislator who had to deal with Dan and Ed:

"They were a pair. They separated things between them. Ed handled the finances of the city and county government, and Dan handled the patronage. They had a marvelous working arrangement, which I saw when I was in the legislature. Dan would say one thing and Ed would say another. On Social Security Dan told me, 'Don't vote unless they put in the osteopaths.' And Ed said, 'Don't pay any attention to Dan, I'll handle him. That's part of Roosevelt's program. Vote for it.' "

After Erastus had been a senator five years, Dan had another thought: Thacher was retiring before his term ended. Did Erastus want to be mayor? He said he did, and he ran, and of course he won.

His early years as mayor were served when Albany was under heavy fire from Thomas E. Dewey, who in 1938 began campaigning on the issue that if elected governor he would destroy the Albany Machine.

When elected in 1942, Dewey went after the Machine with vigor; and his probe of misused funds, judicial chicanery, and much more, lasted two and a half years. Erastus, thirty-five, was drafted into the Army in 1944 at mid-investigation, at a point when married men with dependents were being called up. He had a son, Erastus, and a daughter, Elizabeth. He served seventeen months and was still a buck private, stationed in Czechoslovakia, when he was nominated back home for a second term as mayor.

When he left for the service—with fanfare and a parade—he gave a lift to the boys and girls under fire from Governor Dewey. When he returned, as a private first class and a boyish-looking hero in uniform, it was almost election time, and when the results came in, it was as if the Dewey investigation had never happened. Erastus was reelected by 36,122 votes.

His lone venture after higher office came in 1946, when he ran for lieutenant governor, with James Mead as the gubernatorial candidate. He ran, he told me, because Dan asked him to. The party, at state level, needed help, and Erastus represented a chance of wooing the veterans' vote. He didn't want to run, and Dan didn't think Mead stood a chance of defeating Dewey. But he ran to pay Albany's dues; and, as expected, Dewey and Joe Hanley smeared Mead and Erastus. Erastus returned to City Hall and never again ventured out of it in search of higher office.

The recurring question, a cliché in Albany, is: Why not? Why did a man with such talent, education, money, wit, charisma, and political know-how settle for a career in a middling sort of town like Albany?

Erastus's ready answer was that he never wanted higher office, that he liked Albany, liked its manageable size, could get to know almost everybody, be accessible to almost everybody; and this was true enough. He said he never wanted Congress, and that he realized he didn't after being in the state legislature for six years, more than enough for any man who prized the work ethic as much as he. (He routinely worked a sixty-hour week until he fell ill.)

"I never got very active in the legislature," he told me. "Only two or three issues I had"—and even those were unmemorable to him. As to the governorship, the Albany Machine had three chances at that: with Hackett, Edwin Corning, and then in 1932, when Mayor Thacher emerged as a viable candidate, only to have Franklin Roosevelt's choice, Herbert Lehman, win the day. Erastus would surely have been in line for subsequent consideration, but upstate politicians played a diminishing role in king-making after the 1930s; and Corning's humbling defeat in the 1946 run for lieutenant governor ("I got defeated by more votes than I was ever elected by, added up together"—the losing total was 1,433,201) provided a reality principle that guided his latter-day behavior. He said he was offered a chance to run for governor in 1950 but turned it down. He was also a very dark horse contender to be Harry Truman's running mate in 1948.

What should be considered by those who wanted Erastus to rise to the U.S. Senate or to other exalted benches, is the size of the Albany domain he would have to give up. He controlled the city, the county, and the Board of Education, which together, in 1982, employed 7,200 and had a combined budget of just under $118 million. Legally, Erastus was not an official of the county, but he ran it anyway, as Albany's mayors always have since the early days of the Machine. He knew every line in every department request in the county budget, but his knowledge didn't always translate into clarity for the taxpayer who wanted to discover where his money was going. Republican actuaries developed cataracts looking for the Rosetta Stone that would explain such items as "Elections—$250,000" or "Other expenses—$500,000." "It's not a budget, it's an appropriations bill," said Harold Rubin, a former chief state budget examiner and longtime critic of Erastus.

Whatever it was or wasn't, it was all anybody ever got out of the county. The manipulation of city and county money was attacked periodically by state and federal examiners. A 1982 audit of city finances by an independent auditing firm reported the city illegally used $9.2 million—borrowed for long-term capital projects—to pay for day-to-day operating expenses in 1980 and 1981. Dewey's investigators levied a similar charge against the city in the 1940s probe. The 1982 audit won great attention in the press, but Erastus rebutted the charges and was working to solve the city's fiscal deficit when he fell ill. It was not an issue voters understood or cared much about. Albany-watchers knew it would fade away, that Erastus would not be harmed by it.

"The Mayor has always been the business man," Dan O'Connell told interviewer John Piczak in a 1965 conversation about the traditional way the city's mayors worked. "He took care of business matters, such as tax assessment problems, even though he was not supposed to. That was true, and that's true today. The Mayor took care of city and county business, and we took care of party politics. This is one of the major reasons we have operated so smoothly."

"Corning operates in the same manner?" Piczak asked.

"That's right," said Dan. "Mayor Corning is very personable and businesslike and does a fine job for the people."

Corning himself told Piczak: "I involve myself in both city and county affairs so as to coordinate operations. Things flow smooth that way."

In recent years the county has had a county executive as well as a county attorney and a majority leader of the county legislature, all of whom have had a hand in budgetary and patronage matters. But just as no mayor ever challenged Dan, no lesser executive, city or county, ever challenged Erastus.

Said County Executive Jim Coyne, "I'm basically an organization-type person." Said County Attorney Robert Lyman, "The Mayor is going to make the decision regardless of what the hell anybody has to say anyway." Said Majority Leader Richard Meyers, "There is no doubt about it. If the Mayor feels strongly about it, I feel strongly about it."

A case in point on power: when county legislator David Duncan, an attorney who seemed bound for higher echelons in the Machine, declined to vote for the expulsion of Charlie Ryan as election commissioner (not because he backed Ryan—he claims he did not—but because of a point of law at issue), Duncan found himself in a primary battle when he came up for reelection. Erastus quietly supported Duncan's challenger and Duncan was defeated.

Then in 1973 the son of an ex-sheriff (an enemy of Dan's) ran for sheriff and won. He was John J. McNulty, a Democrat, the first ever to oppose Dan in a primary and win. A savvy Irish pol, McNulty controlled the hefty county-jail patronage, which posed an obvious threat to party harmony, especially after he was re-elected. But in the middle of his second term he ran into trouble with the county legislature over jail-overtime costs, and he resigned, a consummation that could not have been engineered without Erastus's consent.

The Mayor's authority was absolute, and because of such power he was feared by his underlings. In an ambitious series of articles entitled *His Honor, the Boss*, published in the *Times-Union* in October 1979, reporter Alan C. Miller wrote of a conversation he had had with a Democratic committeeman about Albany County politics. The man had to clear it with his ward leader, who wanted to know the questions asked and answers given. About the element of fear in regard to Erastus, the committeeman said, "There is no fear. The Mayor demands a lot of respect and attention." But the committeeman insisted his name not be used and demanded it be scratched out of Miller's notebook.

Miller also spoke with Executive Deputy County Comptroller Robert Hammond, who reported that Albany Associates, Erastus's insurance agency, wrote 90 percent of the county's insurance, or an estimated $1.5 million in annual premiums. These policies were let to public bid, but Miller quoted the Mayor as saying Albany Associates got it because "nobody else wanted to bid."

As might be expected, the conflict-of-interest question was asked occasionally about Erastus's insuring the county, but it was all quite legal as long as he was not a county official.

The quest for money and power has motivated men in the Corning family for a century and a half, but these motives alone do not explain Erastus. They don't explain why he held on to his power *for so long*. I sat with him in his office one afternoon and he took occasional phone calls. One was from a man who wanted to tell him how to run the Fifth Ward. Another came from a woman complaining about rat-infested garbage on Arbor Hill. On another occasion when we talked, he said a black man came to see him one day to get a pistol permit so he'd have a gun when he went to Mississippi. Erastus told him a pistol was worthless if you didn't know how to shoot it and an Albany pistol permit wouldn't be worth anything in Mississippi anyway. But he suggested the man get a used shotgun at a local pawnshop because that was really an effective weapon, and the man went away happy.

He spoke at the Doane Stuart School in Albany one day in

1982, and Henry Wright, a sixth-grade classmate of my son's, asked him a question: What was the worst decision you ever made? He told the audience he'd have to think about that one and would write Henry a letter, which he did, and it said:

> Dear Hank,
>   I have thought what was the worst decision I made. There are very few of them that were really bad and no particular one comes to mind at this time. I think generally I regret when I try to do something to help somebody and it isn't successful. This happens more often than I would like.

The fact that Erastus put himself even through kiddie paces after forty-one years of omnipresence—marching in all the St. Patrick's Day parades, tiptoeing through all the tulip festivals—makes one wonder how he could have borne the repetition. His answer, given on the CBS *Sunday Morning* television show in January 1981—a profile of him he adjudged shallow—was "I early came to the conclusion that what's important to the people is important to me." He also said that the people in Albany were probably more interested in politics than people in any other American city except Washington, D.C.

If anything made sense out of a man of such intelligence slogging through four decades of trivia when he could have been a perfectly useless man-about-town, harassing his broker and abusing his liver, it was his long-held belief in politics as a form of personal salvation and private exaltation. Apart from the satisfaction he derived from being a once-significant, then indispensable, cog in the Machine, the job also gave him privileged access to those higher political levels his Brahmin and Eli boosters had long coveted for him. Thinking only of recent involvement: he was one of Hugh Carey's earliest backers in Carey's first run for the governorship; and Albany's backing was said to be the catalytic element that won Carey the nomination. He was one of the earliest and strongest backers of Mario Cuomo for governor, and boosted him even from a sickbed. When New York City Mayor Ed Koch also entered the race for governor (and gratuitously insulted Albany and all of upstate New York in a *Playboy* interview), Erastus offered Koch one of his own winning campaign slogans: "Keep the Mayor Mayor."

Erastus was also upstate director of Jimmy Carter's reelection campaign in 1980, and while Carter lost the state to Teddy Kennedy in the primary, he didn't lose Albany. He and Walter Mondale carried the county by 22,000 votes. Vice-President Mondale, during a speech to the Democratic National Convention in Manhattan in 1980, said he'd asked for a list of Albany Democratic supporters and Erastus had given him a list of all city employees.

Mondale, vastly amused, recalled the exchange that followed: "I asked him, which ones are Carter supporters? You haven't checked them. He said, 'You don't have to check them.' "

But while Erastus enjoyed such links to high office, he also perceived more clearly than anyone who went before him, in any city in the United States, that the Careys, the Carters, and the Mondales come and go: four-, maybe eight-year flashes in the state or national pan. But City Hall, ah yes, City Hall: that clean (sixty-eight janitors in 1980), well-lighted place—why, a man might inhabit it until he was maybe 287 years old, might he not?

In early 1982 he told a newsman who asked whether he would encourage college graduates to enter politics, "If they've got a thick skin and like it, yes. It's a tough game today. I think it's a little harder than it has been because of some unfortunate experiences on the national level. Some people have said that it isn't as much fun as it used to be, which is a very simplistic way of looking at it. . . . As far as I'm concerned, it's still fun. But I developed a thick skin a long while ago."

This, I believe, goes to the heart of what really drove Erastus all those years: a passion to play the game his father and Dan taught him to play. Psychologists could have studied with profit his urbane, unrufflable facade; his grace under pressure from state investigators specializing in jugular attack, from surly newspaper editors brandishing the moral code, from insurgent Democrats and insufferable Republicans who coveted his cubicle, from beset taxpayers who disapproved of his prestidigitational use of their money, from hapless reformers who thought that cornering him publicly on an issue was a significant achievement: as if words were politically meaningful.

I recall a moment late in 1965 when an angry group of the city's clergy, thirty-two in all, half of them Catholic, ganged up on the Mayor to protest the city's withdrawal of $23,000 in funds from Trinity Institution, a South End social welfare agency that had shaped the neighborhood group movement in the early days of the War on Poverty. The movement was giving the city innumerable headaches, and so Dan and Erastus decided to stop subsidizing it.

The unified clerics seemed to be cranking up a powerfully ill wind for the Machine, and during the meeting with them in his office, Erastus said he would consider restoring the funds. Some of the clerics took this as a positive sign, and some felt the muscle flexing by such a mixed group of priests, ministers, and one rabbi was historic, maybe even a new form of power.

I remember that during a news conference with editors of the *Times-Union* to discuss this story that day, the opinion was voiced that "They got him, they got Erastus." But Dan Button, then executive editor and later a congressman, only shook his head, smiled, and said, "They don't have him. Wait until you see what he says tomorrow."

When tomorrow came a few days later, the Mayor's commitment to reconsidering the matter had flabbed out. He had given the clerics the words they wanted to hear on the day of their wrath. What else did they want from him? Consistency?

Trinity did get back some of the money taken away from it, but only after years had passed, and then only a fragment of the loss.

The War on Poverty had happened because of the infusion of federal funds into the community, a baleful development in the mind of Dan O'Connell. Albany was the last large city in the country to have an antipoverty program, and when I asked Erastus why, he blamed it on the constant changing of federal guidelines. But that was the official story. He followed up this point with a more candid response by remembering the problem that state aid to the county nursing home (the Ann Lee Home) had presented years before to Dan and himself, and to Johnny Dwyer, who was running the Ann Lee and who didn't want the state money.

Said Erastus, "Johnny Dwyer told Dan it would give the state a say in how he ran the home. And it took eighteen months to convince Dan that the state was running it anyway, and if they were saying how to do it, let's get them to pay for some of it."

Dan never liked interference in what he considered his business—the city and the county. He told interviewer John Piczak in 1965 what he thought of the press because of this. Piczak asked him why the press turned against the Machine in the late 1920s, and Dan said, "The newspapers were . . . butting into our business. Whenever we spent any money they wanted to have a say in how and on what. Well we just stopped letting those newspapers have any say in what was spent."

"Did they ever have any say?" asked Piczak.

"No, not since we took over and reorganized the party. You know, those newspapers are the most un-American thing in the U.S."

Erastus remembered that the Machine backed one newspaper during the 1920s as a way of getting its point of view across, but that didn't work out. He couldn't remember which paper it was. In later years the problem was obviated when the city and county used legal advertising as carrot and stick to control the competing Gannett and Hearst papers. I've seen estimates from $50,000 to $300,000 as the amount divided between Hearst's *Times-Union* and Gannett's *Knickerbocker News* for such ads.

There was also the fear at these papers that the Machine would coerce advertisers to favor one publication over the other as it had done successfully in the 1920s in putting the *Sunday Telegram* out of business. And so neither paper was seriously critical of the Machine's behavior during the early 1950s, when I was observing them both from a reporter's perspective, though the *Knickerbocker* was a shade more aggressive in reporting negative news. There were reporters on both papers, covering either City Hall or the County Court House or both, who moonlighted on the city and county payrolls; and it didn't make any difference to the editors of either paper, almost all of whom were Democratic boosters.

Gene Robb came into this situation in 1953 as publisher of the *Times-Union* and remained in that post until his death in 1969. In those sixteen years he became the principal enemy of the Machine, but serious enmity did not really surface until 1960. At first, Robb felt he could not take on the Machine as an adversary because of the carrot game. Lee Robb, who chairs the State Commission on Judicial Conduct, remembered her husband's saying at the time, "I cannot go all the way now. The paper belongs to someone else and I cannot destroy it." He felt, she said, that advertisers susceptible to pressure would put all their ads in the *Knickerbocker* if the *Times-Union* attacked the Machine.

Then in 1960 Robb led the consolidation of the two papers under Hearst ownership, with both continuing to publish. The fear of losing ads then greatly diminished, and Robb opened the news, editorial, and letters columns to reports and comment critical of the Machine, journalistic behavior unseen in Albany for a quarter century. The Machine's response was to withdraw the ads.

I asked Erastus what he thought of Gene Robb and that whole time, for he and Robb had been social peers, fellow Fort Orange Clubmen. "I liked him," Erastus said, "a fine man. We always had a good time together. He was a capable and good newspaperman."

Lee Robb remembered similar sentiments voiced by her husband. "They saw one another at the club and told stories and got on in person. But they were at opposite poles in what they believed. I think it was the first time that Corning ever had an adequate adversary."

The Machine's adversarial attitude hardened when it withdrew the ads. Erastus said it was Dan's decision to withdraw them, and he went along with it. "When you work with someone . . ." he said, and didn't finish the sentence. He quoted Dan's opinion about the paper's criticism: "I don't mind what they're saying, but why pay them, too, for saying it?"

The break with the papers meant open warfare. Robb had been a newsman himself, unlike many publishers, and had strong feelings about the editorial side of the newspapers. After the ads were withdrawn he told me he felt an onus had been lifted from the papers, despite the wallop to the pocketbook.

Robb was at the time president of the American Newspaper Publishers Association, a director of the Associated Press and the Hearst Corporation, and had been Phi Beta Kappa out of the University of Nebraska, with a major in journalism. He also held a law degree from George Washington University and had worked for Hearst in multiple editorial and managerial capacities. Despite his long experience in journalism he did not anticipate the kind of warfare Dan and Erastus, through their district attorney and their grand juries, began to wage.

By May 1963 reporters and editors from both papers had been called before Albany grand juries three times in less than a year. Eight staff members had appeared nineteen times before the grand jury. Robb himself, said his widow, appeared ten or eleven times. In a protest to the grand jury Robb wrote: "Within my thirty-five years as a newspaperman, I have never heard of a comparable situation anywhere in the United States."

One reporter, Edward Swietnicki, was charged with second-degree perjury, not because of any conflict about what he wrote in the press but because he made conflicting statements to the grand jury about what he'd said to his editor about a story. He was tried and acquitted.

His case demonstrated the extremes to which the Machine was willing to carry the war. Its candidates for office focused on the Albany newspapers in a concerted effort to discredit them. When the State Investigations Commission was embarrassing the Machine with its probe into county purchasing practices in 1964, a candidate for reelection to the Assembly took all of his fifteen-minute radio stint to rap the reporting in the newspapers on the SIC hearings. Those hearings were producing testimony about extraordinary markups (as much as 500 percent) on items sold to the county, about outside bidders being denied a fair chance to bid, about fraudulent billings.

The result? The SIC charges faded into history, and the following year Erastus was reelected. His campaign that year deserves a bit of attention for its quaintness. When we talked in 1979, he spoke of the old way of campaigning, buying fifteen-minute television spots once a week, or perhaps six times during the campaign.

The spots cost $300 to $400 for fifteen minutes when he first began using them, in the 1950s. "If you tried to get fifteen minutes today," he said, "they'd laugh at you."

Those broadcasts were "the whole campaign," he said, "and you had to be very careful."

In 1965, a year of prolonged drought, he ran against a man named Jacob Olshansky, an assistant state attorney general and an unknown, who had been critical of the city's water supply, one of the genuinely golden achievements of the O'Connell Machine in the 1920s and early 1930s. Erastus devoted half of his fifteen-minute TV speech to the water issue, attacking the *Times-Union*, which, he said, had been "full of reckless charges, vicious insinuations, loaded questions, half-truths, and absurd recommendations."

He cited five references to water that had appeared in the paper as being false or misleading. The next morning the *Times-Union* rebutted: "Though [the Mayor] attributed [the charges] to the *Times-Union*, they were quotations from a speech by . . . Olshansky, and from the news report of that speech. . . . In each case [the Mayor] omitted reference to his opponent and attributed the references to this newspaper."

The war continued.

The *Knickerbocker News* in these years was edited by Robert G. Fichenberg, and his attacks on the Machine made him, according to Leo O'Brien, the most hated man on either newspaper, as far as the Machine was concerned. Fichenberg remembers a snarleyow response to him by many regular Democrats, but says that Erastus was always cordial and civil when they met in public. Dan Button resigned his *Times-Union* editorship in 1966 to run for Congress as a Republican when Leo O'Brien retired. Button walked through most of the congressional district, ringing doorbells, speaking against the Vietnam War, and dumbfounded everybody by defeating Dan's candidate, Richard J. Conners (now an assemblyman). Button won easily again in 1968, both his victories striking developments; for the Republicans had been so relentlessly humiliated, so neutralized as a party, so bought out with a handful of judgeships, that for decades they had ceased acting like politicians and behaved like pop-up targets whose function was to be instantly shot down every Election Day.

Dan O'Connell once commented on this phenomenon: "There's no sign they'll ever beat us. They're just like we used to be." Dan meant before the takeover in 1921, when Democrats, under the leadership of Patrick (Packy) McCabe, were patsies for the Barnes Machine. But after Button's first victory, the Republicans stopped playing dead and in 1968 elected a state senator, two assemblymen, and, most incredibly of all, a district attorney, leaving Dan and Erastus bereft of that formidable latter office for the first time in their history.

By 1970, however, they were on the comeback trail. They allied themselves, after a redistricting, with Sam Stratton, an improbably popular congressman, to defeat Button on his second bid for reelection. Then they took back the district attorney's office, the Senate seat, and one Assembly seat, leaving only the second Assembly seat still in Republican hands in 1983. Republican hopes rose again in 1973, when Erastus confronted his most dangerous opponent, Carl Touhey, an Irish-Catholic millionaire with a Princeton degree and a winning personality.

Erastus said Touhey caused him more anticipatory worry than anyone he had ever faced. On top of all Touhey's plus factors, the city tax rate had just been doubled (Dan thought Erastus made a mistake doing that). Also, said Erastus when we talked, "there were three SIC investigations—the police, purchasing, and delinquent taxes—all in the period of a year. Plus, Carl was a highly attractive independent businessman whose father, Carl, Sr., had been a Ford dealer, a Democrat, and president of the Chamber of Commerce. So the conditions were not the best for an enthusiastic electorate."

Nevertheless, Erastus won, but by his lowest margin ever: 3,500 votes, and some view that year as the end of the Republican renaissance. In 1979 George Scaringe, county Republican chairman, told a reporter, "After we won [in 1968] we thought we broke the backs of the Democrats. We had to be fools."

Though fortunes regressed for Republicans, the decade had given Albany a heady whiff of the two-party system. For many it was a primal whiff, a nosegay from the Albany newspapers, whose contribution to it, if long overdue, was nevertheless substantial.

Gene Robb's death in 1969 demarcates this volatile era without ending it. An independent press in Albany (the papers have since moved out of the city to suburban Colonie, still in Albany County) is Robb's legacy, and also Dan's and Erastus's, though they had something else in mind.

Erastus would have been as politically febrile as his grandfather the orchid collector had he not believed in confronting hostile realities like the press and converting them to Democracy, Albany style. What's more, there might have been no longevity for the Machine, none of the perquisites that go with power, and probably nothing so complex and paradoxical as himself to write about, had he not been a ruthless warrior.

I remember an instructive scene in *The Roaring Twenties*, when Jimmy Cagney, who after years of sappy pining for Priscilla Lane, finally confronts her, only to hear her plead the case for her new husband, Jeffrey Lynn, a district attorney of sorts who is prosecuting Cagney's ex-partner in bootlegging, Humphrey Bogart. Bogie's name in the film is George, and when Priscilla says it is Jeffrey's job to nail George, Cagney says, "Yeah, and it's George's job not to let him."

Open warfare was obviously an extreme method of preserving power, but Erastus also employed more subtle methods, one of which became visible with a challenge that arose as the war with the press was waning: the amorphous problem presented by the vast, shifting mass of students, 16,000 now, who were populating Albany State University (SUNYA) every year.

I recall that local educators in the 1960s chuckled at what a surprise the Machine was in for because of all these students and faculty. The new folks, went the line, just wouldn't put up with the bossism that appealed so perversely to Albanians. Tom Smith, who teaches in the English Department at SUNYA, does indeed remember Erastus, Dan, and the Machine's being lumped together with the "old politics" that was the target of the anti-establishment movement on campus.

Vincent Reda, a SUNYA student in 1970, also remembered the "tremendous antipathy" students felt toward the Machine, and the attacks on it in the student newspaper, the *Asp*. "The feeling was 'We're going to drive them out . . . that whole gang can't survive this era,' " said Reda. "But eventually that changed and students focused more exclusively on the larger problems, like Nixon and the Vietnam War. It seemed easier to change the world than to change Albany."

Tom Smith remembered one of the turning points, about 1970: "There was a big interview with Corning by two of the *Asp*'s editors. They thought they were going to confront the devil, but he made a great case for the city and himself, and the editors were beguiled and charmed and said that in the article."

Throughout the decade, Erastus's picture turned up regularly on the *Asp*'s front page and he became a coveted object of interviews by students of history, journalism, and political science, whom he received with regularity in his office. He also became sought after as a campus speaker. I recall one miserable winter night early in 1982 when he turned up, visibly weakened by his emphysema, and as he had promised, he submitted himself to an interview by two dozen students, who took notes on his remarks to write stories for their journalism class.

To what end did he put himself through this?

Like the ballerina in the red shoes who couldn't stop dancing, Erastus, until illness flattened him, seemed unwilling, perhaps even unable, to stop speaking, to stop showing up, to stop perpetuating his own mythology and that of the government of which he was sole proprietor; for this was what he did, what he had always done, and there was no end to the people's demand, no end to his success in answering that demand. As a consequence, his ubiquity created its own form of radiance.

"He was," said Richard Vincent, a noted Albany chef and former music critic, "like Joe DiMaggio. He'd turn up and suddenly the whispers would run through the crowd: 'There's Corning . . . Corning's here . . . pssst, pssst . . . there he is . . . over there.' "

Apart from this Erastusian radiance, there was a more traditional political tactic at work in regard to the students: exclusion of their vote. Not until 1980 did SUNYA students win their right to vote from the school address. They had had to go to court to force the Albany Board of Elections to permit them registration. Theretofore, permission was given selectively, parsimoniously.

After the court victory, 1,200 students registered to vote in Albany in 1981, the year of a mayoral election. Only 275 voted, hardly a bloc of significance. It can't be argued that the Mayor's visibility on campus dragged student voters to the polls on his behalf, but his demeanor was certainly a factor in turning aside student wrath.

"There was no more of that tremendous adversary attitude," said Tom Smith. "He was just another political executive, and students felt some kind of awe that he'd lasted so long when nothing else had."

Erastus recalled another facet of his relationship to SUNYA students in which wrath was walking the streets: a protest march by students and others who planned to occupy the post office at Broadway and Maiden Lane, then the principal federal building in the city.

Tom Smith marched in some of those marches, including one that followed closely upon the killing of students at Kent State University in 1970. He remembers students occupying the Plaza at State and Broadway, and hard hats, who were building the Twin Towers on Washington Avenue, dropping stones and nuts and bolts at the marching students, though he recalls no one being hurt. He remembers the same day Erastus remembered— when police were lining the streets and the word was being passed among the marchers to keep cool, do nothing crazy, and the police won't, either.

Erastus credited a book by Buckminster Fuller with helping that day turn out as it did. A professor at SUNYA (not Tom Smith) was in Clapp's bookstore looking for a copy and was told that the Mayor had bought the last one. The idea of a literate mayor pleased the professor, and so he called Erastus and they became good friends; the professor also became an informer, keeping the Mayor in touch with campus fevers and crises. And then came this day when the federal building was to be occupied. State and local police were at the ready, and so were federal troops.

The Mayor recalled being in close touch with Alton G. Marshall, Governor Rockefeller's assistant, who, he said, was in touch with U.S. Attorney General John Mitchell in Washington. Mitchell was being heavy-fisted and wanted to arrest the marchers, said the Mayor. But after Kent State, the vision of mass arrests in Albany, and what that might bring, was unpalatable, and so at the Albany end of events the theme was restraint.

As Mitchell was pressing for the troops to make their move, said the Mayor, his informer came through with the news that leaders of the march would probably disband, or turn around, after achieving whatever their symbolic goal of the moment was; and so, the Mayor said, he told Marshall, "Stall Mitchell ten minutes and they'll turn back." And, said the Mayor, they did.

It might be said that in his own time, in his own way, Erastus occupied SUNYA and clasped it to him. Asked by journalist Paul Grondahl in May 1982 what he thought his campus image was, Erastus said, "I haven't any idea. The one thing I hope is that the students know I'm available and that I will be ready to listen with a sympathetic ear and do what I can to help if possible."

Benevolence rolled off his tongue with such ease that one might have suspected he majored in Modesty, Generosity, and Fluency at Yale. But in fact he was so cautious as a beginner in politics that a speechwriter, an Albany newsman named Leo Doody, did his thinking for him.

"He was everybody's speechwriter," said Erastus, "and had been with the party even as a newspaperman. He wrote the first speech when I ran for mayor, and there was a paragraph I didn't understand. I sent the page down to him and said, 'Look at that, will you? I've read it and read it and read it, and I don't know what the hell it means.' He read it and said to me, 'Erastus, I don't know what it means, either, but it's exactly what I want to say.' "

History might well note this moment as the Mayor's initiation into the pragmatic function of inscrutable communication, at which he eventually became a maestro. His written and verbal skills were formidable, and when he sought to be lucid he was brilliant. But he also had the skills to obfuscate, evade, to carry words around end, or through the middle, or sometimes both at the same time, in order to score his verbal touchdowns. It was yet another way in which he matched wits with his adversaries.

The late Walter Langley, a state senator and one of the 1968 breakthrough Republicans, used to say of Erastus, "He plays the local political reporters like a grand piano."

When the era of the paid fifteen-minute TV press conference faded away, the Mayor looked askance at television. But by 1969

City Hall had a TV room with lights ready for use by TV cameramen, and when the Mayor rolled in from his office next door, the house was full. "The easiest news conference in town," said Robert Lawson, then news director of WPTR radio.

A newsman wondered what had happened to the Mayor. "You used to treat TV akin to a plague, but now you're television's baby." The Mayor said he wasn't avoiding anyone; it just used to be too time-consuming, no place to hold a press conference.

He might have added it was also an election year for him, and he was both subject and object. A reporter asked why he so often said "I don't know" in answer to questions.

"Ninety-nine percent of the time when I say I don't know, I don't know," he said. "Once in a while I might know a little bit, but when you don't know the whole answer, you don't believe in giving half an answer. Nobody should tell people what they don't want to tell them. . . . If you can make it look good so they go away reasonably satisfied, more power to you. Otherwise you either do it that way or just tell them that you're not going to give them the answer."

A reporter told the Mayor that a recent visitor had said the abandoned buildings in Albany made it look like a ghost town or a demolition project, and how did he respond? The Mayor said that a well-known television commentator had come to Albany and seen all the construction and said it was one of the most vital, growing cities in the Northeast. After the press conference the reporter asked the Mayor, "Who was the well-known television commentator?" And the Mayor asked, "Who was the recent visitor?"

Such responses enhanced the legend of his talent. Ken Gordon, a SUNYA student-journalist, interviewed the Mayor and touched on this. Some reporters, he wrote, were talking about the difficulty of pinning down the Mayor, when a *New York Times* man made a bet he could get one straight answer. The *Times* man asked no questions until the press conference was almost over, and then he said, "Excuse me, Mr. Mayor. What is your favorite color?"

"Plaid," said the Mayor.

This was such a good story I wanted it to be true, and so I asked the Mayor about it. "No, not true," he said. "If they asked me, I'd say green. I like the color green. I have three pairs of socks which are not green and I never wear them."

The Mayor, in December 1972, testified for two hours before

the SIC. Under comparable tensions Richard Nixon's sweat trickled guiltily down his nose, a man betrayed by his own juices. Captain Queeg righteously rubbed those steel balls of his together until he lost his bearings. But Erastus behaved differently. It could be said that he gave a plaid performance, whose tone was set with the first question asked by the SIC counsel (hereinafter known as Q.) and the answer from the Mayor (hereinafter known as A.).

> Q. Mr. Mayor, what is your position?
> A. In what fashion?

The Mayor was asked soon after if he knew Dan O'Connell and he said he did.

> Q. And what is Mr. O'Connell's position at this time
>   in the County of Albany?
> A. He is a citizen.

The Mayor admitted he was one of three vice-chairmen of the Albany County Democratic Committee, and the counsel asked:

> Q. Who is . . . in charge of the daily operations of the
>   . . . Committee?
> A. I don't know.
> Q. You don't know who is operating that committee?
> A. No.
> Q. In your position as vice-chairman, has it ever come
>   to your attention who directly runs that committee?
> A. No.

Counsel inquired whether the Mayor knew James Ryan, a close associate of Dan's, a party leader, and onetime county purchasing agent.

> A. James Bryan?
> Q. Ryan, R-Y-A-N.
> A. Yes, James Ryan. Yes, I do.
> Q. How long have you known James Ryan, Mr. Mayor?
> A. Oh, I would say perhaps 20 years, perhaps 25.
> Q. What does Mr. Ryan do for a living, Mr. Mayor?
> A. I don't know.

Questions ranged over the cost of city purchases: $1,200 for a broom worth $224; $988 a month for use of a Jeep that cost the contractor $800 when he bought it used; another contractor's overcharging for street sweeping. The type of city contract signed came in for discussion, and the chairman of the hearing, a man named Curran, was also drawn into the discussion:

> Q. Mr. Mayor, were these not, in fact, cost-plus contract arrangements?
> A. Would you please repeat that question? I don't know. You are getting this double negative in, and I don't know whether to answer that question yes or no.
> Chairman: The question was: Were they cost-plus arrangements?
> A. He said, "Were they not."
> Chairman: Let's try this question, "Were they cost-plus arrangements?
> A. Yes.
> Chairman: Next question.
> Q. Is it not a fact, Mr. Mayor, that as a result of increasing his costs, the contractor we are referring to would increase his profits?
> A. This is the same question, Mr. Curran. He puts through another not in here and I don't know whether to answer him yes or no.
> Curran: Does the cost increase the profits?
> A. That again. You are doing the same thing.
> Curran: As the costs increase, do the profits increase?
> A. I don't know.

Near the end of the Mayor's testimony, the SIC counsel inquired into his personal income:

> Q. Mr. Mayor, how much income did you receive from the insurance agency of which you are president?
> A. I have no idea.
> Q. Are you sure you have no idea as to how much income you receive?
> A. You asked me at the private hearing. I didn't know then and I don't know now. I didn't look.
> Q. Mr. Mayor, you are unable to tell me how much income you received for the year 1971 from Albany Associates?

A. That is correct.
Q. Have you had an opportunity between the time of
your private hearing and today to look this fact up?
A. I could have looked if I wanted. You didn't ask me
to find the information.
Q. Could you give me the total amount of salary and
other payments that you received during the year
1971?
A. No.

At his weekly press conference, held the same day as the SIC
hearing, the Mayor said in response to a question about the SIC
that it was like a "one-way street . . . they can attack you, but
you can't answer."

His nonanswers proved sufficient unto the day and the year,
however. No indictments came from the investigation, and he
was reelected the following November.

When Dan died four years later, another power struggle began
for Erastus: a head-on collision with Dan's vestigial power figures, Jimmy and Charlie Ryan, for control of the party. Four days
after Dan's death Jimmy quit as executive secretary of the party.
Two weeks later Charlie was clandestinely supporting Howard
Nolan, Erastus's mayoral challenger, in an upcoming primary.
The *Times-Union*, based on its own poll showing Nolan leading
by a nearly two-to-one margin, predicted a Nolan victory. Erastus
admitted Nolan was worrisome, but then defeated him, anyway,
and went on to win the election by more than three to one.

The Ryans remained members of the party's executive committee, on which Erastus had replaced Dan as chairman. But
Charlie coveted the chair, seeing himself as Dan's real heir for
supreme party power. Charlie planned to introduce a resolution
during the party's annual full committee meeting in September
1978, calling for a secret ballot to elect a new chairman.

Erastus learned of the move, canceled the full meeting, and in
June called a meeting of the party's five-member executive committee to oust the Ryan brothers from membership. The meeting
was basically Erastus having a conversation with himself. His
two allies were Mary Marcy, ninety years old and out of it, and
Robert Bender, former city housing director, whom Erastus had
named party secretary after Jimmy Ryan's resignation.

In the open balloting for committee chairman, party regulars,
despite loyalty to the Ryans, knew their jobs were in jeopardy

unless they voted for the real power: Erastus. "I got the cheers," Charlie told me, "but Corning got the power." The irony here is that the Ryans, longtime enforcers for Dan, had taught thousands in the party how to fear Dan's first commandment: Thou shalt be loyal, or else.

Charlie Ryan tried again, ran for Common Council president and lost again. "The party will be controlled for years," he then said, "by Corning and Polly Noonan." He added of Noonan, a little-known but formidable power in the party, "I haven't gotten along with her in years."

The press rarely spoke of Dorothea (Polly) Noonan. She had served as Erastus's secretary when he was a state senator in the 1930s, and in subsequent years she worked for various Democratic Senate leaders, serving as the link for legislative patronage from Albany. This position has recently been held by Polly's daughter, Pamela Montimurro, an aide to Senate Democratic leader Manfred Ohrenstein. Polly was a presence at Democratic conventions but held no party office while Dan O'Connell was alive. An old-time committeeman told me Dan wanted Erastus to sever his connection to her, but Erastus refused and she remained a figure of influence.

When Dan died, Polly moved into the limelight. She became president of the Albany Democratic Women's Club, the same position Mary Marcy had held in Dan's era. She downplayed her role as a power broker: "I have no power. I do not advise the chairman [Erastus]. . . . I am a full-time grandmother."

Said Erastus, "I have been friends with her whole family for better than forty years. . . . I respect her judgment. I respect her friendship. . . . But my decisions I make on my own."

Times-Union reporter Alan Miller documented the Noonan connection to Albany power at length, showing that at least five family members besides Polly and Pamela held positions of authority in the city and the county. What Miller's series revealed was how other families, longtime loyalists of Dan's, were threaded through the party at many levels, on into the third generation, but how positions of real power over patronage were controlled, without exception, by people loyal to Erastus.

Polly's public role grew larger as time went on. When Erastus was hospitalized she served as hostess for a fund-raising luncheon for then gubernatorial candidate Mario Cuomo and was also hostess at a campaign party—attended by 2,500 Democrats—in honor of Cuomo's wife, Matilda. When Cuomo was elected governor he repaid some of his debt for Erastus's early support by naming Polly one of three vice-chairpersons of the Democratic State Committee. Also, Polly's daughter, Pamela, was named a member of that committee to fill the vacancy left by Mary Marcy's departure.

Polly's most contentious public moment came in September 1982, when she turned up at a meet-the-candidates night in the Fifteenth Ward to challenge the ward's incumbent leaders, who seemed friendlier to Charlie Ryan than was necessary. Mrs. Frances Perrone, the ward leader's wife, refused to let Polly enter. Polly said it was a public meeting to which she'd been invited. Mrs. Perrone later said that Polly then punched her in the ribs, and that a woman with Polly kicked Mrs. Perrone in the heel, "creating muscle spasms." Polly denied this, and said Mrs. Perrone shoved her. The case turned up in Albany Police Court, Mrs. Perrone alleging assault. She produced a hospital report citing multiple contusions to her ribs and a spasm in her calf muscle. Not quite two months later—immediately after the election—the case came to a hearing. Mrs. Perrone fainted in court, and the judge dismissed her complaint, saying it hadn't risen to the level of a crime. Said Mrs. Perrone, "There's no justice in this state."

Polly's candidates won the day in the election, and the woman who was alleged to have kicked Mrs. Perrone became the new leader of the Fifteenth Ward.

Polly would probably not have become such a limelighter had it not been for Erastus's illness, which removed him from center stage. On June 15, 1982, he entered Albany Medical Center for treatment of his bronchitis and emphysema (the disease of the smoke-filled room that also destroyed Dan O'Connell), to be there "a few days," said a hospital spokesman. He missed the State Democratic Convention, where he was to place Mario Cuomo's name in nomination for governor. A week after entering the hospital he suffered a setback, went into intensive care, and was placed on a respirator for the first time. He missed the visit to Albany by Queen Beatrix of the Netherlands, missed the Democratic National Convention, and for the first time in the modern history of Albany, people were speculating that the Albany Machine, as they had known it most of their lives, just might not be immortal after all.

Erastus was released from the hospital on July 16, a hot day, went home, suffered an asthma attack, and was back on the hospital respirator on July 17. In August he told his aides at City Hall something they never expected to hear: "You've been leaning on me too much. You have to lean on yourself"—this from the supreme autocrat of the modern age. On August 14, doctors put a permanent plastic tube in his throat to ease his breathing. This came only a few days after his wife, Elizabeth, had an aneurysm removed from her neck, and his daughter, Bettina, underwent elective surgery on her arm—all in the same hospital. The Mayor's family had rarely basked in so much personal publicity, his private life having been enduringly swathed in privacy.

On October 6 the Mayor was transferred by ambulance to the Respiratory Care Center of Boston University Medical Center, an unexpected development. Would he resign as chairman of the party? Could he run the city from a Boston hospital, as his aides announced he would? In mid-October he was swiftly and surely reelected chairman of the Albany County Democratic Committee. Couriers carried city business to his Boston hospital room. Jimmy Carter, passing through Boston, called to wish him well. Ronald Reagan wrote him and told him Albany and the nation needed him. The Mayor made his first call from the hospital on November 11. He called Polly. She said he sounded absolutely wonderful.

In December he developed pneumonia and went into intensive care. He recovered and rode his stationary bicycle three miles a day in his hospital room. Oxygen tanks and breathing apparatus were set up in City Hall in preparation for his return, but he developed an irregular heartbeat and in early February a catheter was implanted in his heart to help doctors monitor his life. In late February surgeons removed half of his large intestine to excise a benign tumor that was causing bleeding. About March 4 he suffered a mild heart attack and his condition was downgraded from "stable" to "guarded." A poll taken by a television station indicated that 48.7 percent of Albanians polled felt Erastus should retire and another 20.7 believed he should at least step aside temporarily. He did neither. On March 12 he was operated on for bleeding ulcers at the base of his esophagus.

This prolonged illness focused the city's attention on his legal successor. Handpicked by Erastus himself was an unlikely figure, given the history of the Machine. He was Thomas M. Whalen III, an Irish Catholic, born in 1934, a product of Catholic schools and college, a lawyer in an old Albany law firm, a man committed to social and minority problems—race and drugs, for instance—

in a way that was as anomalous for an Albany politician as was the fact of Catholicism in an heir apparent to City Hall.

Whalen became president of the Common Council, the city's second-highest office, and from there moved into Erastus's chair when Erastus was hospitalized. He shared the provisional leadership with Vincent McArdle, the city's corporation counsel, and with four others, who came to be called "the Kitchen Cabinet." Together these men put forth a new candor in city management—a budget, for instance, in which the true costs of city services were clearly itemized: a vastly different document from the cryptic tables traditionally offered up by Erastus, though it must be added that this new style was obviously achieved with the ailing Mayor's blessing. Very probably he could trust no one else's fiscal imagination to be as hermetically secure as his own.

Whalen's competence and his amiable intelligence, shown during stressful days, were making him quietly popular; and he was clearly the front runner for eventual nomination to succeed the Mayor. But his role as a politician was marginal; and as Erastus grew weaker, a wild scrambling in the party was already under way to oppose Whalen with other candidates. And because he was unschooled in the kind of political cutthroatery that had gone on in Albany since the nineteenth century, one could, in mid-1983, consider his nomination only probable, not forgone.

The ailing Erastus clung to his office tenaciously, allowing his people time to grow and prosper in power, but also extending his own personal hold on the national record of continuous time in office. He was extraordinarily proud of his longevity when we talked. Was it true that there was no one else in America even close to matching his record? Well, he said, someone did call him in 1981 to say that the city manager of Worcester, Massachusetts, had been in office forty-one years also. Erastus phoned the man and found it a mere thirty-one. Absurd.

Nobody else?

"The mayor of Dearborn, Michigan," he said, "a man named Orville Hubbard, the son of Elbert Hubbard, who wrote 'A Message to Garcia,' he was elected in 1941 and took office on January 6, 1942. I had him by five days. He didn't run for reelection in 1977. He was considerably older than me, a veteran of World War One. He used to pass out thimbles with the days of his years in office."

Dearborn, said Erastus, is about the same size as Albany, but with a difference. The Ford Motor Company paid more taxes to Dearborn than the entire tax bill of the city of Albany. "There wasn't one single black resident of the city of Dearborn until a few years ago," he added, the unspoken word being that no black man working in the Ford Motor Company could live in Dearborn. "Hubbard was indicted for civil rights violations and acquitted. He had a stroke in 1974, and the woman he lived with was the only one who stuck by him. And last year [1981] she ran against his successor (Hubbard's former police chief) and was beaten. There are interesting parallels between Albany and Dearborn."

Erastus was, we should recall, a history major at Yale, and he kept up with the past as well as the present in the years after his graduation. He spoke often of Dan O'Connell's interest in history. Dan, he said, "always taught me that it was a very easy thing to do, to spend some time on history, because it saved you so much in making decisions, because so many of the things that you wouldn't know how to handle, if you just looked up past history, you found out how to handle it."

We talked of a pair of Old Albanians, Aaron Burr and Philip Schuyler, and then of Tom Dewey. I remembered Dan saying the American people would never elect a man like Dewey to be president. Erastus said no, Dan's line was they'd never elect men like Burr, Dewey, or Nixon, and Dan was partly wrong. The talk turned to Dewey, and Erastus said that during the 1940s Dewey wouldn't talk to him for two years. Then the President of Chile came to town and protocol advisers told Dewey it wouldn't be right if the Mayor weren't present, and so he and Dewey met and shook hands. He later listened while Dewey delivered a speech in Albany at the Schuyler Mansion, the home of Philip Schuyler, one of America's great generals in the Revolution.

Dewey was criticizing President Truman for firing General Douglas MacArthur, Erastus said. "And then Dewey said, 'That sort of thing couldn't have happened in Revolutionary days.' "

Dewey couldn't have been more wrong. Schuyler, a selfless patriot who could be as overbearing as MacArthur, was relieved of his command by politicians during the Battle of Saratoga, and Horatio Gates was installed to preside over the victory and became a national hero. A despondent Schuyler left the Army. Gates went on to celebrated ineptitude in losing the Battle of Camden, South Carolina.

Erastus said he seemed to be the only man in the room listening to Dewey's speech who knew how all wet it was; and no newsmen covering it caught the error.

"A lot of people paid no attention to Dewey," said Erastus, "but I always did. He was a smart man. I don't know where the hell he got his history, though."

Erastus got a good deal of his history, as he was always fond of saying, from his on-the-job training. Since 1941 he presided over his city's (and county's) response to three wars; the housing and baby booms; the advent of public housing and urban renewal; the civil rights movement; the sexual revolution; the decline of belief; the decline of railroads and the growth of highways; the mortification and banishment of the Studebaker, the Hudson, the Terraplane, the De Soto, the Packard, the Edsel, the Corvair, and the Bug; the drug wars; the impaction of black ghettos; the welfare state; civil service; the age of television; the jet age; the space age (no votes out there); the collapse and renewal of Downtown; the flight to the suburbs; shopping centers sapping the city retail core; Governors Lehman, Dewey, Harriman, Rockefeller, Wilson, Carey, and Cuomo; Presidents Roosevelt, Truman, Eisenhower, Kennedy, Johnson, Nixon, Ford, Carter, and Reagan; Albany Catholic Bishops Gibbons, Scully, Maginn, Broderick, and Hubbard; Popes Pius XI, Pius XII, John XXIII, Paul VI, John Paul I, and John Paul II; Soviet leaders Stalin, Beria, Malenkov, Khrushchev, Brezhnev, and Andropov. He held power longer than Trujillo, Franco, Perón, Batista, Somoza, Napoleon, Hitler, Mao Tse-tung, Catherine the Great, Peter the Great, Henry VIII, Ferdinand and Isabella, Ethelred II, and in 1983 he surpassed Augustus Caesar. (Yes, he told me, but did Augustus smoke tobacco?)

Perhaps Lena Horne, Katharine Hepburn, Bette Davis, Laurence Olivier, Count Basie, Ella Fitzgerald, Perry Como, and Frank Sinatra could claim a similarly triumphant span, but getting elected every four years was never their problem.

The
Last Word

*I*t is early June now, and Erastus Corning is dead, buried, mythologized, and on his way to apotheosis. He died stoically suffering the tortures of Job, and flagellating himself psychologically, like Tolstoy's Ivan Ilych. He died amid a hubbub of love and accolades that elevated him to the status of Great Man. He was buried with all the funereal pomp and dignity the Episcopal High Church can bestow on its most exalted members. People close to him felt their father had died, that State and Pearl, the crossroads of the city's heart, had been stolen. The press, whose mortal enemy he had been for twenty years or more, outdid itself in eulogizing him. Let it not be said that the good he did was interred with his bones: it was in all the papers, on all the channels. Those who viewed him as an evil figure, a corrupt and venal politician with a thirst for vengeance, a punitive user of power to banish or destroy those who contravened his Machine, gnashed their teeth at the eulogistic flood, and at what they saw as the great prestidigitator's greatest trick of all: crawling inside his own inherited hat and turning himself into a saint.

Is saintliness, too, in the eye of the beholder? Was it really sleight of hand? Well, he had changed somewhat. He had chosen a self-described Kennedy liberal, Tom Whalen, as his successor.

He had altered the way the city did business: "The Mayor decided to do away with kickbacks," said an intimate. "The party is flush." After Dan's death he had also gone public in odd ways: reviewing a book at the public library, *Celebrations of Life*, by one of his heroes, René Dubos, the French microbiologist-philosopher, and proving his intellectual capabilities to a generally unsuspecting public. Why had he never reviewed a book before? "Nobody ever asked me." In his senior years he had also enjoyed basking in the warm glow of elder-statesmanhood. Mario Cuomo, as a gubernatorial candidate, said there was only one man for whom he would step aside again to serve as lieutenant governor if that man decided to run for governor. "And that is Erastus Corning," said Cuomo, "the greatest Mayor this state has ever seen." Even Erastus's old enemies from decades gone were allowing him points for having changed, for having deep-sixed Dan's crude style and restored gentility and a new degree of openness to city government. These old foes had mellowed, and they said Erastus had, too. If it wasn't the whole truth, it at least looked like it, and so the stage was made ready for the dance of the eulogies.

He died Saturday, May 28, 1983, at 12:20 p.m., in University Hospital in Boston, and, though he had been grievously ill, his death was not expected. He'd been worse the previous week and was still thinking of coming home, as he had been since January. Few believed he'd make it, but he thought he would. Doctors called him a "cheerful, hardworking patient" who pursued his rehabilitation with gusto. He was, they said, "tenacious and strong-willed." His medical bills for his prolonged illness were said to have totaled more than $1 million already. In January he had summoned his Albany tailor of twenty-two years' standing, Angelo (Joe) Amore, to Boston to alter two custom-made suits. Wheelchair ramps and railings were being planned for his home on Corning Hill. A concrete pad for oxygen talks was installed at his home and a specially equipped van was purchased so he could drive himself home when the time came. But he never wore the suits, never rode in the van, never left the hospital. He lost his voice, then lost the use of his hands to write notes to visitors. He weighed, so it was said, well under a hundred pounds, was breathing with the aid of a respirator, and was being fed intravenously. He died of a pulmonary embolism, a blood clot that traveled from his legs or abdomen to his lungs, and there triggered a fatal heart attack. On October 9 he would have been

seventy-four years old. His casket was closed as part of the Episcopal ritual when he lay in state in the Cathedral of All Saints
at Swan and Elk streets, but it would have been closed under any
circumstances. An associate said he was so wasted no one would
have recognized him.

On Tuesday, the day he lay in state, it was Democratic weather,
which is to say it rained all day. The cathedral doors were opened
at midmorning, and after a private prayer service for the Corning
family, the people of the city came to pay their respects. Television crews set up shop across Swan Street from the cathedral's
main entrance; inside, camera arrangements were on a pool basis,
two cameras fixed, not moving. Also, seventy-six chairs were
assembled in the left aisle in what newspeople were already calling "the cage." Because of their positions, the cameras would not
be able to focus during the ceremony on the faces of the Corning
family, for, as always, the family wanted to keep its life as private
as possible. Some TV newsmen were asked not to focus undue
attention on Polly Noonan, who would be in the fifth row during
the funeral service on Wednesday. When Governor Cuomo arrived for the morning prayer service he embraced Polly, and a
city official asked that this encounter also be downplayed by TV.
But it was not. A notice appeared in the newspapers that the
Albany County Democratic Women's Club, over which Polly
presided, would meet in a body Tuesday at 7:00 p.m. to pay its
respects.

No one knew what sort of crowd to expect. The last state
funeral in the city had been on March 10, 1926, for William S.
Hackett, the Machine's first mayor, an enormously popular man.
Services were held two blocks from All Saints Cathedral, at Em-
manuel Baptist Church on State Street, near Swan. Fifty thousand
people lined the streets to greet his casket coming back from
Cuba, where he'd died, and another fifty thousand turned out for
the funeral, or so it was estimated by his eulogists. Forty thousand, they said, filed past the bier as it lay in state in the City
Hall rotunda. Fifty thousand was also the estimate of those who
had viewed Abraham Lincoln's casket in 1865 when he lay in
state in Albany at the old Capitol, with thousands more turned
away when the doors were closed.

Erastus Corning would draw no such crowds in the age of
television, when people could gain intimate access to the funeral
proceedings on their home screens. By the time the funeral ceremony began, perhaps some nine thousand to ten thousand peo-

ple would have passed through the cathedral, more than five thousand signing their names and addresses in three ledgers at the back of the church. Some signed for two as "Mr. and Mrs." Many didn't sign at all.

They came down the center aisle and walked to the altar where Erastus lay, his casket covered by a white pall with a brocaded red cross, the same pall used for all funeral services at the cathedral. A folded American flag lay atop the pall. Throughout the day, students, state troopers, soldiers, city police, and firemen took turns standing vigil, three on each side of the casket. Light came in through the vast and splendid stained-glass window on the east facade of the church; also from the floodlights trained on the main altar, and from the cathedral's many wall sconces. An organist kept up a steady flow of dirges and hymns, and the formality of it all had the effect on a visitor of lofting Erastus far above the street-level politics to which he had given so much of his life.

This cathedral was, in one way, a Corning province, though by one cleric's count the Mayor turned up at services only about twice a year. Elizabeth Corning, on the other hand, was a weekly presence, and more. Erastus's great-grandfather had bought the land between Swan and Hawk streets on which the cathedral would eventually rise, as well as land across Elk Street and down into the hollow of Spruce Street—toward Gander Bay, where the Irish poor dwelt—and had given it to the Episcopal diocese established by that most energetic and willful cleric, William Croswell Doane, the first Episcopal Bishop of Albany. An Episcopal historian, Canon George E. DeMille, wrote: "As a founder of the cathedral of All Saints, [Corning] ranks second only to the bishop."

Corning died in 1872 after giving the land (his son, Erastus, Jr., continued as Doane's chief patron) and also establishing the financial foundation that enabled Doane to create the cathedral, St. Agnes School, Child's Hospital, and a sisterhood that served both school and hospital. Ground was broken for the cathedral on June 3, 1884, and after four years, and at a cost of $320,000, the formidable and beautiful structure was dedicated on November 20, 1888.

Because of the diocese's chronic shortage of funds, Doane never acquired the remainder of the block where the cathedral stands, so in a hurry to build was he. In 1913 the cathedral would be eclipsed by the State Education Building, in whose shadow it so elegantly stands today. Bishop Doane (who died in that dark year of 1913) and the early Cornings had made their exceptional mark on Albany's history and landscape; but the caprice of fate would relegate their glory to a side street, just as it would ravage the body of our Erastus when he was at the peak of his political glory.

At six-thirty in the evening of Erastus's wake, after an afternoon of desultory visiting, the crowds started to arrive in groups— the Sons of Italy, a dozen veterans in overseas caps, a half-dozen nuns. State Senator Howard Nolan, who primaried the Mayor in 1977, turned up; so did Police Justice Tom Keegan, who used to fish with the Mayor. A black man came in on crutches. Men in work clothes, kids in jeans, and women with babies came down the aisle. Ed McMahon, a reporter for the *Knickerbocker News*, came by to report that the longtime caretaker at the Corning estate, Bela Kollarits, seventy-four, who had entered the hospital the same day as Erastus, suffering from emphysema, as was Erastus, had died on May 28, as did Erastus. The second death intensified Elizabeth Corning's distress.

By seven o'clock the cathedral's center aisle was constantly full of people, two and three abreast from altar to door, and the side aisles were full as well. Polly Noonan arrived, wrapped in a raincoat, her brown hair piled high in an upswept coiffure. At the prayer service the previous day, she'd arrived with her husband and the secretary of the County Democratic Committee, had sat through the service, and then, when leaving, had broken away from her husband's side and run out of the church alone. Now she came down the aisle supported by the arms of two other women and followed by at least one hundred and fifty Democratic women who, after stopping at the Mayor's casket, all stood in line to sign the book. One hundred and twenty-five VFW members arrived in parade formation at seven-thirty and that was the peak. The family came to pray at nine o'clock, and then the doors closed for the night.

The sun rose and shone on Erastus's final morning among the living. As it had been with Dan, so it would be with the Mayor: the "biggies," as the press called them, would not turn up. Jimmy Carter, for whom Erastus had been upstate campaign manager, was traveling. Fritz Mondale, whom Erastus had planned to support for president in 1984, called to find out Erastus's favorite charity. Teddy Kennedy wasn't heard from. The state was well represented: Governor Cuomo came and would read the epistle at the service. Senators Daniel Patrick Moynihan and Alfonse D'Amato arrived, then ex-Governor Hugh Carey, Congressman

Sam Stratton, who flew home from Paris to attend, ex-Congressman Ned Pattison, the new Albany Mayor, Tom Whalen, who'd been inaugurated May 29, and a swarm of local politicians who were the cogs, wheels, nuts, bolts, and screws of the Machine.

The cathedral seated four hundred people normally, but extra chairs were brought in to accommodate the throng, and the final estimate was thirteen hundred, the last to arrive—just before City Human Resources Commissioner Jack McEneny closed the doors—being a black youth with his hat on backward. McEneny told him to take off his hat and then the service began. It was ecumenical: Presbyterian and Baptist clergymen, a Jewish rabbi, the Roman Catholic Bishop, Howard Hubbard, the Episcopal Bishop, Wilbur E. Hogg.

By Episcopal tradition no eulogy was permitted, but the cathedral's dean, David S. Ball, referred to the Mayor repeatedly in his sermon. Mario Cuomo, from the Epistle of St. Paul to the Corinthians, invoked him obliquely when he read: "Then cometh the end, when he shall have delivered up the kingdom to God, even the Father; when he shall have put down all rule and all authority and power. For he must reign, till he hath put all enemies under his feet. The last enemy that shall be destroyed is death."

But not even Erastus Corning had that kind of clout, and he was wheeled slowly down the aisle to the door, at which point the pallbearers carried him to the hearse. The identity of the bearers had been a closely guarded secret until ten-thirty on the morning of the funeral. They were five: his children, Erastus Corning III, forty-nine, and Elizabeth (Bettina) Dudley, forty-four; and his grandchildren: Amy Corning, Theodore Robert Dudley, and Erastus Christopher Dudley. It is not unheard of for children to be bearers for their parents but it was wholly unexpected on this occasion.

"The Corning family upstaged everybody with the unbelievable choice of pallbearers," said Jack McEneny, a principal coordinator of the funeral arrangements. "In the final analysis he was given to the city by the Corning family, and taken back by the Corning family."

The presence of Erastus III was a particularly poignant development, for the Mayor had told a newsman that he'd been estranged from his son for years. The newsman is Ed Dague, anchorman for WRGB-TV, Schenectady. He'd first put the question to the Mayor at his 1982 inauguration for an eleventh term.

The Mayor's children, by tradition, lined up beside him as he took the oath of office, but his son was missing that year. Where was he? The Mayor didn't know. "Somewhere between New York and Hawaii," he said. "He never calls me."

Said Dague, "He said he had not been a very good father and that his son didn't share his interest in politics." He told Dague he'd been busy, first as a legislator, then as Mayor, when his son was growing up. Then came the war and he was away a year and a half, and when he came home his son was getting ready to go off to boarding school.

"He was very emotional about this," Dague recalled. "He felt he missed entirely his son growing up, and his son resented that, and was bitter. 'I feel I'm a failure as a father,' he said, and he added that he tried harder with Bettina."

Bettina was a frequent visitor to the Mayor during his year of illness, but it was not until he was transferred to the Boston hospital that Erastus III came to see him; and he came about three times, Dague said. And now here he was, carrying his father's devastated body down the steps of the church to the hearse. He is not as tall a man as his father; is of slight build, with thick and solidly gray hair down to his collar. His face on that morning, from a distance, showed the solemnity of a mourner, and also a strong resemblance to his father's most famous face.

As the children and grandchildren hoisted the casket into the hearse, Elizabeth Corning stared with extreme sadness visible on her gaunt and lined face. A photographer captured her at that moment, and in her expression one can read not a tearful grief but a resignation, a culmination. A friend of the Cornings once asked her how she felt about coming to Albany as a bride, and she told him, "I was so in love with Erastus, I couldn't see Albany."

The door of the hearse was closed, the family settled into the Mayor's black limousine bearing the license plate "A," and the procession began. It moved south on Swan Street past a block-long crowd that was standing ten deep behind a police line. It moved onto Washington Avenue, which had been closed to traffic, and eastward past several platoons of police standing at attention on either side of the avenue down to the Capitol. When the cortege reached City Hall the hearse paused briefly near the Mayor's parking space, while the carillon in City Hall tower played "God Bless America." Then the cars moved down State Street to Broadway, and north to Albany Rural Cemetery, where Erastus was buried privately among his ancestors. No newsmen were allowed past the cemetery's main gate.

It was a splendid event: the ancestral cathedral, the panoply of the lying-in-state, the playing out of the Christian ritual, the aptness even of the final hymn, "Albany" (sometimes called "Ancient of Days"), written by Bishop Doane in 1886:

> O holy Jesus Prince of Peace and Saviour,
> To thee we owe the peace that shall prevail,
> Stilling the rude wills of men's wild behavior,
> And calming passion's fierce and stormy gale.

It was an event splendid in its elegance, its aristocratic restraint, its privacy, its aloof refusal to buck the stormy gales below. But with that said, it should also be noted that "God Bless America" would have been more apt for Richard Nixon's passing; that the whole spectacular funeral left out something important about Erastus: the excess element of his personality that they could never stuff into such a stylized coffin. Yes, he was an Episcopal Connecticut Yankee aristocrat by derivation, but if anyone thinks that is all he was, then they did not see the man in action, have not heard the stories. His complexity needs a novelist's freedom of space and language in order to have justice done to it. He was as much a rough-and-tumble political paddywhack Irishman by association, by assimilation, by preference, and by paternal matrix, as he was a baronial blueblood.

His friends recalled certain elements of this in sidewalk conversation before and after the ceremonials. He was, for instance, toastmaster for a group called the Fifth Estate, a mix of newsmen and politicians that had as its motto an immortal line pronounced first by an Albany lawyer named Charlie Torche: "Honesty is no substitute for experience." He once asked the press to turn off its cameras and put down its pencils while he said something off the record, and when all complied he called one of the newsmen present an "unadulterated fuckhead" and then resumed his on-the-record session. The drinking stories about him are legion, but one has some enduring elements to it. It was his custom, when he was a new, twenty-seven-year-old legislator in 1936, to go to lunch, drink merrily, come back to work happy, and do no work all afternoon. Polly Noonan, then his new twenty-year-old secretary, had been recommended to him by Dan's close associate,

Mary Marcy. Polly put up with the afternoons just so long, then went to Dan and told him she wanted another job, couldn't stand working for Erastus. Dan called in Erastus, told him to straighten up, Erastus cajoled Polly into staying on, and on May 19, nine days before Erastus died, he and Polly celebrated their forty-seventh year of friendship and association.

There are too many stories to recount them all here, but two more demand inclusion. Ed Dague said to the Mayor on camera one day, "With all due respect . . . you hold such power that if you told the Common Council to meet in pink lingerie, they would."

"I think you go too far," said Erastus. "In blue lingerie, perhaps, but pink is too much."

The second story comes equipped with a setting: the Fort Orange Club. It is lunchtime, and the funeral has just ended. Erastus is en route to the cemetery, and the club's dining room begins to fill up with blue-suited men who've just come from the cathedral. In the foyer is a framed picture of Erastus, with a legend noting that he was club president from 1967 to 1969. The frame is draped in black. Carl Touhey and his son Charlie both arrive, and then Hugh Carey. Harry Rosenfeld, editor of Capital Newspapers, is here, having only recently written a line about Erastus that spoke for many, especially the members of this club: "Some of the salt and savor has departed from this community." Gene Sarazen, the former golf champ, comes in briefly to use the men's room. He is eighty-one, can still hit his age for eighteen holes, and played often with Erastus after the two met socially near Albany. At one table Pat McKenna, an Albany builder, is telling a golf story about the Mayor. Pat was partners with Erastus, each of them with an eight or ten handicap, and the match against two others hinged on Erastus's sinking a long putt.

"He was a diabolical putter," said Pat. "The son of a bitch could knock 'em in from all over. I yelled to him. 'Knock that ball in.' He looked at me and his face changed. Then, with his hickory-shafted putter, he sank the ball and said to me, 'I hate like hell to be told what to do.' "

It fell to him in life to tell others, but he decided when he entered the hospital that he hadn't told them often enough, that he'd lived the wrong way for forty years, hadn't built an organization that could stand on its own feet, that could function without his guidance, hadn't allowed others enough responsibility, had been too much of a boss.

The Machine, not surprisingly, survived Erastus's illness, but the question remains: Will it survive his death? Tom Whalen inherits a city more deeply in debt than any other in the state, and the party chairman, Leo O'Brien (no relation to the late Congressman), inherits a party that is alive with pride, covetousness, lust, anger, gluttony, envy, and sloth, but that is also overflowing with political wisdom, experience, power, aggression, money, Irishness, Catholicity, miscellaneous ethnicity, Democracy, the good will of the electorate, and Mario Cuomo as a friendly neighbor up the block.

The committeeman system, on which the party functions, will survive, but with obviously divided allegiances among the members; and a meritorious and charismatic candidate will probably be essential to the perpetuation of party power. The membory of how close Carl Touhey came to winning in 1973 is still very fresh.

The city is alive now, politically, in an entirely new way: a wrestling match among Democrats, with no holds barred, in the offing—something unseen in Albany since the age of Warren Harding, Prohibition, the Black Sox scandal, and the dawn of the age of radio. The strong possibility also exists that the new regime under Whalen will deviate sharply from the course charted by Dan O'Connell and followed by Erastus, and become an open and responsive and responsible government that might even please reformers. We will all wait and see.

But now it is necessary to end the story, at least for the time being. There is more to come, and maybe one day we will have some of it. But what we have, tangibly, audibly, is the last word. It comes in a videotaped obituary prepared by Ed Dague, who spoke perhaps thirty or forty times with the Mayor in person or on the phone during the last year of his life, who covered the two hundred weekly press conferences the Mayor gave from 1968 forward. The taped images accumulate and enhance a memory already vivid with a lifetime of mind's-eye imagery; and what it is, is a riffling of that penny game at the carnival in which the pictures snap before us and give us the illusion of movement— of Erastus Corning aging: gangly, long-faced youth become dashing political prince of the city, become gray eminence in full flood, become bedridden emphysemiac, become taut skin over old bones. His voice changes during ten thousand public speeches: now a high-pitched clavichord of uncertain range, now a resonant cello of absolute virtuosity.

And then, in January 1982, the voice becomes rickety and racked, too hyper, perhaps from medicinal drugs, too feeble in timbre to be instantly recognizable as his own anymore. The voice reflects in what it says the unacceptability of death as an alternative. "The doctors took a lot of photos today," it says. "I exhausted them. Things look very good." And then it adds the postscript "Say hello to people. Tell 'em things are going along."

Erastus Corning never said anything for the record after that. There the O'Connell-Corning Machine goes off the air, and the rest is memory and hearsay.

Mary McDonald and Bill Kennedy (Sr.)
at St. Agnes's Cemetery sometime in the 1920s.

PART

6

CLOSING TIME

Debts
and Butterings

*B*efore we go any further it is important to acknowledge some people and places that helped us get to this point. Acknowledgments usually turn up at the beginning of the book and the reader skips them in a rush to get to the action. Ours are strategically placed here like a tray of chocolate dessert candies, Martha Washington butter creams, for instance, so they can be savored.

For twenty years I've wanted to write a book like this, one that encompassed the history and the journalism and some of the random memories that have obsessed me. But I might never have done it had it not been for Susanne Dumbleton, who with her partner in Albany's Washington Park Press, Anne Older, decided to republish some old articles I wrote on Albany neighborhoods in 1964. I agreed to update the articles but when I set out to do that I found them all misshapen by time and their prose as flat as Mesopotamian root beer. The book became a new venture, with the old work remaining only as a foundation and Sue turned into both editor and energetic researcher. My editor at The Viking Press, Cork Smith, read the finished product and found it of sufficient general interest that a copublishing venture came into existence, and so now you can buy this book in Kansas City as well as Albany. I hope.

Much of the research was done at the Albany Institute of History and Art (presided over by Norman Rice, who has been helpful since my Albany research began in the early 1960s) and at the Albany Public Library's Pruyn Room, which, like the Institute, is a treasure chest of Albany history. Edgar Tompkins and his library staff have been preposterously kind and helpful to me. The library was once seriously flawed, as I noted some years ago, its lone recording of the voice of a writer for whom I have great admiration having been stolen but not replaced. I am pleased to report that in early 1983 the recording is back on the shelf, and so the library is once again perfect in all respects.

I have pillaged hundreds of books to create this work. The authors and editors to whom my debt of fact and insight is largest are five: Joel Munsell, George Howell, Jonathan Tenney, and Cuyler Reynolds, who are dead, and Morris Gerber, who isn't. Gerber has published four volumes of *Old Albany*, picture histories with some text, all zany books, lacking indexes or comprehensible organization and captioning, but, even so, wonderful time machines for reentering the city that was. Joel Munsell edited the *Annals* and *Collections* of Albany, primary sources for verifying the city's past. Howell and Tenney edited the bicentennial history that took Albany up through 1886, quite coherently. And Cuyler Reynolds edited the *Albany Chronicles*, the most indispensable book on the shelf for finding your way through Albany time. The *Chronicles* is really a collection of extended headlines, a chronological record of events, letting us know when the Hudson opened to river traffic in 1832 (that was March 23, and the last ice passed out at Kinderhook) or when and where Jenny Lind sang here (Third Presbyterian Church on Clinton Square, July 9 and 11, 1851).

Reynolds takes us up through 1906 and stops, and no one since has carried on with this work, which is a pity, and which some worthy citizen should remedy with a subsidy. State University's library students would love a chance to do this for a stipend, or so I am told by Bill Katz of the university's library school, and Bill has never lied to me. We should have a chronology that takes us up through the city's tricentennial—1986—celebrating its birth as a chartered city. There are three years left. Is there a philanthropic antiquarian in the audience?

I would also like to thank Edgar S. Van Olinda, who is dead, and who should be reconstituted. He wrote a column in the *Times-Union* for maybe fifty years, recounting how it was in the good old days in Albany. Eddie, which nobody but me called him (I know this because I once phoned him at home and when I asked for Eddie his wife thought I had the wrong number; everybody else called him Van), loved the city, loved music, washed dishes with John Philip Sousa at Mrs. Schaeffer's theatrical boardinghouse at Lark Street and Central Avenue, and sang "Will You Love Me in December as You Did in May?" for Jimmy Walker. Al Smith was also there the night Eddie sang the song Walker wrote in 1905, and which became Walker's trademark. All three were sitting in Keeler's bar at the time, and Walker's response was "I've heard it sung better, I've heard it sung worse. You are in between." Eddie did not report on Smith's response but he added that Smith was quiet in those days because he was advocating national censorship to keep sexy writing away from children. It was typical of Eddie to mix Smith and Walker, who belonged together, with song and sex censorship, which did not. He was the city's champion non sequitourist.

Nevertheless, he should be republished, for he was the chronicler of an age: very readable, factually untrustworthy now and then, but relentless about exploring life on the sunny side of State, Pearl, and Broadway. It would be a lovely book because with Eddie it is not the facts but what shines through the facts that matters.

I would like to thank two people I don't know, John Piczak and James Riedel, for giving me a bit of access to Dan O'Connell and Erastus Corning that I hadn't had before. Piczak interviewed Dan and Erastus in 1965 and wrote reports on what they told him, and those are on file at Riedel's bailiwick, the Department of Political Science in the Graduate School of Public Affairs at State University in Albany, along with much more valuable local history.

I have already thanked C. R. (Tip) Roseberry numerous times for his help. He is the best and most voluminous reporter on Albany history I have ever come across, and his work on Albany neighborhoods has helped me shape my own. He has probably been known to make a mistake but never through indifference to the facts. He is a scrupulous researcher and a superior historical journalist, and he wrote a fine book about the Capitol. His stories in the *Times-Union*, covering so many facets of the city, are an invaluable record of history to which attention should be paid. He should be collected. His articles should also be made the subject of a bibliography as soon as possible to make life easier for people like me who look things up as a way of life.

I would like to thank Bill Lowenberg for talking about old newspaper days with me. We worked together on the *Times-Union*, but he remembers the way it was in the age before I was old enough to hang out in the dingy newsrooms on Beaver Street, which used to be Newspaper Row. Those were the days when the politicians had shameful control of the papers and if you put a hostile question to the Mayor he would call George Williams (the *Times-Union*'s managing editor) and when you got back to the office George would ream you sideways for insubordination to an elected Democrat, take the City Hall story away from you, and send you out to cover the manure auction in East Greenbush. I would also like to thank the *Times-Union* for running my original neighborhood articles, and also for publishing itself every day of my life, especially on the days it employed me. I withhold thanks from certain editors who are either dead or gone. They know who they are, even if they are dead.

I would like to send good wishes to the anonymous judges at the National Endowment for the Arts for giving me money that helped me to write this book and part of a new novel. Nobody ever gave me money before they did, except my mother and father. And what I got from them I spent thirty-five years ago.

I owe a debt to Vinny Reda, who helped in the research, typed about a thousand pages, and caught me in so many solecisms and innovative spellings that he grew surly with authority. However, he is the principal figure in our set who can carry a tune without straining any of his ligaments, and so his presence is essential at significant social gatherings and I think it unwise to dwell further on his editorial arrogance.

I owe another debt to Leo O'Brien, who is dead and I wish he weren't because he might enjoy this book. He thought I should have written it a long time ago. So do I. However it is done now, almost, and Leo is a presence in it and yet he can't see it. We had some long talks just before he died and if you scout around in these pages you may catch a note or two of his O'Brienian syntax.

It is also essential to acknowledge the gift my wife, Dana, has for keeping me as happy as any writer can ever expect to be, and who is very good at putting together superior children, which she has done three times without losing her talent for making unbearably good cognac chicken and running a business and teaching dance and managing our precarious finances in a way that kept us out of debtor's prison. Kurt Vonnegut once said all writers' wives are beautiful, and that is always true if you sometimes squint. With Dana there is no need for squinting. She is always gorgeous no matter which way or how often you look at her.

Now, please move along to the next page.

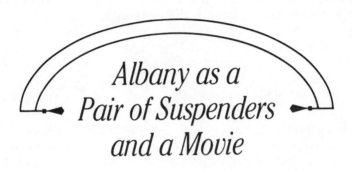

Albany as a
Pair of Suspenders
and a Movie

Now that you are here it is time
to say that this book is getting ready to come to a stop. It's silly
to say it's the end, for what I really should do is go back to page
one and start over and add all the things I've left out or am just
discovering. Writers who confront history on the page should be
subsidized for life so they can get it right. Of course you can't
get it right. You can only get it your way; and with a city whose
history is almost as old as the country's, you certainly can't get
it all. But I've done what I can, given the fact that I am nine
months late with the manuscript. Writers who confront history
on the page should be given a permanently flexible deadline that
expands like a good pair of suspenders.

I can't imagine anybody being satisfied with this book. I certainly am not. I just realized, for instance, that I haven't yet
mentioned Nick Bochvaroff. What an oversight! I think I'll mention him. He ran a penny-candy store and grocery on Broadway
at the foot of North Third Street in North Albany. He wore a
long white apron and had a thick black mustache, and when he
dressed up and went to mass at Sacred Heart Church he wore a
brown double-breasted suit and a brown homburg of a European
style. A Ukrainian homburg, perhaps. He looked more natural in
the apron and I liked him and his store enormously. He sold

Garcia Vegas and Sweet Caporals and Spuds and Grade A's and maple bells and Hershey kisses and he fought the summer fly problem with about six flypaper strips that hung from his ceiling over the vegetables and the wonderful marble-topped soda fountain where he made the best pineapple sundaes in North Albany. When I couldn't make up my mind about candy he would curse at me. "Cheesa cracks, soup patatas, make uppa you mind," he'd say.

It is amazing what you can leave out of a book if you don't think it through. Now that Nick is included I have decided that this book is as thought through as it is going to be. I used to quote Faulkner as saying you didn't finish a book, you abandoned it. I later found out Valery said that first about a poem. Before Valery it was Balzac. Before Balzac it was somebody else who ran out of time. Writers who run out of time should be grateful. They then can get on to the next problem.

The next problem is the second person I almost abandoned without a proper farewell. He is my mother's brother, Pete McDonald, a presence in all my books because of the immense vitality that emanated from him, and because of his enthusiasm for that part of life that appeals to the soul's desire to be an outlaw (not a criminal, an outlaw). He loved the Albany nighttime and its music and its gambling, and he was imbued all his life with a sense of raffish play that was infectious. He was the opposite of tactful, and was disliked for life by many whom he had insulted by revealing the truth about them. He said of one pretentiously dressed woman, "She wouldn't look good in Tiffany's window." He held grudges and punched out his antagonists and when he drank he was impossible. But I always sought his company because everything he said either informed me or made me laugh. He had no time for trivia, no patience for repetition, and he had an insightful eye. I think he had the raw material for becoming a good writer if he'd only known early on that people did such things as write books in this world. Of course he wouldn't have had the patience. He was too fond of action. He developed Parkinson's disease and cancer and then he had a stroke and declined slowly and torturously, but with all his reasoning powers intact. He was dying, at home, and my Aunt Marge called me and told me to come over. It was winter and when my wife and I walked in and saw him, lying on his back, breathing with great difficulty, probably in pain, surely in grave discomfort, clearly terminal and focusing on that, or perhaps focusing only on the pain, I said what

I usually said: "Whataya say, Pete," and he looked me over, raised a finger and pointed at my chest, and said, "I like it," and turned his gaze away and gave his attention back to what was going on in his body and his brain and his soul. He was talking about my scarf when he pointed, the only thing he could have been talking about. It was a red-and-blue scarf, colorful and long but not gaudy. I'd worn it a great deal and he'd probably seen it before; but what he was saying was that he liked my style: I looked dressed up to him, the way he always liked to look, and did look, when he was on the town. I then told him all my news—what was going on with my book, which was going to be published later in the year and which I had already read to him in pieces because I knew he wouldn't live to see it in print. He thought it'd be a best-seller. He said he'd bet on that, which explains why he was usually broke. Marge said she thought Pete had been in a coma before my wife and I walked in that night, and that he snapped out of it to be with us, to listen to what I had to say. When we left, she said, he sank back into his last four silent hours, and then he died.

I am getting to the stopping point now, and can see daylight.

The light is illuminating Colonie Street and St. Agnes Cemetery, and it is doing that because of Joe Brennan, who is given special attention elsewhere in this book. Joe had lived on Arbor Hill, where my parents were born and raised. Maybe you knew I was going to get around to thanking my parents for inventing me, but even if you didn't, here I am, around to it. Joe remembered them both before I was a consideration in the back of somebody's inventive impulses.

Joe remembered my father on Van Woert Street in the century's first decades, remembered him being short and thin, which he was, and being a natty dresser, which he was, and Joe remembered his nickname, Licory, my father's way of saying Licorice when he was a little kid. Joe remembered my mother, Mary McDonald, and my aunt, Katherine McDonald, when they lived at 142 Colonie, above Ten Broeck Street.

"I remember them all their life," Joe said. "I was never in their company. I never talked to them. I remember one was dark and one was red-haired. I remember the dark one was very good-looking. They were nice, refined girls. Quiet, unassuming girls. They went along, not loud. I see them within the parish lines. I see them going and coming from school. And I see them when they used to walk to work in North Albany later in life."

The dark one was my mother, Mary, and she was a knockout. Katherine was also a pretty and striking redhead, with hair down to the middle of her back, but always worn in a bun. Mary had a universal beauty, and this is not mother worship. It is verifiable from a hundred old photos of her in all her years as a girl and a young woman. I know a knockout when I see one and she was a knockout.

I found one picture in which she and Katherine are standing in the sunlight of an alley off Colonie Street, dressed almost like twins, with long skirts, gaiters over their pointy shoes, and belted jackets with white, feathered, boalike collars. In another photo they are holding their hats and both are wearing white-collared blouses and are arm in arm with their friend Florence Lynch, who is putting on a little weight.

I had always looked at these photos as still lifes, the moment caught and held forever. I become very excited by old photos, not only of my family, but of anybody's family, of anybody.

But all that is nothing compared to the excitement Joe Brennan gave me. When I listened to him talk about watching the McDonald girls walk down Colonie and up Pearl, his talk became an animating principle and superseded all the photos of those girls that I'd ever looked at. Now they walk where before they'd only stood still. They link arms after the shutter clicks and they walk back up the hill with the wind blowing the feathers on their collars. They take small steps because their skirts are so tight around their ankles. They are a movie.

There is a photo of my mother and father at the cemetery sitting on a bench and the sun is in my father's eyes but not my mother's because the marvelous hat she is wearing is shading them. She's wearing her fox collar. Pop has on his sailor straw with its band almost as wide as the crown, a single-breasted dark suit with peak lapels, a vest, a pocket handkerchief, a flower, and ankle-high shoes with classy pointed toes. They both look very young. There is nothing on the reverse side of the photo to let anybody know what they are doing at the cemetery.

Perhaps it is 1921. My father has been out of the Army two years and is living at Electric Park on Kinderhook Lake in Columbia County with friends. My mother is living with her brother and sister and her mother on Colonie Street. Her father died in 1918, after a lingering battle with pneumonia. Perhaps the photo is not 1921. If I knew fashions better I would be more precise. It could be 1924 or even later, but I want it to be 1921 because my father is smitten with my mother and is writing her postcards from Electric Park. They are tinted cards and they show the main midway and a rowboat on the lake.

"Wishing one more chance to send gladdest of greetings to a friend," he writes her. It's Memorial Day, 1921—May 31. A week later, June 6, he sends her another card: "Old Pal, why don't you answer me? Bill."

On June 17 he writes her again: "Dear Friend Mary, Your card of the 13th received this a.m. and very glad to hear from you. I'll say it was somewhat of a surprise. How about it!"

Not much is going on in Electric Park, he says, as it is full of hicks who retire at ten p.m. "You know me . . . my feet just about ache for a good dance. I suppose you are very good at the new one called the Homme. Sometime when you are at leisure, if you care to let me know, we will step out." He signed it Sincerely.

I take it this message was not received negatively on Colonie Street. I take it Mary McDonald found a way to let Bill Kennedy know she was at leisure. And they did step out. I am here to tell about that.

Photo Credits

Pages ii – iii photograph by Michael Fredericks, Jr. © 1983 Michael Fredericks
Title page. Collection of McKinney Library, Albany Institute of History and Art (hereafter AIHA)
Part I. Albany Public Library
Part II. AIHA
Part III. AIHA
Part IV. Morris Gerber Collection
Part V. Bernie Kolenberg, Capital Newspapers
Part VI. Author's collection
1. AIHA
2. AIHA
3. AIHA
4. AIHA
5. Courtesy Congregation Beth Emeth, Albany, N.Y.
6. AIHA
7. AIHA
8. Morris Gerber Collection
9. Morris Gerber Collection
10. AIHA
11. AIHA
12. AIHA
13. AIHA
14. AIHA
15. AIHA
16. AIHA
17. AIHA
18. Bob Richey, Capital Newspapers
19. Photograph by Michael Fredericks, Jr., for Washington Park Press
20. AIHA
21. AIHA
22. AIHA
23. AIHA
24. Morris Gerber Collection
25. AIHA
26. The Bettmann Archive
27. Author's collection
28. Author's collection
29. Wide World Photos, Inc.
30. Capital Newspapers
31. Capital Newspapers
32. Capital Newspapers
33. Capital Newspapers
34. Capital Newspapers
35. AIHA
36. AIHA
37. Morris Gerber Collection
38. Bob Richey, Capital Newspapers
39. Bob Wilder, Capital Newspapers
40. Capital Newspapers
41. Capital Newspapers
42. Capital Newspapers
43. Courtesy Lee Robb
44. AIHA
45. The Bettmann Archive
46. Bob Paley, Capital Newspapers
47. Donald Doremus, New York State Office of General Services, Promotion, and Public Affairs
48. Photograph by Michael Fredericks, Jr., for Washington Park Press
49. Photograph by Michael Fredericks, Jr., for Washington Park Press
50. Photograph by Michael Fredericks, Jr., for Washington Park Press
51. UPI
52. Capital Newspapers
53. Photograph by Michael Fredericks, Jr., for Washington Park Press
54. UPI
55. Capital Newspapers

Index

Albani, Madame, 102–103

Albany: assessment practices in, 279–280; chartered, 14, 155; first mayor of, 85, 155; naming of, 6, 155; poverty programs of, 166, 173–74, 277–278, 342 (*see also* Housing). *See also* Albany city agencies

Albany Academy(ies), 62, 108, 121, 150, 229; Female/for Girls, 62, 122; of the Holy Names, 125; Jewish, 218; of the Sacred Heart, 109; St. Joseph's, 99, 100. *See also* Christian Brothers Academy (CBA)

Albany Area Housing Opportunities (AAHO), 320–21. *See also* Housing

Albany Associates insurance company, 315, 339, 353

Albany city agencies: Board of Education, 103, 283, 316, 337; Board of Elections, 349; Client Council, 263; Common Council, 27, 45, 57, 68, 142–43, 284, 355, 358, 369; Council of Community Services, 259; Housing Authority, 51, 320; Police Department, 158, 195, 203, 206–207, 276, 278–79, 281; Public Library, 8, 10–12, 230, 376

Albany colleges: Junior College, 126; Law School, 126, 248; Medical, 126, 128, 243, 244; of Pharmacy, 126; Teachers, *see* State University of New York at Albany (SUNYA)

Albany Country Club, 108, 111, 118, 226

Albany County, 97, 156, 338–39; SIC investigation of, 45, 48–49, 288, 292, 345, 346, 352–54; and South Mall, 313–14, 316

Albany County agencies and organizations: County Jail, 78; Court and Court House, 50, 92, 108, 293; Democratic Committee, *see* Democratic party; Historical Association, 102; Welfare Department, 162, 309, 310

Albany Felt Company, 31, 331

Albany High School, 92, 108, 125, 152, 229, 248, 256

Albany Institute of History and Art, 12, 14, 41, 183, 331, 376

Albany newspapers: *Argus,* 25, 107, 143; *Atlas and Argus,* 69, 70, 71; *Capitol,* 257; *Daily Advertiser,* 59, 217; *Daily Herold* (German-language), 243, 250; *Evening Jour-*